Literacy & Language Instruction to Advance All Learners

- **Develop Foundational Skills**
- **Read Complex Texts**
- **Speak and Write Using Text Evidence**
- **Teach the Writing Process**
- **Differentiate Instruction to Support All Learners**
- **Seamlessly Integrate English Language Development and Literacy**

Development Team

Authors
Peter Afflerbach, Ph.D., University of Maryland
Silvia Dorta-Duque de Reyes, M.A.,
    Benchmark Education Company
Queta Fernandez, Spanish Literacy Consultant
Linda Hoyt, M.A., Author and Literacy Consultant
Adria Klein, Ph.D., California State University, San Bernardino
Carrie Smith, M.S., Benchmark Education Company

Contributing Authors
Farah Assiraj, M.A., Boston Public Schools
Jorge Cuevas Antillón, M.A.,
    San Diego County Office of Education
Erin Bostick Mason, M.A. Ed.,
    California State University, San Bernardino
Marjorie McCabe, Ph.D.,
    California State University, San Bernardino
Jill Kerper Mora, Ph.D., San Diego State University
Jeff Zwiers, Ed.D., Stanford University

Linguistic Consultants
Sandra Ceja, InterLingual SoLutions
Youniss El Cheddadi, Arabic Department,
    San Diego State University
Lilly Cheng, Ph.D., University of California, San Diego

Benchmark ADVANCE
BENCHMARK EDUCATION COMPANY
145 Huguenot Street • New Rochelle, NY 10801

For ordering information, call Toll-Free 1-877-236-2465 or visit our website at www.benchmarkeducation.com.

©2018 Benchmark Education Company, LLC. All rights reserved. Teachers may photocopy the reproducible pages for classroom use. No other part of the guide may be reproduced or transmitted in any form or by any means, electronic or mechanical, including photocopy, recording, or any information storage or retrieval system, without permission in writing from the publisher. Printed in Guangzhou, China. 4401/1216/CA21601873
ISBN: 978-1-5125-2295-2

Table of Contents
Units 3 & 4

Program Overview

Literacy & Language Instruction to Advance All Learners
Grade 2 Components

Unit 3:
Plants and Animals in Their Habitats

How do living things get what they need to survive?

Unit 4:
Many Characters, Many Points of View

How can a story change depending on who tells it?

Additional Resources

- *Connect Across Disciplines Inquiry Projects*
- *Preteach/Reteach Routines*
- *Small-Group Texts for Reteaching Strategies and Skills*
- *Collaborative Conversation*
- *Access and Equity: Meeting the Needs of Students with Disabilities and Students Who Are Advanced Learners*

- *Contrastive Analysis of English and Nine World Languages*
- *Vocabulary with Spanish Cognates*
- *Managing an Independent Reading Program and Recommended Trade Books*

Literacy & Language Instruction to Advance All Learners

Teach reading, writing, speaking, and listening and successfully reach each one of your students.

Benchmark Advance provides resources and effective instruction to support all components of a best-practice literacy block. And the program's amplified English language support ensures success for English learners.

Build a Solid Literacy Foundation

Develop Foundational Skills

Explicit, systematic instruction lays the groundwork for literacy achievement.

Kindergarten–Grade 2:

Phonological Awareness, Phonics, and High-Frequency Words
- First 20 days Foundations and Review
- Daily explicit lessons in every unit
- Decodable reading practice
- Hands-on manipulatives
- Application in context: shared reading and small-group reading

Print Concepts and Fluency
- First 20 days Foundations and Review
- Daily Shared Reading
- Small-group leveled reading and reader's theater

Grades 3–6:

Multi-Syllabic Phonics and Word Analysis
- Explicit lessons in every week
- Word study passages for practice in context
- Practice activities to support vocabulary development

Fluency
- Small-group leveled reading
- Reader's heater for repeated oral reading practice

Read Complex Texts

Students encounter complex texts in multiple resources.

Kindergarten–Grade 1:
- Interactive Read-Alouds of Authentic Texts
- Mentor Read-Alouds to build strategies and vocabulary
- Extended Read-Aloud Big Books to practice strategies
- My Shared Readings, Decodable Texts, Leveled Texts, and Reader's Theater for hands-on reading practice

Grades 2–6:
- Interactive Read-Alouds of Authentic Texts
- Texts for Close Reading Short and Extended Reads
- Reader's Theater for repeated oral reading practice

Spread of My Shared Readings
Read-Aloud Handbook

Texts for Close Reading
Read-Aloud Handbook

Students read and annotate their own texts to create a portfolio or their thinking and writing.

iv

Program Overview

Speak and Write Using Text Evidence

Students discuss and write about texts to show their understanding.

- Text evidence questions provided for every selection.
- Collaborative conversation is integrated into daily lessons.
- Explicit mini-lessons teach writing to sources.

Teach the Writing Process

Students engage in process writing of all three text types–plus poetry!

- Author's craft mini-lessons provided every day.
- Explicit instruction for language conventions.
- Built-in conferring support for teachers.
- Independent online process writing modules available.

Differentiate Instruction to Support All Learners

Support and advance all students through small group instruction and independent practice.

Resources to Support Flexible Grouping:

- Guided reading groups
- Strategy groups
- Heterogeneous reader's theater groups
- Literature circles
- Intervention groups

Seamlessly Integrate English Language Development and Literacy

Raise the bar for English Learners by amplifying core instruction.

Language support during Core ELA lessons:

Strategies at three intensity levels–light, moderate, and substantial–support English learners to engage meaningfully in core ELA lessons.

Teachers begin with light support and intensify the scaffolding only as needed, supporting ELs to participate at the same level of rigor as other students.

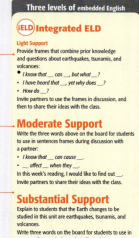

Focused English Language Development

All English language study is based on the same complex texts students read during core instruction. Texts are visually amplified to support comprehension, and English grammar and vocabulary are taught using examples from the complex texts.

Grade 2 Components

Whole Group

Texts for Close Reading

Student
Print & E-Books

Unit 1   Unit 2   Unit 3   Unit 4   Unit 5   Unit 6   Unit 7   Unit 8   Unit 9   Unit 10

Teacher
Print, E-Guides & Digital Tools

Units 1 & 2   Units 3 & 4   Units 5 & 6   Units 7 & 8   Units 9 & 10   Read-Aloud Handbook   Grammar, Spelling & Vocabulary Activity Book

Phonics Resources

Letter Cards   High-Frequency Word Cards   Frieze Cards   Sound-Spelling Cards   Phonics & High-Frequency Words Activity Book   Decodable Passages

Assessment

Print & Online Assessments

Weekly and Unit Assessments   Interim Assessments and Performance Tasks   Informal Assessments   Assessment Reporting Platform

Focused ELD

Student
Print & E-Books

Texts for English Language Development, Units 1–10   Think-Speak-Listen Conversation Flip Book

Teacher
Print & E-Guides

English Language Development Teacher's Resource System   English Language Development Assessment

Program Overview

Small Group

Leveled Texts (7 titles per unit)

Student
Print & E-Books

Unit 1   Unit 2   Unit 3   Unit 4   Unit 5   Unit 6   Unit 7   Unit 8   Unit 9   Unit 10

Teacher Guides and Text Evidence Question Cards
(7 of each per unit)

Teacher
Print, E-Guides & Digital Tools

Unit 1   Unit 2   Unit 3   Unit 4   Unit 5   Unit 6   Unit 7   Unit 8   Unit 9   Unit 10

Reader's Theater (2 scripts per unit)

Student
Print & E-Books

Unit 1   Unit 2   Unit 3   Unit 4   Unit 5   Unit 6   Unit 7   Unit 8   Unit 9   Unit 10

Teacher
Print, E-Guides & Digital Tools

Reader's Theater
Teacher's Handbook, Units 1–10

Intervention

Quick Check Assessments
Print & E-Guides

  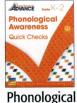  

Foundational Skills Screeners | Fluency | Print Concepts | Phonological Awareness | Phonics and Word Recognition | Reading | Language

Intervention Mini-Lessons
Print & E-Guides

Fluency | Print Concepts | Phonological Awareness | Phonics and Word Recognition | Reading | Writing and Language Handbook | Mentor Text

---

Benchmark UNIVERSE

Digital Learning Portal
Interactive Resources & Instruction for the Entire Program

E-Planner
Plan & Manage Student Groups

Video
Multimedia to Reinforce Unit Topic

Weekly Presentations
Collected Resources for Whole-Group Instruction

E-Books
Whole-Group and Small-Group Texts

Home to School
Take-Home Letter and Activities

Online Assessments
Test-Taking Environment for Students
Reporting Platform for Teachers

vii

Exploring the Program Digitally

The Digital Teacher Experience. Powered by Benchmark Universe™

YOUR DASHBOARD One place to access all of your content, planning, and management tools

- Assignments
- Messages
- Manage Students
- Help
- Book Reviews

Manage classes and assignments, and message students. Students can also review books and share those reviews.

Benchmark Advance™
Provides access to the digital content library for the ELA/ELD program
See pages 26–27.

Benchmark Adelante™
Provides access to the digital content library for the SLA/SLD program

English Language Development
Digital content library for your designated ELD components

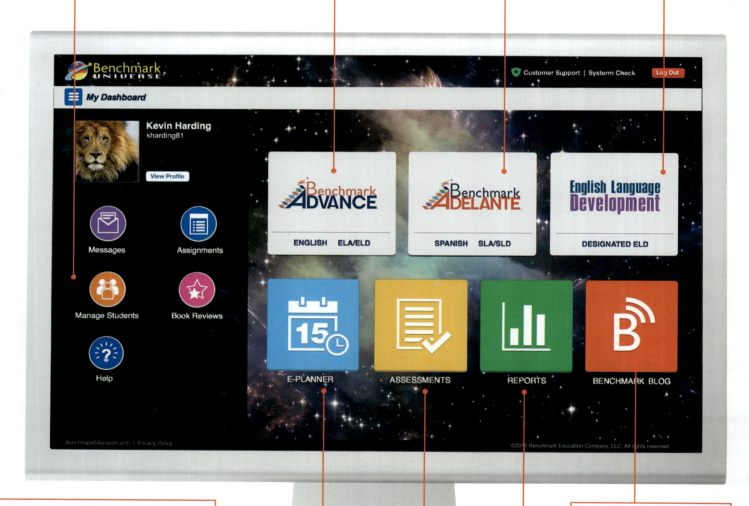

- E-Planner
- Assessments
- Reports

The E-Planner includes filtering by standard and a drag-and-drop feature. Online assessment with reporting can be used to track mastery by standard or by skill.

BENCHMARK Blog
Resources, tips and tricks, and professional development articles published throughout the year

UNIT 3

Plants and Animals in Their Habitats

Essential Question

How do living things get what they need to survive?

Enduring Understanding:

The habitats of living things provide what they need to survive.

In this unit, students read and compare selections about plants and animals to understand how living things get what they need in their habitats.

Unit Strategies and Skills

Unit 3

	WEEK 1	WEEK 2	WEEK 3	
Metacognitive	Determine Text Importance	→ Determine Text Importance	→ Determine Text Importance	
Reading	Identify the Main Topic of a Text	→ Identify the Main Topic of a Text		✔
	Explain How Images Contribute to and Clarify a Text	→ Explain How Images Contribute to and Clarify a Text		✔
	Use Text Evidence to Draw Inferences	→ Use Text Evidence to Draw Inferences		✔
	Recount Key Story Events	→	Recount Story Events	✔
	Describe the Overall Structure of a Story	→	Describe the Overall Structure of a Story	✔
	Compare and Contrast Key Points in Two Texts on the Same Topic	→ Compare and Contrast Key Points in Two Texts on the Same Topic to Make Connections Across Texts	→ Compare and Contrast Key Points in Two Texts on the Same Topic	✔
Vocabulary	Distinguish Shades of Meaning Among Related Adjectives	→	Distinguish Shades of Meaning Among Related Adjectives	✔
		Determine the Meaning of Words and Phrases		

	WEEK 1	WEEK 2	WEEK 3	
Writing	Writing to Sources: Informative Report	Writing to Sources: Informative Report	Writing to Sources: Informative Report	✔
Conventions of English	Produce Complete Compound Sentences	Capitalize Holidays and Geographic Names	Create Compound Sentences / Check and Correct Capitalization	✔
Phonics/Word Study	Long **u: ew, ue, u, u_e**	**r**-Controlled Vowel **ar**	**r**-Controlled Vowels **er, ir, ur**	✔
Fluency	Read on-level text with purpose and understanding.	Read on-level text with purpose and understanding.	Prosody: Speed/Pacing–Varied* / Inflection and Intonation–Stress*	
Speaking and Listening	Participate in Collaborative Conversations / Recount or Describe Key Details / Ask and Answer Questions to Gather Information or to Clarify			

✔ = Strategies and skills are assessed on the Unit Assessment. Skills with no check mark are *not* assessed in this unit.

* See Reader's Theater Teacher's Handbook

UNIT 3 Differentiated Instruction Planner *Meeting th*

Small-Group Reading Instruction Options:

☐ Unit-Specific Leveled Texts for Differentiated Instruction

Group students by instructional reading level to guide and expand their skills and strategies. Use the lesson-specific Teacher's Guide and Text Evidence Question Card for each title.

| 310L F/9 | 370L F/9 | 390L F/10 | 380L F/10 | 440L J/18 | 510L M/28 | 300L K/20 |

☐ Close Reading of Complex Text

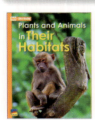

Reread complex texts in the unit's *Texts for Close Reading*. Use the text-evidence questions aligned to DOK levels provided online.

☐ Reader's Theater

Group students heterogeneously for multi-leveled reader's theater experiences that build fluency and comprehension. Use the 5-day lesson plans provided, pages 32–43.

☐ Literature Circles

Select trade books for groups based on their interests and reading abilities. See the Unit 3 Recommended Trade Books on page AR82.

☐ Reading Strategy Instruction

Group students for additional modeling and guided practice with specific strategies from the unit. See Small-Group Texts for Reteaching Strategies and Skills on pages AR18–AR25.

☐ English Language Development

Preview or review the unit selections with amplified visual support, and build English language skills based on the readings.

☐ Intervention

Select appropriate intervention lessons based on data from your weekly, unit, and interim assessments as well as informal assessments.

Plants and Animals in Their Habitats

Essential Question: How do living things get what they need to survive?

WEEK 3

- Keeping Warm
- I, Mouse

Shared Read 3:
"A City Park Habitat," p. 16
Informational Science, 590L

Shared Read 4:
"A New Home for Margie," p. 17
Animal Fantasy, 400L

Shared Read 5:
"Burt the Sea Turtle," p. 28
Animal Fantasy, 510L

Shared Read 6:
"The Monarchs' Journey," p. 29
Informational Science, 500L

Extended Read 1:
Habitats Around the World," pp. 18–25
Informational Science, 560L

Extended Read 2:
"Lost in the Desert," pp. 30–37
Realistic Fiction, 450L

 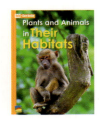 

- G/12
- H/14
- I/16
- M/28

- K/20
- L/24
- N/30
- P/38

Reader's Theater Teacher's Handbook

d Text Evidence
ach title

Informative Report
e Prompt
ns, and Details in a Source Text
Notetaking from a Media Source

riting
and Geographic Names

Writing to Sources: Informative Report
- Introduce Your Topic
- Draft and Develop Your Points and Include a Conclusion
- Revise to Improve Sentence Fluency by Creating Compound Sentences
- Check and Correct Capitalization
- Evaluate and Reflect on Writing

Word Study Read:
"An Ocean Visit," p. 26
Personal Narrative, 450L

For additional practice, see:
"Shark Teeth"

Word Study Read:
"Kurt's Big Trip," p. 38
Realistic Fiction, 290L

For additional practice, see:
"Everglades," "Visit the Everglades," "The Hurt Turtle"

Foundational Skills Screeners

Assess students' proficiency in Print Concepts, Phonological Awareness, Phonics, and Fluency.

Quick Checks

Monitor students' progress using focused informal assessments.

Digital Learning Portal
Interactive Resources & Instruction for the Entire Program

E-Planner
Plan & Manage Student Groups

Video
Multimedia to Reinforce Unit Topic

Weekly Presentations
Collected Resources for Whole-Group Instruction

E-Books
Whole-Group and Small-Group Texts

Home to School
Take-Home Letter and Activities

Online Assessments
Test-Taking Environment for Students
Reporting Platform for Teachers

UNIT 3

Components at a Glance

		WEEK 1	**WEEK 2**
Interactive Read-Aloud	10 MINUTES PER LESSON	**Metacognitive Strategy:** Determine Text Importance Conduct an interactive read-aloud at any point in your literacy block. Over the course of the unit, you may choose a recommended trade book or from these selections provided in the Read-Aloud Handbook:	• Worms to the Rescue • In the Garden • Fly Away, Ladybug!
Shared Reading	10 MINUTES PER LESSON	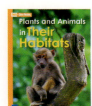  **Shared Read 1:** "News About Scorpions," p. 4 Informational Science, 680L **Shared Read 2:** "All the Penguins," p. 5 End-Rhyme Poem, NP	 
Reading Mini-Lessons	10 MINUTES PER LESSON	 **Short Read 1:** "The Coldest Place on Earth," pp. 6–9 Informational Science, 630L **Short Read 2:** "Postcards from Alex," pp. 10–13 Animal Fantasy, 470L	
Small-Group Reading	15–20 MINUTES PER GROUP	 310L F/9 370L F/9 390L F/10 380L F/10 440L J/18 510L M/28 300L K/20	Teacher's Guide ar Question Card for
Writing and Language Mini-Lessons	10 MINUTES PER LESSON	 **Writing to Sources: Informative Report** • Read a Mentor Informative Report • Read and Analyze the Source Text Organization • Listen and View to Find Facts and Details • Draft **Conventions of Language** • Produce Complete Compound Sentences	 **Writing to Source** • Read and Analyze • Find Facts, Definiti • Active Viewing and • Organize Your Idea **Conventions of W** • Capitalize Holidays
Phonics/Word Study Mini-Lessons	15–20 MINUTES PER LESSON	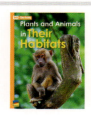 **Word Study Read:** "The Deserts of Utah," p. 14 Informational Science, 470L **For additional practice, see:** "'More About Utah," "Camping Out," "The Rescue Park"	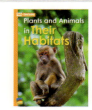 
Assessment 		 **Interim Assessment 2,** p. 37 Administer the test after students have completed the unit.	 **Week 1,** p. 63 **Week 2,** p. 69 **Unit 3,** p. 77 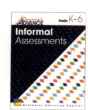 **Informal Assessments** Conduct and document meaningful, ongoing observations using informal assessments.

...he Needs of All Learners

Independent and Collaborative Activity Options:

Read Independently

Make a range of informational and literary texts available for students to self-select based on their interests including:
- previously read leveled texts and e-books.
- books and magazines related to Plants and Animals in Their Habitats.
- trade fiction and nonfiction titles.

Confer with individuals or groups to support their reading development.

Read Collaboratively

Engage students in one or more of the following fluency-building activities, including:
- partner reading of previously read leveled texts.
- partner or trio listening and reading along to an e-book.
- small-group rehearsal of Unit 3 Reader's Theater scripts.

Write Independently

Have students complete the Independent Writing tasks specified at the end of each day's writing mini-lesson. Look for the ✓

Conduct Research

Assign groups of students one of the unit-related Connect Across Disciplines Inquiry Projects to complete during the three-week unit (see pages AR2–AR3).
- Label a U.S. Map
- Make a Habitat Mural
- Create a Zoo Exhibit (Challenge Project)

Apply Understanding

Assign an informal assessment activity to help you evaluate students' mastery of targeted strategies and skills. Look for the ✓

Answer Questions Using Text Evidence

Assign questions from the Text Evidence Question Card to individuals or partners based on the leveled texts they have read.

Skill Practice

Assign pages from the Grammar, Spelling, and Vocabulary Activity Book.

Assign pages from the Phonics and High-Frequency Words Activity Book.

Build, Reflect, Write

At the end of each week, ask students to reflect on their understanding of the weekly selections and their ideas related to the unit Essential Question by completing the "Build Knowledge" and "Reflect" sections of the Build, Reflect, Write page.

Unit 3 Writing & Vocabulary

Writing to Sources: Informative Text

In Week 1, teachers guide students through an analysis of a Mentor Informative Text and how to apply that analysis to their writing. In Week 2, teachers guide students to read and analyze a new prompt based on their *Texts for Close Reading*. Students then plan and organize their own writing in response to this prompt. In Week 3, teachers guide students to draft, revise, and edit their response to the writing prompt.

Week	Focus	Daily Writing Mini-Lesson	Page
1	Organize Ideas	Read a Mentor Informative Text	10
		Read and Analyze the Source Text Organization	18
		Read to Find Facts and Details	26
		Listen and View to Find Facts and Details	34
		Conventions of Language: Produce Complete Compound Sentences	40
2	Draft	Read and Analyze the Prompt	50
		Find Facts, Definitions, and Details in a Source Text	58
		Active Viewing and Notetaking from a Media Source	66
		Organize Your Ideas	72
		Conventions of Writing: Capitalize Holidays and Geographic Names	78
3	Revise, Edit, and Publish	Introduce Your Topic	88
		Draft and Develop Your Points and Include a Conclusion	96
		Revise to Improve Sentence Fluency by Creating Compound Sentences	104
		Check and Correct Capitalization	110
		Evaluate and Reflect on Writing	114

Vocabulary Instruction

Build students' vocabulary related to the unit topic using explicit vocabulary mini-lessons and vocabulary routines.

Week	Lesson Type	Vocabulary Words from *Texts for Close Reading*	Instruction
1	Build Vocabulary	**"All the Penguins":** big (p. 5) **"Postcards from Alex":** big (p. 12) **Related Words:** gigantic, huge, large, enormous, delicious, tasty, cold, freezing, chilly, hot, dry, sizzling, warm, fiery, sun-baked, burnt, dusty, large, tired, exhausted, drowsy, sleepy	**Day 4:** Distinguish Shades of Meaning Among Related Adjectives, p. 32
	Phonics & Word Study	use, few, cute, huge, cube, music, rescue, menu, fuel, January	**Days 1–5:** Long **u: ew, ue, u, u_e**, pp. 12–13, 20–21, 28, 36, 42–43 *Word Study vocabulary words are also the week's spelling words.*
	Making Meaning with Words	**"The Coldest Place on Earth":** barren (p. 6), harsh (p. 6), fragile (p. 8), huddle (p. 9) **"Postcards from Alex":** desert (p. 13)	Use the routine on pp. AR13–AR14 to introduce these words. Have students complete the "Making Meaning with Words" glossary on the inside back cover of the *Texts for Close Reading*.
2	Build Vocabulary	**"The Coldest Place on Earth":** blubber (p. 7) **"The Deserts of Utah":** habitat (p. 14) **"A City Park Habitat":** habitat (p. 16) **"Habitats Around the World":** habitat (pp. 18, 19, 21, 23, 25), grasslands (pp. 19, 20, 25), savanna (p. 20) blubber (p. 21), tundra (pp. 21, 22, 25), coral (pp. 24, 25), prairies (p. 19) **Related Words:** prairie, savannas	**Day 3:** Determine the Meaning of Words and Phrases, p. 63
	Phonics & Word Study	car, star, march, smart, hard, farm, large, shark, garden, yard	**Days 1–5: r**-Controlled Vowel **ar**, pp. 52–53, 60–61, 68, 74, 80–81 *Word Study vocabulary words are also the week's spelling words.*
	Making Meaning with Words	**"Habitats Around the World":** thaws (p. 22), shallow (p. 24)	Use the routine on pp. AR13–AR14 to introduce these words. Have students complete the "Making Meaning with Words" glossary on the inside back cover of the *Texts for Close Reading*.
3	Build Vocabulary	**"The Coldest Place on Earth":** freezing (pp. 7, 8, 9) **"Postcards from Alex":** freezing (p. 11) **"The Deserts of Utah":** cool (p. 14) **"Habitats Around the World":** hot (pp. 20, 23) **"Lost in the Desert":** cool (p. 32), quiet (pp. 34, 36), happy (p. 36), afraid (p. 36), silly (p. 37) **Related Words:** loudly (p. 36), loud, earsplitting, silent, hushed, peaceful, hotter (p. 31), starving, delighted, terrified, goofy	**Day 3:** Distinguish Shades of Meaning Among Related Adjectives, p. 101
	Phonics & Word Study	bird, hurt, her, nurse, girl, shirt, burn, third, never, winter	**Days 1–5: r**-Controlled Vowels **er, ir, ur**, pp. 90–91, 98–99, 106, 112, 116–117 *Word Study vocabulary words are also the week's spelling words.*
	Making Meaning with Words	**"Lost in the Desert":** peered (p. 32), fled (p. 37), terror (p. 37)	Use the routine on pp. AR13–AR14 to introduce these words. Have students complete the "Making Meaning with Words" glossary on the inside back cover of the *Texts for Close Reading*.

©2018 Benchmark Education Company, LLC

Grade 2 • Unit 3

Week 1 Mini-Lessons at a Glance

	Day 1	Day 2
Reading Mini-Lessons	Introduce Unit 3: Plants and Animals in Their Habitats (10 Min.), p. 4 SL.2.1a, SL.2.1b, SL.2.2, L.2.4 Shared Reading (10 Min.), p. 6 RF.2.4b, RF.2.4c "The Coldest Place on Earth": Identify the Main Topic of a Text (15 Min.), p. 8 RI.2.1, RI.2.2	Shared Reading (10 Min.), p. 14 RF.2.3f, RF.2.4a, RF.2.4b Explain How Images Contribute to and Clarify a Text (15 Min.), p. 15 RI.2.5, RI.2.7, SL.2.2 Use Text Evidence to Draw Inferences (15 Min.), p. 16 RI.2.1, RI.2.5
Writing and Language Mini-Lessons	Write an Informative Report: Read a Mentor Informative Report (15 Min.), p. 10 W.2.5	Write an Informative Report: Read and Analyze the Source Text Organization (15 Min.), p. 18 W.2.5
Phonics/Word Study Mini-Lessons	Long u: ew, ue, u, u_e (15 Min.), p. 12 RF.2.3a, RF.2.3b, RF.2.3c, RF.2.3e, RF.2.3f, L.2.2d • High-Frequency Words: *again, below, carry, does, eight, find, house, laugh, mother, school* • Weekly Spelling Words: *use, few, cute, huge, cube, music, rescue, menu, fuel, January*	Long u: ew, ue, u, u_e (15 Min.), p. 20 RF.2.3a, RF.2.3b, RF.2.3c • High-Frequency Words: *again, below, carry, does, eight, find, house, laugh, mother, school*

Short Read 1: "The Coldest Place on Earth"

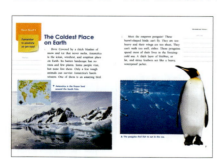

Informational Science

Quantitative — Lexile® 630L

Qualitative Analysis of Text Complexity

Purpose and Levels of Meaning ❶
• Text purpose is simple: to describe the life of penguins in Antarctica.

Structure ❷
• The text structure is straightforward and sequential.
• Readers encounter a map.

Language Conventionality and Clarity ❷
• Sentences are mostly simple, and technical language is explained through context, labeled images, or direct definition.

Knowledge Demands ❷
• For full comprehension, readers will benefit from an awareness of extreme polar conditions.

**Total QM: 7
Moderate Complexity***

*The texts in *Benchmark Advance* are qualitatively evaluated based on their grade-level placement in the program. Reader maturity and age appropriateness are key considerations in the subjective use of the rubrics.

Day 3	Day 4	Day 5
Shared Reading (10 Min.), p. 22 RL.2.4, RF.2.3d, RF.2.4b, L.2.4c	**Shared Reading (10 Min.), p. 29** RF.2.3b, RF.2.4a, RF.2.4b, RF.2.4c	**Shared Reading (10 Min.), p. 37** RI.2.1, RF.2.3d, SL.2.2, SL.2.3
"Postcards from Alex": Recount Key Story Events (15 Min.), p. 24 RL.2.1, RL.2.5	**Describe the Overall Structure of a Story (15 Min.), p. 30** RL.2.1, RL.2.5 **Build Vocabulary: Distinguish Shades of Meaning Among Related Adjectives (10 Min.), p. 32** RL.2.4, L.2.5b	**Compare and Contrast Key Points in Two Texts on the Same Topic (15 Min.), p. 38** RI.2.9, SL.2.1a, SL.2.1b, SL.2.1c
Write an Informative Report: Read to Find Facts and Details (15 Min.), p. 26 W.2.7, W.2.8	**Write an Informative Report: Listen and View to Find Facts and Details (15 Min.), p. 34** W.2.7, W.2.8	**Conventions of Language: Produce Complete Compound Sentences (15 Min.), p. 40** L.2.1f
Long u: ew, ue, u, u_e (10 Min.), p. 28 RF.2.3b, RF.2.3c, RF.2.3e, RF.2.3f, L.2.2d • High-Frequency Words: *again, below, carry, does, eight, find, house, laugh, mother, school*	**Long u: ew, ue, u, u_e (20 Min.), p. 36** RF.2.3b, RF.2.3c, RF.2.3d, RF.2.3e, RF.2.3f, L.2.2d • High-Frequency Words: *again, below, carry, does, eight, find, house, laugh, mother, school*	**Review and Assess Long u: ew, ue, u, u_e (20 Min.), p. 42** RF.2.3a, RF.2.3b, RF.2.3c, RF.2.3e, RF.2.3f, L.2.2d • High-Frequency Words: *again, below, carry, does, eight, find, house, laugh, mother, school*

Short Read 2: "Postcards from Alex"

Animal Fantasy

Quantitative	Lexile® 470L

Qualitative Analysis of Text Complexity

Purpose and Levels of Meaning ❷
- The story has a clear moral: travel is good because it helps you appreciate home.

Structure ❸
- This story with anthropomorphic characters is told mostly through letters.
- Readers must navigate two different modes and interpret illustrations for full understanding.

Language Conventionality and Clarity ❷
- Sentences are mostly simple and the vocabulary is familiar, with a few foreign place names like Chile and the Amazon.

Knowledge Demands ❷
- Readers will benefit from familiarity with the Amazon and its creatures—especially the anteater, which is only identifiable through illustration.

Total QM: 9 Moderate Complexity*

©2018 Benchmark Education Company, LLC

Grade 2 • Unit 3 • Week 1

DAY 1

UNIT INTRODUCTION

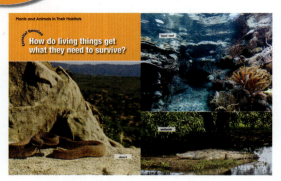

Texts for Close Reading, pp. 2–3
Unit Introduction

Student Objectives

I will be able to:
- Share what I know about living things.
- Participate in a group discussion.

Additional Materials

Weekly Presentation: Unit 3, Week 1
- Unit 3 Video
- Guiding Questions/Initial Ideas Chart

Observation Checklist for Collaborative Conversation

As peer groups discuss the Essential Question, use the questions below to evaluate how effectively students communicate with one another. Based on your answers, you may wish to plan future core lessons to support the collaborative conversation process.

Do peer groups . . .
- ❏ stay on topic throughout the discussion?
- ❏ listen respectfully?
- ❏ build on the comments of others appropriately?
- ❏ pose or respond to questions to clarify information?
- ❏ support their partners to participate?

Introduce Unit 3: Plants and Animals in Their Habitats (10 MIN.) SL.2.1a, SL.2.1b, SL.2.2, L.2.4

Pose Essential Question

Ask students to access the introduction to "Plants and Animals in Their Habitats" in their texts or on their devices. Explain that as students read, they will find ideas that help to answer the question. Invite a volunteer to read aloud the Essential Question:

> **How do living things get what they need to survive?**

Explain to students that over the next three weeks, they will read informational texts, stories, and a poem that describe how plants and animals that live in different habitats around the world have adapted to survive in their respective habitats.

View Multimedia and Build Vocabulary

Display or have students access the Unit 3 Video on their devices.

Ask students which images from the video stood out to them, and why they remember the images. Add new ideas to your class list. Write the domain-specific vocabulary words **habitat**, **shelter**, and **adapt** on the board. Replay the video and ask students to use audio and video clues to determine the meaning of these words.

Collaborative Conversation: Peer Group

To guide their thinking as they begin Unit 3, ask peer groups to generate questions about what living things need in order to survive. Remind them that a strong, thoughtful question has more than one right answer. You may wish to have each group designate a discussion facilitator, scribe, timekeeper, and encourager. Model framing interesting, thoughtful questions that can be answered in more than one way.

- *I wonder how animals that live in a desert _____.*
- *I wonder what kind of _____ affects the way _____.*

Share

Have each group's scribe share guiding questions and ideas their group generated. Capture questions and ideas on a class Guiding Questions/Initial Ideas Chart. Invite other groups to add their ideas. This is an ideal time to reinforce students' ability to build on the ideas of others in constructive ways. If necessary, provide additional modeling.

Say: *[Name] listened thoughtfully before raising a hand to comment. That's a great way to show respect for everyone's ideas.*

Use the brief conversation to help you benchmark students' knowledge around the unit topic and to build their interest.

Guiding Questions	Initial Ideas
How do living things get food?	Some animals hunt other animals. Plant roots take in food from the soil.
How do living things stay safe?	Some animals run away from hunters. Some plants have spines to protect them.
How do living things stay warm or cool?	Animals that live in cold lands have thick fur. Animals that live in hot lands stay underground.

Sample Guiding Questions/Initial Ideas Chart

---

iELD Integrated ELD

Light Support

Introduce the topic for the week: **living things.** Elicit unusual animal names, verbs, and verb phrases: **stay warm, stay cold, stay safe, catch food, hide from.**

Have students complete question frames.

I have always wondered _____.

I have always wanted to know _____.

I have always wanted to ask _____.

Moderate Support

Elicit animal names. Have students ask questions about animals. Model completing a question frame: *How do snakes stay safe?* Then have students work with the following frames to ask questions:

What do _____?

Where do _____?

How do _____?

Why do _____?

When do _____?

Substantial Support

Present, list, and review verbs. Students echo-read and role-play meanings.

Verbs: **live, eat, find, move, go, see, hear, smell, like, feel.**

Model forming a question using the word **eat.**

Say: *When do living things eat?*

Help students use the verbs to complete question frames.

What do living things _____?

Where do living things _____?

Why do living things _____?

How do living things _____?

SL.2.1a Follow agreed-upon rules for discussions (e.g., gaining the floor in respectful ways, listening to others with care, speaking one at a time about the topics and texts under discussion). **SL.2.1b** Build on others' talk in conversations by linking their comments to the remarks of others. **SL.2.2** Recount or describe key ideas or details from a text read aloud or information presented orally or through other media. **L.2.4** Determine or clarify the meaning of unknown and multiple-meaning words and phrases based on grade 2 reading and content, choosing flexibly from an array of strategies.

©2018 Benchmark Education Company, LLC

Grade 2 • Unit 3 • Week 1

DAY 1

SHARED READING

Texts for Close Reading, p. 4
"News About Scorpions"

Student Objectives

I will be able to:
- Read an informational text.
- Identify and annotate key details in a text.

Additional Materials

Weekly Presentation: Unit 3, Week 1

Shared Reading (10 MIN.) RF.2.4b, RF.2.4c

Introduce the Text

Display and read aloud the title of the informational text "News About Scorpions." Invite students to work with a partner to infer what the text will be about. Encourage them to focus on the title and the photograph as they preview.

Model Fluent Reading: Rate/Pausing

Explain that readers must pause when they come to a comma, because commas separate ideas, clauses, or items in a list. Read the first paragraph aloud. Read the text fluently, pausing slightly between phrases, clauses, and sentences. Have students echo-read the second paragraph after you.

Model Determine Text Importance

Tell students that they will be reading informational texts in this unit, both short and longer. Stress that a key reading strategy for informational texts is Determine Text Importance. Different parts of one text will usually vary in importance. Tell students that it is important to consider text importance before, during, and after reading. Model determining text importance as you preview "News About Scorpions."

Sample modeling. *Right away I know that the title is important. It tells me what the subject of the text is—scorpions. I have heard of scorpions, but I really don't know anything about them. I see at a glance that this text is short, so I know that I'll have to read very carefully so that I don't miss any important information. The photograph is important—I think that must be a scorpion. There's no caption with the picture, which is too bad. Photo captions usually tell what is being shown or explain what is happening, and that's very important text.*

Tell students that throughout this unit they will be practicing Determine Text Importance on a variety of read-aloud and shared reading texts.

SHARED READING

WEEK 1 • DAY 1

Transfer Skills to Context: Annotate Key Details ⓘELD

Model identifying the key details in paragraph 1 as you underline them.

Sample modeling (paragraph 1). *One important question to ask about this topic is, "What is a scorpion?" I'll reread to find and underline details that answer that question. One answer in the text is that it's "a scary creature to run into." I'll underline that.*

Ask student to identify other key details in paragraph 2 that describe scorpions.

Transfer Skills to Context: Words with long i

Ask students to pay attention to each of these words with the long **i** vowel sound in "News About Scorpions." Have them say the word and name the letter(s) that spell the long **i** sound: **spiders**, **like**, **tiny**, **dry**, **night**.

ⓘELD Integrated ELD

Light Support

Provide visual support, and cognates for key vocabulary and science facts: **scorpion, arachnid, prey (presa), habitat, insects (insectos), aggressive (agresivo)**.

Have students draw conclusions about scorpions. Provide a sentence starter and additional sentence frames.

Some people think scorpions . . .

seem _____, because _____.

look like _____, because _____.

might be _____, because _____.

Moderate Support

Introduce key vocabulary, such as **eight legs, scorpion, habitats, insects, tails, pincers; sting, cornered, search, deadly, poisonous**. Ask questions to probe the reading.

Ask: *Why do you think scorpions search for prey at night? What can happen if a scorpion is cornered?*

Substantial Support

Provide visual support, and cognates for key vocabulary and science facts: **scorpion, arachnid, prey (presa), habitat, insects (insectos), aggressive (agresivo)**.

Model asking a simple question using the word **habitat**.

Ask: *Where is a scorpion's habitat?*

Help students use key vocabulary to ask original questions.

What cornered the _____?

How did the scorpion sting the _____?

RF.2.4b Read on-level text orally with accuracy, appropriate rate, and expression on successive readings.
RF.2.4c Use context to confirm or self-correct word recognition and understanding, rereading as necessary.

©2018 Benchmark Education Company, LLC

Grade 2 • Unit 3 • Week 1

DAY 1 — SHORT READ 1 MINI-LESSON

Texts for Close Reading, pp. 6–9
"The Coldest Place on Earth"

Student Objectives

I will be able to:
- Read an informational text.
- Identify and underline key details.

Additional Materials

Weekly Presentation: Unit 3, Week 1
- Key Details and Main Idea Chart

Ways to Scaffold the First Reading

Use your observational assessment to determine the intensity of scaffolding your students need.

IF . . .	THEN consider . . .
Students are English learners who may struggle with vocabulary and language demands . . .	**Read the text TO students.** • Conduct a before-reading picture walk to introduce vocabulary and concepts. • Stop after meaningful chunks to define unfamiliar words and paraphrase difficult sentences.
Students are struggling readers who may decode with little comprehension . . .	**Read the text WITH students.** • Stop after meaningful chunks to ask **who, what, when, where, how** questions. • Work with students to define unfamiliar words and paraphrase key ideas.
Students need some support to read unfamiliar texts with comprehension . . .	**Have students PARTNER-READ.** Partners should: • take turns reading aloud meaningful chunks. • ask each other **who, what, when, where, how** questions about the text. • circle unfamiliar words and define them using context clues.

"The Coldest Place on Earth": Identify the Main Topic of a Text

(15 MIN.) RI.2.1, RI.2.2

Preview the Text

Display and ask students to open to "The Coldest Place on Earth." Allow time for students to preview the title, the text, photographs, and captions before they read. Invite students to turn and tell a partner about important text they noticed based on their preview. Sample modeling if necessary.

Sample modeling. Before I read a text, I preview it. I read and think about the title. I look at the illustrations. Sometimes I skim the text, and I make predictions. I also determine text importance by noticing captions, labels, and bullets. I see a map and a photograph on page 6. There is a caption, and I think it probably explains the map and photograph. I think that is pretty important to understanding the text.

Model

Have students follow along as you read aloud the first two paragraphs. Model identifying and annotating key details.

Sample modeling (paragraph 1). This paragraph is about Antarctica, the place itself. I'll underline details that describe Antarctica: **iciest, windiest, and emptiest place on Earth.** *Other details are about how hard it is for living things to survive there, so I'll underline* **a few tough animals** *and* **an amazing bird.**

Sample modeling (paragraph 2). Paragraph 2 introduces me to the emperor penguin. I'll ask myself, "What is most important to understand about emperor penguins?" I'll underline key details about emperor penguins: **can't fly, spend most of their lives in the freezing-cold sea.**

Grade 2 • Unit 3 • Week 1 ©2018 Benchmark Education Company, LLC

SHORT READ 1 MINI-LESSON

Guided Practice

Allow students time to read the rest of the text. Refer to the "Ways to Scaffold the First Reading" sidebar if your students need support to read the text. Pose text-dependent questions to guide their thinking as they look for key events. For example:

- What is paragraph 3 mostly about? What details support the main idea?
- Which detail in paragraph 4 is more important—"tap, tap, crack!" or "eggs hatch"? Why?

Display a blank Key Details and Main Idea Chart and work with students to begin filling it out. During discussion, remind students to take turns respectfully and to connect their ideas to what they heard from previous speakers.

Section	Key Details (paragraph)	Main Idea
Paragraphs 1–2	Antarctica is the "iciest, windiest, and emptiest place on Earth." (1) Emperor penguins "can't fly," but "spend most of their lives in the freezing-cold sea." (2)	Emperor penguins are flightless birds that are tough enough to survive in cold, icy Antarctica.
Paragraphs 3–4	"Each mother lays one egg." (3) The father keeps the egg warm.(3) When the eggs hatch, the mothers "cares for their chicks." (4)	Emperor penguin parents share the job of caring for their egg and the hatched chick.

Sample Key Details and Main Idea Chart

During independent time, ask students to reread paragraph 3 and find the question in it. Have them write a sentence that answers the question using details in the paragraph.

 **Integrated ELD**

Light Support
Have students echo-read "The Coldest Place on Earth" and find key phrases such as the following:

can't fly	act like	come back
can't walk	lay eggs	care for

Help groups say, read, write, and present original sentences using key phrases.

Moderate Support
Students echo-read "The Coldest Place on Earth" and find key vocabulary such as the following:

tap	return	breaking
crack	stay	freezing

Have students use at least two key vocabulary words in one original sentence.

Substantial Support
Students echo-read "The Coldest Place on Earth" and find key vocabulary such as the following:

survive	waddle	keep
spend	wiggle	huddle

Write key vocabulary words on cards. Use photos and the text, along with gestures and simple phrases, to discuss meaning. Students role-play to show comprehension. Groups present assigned words and then switch cards. Model presenting the word **huddle**.
Say: *This is the word* **huddle**.
Here it is in the story. (point to the word)
To **huddle** *means to come together tightly.*
The penguins **huddle** *when they are cold.*

RI.2.1 Ask and answer such questions as who, what, where, when, why, and how to demonstrate understanding of key details in a text. **RI.2.2** Identify the main topic of a multiparagraph text as well as the focus of specific paragraphs within the text.

DAY 1

WRITING TO SOURCES

Write an Informative Report: Read a Mentor Informative Report (15 MIN.) W.2.5

Engage Thinking

Tell students they will be writing an informative text over the next three weeks. In an informative text, a writer provides facts about a topic and includes details that support those facts. Definitions of important words are also part of the text. For example, an informative report about an animal would include facts, such as where the animal lives and what it eats, and the meaning of any difficult words the author uses.

Read and Analyze the Prompt

Display and distribute copies of Mentor Writing Prompt and Mentor Informative Report. Read the writing prompt aloud.

Sample think-aloud. *This prompt tells me what to write—an informative report about how emperor penguins survive in Antarctica. The prompt directs me to include facts and the meanings of important words that I learn from two different sources.*

Read and Analyze the Mentor Text

Display and/or distribute the informative text "Emperor Penguins in Antarctica." Tell students this as written in response to the prompt. Ask students to listen and follow along as you read it.

Mentor Writing Prompt

Write an informative report that describes how emperor penguins survive Antarctica's harsh winters. Support your ideas with facts and definitions from "The Coldest Place on Earth" and information from "Adapting to Survive."

Student Objectives

I will be able to:
- Read and analyze a writing prompt.
- Read and analyze the features of an informative text.

Materials

Weekly Presentation: Unit 3, Week 1
- Mentor Writing Prompt
- Mentor Informative Report
- Facts, Details, Definitions Chart
- Informative Report Anchor Chart

Informative Report Anchor Chart

To write an informative report, writers…
Include facts, details, and content words
- State facts about the topic
- Include descriptive details to support the facts
- Define content words

Emperor Penguins in Antarctica

The emperor penguin is one tough bird! It lives all year in Antarctica, one of the coldest places on Earth. It has adapted in interesting ways so that it can live there.

From reading "The Coldest Place on Earth," I learned that Antarctica is "the iciest, windiest, and emptiest place on Earth." In "Adapting to Survive," I saw and heard that penguins are the only animals "to live in Antarctica all year round" and that other birds leave when winter comes.

I learned from the text that a "thick layer of blubber, or fat," protects and keeps the bird warm. I heard in the video that "four layers of waterproof feathers and another layer of fat underneath" act like a thick suit to keep them warm and dry when they swim in the icy sea.

I read that huddling close together also helps emperor penguins stay warm. In the cold, dark days of winter, "the fathers huddle together" against the freezing wind. They are also holding eggs! Fathers keep the eggs warm, and the mothers dive into the icy water to find food.

Winter in Antarctica is harsh, but emperor penguins don't think so. They stay warm. They lay eggs. For two months, they wait for their babies to hatch. The long, dark days are soon over, and all the penguins return to the sea together.

Mentor Informative Report

10 Grade 2 • Unit 3 • Week 1 ©2018 Benchmark Education Company, LLC

WRITING TO SOURCES

WEEK 1 · DAY 1

Point out that "Emperor Penguins in Antarctica" exemplifies these informative text features: states facts about Antarctica and emperor penguins, includes descriptive details, and defines important words.

Begin a two-column chart to record the facts, descriptive details, and defined words in the informative text. Model how to find one example of each and record it in the chart.

Facts	Emperor penguins live in Antarctica.
Descriptive Details	Antarctica is cold and icy.
Definitions	Blubber: a thick layer of fat

Sample Facts, Details, Definitions Chart

Share Your Understanding

Bring students together and invite partners to share their ideas, adding their findings to the two-column chart. Then create an anchor chart like the sample provided.

☑ Quick Write

During independent time, have students independently answer the following question: *What types of information are included in informative texts?* Use students' writing to evaluate their understanding of the genre.

---

iELD Integrated ELD

Light Support
Ask students to find words that describe the weather in Antarctica (**freezing, harsh, icy**) or ways that emperor penguins adapt to the cold (**blubber, feathers, huddle**). Model the correct pronunciation of the words, as needed, and have students repeat. Have students demonstrate their understanding of each descriptive word by using it in a sentence.

Moderate Support
Have students find and pronounce words that describe the Antarctic weather and how emperor penguins stay warm. Model the correct pronunciations, as needed, and discuss the word meanings. Then help students use the words in context by providing sentence frames for them to complete. For example:
Antarctica is a _____ place. (**freezing, harsh, windy, barren**)
_____ *helps keep emperor penguins warm.* (**huddling, feathers, blubber**)

Substantial Support
Write and display the words **harsh, icy, freezing, huddle, blubber,** and **feathers**. Pronounce each word clearly, and use visuals, actions, and examples to help students understand its meaning. Then ask questions that allow students to demonstrate their understanding and provide sentence frames to help them respond by using the appropriate words. For example:
Which word tells how cold the weather is in Antarctica? The Antarctic weather is _____.
Which word tells how the penguins stay warm? The penguins _____ together to keep warm.

W.2.5 With guidance and support from adults and peers, focus on a topic and strengthen writing as needed by revising and editing.

Long u Frieze Card and Sound-Spelling Card

Student Objectives

I will be able to:
- Identify, blend, and spell words with long **u**.
- Learn and read high-frequency words.

Additional Materials

- Letter cards: **b, c, e, s, t, u**

Weekly Presentation, Unit 3, Week 1
- Long **u** frieze card
- Long **u** sound-spelling card
- High-frequency word cards: **again, below, carry, does, eight, find, house, laugh, mother, school**
- Review high-frequency word cards: **good, many, near, off, people, right, that, two, under, very**

For additional word study/decodable practice, see: *More About Utah*, *Camping Out*, and *The Rescue Park*.

Long u: ew, ue, u, u_e (15 MIN.) RF.2.3a, RF.2.3b, RF.2.3c, RF.2.3e, RF.2.3f, L.2.2d

Spelling-Sound Correspondences

Introduce: Long u
Display the long u frieze card.

Say: *This sound is /ū/. The /ū/ sound is spelled many ways:* **ew, ue, u, u_e**.

Model: ew, ue, u, u_e
Point to each spelling on the card and provide a sample word: **ew** as in **few**, **ue** as in **fuel**, **u** as in **unit**, **u_e** as in **fuse**. Write each sample word and underline the long **u** spelling.

Say: *Look at the first word I wrote:* **f-e-w.** *I see long **u** spelled **ew**. Listen and watch as I sound out the word:* **/fuuu/, few**.

Run your hand under the word as you sound it out.

Practice: few, fuel, unit, use
Repeat the long **u** words one at a time. Ask students to write each word and underline the long **u** spelling.

Blend Words

Model: Long and short u
Display the letter cards for **cut**. Model how to blend the sounds together as you run your hand under each letter.

Say: *This is the letter* **c**. *It stands for /k/. This is the letter* **u**. *It stands for /u/. Listen as I blend these sounds together:* **/kuuu/**. *This is the letter* **t**. *It stands for /t/. Now listen as I blend all three sounds together:* **/kuuut/, cut**. *Say the word with me:* **cut**.

Model adding an **e** to the end to make the word **cute**.

Say: *I can add an* **e** *to the end to make the vowel team* **u_e**. *The vowel team* **u_e** *stands for the long* **u** *sound. Listen as I blend the new word:* **/kuuut/**. *Say the word with me:* **cute**.

Continue modeling the words **cub, cube** and **us, use**.

Practice: huge, menu, few, fuel, rescue
Write each word. Have students read aloud together to blend the sounds. Point out the two syllables in the words **menu** and **rescue**. Provide corrective feedback, as needed.

PHONICS & WORD STUDY

WEEK 1 · DAY 1

Spelling (iELD)

Pretest

Say each spelling word. Read the sentence and say the word again. After the pretest, write each word as you say the letters. Have students check their work.

use	Can you **use** some help on your project?
few	I only have a **few** crayons left in the box.
cute	My dog is so **cute**!
huge	An elephant is a **huge** animal.
cube	A box is in the shape of a **cube**.
music	I like to listen to **music** when I exercise.
rescue	I watched the firefighter **rescue** the cat from a tree.
menu	What is your favorite meal on the **menu**?
fuel	We need to get **fuel** for the car.
January	**January** is the first month of the year.

High-Frequency Words

Introduce: *again, below, carry, does, eight, find, house, laugh, mother, school*

Use the following routine: Write simple sentences using each high-frequency word. Underline the word and discuss important features about it. Say the word and have students repeat it. Then spell the word with students as you point to each letter. Finally have students write the word as they spell it aloud.

Practice

Display the high-frequency word cards. Have students work with a partner to write sentences using the words. Then have volunteers read a sentence and identify the high-frequency word.

Review: *good, many, near, off, people, right, that, two, under, very*

Review last week's words using the high-frequency word cards. Mix and display one word card at a time as students read aloud together each word.

(iELD) Integrated ELD

Light Support

Elicit unusual animal names, such as moths.
Model asking questions using sentence frames. Then have students think of original questions.
I have always wondered _____?
I have always been curious _____?

Moderate Support

Elicit unusual animal names. Model asking questions.
Ask: *Why do wolves howl?*
Have students complete the following question frames to ask question about the story:
What do _____?
Where do _____?
How do _____?
Why do _____?

Substantial Support

Introduce the nouns **frogs** and **butterflies.**
Use a sentence strip to model formulating questions.
Point out the initial question word and final question mark explicitly.
When do frogs sleep?
Model forming questions using the following frames:
What do _____ eat?
Where do _____ live?
Why do _____ hide?
How do _____ change?

RF.2.3a Distinguish long and short vowels when reading regularly spelled one-syllable words. **RF.2.3b** Know spelling-sound correspondences for additional common vowel teams. **RF.2.3c** Decode regularly spelled two-syllable words with long vowels. **RF.2.3e** Identify words with inconsistent but common spelling-sound correspondences. **RF.2.3f** Recognize and read grade-appropriate irregularly spelled words. **L.2.2d** Generalize learned spelling patterns when writing words (e.g., cage → badge; boy → boil).

©2018 Benchmark Education Company, LLC

Grade 2 • Unit 3 • Week 1   **13**

DAY 2 — SHARED READING

Texts for Close Reading, p. 4
"News About Scorpions"

Student Objectives

I will be able to:
- Read an informational text.
- Identify and annotate the main idea.

Additional Materials
Weekly Presentation: Unit 3, Week 1

---

iELD Integrated ELD

Light Support
Review "News About Scorpions." Elicit, post, and have students echo-read key details for each paragraph. Students complete the sentence frame for each paragraph to determine the main idea: *Since I read that _____, I think the main idea of this paragraph is _____.*
Encourage students using the following prompts.

Paragraph 1	Paragraph 2
Detail: poisonous and deadly sting	**Detail:** search for prey at night
Main idea: describe scorpions	**Main idea:** describe how scorpions get food

Moderate Support
Present as above.

Paragraph 1	Paragraph 2
Detail: have pincers; look like lobsters	**Detail:** warm, dry habitats
Main idea: discuss what scorpions are like	**Main idea:** discuss where scorpions live

Substantial Support
Present as above.

Paragraph 1	Paragraph 2
Detail: curved tails	**Detail:** catch food at night
Main idea: tell what scorpions are like	**Main idea:** describe how scorpions get food

---

Shared Reading (10 MIN.) RF.2.3f, RF.2.4a, RF.2.4b

Reread for Fluency: Rate/Pausing

Partner reading: Assign partners to read aloud "News About Scorpions" to each other. Remind students to read at a speed that sounds like natural speech and to be mindful of punctuation marks that signal when to pause or stop briefly as they read.

Collaborative Conversation: Determine Text Importance

Remind students that yesterday you showed them how you used the Determine Text Importance reading strategy while you previewed "News About Scorpions." Tell them that today partners will practice the strategy as they read the text. Stress how important it is that they determine what text and text features are important as opposed to what are merely interesting. By doing that, readers can distinguish between what they need to read carefully and what they may pay less attention to. If necessary, guide partners with questions. For example:

- *Do you think it is important to know the scorpions are poisonous?*
- *In a text about an animal, is news about how it eats and hunts important?*

Transfer Skills to Context: Annotate Main Idea

Remind students that yesterday they underlined the key details in the text. Model how you identify the main idea of a paragraph by looking at the key details. For example:

Sample modeling. *In paragraph 1, I underlined details that describe a scorpion: curved tail, eight legs, poisonous sting, in the arachnid family, pincers. The main idea of this paragraph is "What is a scorpion?" I will write the main idea down.*

Ask students to identify and annotate the main idea of paragraph 2 by looking at the key details they underlined.

Transfer Skills to Context: Long u Vowel Team Syllable Pattern

Point to the word **News** in the title and ask students to read it aloud with you.

Ask: *What vowel sound do you hear in* **news***? What two letters spell that sound?*

Then display these words for students to read aloud, repeating the vowel sound for **ew** in each: **threw**, **mew**, **chew**, **dewdrop**, **renew**, **grew**.

RF.2.3f Recognize and read grade-appropriate irregularly spelled words. **RF.2.4a** Read on-level text with purpose and understanding. **RF.2.4b** Read on-level text orally with accuracy, appropriate rate, and expression on successive readings.

Explain How Images Contribute to and Clarify a Text (15 MIN.) RI.2.5, RI.2.7, SL.2.2

SHORT READ 1 MINI-LESSON

WEEK 1 · DAY 2

Engage Thinking

Explain to students that informational texts may include maps and photographs. Maps and photographs help them understand main ideas in a text. Explain that a map is a drawing that shows a part of Earth's surface.

Model iELD

Display the opening page of "The Coldest Place on Earth." Model how the text, the map, and the captioned photograph help you build your knowledge about Antarctica.

Sample modeling (photograph and caption). *The text tells me that Antarctica is the iciest, windiest, and emptiest place on Earth. The photograph shows an empty, frozen land, with snowy mountains and an ice-filled sea. The caption tells me that Antarctica is the land around the South Pole. The map helps me understand where Antarctica is located.*

Sample modeling (map). *I see that the labels on the map identify the different continents and major oceans. The compass rose shows that north is at the top and south is at the bottom. I see Antarctica all the way at the "bottom" of the world, far away from the other lands. This helps me understand when the text tells about how empty and barren the landscape is.*

Guided Practice

Have students continue reading and make connections between the information in the text, photographs, and captions. Pose text-dependent questions to guide students' thinking.

- *The text describes the emperor penguin's body. How does the photograph on page 7 help you understand that information?*
- *Read about what the father penguins do. What does the photograph on page 8 show? What additional fact is in the caption?*

Reflect on the Strategy

Ask students to turn to a partner to answer this question: *Why should you pay attention to maps, photographs, and captions when you are reading a text?*

☑ Show Your Knowledge

During independent time, ask students to use information from paragraph 1 and the map to write a new caption for the photograph shown on that page.

Texts for Close Reading, pp. 6–9
"The Coldest Place on Earth"

Student Objectives

I will be able to:
- Use text and graphics features to understand ideas in a text.
- Explain the purpose of a map.

Additional Materials

Weekly Presentation: Unit 3, Week 1

iELD Integrated ELD

Light Support
Discuss and read the map, photo, and caption on the opening page of the text. Find Antarctica as a group. Have partners present simple sentences that show how the map helps them understand the photo. Provide sentence frames.
The compass rose _____.
The continent, _____, is _____ and _____.
The location of _____ is _____.

Moderate Support
Discuss and read the map, photo, and caption on the opening page of the text. Students discuss how the map helps them understand the text. Use these sentence frames:
The compass rose helps me _____.
I see the _____, Antarctica, and it is _____.

Substantial Support
Discuss and read the map, photo, and caption on the opening page of the text. Students discuss and echo-read key vocabulary for reading maps: **compass rose, location, south.**
Students orally complete sentences about the photo caption and the map.
The _____ (compass rose) helps me find the _____ (location) of Antarctica, which is in the _____. (south)

RI.2.5 Know and use various text features (e.g., captions, bold print, subheadings, glossaries, indexes, electronic menus, icons) to locate key facts or information in a text efficiently. **RI.2.7** Explain how specific images (e.g., a diagram showing how a machine works) contribute to and clarify a text. **SL.2.2** Recount or describe key ideas or details from a text read aloud or information presented orally or through other media.

©2018 Benchmark Education Company, LLC

Grade 2 · Unit 3 · Week 1   **15**

DAY 2

SHORT READ 1 MINI-LESSON

Use Text Evidence to Draw Inferences

(15 MIN.) RI.2.1, RI.2.5

Engage Thinking

Explain to students that readers must use the information they find in a text to figure out ideas that the author doesn't directly state. Guide students to understand that asking questions about what is directly stated in a text helps readers figure out answers that are not directly stated.

Texts for Close Reading, pp. 6–9
"The Coldest Place on Earth"

Student Objectives

I will be able to:
- Draw inferences about animals in their habitats.
- Identify text evidence that helped me draw an inference.

Additional Materials

Weekly Presentation: Unit 3, Week 1
- Inferences and Evidence Chart

Model

Model identifying and using what is directly stated in "The Coldest Place on Earth" to draw inferences about the information. Reread paragraph 2 and the photo caption.

Sample modeling. *When I read the details "can't fly" and "can't walk too well," I wonder, How do these penguins move? The text says, "These penguins spend most of their lives in the freezing-cold sea." The photo caption tells me that they eat fish they find in the sea. I can draw the inference that penguins are skillful swimmers and hunters.*

Sample modeling. *When I read the detail about the penguin's "barrel-shaped body," I wonder, Why might it have a body shaped like a barrel? I know that a round shape that is narrow at both ends, like a barrel, moves fast in water. I can draw the inference that the penguin's body shape gives it speed underwater.*

Guided Practice

Ask students to reread the rest of the text to answer questions that require them to draw inferences:

- *Why does the father penguin keep the egg on top of his feet?*
- *What does the father penguin eat while he takes care of the egg?*
- *How does huddling keep the penguins warm?*

Use students' responses to create an Inferences and Evidence Chart showing inferences made from text evidence.

Inferences	Text Evidence (paragraph)
The father keeps the egg on top of his feet so that it can be warmed by his belly.	"right under their bellies" (3) "eggs stay safe and warm" (3)
The father penguin doesn't eat anything while he takes care of the egg.	After mothers return, "it's the fathers' turn to eat." (4)
Huddling keeps the penguins warm because their bodies give off heat. When they crowd together, they share their body heat.	"All the fathers huddle together to keep each other warm." (4) "The fathers take turns standing on the inside of the huddle, out of the wind." (caption)

Sample Inferences and Evidence Chart

16   Grade 2 • Unit 3 • Week 1

©2018 Benchmark Education Company, LLC

SHORT READ 1 MINI-LESSON

WEEK 1 • DAY 2

Reflect on the Strategy

Ask students to reflect on the strategy by discussing different ways to complete this statement: *When you draw inferences, you _____.*

 Show Your Knowledge

During independent time ask students to reread paragraph 2 and to draw an inference about how the penguins stay warm in the icy sea. Have them point to evidence in the text and/or a photo that led them to their inference.

Challenge Activity. Have students use the internet to read about the Antarctic fur seal. Then have them write two or three sentences about the animal and its habitat, including at least one sentence with an inference.

 **Integrated ELD**

Light Support
Ask students to echo-read the Inferences and Evidence Chart in Guided Practice. Have each student complete the sentence frame below.
Because _____, the implication is _____.

Moderate Support
Students echo-read the Inferences and Evidence Chart in Guided Practice, and complete the sentence frame below.
Since _____, I can infer _____.

Substantial Support
Students echo-read the Inferences and Evidence Chart in Guided Practice, and complete the sentence frame below.
When I read that _____, I concluded _____.

RI.2.1 Ask and answer such questions as who, what, where, when, why, and how to demonstrate understanding of key details in a text. **RI.2.5** Know and use various text features (e.g., captions, bold print, subheadings, glossaries, indexes, electronic menus, icons) to locate key facts or information in a text efficiently.

©2018 Benchmark Education Company, LLC

Grade 2 • Unit 3 • Week 1

DAY 2

WRITING TO SOURCES

Write an Informative Report: Read and Analyze the Source Text Organization (15 MIN.) W.2.5

Mentor Writing Prompt

Write an informative report that describes how emperor penguins survive Antarctica's harsh winters. Support your ideas with facts and definitions from "The Coldest Place on Earth" and information from "Adapting to Survive."

Student Objectives

I will be able to:
- Identify facts and details from a source text that are used in an informative text.
- Identify and write about parts of an informative text.

Materials

Weekly Presentation: Unit 3, Week 1
- Analyze the Source Text
- Informative Report Anchor Chart

Informative Report Anchor Chart

To write an informative report, writers…
Include facts, details, and content words
- State facts about the topic
- Include descriptive details to support the facts
- Define content words

Include an introduction, body, and conclusion
- Give background information in the introduction
- Provide facts and details in the body
- Sum up the ideas in the conclusion

Engage Thinking

Remind students that yesterday you read them a writing prompt and an informative report written in response to that prompt. Then you analyzed the features included in an informative report: facts, details, and content words.

Tell students that you relied on two sources for the facts, details, and definitions that you used in the informative report. Today, you will show them how you used information from the source text "The Coldest Place on Earth" in your report.

Model

Display Analyze the Source Text, Excerpt 1 and distribute copies to students. Read aloud the first Mentor Informative Text Excerpt. Model how you used background information from the source text to write an introduction. Make students aware that in your report you are also citing information you saw and heard in the media source.

Say: *I needed to give background information about Antarctica and emperor penguins. I found information about both in the opening paragraph of "The Coldest Place on Earth." Let's read the source text. I'll highlight the information I used.*

Ask students to highlight the same information on their copies as you read aloud. Point out that you did not include every idea, and you used your own words.

Mentor Informative Text Excerpts	Source Text Excerpts: "The Coldest Place on Earth"
1. The emperor penguin is one tough bird! It lives all year in Antarctica, one of the coldest places on Earth. It has adapted in interesting ways so that it can live there. From reading "The Coldest Place on Earth," I learned that Antarctica is "the iciest windiest, and emptiest place on Earth." In "Adapting to Survive," I saw and heard that penguins are the only animals "to live on the Antarctic all year round" and that other birds leave when winter comes.	1. *Brrrr.* Covered by a thick blanket of snow and ice that never melts, Antarctica is the iciest, windiest, and emptiest place on Earth. Its barren landscape has no trees and few plants. Some people visit, but none live there. Only a few tough animals can survive Antarctica's harsh winters. One of them is an amazing bird.

Analyze the Source Text, Excerpt 1

18 Grade 2 • Unit 3 • Week 1 ©2018 Benchmark Education Company, LLC

Next, read aloud Mentor Informative Text Excerpt 2.

Say: *As I continued to write, I made sure I answered the prompt. The source gives a lot of information about emperor penguins, but I only needed the facts related to how they survive winter. Watch as I highlight these facts in the source.*

Read aloud Source Text Excerpt 2, highlighting the information that you used in the informative report. Have students highlight their copies. Remind them that you included only the relevant facts and details from the source text and you used your own words.

Mentor Informative Text Excerpts	Source Text Excerpts: "The Coldest Place on Earth"
2. I learned from the text that a "thick layer of blubber, or fat," protects and keeps the bird warm. I heard in the video that "four layers of waterproof feathers and another layer of fat underneath" act like a thick suit to keep them warm and dry when they swim in the icy sea.	2. Meet the emperor penguin! These barrel-shaped birds can't fly. They are too heavy and their wings are too short. They can't walk too well, either. These penguins spend most of their lives in the freezing-cold sea. A thick layer of blubber, or fat, and shiny feathers act like a heavy, waterproof jacket.

Analyze the Source Text, Excerpt 2

Peer Practice

Have students work in pairs to compare the last two excerpts of the mentor and source text. Ask the partners to highlight the facts and details from the source that are used in the mentor text. Remind students that the mentor text also cites the media source at times to support a point the source text supports.

Share Your Understanding

Bring students together and invite partners to share their findings. Remind them that an author uses sources to write an informative report, but chooses only the facts that fit the topic and uses his or her own words. Help students understand that in an informative report, the introduction gives background information about the topic (excerpt 1). The body paragraphs (excerpts 2 and 3) give facts and details, and a conclusion sums things up (excerpt 4).

Add these points to the anchor chart you started yesterday.

Quick Write

During independent time, have students answer the following question: *What are the different parts of an informative report and what information is included in each part?* Use students' writing to evaluate their understanding of the genre.

W.2.5 With guidance and support from adults and peers, focus on a topic and strengthen writing as needed by revising and editing.

iELD Integrated ELD

Light Support
Ask students to choose and list the important ideas from the third excerpt of the source text that they might include in an informative report. Guide them to express each idea in their own words.

Moderate Support
Help students find information about Antarctica's weather in the first source text excerpt. Provide sentence frames to help them express the facts in their own words. For example:
The author says that Antarctica is the iciest, windiest, and emptiest place on Earth.
I can say that Antarctica is a _____ and _____ place.

Substantial Support
Help students find words and phrases in the first source text excerpt that describe Antarctica (**blanket of snow and ice, iciest, windiest, emptiest, barren, harsh**). Together, write and define each word or phrase, using examples, visuals, and actions or gestures to reinforce students' understanding of its meaning. Then have students quick-draw an Antarctic scene. Provide sentence frames to help them describe their sketch using some of the terms. For example:
Antarctica is a very _____ place.
It has lots of _____ and _____.

DAY 2

PHONICS & WORD STUDY

Long *u* Frieze Card and Sound-Spelling Card

Student Objectives

I will be able to:
- Blend, build, and read words with long **u** and long **i**.
- Practice high-frequency words.

Additional Materials

- Letter cards: **b, c, e, f, i, l, m, p, r, s, t, u, w**

Weekly Presentation: Unit 3, Week 1
- Long *u* frieze card
- Long *u* sound-spelling card
- High-frequency word cards: **again, below, carry, does, eight, find, house, laugh, mother, school**

For additional word study/decodable practice, see: *More About Utah, Camping Out,* and *The Rescue Park.*

Long u: ew, ue, u, u_e (15 MIN.) RF.2.3a, RF.2.3b, RF.2.3c

Review long u

Display the long **u** frieze card. Review the long **u** sound spelled **ew** as in **few**, **ue** as in **fuel**, **u** as in **unit**, and **u_e** as in **use**. Point to each spelling-sound.

Say: *What are the letters? What sound do they stand for?*

Blend Words

Model: fuel

Display letter cards for **fuel**. Model blending.

Say: *This is the letter **f**. It stands for /f/. These are the letters **ue**. They stand for /ū/. This is the letter **l**. It stands for /l/. Listen as I blend these sounds together: /fūūūl/, fuel. Say the word with me: fuel.*

Practice: few, use, rescue, music

Use the same routine to guide student practice.

Build Words

Model: cut, cute, cube, cub

Display the letter cards for **cut**. Blend the sounds: /kuuut/, cut.

- Add the **e** to the end and repeat with **cute**.
- Replace the **t** with **b** and repeat with **cube**.
- Delete the **e** and repeat with **cub**.

Practice: pew, few, fuel; us, use, muse, mule

Use the same routine to guide student practice.

20 Grade 2 • Unit 3 • Week 1

©2018 Benchmark Education Company, LLC

PHONICS & WORD STUDY

WEEK 1 · DAY 2

Spelling (iELD)

Closed Sort: *use, few, cute, huge, cube, music, rescue, menu, fuel, January*
Write and display each word on an index card. Ask students to read and spell together each word. Have students sort the cards according to sound/spelling. When completed, have students read aloud together and spell the words. Ask students what they notice about the long **u** spellings (e.g., other words with the **u_e** spelling).

High-Frequency Words

Review: *again, below, carry, does, eight, find, house, laugh, mother, school*
Display the high-frequency word cards. Have students read and spell each word. Focus on common spelling patterns, such as the long **i** in **find**. Have students generate other long **i** words spelled with **-ind**.

Review Long i

Model: light, lightning
Write the word **light** and ask students to identify the vowel sound and spelling. Point out that the letters **igh** are a team, which means they stand for one sound, and that this kind of syllable is called a vowel team syllable.

Write the word **lightning**. Underline each vowel spelling. Explain that a vowel team must stay in the same syllable. Have a volunteer divide the word into syllables. Then have students use the syllables to read the word.

Practice: fly, flying, find, finding, try, trying, tried
Use the same routine to guide student practice.

(iELD) Integrated ELD

Light Support
Review the spelling words. Emphasize the long **u** sound and the different spellings (**ew, ue, u, u_e**). Assign each group 3–4 spelling words. Ask groups to write the words on separate cards, and present them. Tell students to write two sentences using as many spelling words as possible in each sentence. Students can use gestures or simple drawings to portray sentences and show comprehension.

Moderate Support
Review the spelling words. Emphasize the long **u** sound and the different spellings (**ew, ue, u, u_e**). Assign each group 3–4 spelling words. Groups write the words on separate cards, and present them. Pairs write two sentences using as many spelling words as possible in each sentence. Students act out sentences to show comprehension.

Substantial Support
Review the spelling words. Emphasize the long **u** sound and the different spellings (**ew, ue, u, u_e**). Assign each group 3–4 spelling words. Groups write the words on separate cards, and present them. Model presenting the word **fuel**.
Say: *One of our words is fuel, f-u-e-l.*
It has the long u sound.
In this word, the letters u-e make the long u sound.
Gasoline is a fuel.

RF.2.3a Distinguish long and short vowels when reading regularly spelled one-syllable words. **RF.2.3b** Know spelling-sound correspondences for additional common vowel teams. **RF.2.3c** Decode regularly spelled two-syllable words with long vowels.

DAY 3

SHARED READING

Texts for Close Reading, p. 5
"All the Penguins"

Student Objectives

I will be able to:
- Read a poem about animals in their habitat.
- Read at correct rate.
- Identify root words.

Additional Materials

Weekly Presentation: Unit 3, Week 1

Shared Reading (10 MIN.) RL.2.4, RF.2.3d, RF.2.4b, L.2.4c

Introduce the Text

Display "All the Penguins" and read aloud the title of the poem. Point out to students that "Plants and Animals in Their Habitats" is mostly an informational text unit. Explain that literary texts such as stories and poems can help to deepen readers' appreciation of a real-life topic such as life science.

Model Fluent Reading: Rate/Pausing

First Reading. Read the first two stanzas of the poem aloud at a lively rate, with natural pauses for punctuation, line endings, and stanza breaks. Have students read along with you for the last two stanzas. Tell them that they will read at a speed that is not too fast and not too slow, but just right to help listeners visualize the penguins. Remind them to pause at natural stopping places, including at commas, end marks, and stanza breaks.

Model Determine Text Importance

Remind students that earlier in the week you practiced the Determine Text Importance reading strategy on "News About Scorpions." Tell them that determining text importance when reading a poem is different. Poems usually don't present hard factual evidence in order to inform readers. More often, poems are meant to be fun and entertaining. Therefore, determining text evidence for "All the Penguins" will involve both identifying important words and phrases and also identifying the text that makes the poem enjoyable. Model determining the important text on the first stanza.

Sample modeling (stanza 1). *I know that to determine text importance, I'll need to think about what I have already learned about penguins this week. I know from reading "The Coldest Place on Earth" that they are excellent swimmers, so I can understand why they might be **jumping in the sea** together. I will write "excellent swimmers" in the margin. Also, when I read, it was fun stressing the rhyming words at the end of lines 2 and 4. I'll note that **sea** and **playfully** are important words in this stanza.*

22 Grade 2 • Unit 3 • Week 1   ©2018 Benchmark Education Company, LLC

SHARED READING

WEEK 1 · DAY 3

Transfer Skills to Context: Annotate Rhythm

Explain to students that the lines in a poem have a **beat**—a rhythm made by stressing some syllables more than others. Think aloud as you mark the stressed syllables in the first stanza—stress every other beat.

Sample modeling (stanza 1). I'll read aloud the first four lines and clap along to listen for the beats. I can mark the syllables that I stress most in each line: They' are play' ing on' an ice' patch, / They' are jump' ing in' the sea'. / All' the pen' guins are to ge' ther, / Hav' ing fun' so play' ful ly'!

Encourage students to clap along to listen for stressed syllables and the rest of the lines.

Transfer Skills to Context: Use Root Words

Explain to students that they can use root words to figure out the meaning of a longer word. Point out the word **playfully** in the fourth line of the poem. Discuss how this word is made up of three parts: a root word, a suffix, and another suffix. Underline the root word **play** in **playfully**. Explain that looking for root words will help them read and understand longer words.

---

iELD Integrated ELD

Light Support
Display "All the Penguins." Preview the photos, discuss the penguins' habitat, then read and have students echo-read key vocabulary.

icy water	cold and clean air
snow	never come inside

Ask students to read the text and add words to the chart that could help them talk about the penguins' habitat. Students use sentence frames to make inferences about the penguins' habitat.
Since _____, I think their habitat _____.
I see _____ and _____, so I think their habitat ____.

Moderate Support
Present as above.

Antarctic	land
cold and clean	sea

Their habitat is _____ both _____ and _____.
The penguins live _____.

Substantial Support
Present as above.

ice patch	home
cold	clean

Say: *Let's discuss the penguins' habitat.*
Their habitat seems cold, because I see an ice patch.
Their home looks clean, because I don't see any garbage.
Have students complete the following sentence frame to make an inference about the penguins' habitat:
Their _____ looks/seems _____, because _____.

RL.2.4 Describe how words and phrases (e.g., regular beats, alliteration, rhymes, repeated lines) supply rhythm and meaning in a story, poem, or song. **RF.2.3d** Decode words with common prefixes and suffixes. **RF.2.4b** Read on-level text orally with accuracy, appropriate rate, and expression on successive readings. **L.2.4c** Use a known root word as a clue to the meaning of an unknown word with the same root (e.g., addition, additional).

©2018 Benchmark Education Company, LLC

Grade 2 · Unit 3 · Week 1   **23**

DAY 3

SHORT READ 2 MINI-LESSON

Texts for Close Reading, pp. 10–13
"Postcards from Alex"

Student Objectives

I will be able to:
- Read an animal fantasy about different habitats.
- Identify and annotate important details in the story.

Additional Materials

Weekly Presentation: Unit 3, Week 1
- Sequence of Events Chart

Ways to Scaffold the First Reading

Use your observational assessment to determine the intensity of scaffolding your students need.

IF . . .	THEN consider . . .
Students are English learners who may struggle with vocabulary and language demands . . .	**Read the text TO students.** • Conduct a before-reading picture walk to introduce vocabulary and concepts. • Stop after meaningful chunks to define unfamiliar words and paraphrase difficult sentences.
Students are struggling readers who may decode with little comprehension . . .	**Read the text WITH students.** • Stop after meaningful chunks to ask *who, what, when, where, how* questions. • Work with students to define unfamiliar words and paraphrase key ideas.
Students need some support to read unfamiliar texts with comprehension. . .	**Have students PARTNER-READ.** Partners should: • take turns reading aloud meaningful chunks. • ask each other *who, what, when, where, how* questions about the text. • circle unfamiliar words and define them using context clues.

"Postcards from Alex": Recount Key Story Events (15 MIN.) RL.2.1, RL.2.5

Preview the Text ⓘELD

Display and ask students to open to "Postcards from Alex." Tell students that this text is an animal fantasy—the kind of literary story in which animals think and talk like people. Model the importance of previewing the text.

Sample modeling. *Before I read a text, I preview it. I read the title and look at the illustrations. Sometimes I skim the text. Sometimes I determine text importance by thinking about why the author wrote the text. As I skim this story, I see animals as cartoon characters, and I also see illustrations that have writing on them like a postcard. I think the author wrote this text to entertain and maybe inform a little.*

Model

Display the story and ask students to follow along as you read, think aloud, and annotate paragraphs 1–4.

Say: *When we think about what happens in a story, we need to find and identify the key events. We can use details in the story to summarize the key events in sequence. We can also use details to determine text importance.*

Sample modeling (paragraph 1). *The story begins with a conversation between two armadillos. I learn from Juan's question that Alex is going to leave his home in the Amazon rain forest. That question gives an important detail, so I'll underline it.*

Sample modeling (paragraphs 2–4). *As their conversation continues, I learn why Alex wants to leave, so I'll underline those details: <u>damp</u>, <u>too warm</u>. His last comment describes what he plans to do—he'll send postcards from the places he goes—so I'll underline it.*

Display a blank Sequence of Events Chart and fill out the first key event.

Story Event 1	Story Event 2	Story Event 3	Story Event 4
Alex the armadillo is leaving his home in the rain forest because it is too damp and warm. He will send postcards to Juan from the places he goes.			

Sample Sequence of Events Chart

24 Grade 2 • Unit 3 • Week 1   ©2018 Benchmark Education Company, LLC

SHORT READ 2 MINI-LESSON

WEEK **1** · DAY **3**

Guided Practice

If your students need support to understand the text, refer to "Ways to Scaffold the First Reading." Pose text-dependent questions to guide students' thinking. For example:

- *How do you know that Alex wants to leave the rain forest?*
- *Why does Alex want to leave? Where did you learn that?*

Have students read Alex's first and second postcards. Have them annotate key story events and determine text importance. Have them underline the key details and/or write why text is important in the margins.

Give students time to read and annotate. Observe their annotations to assess their ability to identify details about key events and to determine text importance. Pose text-dependent questions to guide students' thinking as they look for details to underline. For example:

- *Where does Alex go first? What problem does he find there?*
- *Where does Alex go after that? What problem does he find there?*

Guide students to use their annotations to summarize key story events and to finish filling in the chart.

Story Event 1	Story Event 2	Story Event 3	Story Event 4
Alex the armadillo is leaving his home in the rain forest because it is too damp and warm. He will send postcards to Juan from the places he goes.	Alex visits a mountain in Chile, but it is too cold for him there.	Alex visits a city, but he can't burrow into the sidewalks there.	Alex visits a desert, but it is too hot and dry, and there are no ants to eat. He is coming home to the rain forest.

Sample Sequence of Events Chart

☑ Show Your Knowledge

Ask students to read Alex's last postcard and underline the important details that describe the last key event. Have them write one or more sentences summarizing the ending of the story. Use their work to evaluate their strategy development and help you make instructional decisions.

(iELD) Integrated ELD

Light Support
Preview "Postcards from Alex." Discuss the habitats using the sentence frame *Alex's postcard about the _____ said that _____.* As students complete the sentence frame, have them point to key illustrations or role-play to show comprehension.
Use the illustrations to discuss, present, elicit, and list key vocabulary about each habitat. Use words from the charts to prompt discussion.

rain forest	mountain	city	desert
rainy	chilly	no place to sleep; tired	land; not a drop of water

Moderate Support
Present as above. Provide the sentence frame *Alex told Juan that the _____ was/had _____.*

rain forest	mountain	city	desert
damp	freezing	sidewalks	dry

Substantial Support
Present as above. Provide the sentence frame *Alex wanted to leave _____, because _____.*

rain forest	mountain	city	desert
warm	cold	garbage	hot

RL.2.1 Ask and answer such questions as who, what, where, when, why, and how to demonstrate understanding of key details in a text. **RL.2.5** Describe the overall structure of a story, including describing how the beginning introduces the story and the ending concludes the action.

©2018 Benchmark Education Company, LLC

Grade 2 · Unit 3 · Week 1   **25**

DAY 3

WRITING TO SOURCES

Write an Informative Report: Read to Find Facts and Details (15 MIN.) W.2.7, W.2.8

Mentor Writing Prompt

Write an informative report that describes how emperor penguins survive Antarctica's harsh winters. Support your ideas with facts and definitions from "The Coldest Place on Earth" and information from "Adapting to Survive."

Student Objectives

I will be able to:
- Identify how notes taken by a writer match the information in a source text.
- Take organized notes from a source text.

Materials

Weekly Presentation: Unit 3, Week 1
- Source Text Notetaking Chart
- Informative Report Anchor Chart

Informative Report Anchor Chart

To write an informative report, writers…
Include facts, details, and content words
- State facts about the topic
- Include descriptive details to support the facts
- Define content words

Include an introduction, body, and conclusion
- Give background information in the introduction
- Provide facts and details in the body
- Sum up the ideas in the conclusion

Start by taking notes on source texts
- Create an organized notetaking form
- Fill in the form with information taken from the source text
- Take notes using the writer's own words

Engage Thinking

Remind students that yesterday they identified facts and details from a source text that were used in the Mentor Informative Report about Antarctica and emperor penguins.

Say: *I didn't include all the facts from the source text in the informative report. I focused on what the prompt said to write about. I took notes to organize the information and stay on topic. Today I will show you my notetaking strategy.*

Model

Display the Source Text Notetaking Chart and distribute copies to students.

Say: *Before I started writing my informative report, I studied the writing prompt carefully and thought about what kind of information I would need to look for in the source text. Then I made a notetaking form I could use. I wrote the big idea at the top of the form to help me stay focused. I knew that the first thing I needed to do was give readers some background information about winters in Antarctica and the kind of animal that emperor penguins are. I created a section for this on my notetaking form.*

Display "The Coldest Place on Earth" and have students turn to this selection in their Texts for Close Reading.

Say: *I used "The Coldest Place on Earth" for one of my information sources. Let's look for the background information in this source text. I found it in the first paragraph. As I read this paragraph, I wrote these notes about Antarctica: "It's frozen all year. It's the iciest place on earth. People do not live there." I also found information about emperor penguins and took this note: "They are remarkable birds."*

Model writing the source text title and notes in the appropriate sections of the notetaking form. Point out that the notes are written in your own words. Then have students fill in the same section using their own words.

Peer Practice

Have partners read the second paragraph of the source text to find a fact that explains why emperor penguins can survive winter in Antarctica. Ask them to take notes about the fact and the details that support that fact in the "Facts and Details" section. If they come across a word that they think should be defined for readers, have them write that information in the "Words to Use and Define" section. Encourage students to take notes in their own words.

---

26 Grade 2 • Unit 3 • Week 1   ©2018 Benchmark Education Company, LLC

Share Your Understanding

Bring students together and invite partners to share their notes. Discuss the importance of taking good notes when reading a source text. Guide students to understand that creating a notetaking form, filling it in with information from the source text, and using their own words to write their notes are strategies that will help them take focused, organized, and detailed notes.

Include these points on the anchor chart you've been creating.

Quick Write

During Independent time, have students answer the following question: *How is a notetaking form helpful when you write an informative report?* Use students' writing to evaluate their understanding of the usefulness of a notetaking form.

---

iELD Integrated ELD

Light Support
Have students add any unfamiliar words from the source text to their notes. Discuss the word meanings, as needed. Then, to help students remember the meanings, ask them to create a brief sketch for each word or write a sentence using the word.

Moderate Support
Help students determine facts from the source text, then use those facts to help students structure their thoughts as they take notes.
Say: *The second paragraph leads readers to discover one important fact about emperor penguins and the cold weather of Antarctica—their bodies are built to survive in freezing conditions. This fact is supported by two details that explain how the penguins stay warm. What are those two details?*
(penguins have a thick layer of blubber and they are covered with waterproof feathers).
Encourage students to respond orally to your prompts before they jot down notes using their own words.

Substantial Support
Guide students in finding details in the source text that support facts about how emperor penguins survive the winters of Antarctica. Supply sentence frames to help students state the details in complete thoughts.
Say: *The last sentence in the second paragraph is about how emperor penguins stay warm in the freezing cold. The fact suggested by this sentence is that penguins have bodies that help them survive winter. These two details support this fact:*
Emperor penguins have a layer of _____.
(blubber, or fat)
The penguins' feathers are _____. (waterproof)

W.2.7 Participate in shared research and writing projects (e.g., read a number of books on a single topic to produce a report; record science observations). **W.2.8** Recall information from experiences or gather information from provided sources to answer a question.

DAY 3

PHONICS & WORD STUDY

Texts for Close Reading, p. 14
"The Deserts of Utah"

Student Objectives

I will be able to:
- Blend, read, and spell words with long **u**.
- Read word study (decodable) text.
- Practice high-frequency words.

Additional Materials

- Letter cards: **c, e, e, f, m, n, r, s, t, u, w**
- Long **u** frieze card
- Long **u** sound-spelling card

Weekly Presentation: Unit 3, Week 1
- High-frequency word cards: **again, below, carry, does, eight, find, house, laugh, mother, school**
- Review high-frequency word cards: **good, many, near, off, people, right, that, two, under, very**

For additional word study/decodable practice, see: *More About Utah, Camping Out,* and *The Rescue Park.*

Monitor Student Reading of Word Study (Decodable) Text

As students read the word study (decodable) text and answer questions, ask yourself these questions:

Are students able to . . .
- ❏ blend and read long **u** words in the text?
- ❏ read new high-frequency words with automaticity?
- ❏ demonstrate comprehension of the text by answering text-based questions?

Based on your observations, you may wish to support students' fluency, automaticity, and comprehension with additional decodable reading practice during intervention time.

Long u: ew, ue, u, u_e (10 MIN.) RF.2.3b, RF.2.3c, RF.2.3e, RF.2.3f, L.2.2d

Blend Words

Practice: use, cute, few, rescue, menu
Display pocket chart letter cards for the word use. Model how to blend the sounds to say the word. Use the same routine with other long **u** words to guide student practice.

Read Word Study (Decodable) Text

Introduce the Text
Read the title "The Deserts of Utah" aloud. Stop when you come to the word **Utah**. Model dividing the word to decode it syllable by syllable. Point out the open first syllable and the long **u** spelling **u**.

Read the Text
Ask students to read the text. If students need modeling, guide them to blend decodable words and read high-frequency words. You may wish to conduct a second reading, having partners read to each other while you circulate and monitor the reading.

Connect Phonics to Comprehension
Ask some or all of the following questions:
- *What different land areas can you find in Utah?*
- *How are the jackrabbit and the leopard lizard alike?*
- *How does the cactus survive in the desert?*

Spelling

Write the definitions. Have students copy the definitions and then write the spelling words that go with them.

1. not many (few)
2. the first month of the year (January)
3. very big (huge)
4. to save from harm or danger (rescue)

High-Frequency Words

Practice: *again, below, carry, does, eight, find, house, laugh, mother, school*
Draw a ladder with ten rungs. Write a high-frequency word on each rung. Have students take turns climbing the ladder by reading the words.

Review: *good, many, near, off, people, right, that, two, under, very*

RF.2.3b Know spelling-sound correspondences for additional common vowel teams. **RF.2.3c** Decode regularly spelled two-syllable words with long vowels. **RF.2.3e** Identify words with inconsistent but common spelling-sound correspondences. **RF.2.3f** Recognize and read grade-appropriate irregularly spelled words. **L.2.2d** Generalize learned spelling patterns when writing words (e.g., cage → badge; boy → boil).

28 Grade 2 • Unit 3 • Week 1   ©2018 Benchmark Education Company, LLC

Shared Reading (10 MIN.) RF.2.3b, RF.2.4a, RF.2.4b, RF.2.4c

SHARED READING

WEEK 1 • DAY 4

Reread for Fluency: Rate/Pausing

Partner reading. Ask partners to alternate reading the four verses of the poem "All the Penguins" and then switch roles. Remind them that commas and end marks signal pauses.

Collaborative Conversation: Determine Text Importance

Remind students that yesterday you showed them how you determined text importance as you read the first stanza of "All the Penguins." Tell them that today they will work with partners to determine text importance in stanzas 2–4. You might want to challenge students with leading questions based on the poem. For example:

- *What are the penguins doing in the poem? What text told you that?*
- *Describe the habitat penguins live in. What text gave you that information.*
- *Which text makes the poem entertaining and enjoyable? What words rhyme?*

Transfer Skills to Context: Annotate End Rhyme

Explain to students that in this poem, rhyming words appear at the ends of lines. One reason poets use end rhymes is to make a poem fun to read aloud and easier to remember. Model identifying and underlining end rhymes in lines 1–4.

Sample modeling (lines 1–4). *I'll read aloud the first four lines and listen for end rhymes. I hear the same vowel sound in **sea** and the syllable **ly** in **playfully**. I'll underline lines 2 and 4 that have end rhymes.*

Ask students to listen for end rhymes in the rest of the poem and to circle the rhyming words. They should annotate **between/clean**, **side/inside**, **home/roam**.

Transfer Skills to Context: Long e Vowel Team Syllable Patterns

Ask students to find words in the poem in which two vowel letters spell the long **e** sound. They should identify the words **sea**, **between**, and **clean**. Ask them to name the two vowel letters in each word.

Texts for Close Reading, p. 5
"All the Penguins"

Student Objectives

I will be able to:
- Read a poem.
- Recognize and annotate end rhymes.

Additional Materials

Weekly Presentation: Unit 3, Week 1

iELD Integrated ELD

Light Support
Write words on cards: **feast, leave, each, between, seed, need.** Pairs use the target words in sentences and explain word meanings.

Moderate Support
Write words on cards: **feast, leave, each, between, seed, need.** Students role-play word meanings to show comprehension. Record and have students echo-read original sentences using the target words.

Substantial Support
Review long **e** vowel teams **ee** and **ea**. Write words on cards: **feast, leave, each, between, seed, need.** Hold up a card. Students repeat after you.
Discuss word meanings. Students act out meanings to show comprehension. As a group, practice using the words in sentences.

RF.2.3b Know spelling-sound correspondences for additional common vowel teams. **RF.2.4a** Read on-level text with purpose and understanding. **RF.2.4b** Read on-level text orally with accuracy, appropriate rate, and expression on successive readings. **RF.2.4c** Use context to confirm or self-correct word recognition and understanding, rereading as necessary.

DAY 4

SHORT READ 2 MINI-LESSON

Texts for Close Reading, pp. 10–13
"Postcards from Alex"

Student Objectives

I will be able to:
- Identify the elements found in a story.
- Explain and identify a problem in a story.

Additional Materials

Weekly Presentation: Unit 3, Week 1
- Story Map

Describe the Overall Structure of a Story (15 MIN.) RL.2.1, RL.2.5

Engage Thinking

Review with students their completed Story Events Chart for the fantasy "Postcards from Alex" from yesterday. Explain that they are now going to describe the overall story structure. Tell students to look at "Postcards from Alex," along with the Story Events Chart they completed. Review the key events.

Model

Point to details in the text as you model analyzing story structure for the elements of setting, character, problem, events, and solution.

Sample modeling. *When I read a story, I like to find out what problem the main character is faced with and how the character will solve it. In the first two paragraphs of this story, I learn that the main character is Alex the armadillo, and his problem is that he does not want to live in the Amazon rain forest anymore. The key events are that Alex visits different places but each habitat does not meet his needs. At the end of the story, Alex decides that the rain forest is the best home for him.*

Guided Practice

Display a blank Story Map. Work with students to analyze the story structure. Pose text-dependent questions to guide students, pointing out relevant details in the text and illustrations.

Story Title: "Postcards from Alex"	
Settings Amazon rain forest mountain in Chile city desert	**Characters** Alex the armadillo (main character) Juan the armadillo (Alex's friend)
Problem: Alex doesn't want to live in the rain forest anymore because it is too damp and warm.	
Key Events 1. Alex is too cold on the mountain in Chile. 2. Alex can't dig a burrow on city sidewalks. 3. Alex can't find water or food in the desert.	
How the Problem Is Solved Alex decides that the rain forest is the best home for him.	

Sample Story Map Reflect on the Strategy

Ask partners to work together to generate one or two questions that readers can ask about a story's problem and solution. Together, they should decide why the questions are helpful.

30 Grade 2 • Unit 3 • Week 1

©2018 Benchmark Education Company, LLC

SHORT READ 2 MINI-LESSON

WEEK 1 • DAY 4

 **Show Your Knowledge**

During independent time, display this sentence: *The settings are especially important in the story "Postcards from Alex."* Ask students to write one or two sentences to support that statement.

Challenge Activity. Have students write and illustrate a postcard that Juan might have sent to Alex.

iELD Integrated ELD

Light Support
Display "Postcards from Alex." Students sequence key events on sentence strips. Review signal words. Groups narrate events in the correct order.

To begin with	leaves the rain forest; goes to the mountains in Chile
After that	travels to the city; doesn't like it
In the end	leaves the desert; it's too hot; he goes back to the rain forest

Moderate Support
Display "Postcards from Alex." Students sequence key events on sentence strips. Review signal words. Groups narrate events in the correct order.

starts	visits the mountains in Chile
then	takes a trip to the city
finally	winds up in the desert

Alex starts his adventure when he _____.
Then he _____.
Finally, he _____, and he decides to _____, because _____.

Substantial Support
Display "Postcards from Alex." Students echo-read and sequence sentence strips with key events. Review signal words. Groups role-play and narrate events in the correct order.

1	Alex goes to the mountains.
2	Alex goes to the city.
3	Alex goes to the desert.

After Alex leaves the rain forest, he _____.
Then Alex _____.
Before Alex goes home to _____, he _____.

RL.2.1 Ask and answer such questions as who, what, where, when, why, and how to demonstrate understanding of key details in a text. **RL.2.5** Describe the overall structure of a story, including describing how the beginning introduces the story and the ending concludes the action.

©2018 Benchmark Education Company, LLC

Grade 2 • Unit 3 • Week 1   31

DAY 4

SHORT READ 2 MINI-LESSON

Texts for Close Reading, pp. 10–13
"Postcards from Alex"

Student Objectives

I will be able to:
- Distinguish shades of meaning among related adjectives.
- Share my understanding in partner conversations.

Additional Materials

Weekly Presentation: Unit 3, Week 1
- Shades of Meaning Chart

Build Vocabulary: Distinguish Shades of Meaning Among Related Adjectives (10 MIN.) RL.2.4, L.2.5b

Engage Thinking

Tell students that today they are going to work with related adjectives—words that describe nouns. Related adjectives generally mean the same thing but to varying degrees. Related adjectives have varying shades of meaning.

Model

Ask students for adjectives that are related to the word **big**. Discuss what might be described with each one, and how the meanings differ. For example: **gigantic**, **huge**, **large**, **enormous**. Explain that in this mini-lesson, students will learn how adjectives with similar definitions can convey meanings.

Read aloud paragraphs 3 and 4 of "Postcards from Alex." Model comparing and contrasting the meanings of the adjectives **delicious** and **tasty**.

Sample modeling (paragraphs 3, 4). *Juan uses the adjective **delicious** to describe insects. Alex uses the adjective **tasty**. I know that both **delicious** and **tasty** are adjectives that describe things that are pleasant to eat. The adjective **delicious** has a slightly stronger meaning than **tasty**. I think that tasty foods are good, but delicious foods are very good.*

Guided Practice

Reread Alex's first postcard with students. Draw their attention to these three adjectives: **cold**, **freezing**, **chilly**. Then ask students to answer these questions and give reasons:

- *What is the difference between feeling cold and feeling chilly?*
- *What is the difference between a chilly day and a freezing day?*
- *From least to most cold, how would you order the adjectives **cold**, **freezing**, and **chilly**?*

Reread Alex's last postcard with students. Ask them to find two adjectives that describe the desert (**hot, dry**). Display each of the following phrases and list of three adjectives. Ask students to substitute each listed word for the adjective **hot** or **dry**. Discuss shades of meaning by talking about how the adjectives might be ordered from least to most. Encourage varied responses.

- a hot desert (sizzling, warm, fiery)
- a dry desert (sun-baked, burnt, dusty)

32   Grade 2 • Unit 3 • Week 1

Add the information to a class chart.

Word from Text	Words Ordered from Least to Most
hot	warm, hot, fiery, sizzling
dry	dry, dusty, sun-baked, burnt

Shades of Meaning Chart

Reflect on the Strategy

Assign partners this discussion question: *If adjectives with similar definitions, like **big** and **large**, can convey different meanings, how does a writer decide which one to use?*

After discussion, call on partnerships to share their ideas with the whole class.

Show Your Knowledge

During independent time, ask students to reread Alex's second postcard, sent from the city. Draw their attention to the word **tired** in the closing.

Ask: *From least to most tired, how would you order the adjectives **exhausted, drowsy**, and **sleepy**?*

Challenge Activity. Invite students to create a continuum of adjectives with similar meanings, listing words from least to greatest intensity. For example, students could list synonyms for **small**, such as **little, tiny, miniature,** and **petite**.

SHORT READ 2 MINI-LESSON

WEEK 1 • DAY 4

iELD Integrated ELD

Light Support
Review the settings in "Postcards from Alex," and the concept of varied levels of meaning among related adjectives.
Create a word bank of adjectives that range from least to most and have students echo-read. Use visual support, role-playing, or gestures to explain word meanings.

feel . . .	cold	chilly	freezing

Students use the word bank to complete sentence frames.
At first I was _____ in the mountains.
After that, I was _____ in _____.
I left the _____ because I was _____.

Moderate Support
Create a word bank of adjectives that range from least to most and have students echo-read. Use visual support, role-playing, or gestures to explain word meanings.

feel . . .	warm	hot	boiling

Students use the word bank to complete sentence frames.
It was boiling in the desert.
It was _____ in the _____.

Substantial Support
Review the settings in "Postcards from Alex," and the concept Shades of Meaning Among Adjectives.
Students use the word bank to complete sentence frames. Use visual support, role-playing, or gestures to explain word meanings.

taste . . .	good	tasty	delicious

Model using adjectives in sentences and act out meanings.
In the city, the insects were good.
In the mountains, the insects were tasty.
In the rain forest, the insects were delicious.
Students use each adjective in a sentence and role-play meanings.

RL.2.4 Describe how words and phrases (e.g., regular beats, alliteration, rhymes, repeated lines) supply rhythm and meaning in a story, poem, or song. **L.2.5b** Distinguish shades of meaning among closely related verbs (e.g., toss, throw, hurl) and closely related adjectives (e.g., thin, slender, skinny, scrawny).

DAY 4

WRITING TO SOURCES

Mentor Writing Prompt

Write an informative report that describes how emperor penguins survive Antarctica's harsh winters. Support your ideas with facts and definitions from "The Coldest Place on Earth" and information from "Adapting to Survive."

Student Objectives

I will be able to:
- Identify how notes taken by a writer match the information in a media source.
- Take organized notes after viewing a media source.

Materials

Weekly Presentation: Unit 3, Week 1
- Media Source Notetaking Chart
- "Adapting to Survive" Media Source
- Informative Report Anchor Chart

Informative Report Anchor Chart

To write an informative report, writers…
Include facts, details, and content words
- State facts about the topic
- Include descriptive details to support the facts
- Define content words

Include an introduction, body, and conclusion
- Give background information in the introduction
- Provide facts and details in the body
- Sum up the ideas in the conclusion

Start by taking notes on source texts
- Create an organized notetaking form
- Fill in the form with information taken from the source text
- Take notes using the writer's own words

Take notes on media sources
- Create an organized notetaking form
- Watch and listen for facts and the details that support them
- Fill in the form with information learned from the media source
- Take notes using the writer's own words

Write an Informative Report: Listen and View to Find Facts and Details

(15 MIN.) W.2.7, W.2.8

Engage Thinking

Recall with students that yesterday you used the source text to find facts and details for your informative report on emperor penguins. You showed them how you created a notetaking form and used it to record and organize your notes. Tell students that today you will use a second source to learn about the penguins.

 Model

Display the Media Source Notetaking Chart and distribute copies to students.

Say: *The second source that I used to get information about emperor penguins was a slide show, which is a type of media source. I know that when viewing a media source, I have to use my eyes and ears. I need to watch and listen closely to learn the facts and details that are included in the source. So I set up my notetaking form to include sections in which I could take notes on what I saw and heard in the slide show. Let's view the media source together, then I'll share some notes that I took for my informative text.*

Play "Adapting to Survive." Encourage students to watch and listen closely to the slide show.

Say: *I learned in the slide show that emperor penguins have layers of waterproof feathers and a layer of fat that keeps them warm. The close-up of the emperor penguin's feathers helped me understand this. I also saw other bird species traveling off for the winter. I wrote this in my notes: "Emperor penguins are the only animal that lives in Antarctica year-round. They stay warm and dry because of four layers of waterproof feathers and a layer of fat. Other birds leave when winter comes."*

Model writing these notes in the "Facts and Details I See" section on the notetaking form. Remind students to use their own words when filling in their own forms.

Say: *I also heard details from the narrator. One thing I heard was that Antarctica is actually a desert and that there are only two seasons, summer and winter. In the winter, there is no sunshine and it is extremely cold. I wrote this fact on my form: "Antarctica is one of the harshest and most extreme climates on Earth."*

Model writing these notes in the "Facts and Details I Hear" section. Have students use their own words to add the notes to their form.

Grade 2 • Unit 3 • Week 1

Peer Practice

Have partners take notes from the media source. Remind them to listen and watch for important facts and the details that support them and to use their own words when writing their notes.

Facts and Details I See	Facts and Details I Hear
Four layers of waterproof feathers keep emperor penguins warm and dry.	Antarctica is a desert.
Other bird species leave Antarctica when winter comes.	Antarctica has only two seasons: winter and summer.

Sample Media Source Notetaking Chart

Share Your Understanding

Bring students together and invite partners to share their notes.

Ask: *What are some things you can do to take good notes when using a media source?*

Guide students to understand that creating a notetaking form, watching and listening carefully, filling in the form with information learned from the source, and using their own words will help them take good notes.

Add these points to the anchor chart.

Quick Write

During independent time, have students answer the following question: *Why is it important to watch and listen carefully to a media source?* Use students' writing to evaluate their understanding of the importance of paying close attention to media sources.

WRITING TO SOURCES

WEEK 1 · DAY 4

iELD Integrated ELD

Light Support
After viewing the slide show, have partners take turns asking and answering questions about emperor penguins. Model for them how to focus their exchanges on the facts and details they saw and heard in the media source. For example, ask: *Why are emperor penguins the only animal that spends the winter in Antarctica?*

Moderate Support
Play the slide show, breaking it into shorter segments to help students focus on a few facts and details at a time. Before playing each segment, provide prompts to signal what information students should be expecting to learn. For example: *This section tells a fact about Antarctica's climate. You will hear two details about that fact.* After viewing the segment, have students identify the facts and details. If needed, provide sentence frames for students to use when filling in their forms.

Substantial Support
Pause the slide show frequently to direct students to specific facts that are supported by details. Guide them to restate each fact and work with a partner to record it. Then provide sentence frames for students to use in saying and recording the details.

W.2.7 Participate in shared research and writing projects (e.g., read a number of books on a single topic to produce a report; record science observations). **W.2.8** Recall information from experiences or gather information from provided sources to answer a question.

DAY 4

PHONICS & WORD STUDY

Student Objectives

I will be able to:
- Blend multisyllabic words with long **u**.
- Spell words with long **u**.
- Read high-frequency words.

Additional Materials

- Long **u** frieze card
- Long **u** sound-spelling card

Weekly Presentation: Unit 3, Week 1
- High-frequency word cards: **again, below, carry, does, eight, find, house, laugh, mother, school**

For additional word study/decodable practice, see: *More About Utah, Camping Out,* and *The Rescue Park.*

Long u: ew, ue, u, u_e (20 MIN.) RF.2.3b, RF.2.3c, RF.2.3d, RF.2.3e, RF.2.3f, L.2.2d

Read Multisyllabic Words

Model: rescue

Explain that when a vowel team such as **ew** or **ue** appears in a long word, the vowel team remains in the same syllable. This is because the two letters in the vowel team stand for one vowel sound. Model using the word **rescue**.

- Write the syllable **res** and point out that it's a closed syllable (short vowel sound).
- Add the syllable **cue**. Point out the long **u** vowel team **ue**.
- Circle the vowel spellings **e** and **ue**. Tell students you will divide the word before the two consonants in the middle: **res/cue**.
- Blend the syllables to read the word.

Practice: music, value, fewer, reuse, refuel, human, unit

Use the same routine to guide student practice.

Spelling

Opposites

Write the opposites. Read the words, and ask students to find a spelling word that means the opposite.

- many _____ (few)
- ugly _____ (cute)
- little _____ (huge)
- in danger _____ (rescue)

High-Frequency Words

Review: *again, below, carry, does, eight, find, house, laugh, mother, school*

Display the high-frequency word cards. Read each word and have students repeat the word out loud together and spell it. Have students sit in a circle. Pass the cards, one at a time. Each student reads the word and uses it in a sentence before passing the card.

RF.2.3b Know spelling-sound correspondences for additional common vowel teams. **RF.2.3c** Decode regularly spelled two-syllable words with long vowels. **RF.2.3d** Decode words with common prefixes and suffixes. **RF.2.3e** Identify words with inconsistent but common spelling-sound correspondences. **RF.2.3f** Recognize and read grade-appropriate irregularly spelled words. **L.2.2d** Generalize learned spelling patterns when writing words (e.g., cage → badge; boy → boil).

Shared Reading (10 MIN.) RI.2.1, RF.2.3d, SL.2.2, SL.2.3

Determine Text Importance (iELD)

Remind students that they have been determining text importance all week on texts and sections of texts. Tell them that readers should identify big ideas, themes, and important information when they read. To do that, they must determine the importance of certain text and text features and separate that from less importance text. Remind students to beware that interesting or amusing bits of text may stick out, but readers must determine whether that text is really important—it supports a big idea—or merely interesting.

Model sorting out unimportant text from "News About Scorpions."

Sample modeling. *I read the text through once, and I decided that almost all the text was important. The text is short, and almost every sentence provides important facts and details about scorpions—which is the author's purpose. The text has a great picture of a scorpion, so I understand what scorpions look like. Now I am wondering about the last sentence of paragraph 1. Is it really important that some people think they look like tiny lobsters? I think that's amusing, but it isn't really important as the rest of the text.*

Transfer Skills to Context: Adjectives

Review that adjectives are words that describe things. Explain to students that some adjectives describe how many of something. Ask students to identify adjectives in "News About Scorpions" that answer the question "How many?" (**eight**, **some**)

Build and Reflect

During independent time, tell students to think about the Week 1 selections, and ask them to complete the "Build, Reflect, Write" activity on page 15 to help them think more about how animals survive in their habitats.

SHARED READING

WEEK 1 • DAY 5

Texts for Close Reading, pp. 4–5 "News About Scorpions" and "All the Penguins" and "All the Penguins," p. 5

Student Objectives

I will be able to:
- Identify adjectives that tell how many.
- Answer questions about what I have learned.

Additional Materials

Weekly Presentation: Unit 3, Week 1

iELD Integrated ELD

Light Support
Scaffold before reading "News About Scorpions." Students partner-read and take turns reading aloud meaningful chunks; use context clues to define new words: **aggressive, curved tail, realize, cornered.** Read and monitor their rate.

Moderate Support
Scaffold before reading "News About Scorpions." Read with students. Stop after meaningful chunks; discuss vocabulary and language: **tiny lobsters, pincers, eight legs, active.** Model and explain reading with the correct rate. Students echo-read.

Substantial Support
Scaffold before reading "News About Scorpions." Read to students. Conduct a pre-reading picture-walk; discuss vocabulary and context: **poisonous, scorpion, arachnid, habitats.** Emphasize rate and accuracy. Students echo-read.

RI.2.1 Ask and answer such questions as who, what, where, when, why, and how to demonstrate understanding of key details in a text. **RF.2.3d** Decode words with common prefixes and suffixes. **SL.2.2** Recount or describe key ideas or details from a text read aloud or information presented orally or through other media. **SL.2.3** Ask and answer questions about what a speaker says in order to clarify comprehension, gather additional information, or deepen understanding of a topic or issue.

DAY 5

CROSS-TEXT MINI-LESSON

Texts for Close Reading, pp. 6–13 "The Coldest Place on Earth" and "Postcards from Alex"

Student Objectives

I will be able to:
- Compare and contrast two texts.
- Participate in discussions about two texts.

Additional Materials

Weekly Presentation: Unit 3, Week 1
- Compare-and-Contrast Chart

Compare and Contrast Key Points in Two Texts on the Same Topic (15 MIN.) RI.2.9, SL.2.1a, SL.2.1b, SL.2.1c

Engage Thinking

Display "The Coldest Place on Earth" and "Postcards from Alex." Remind students that there are main ideas in these texts. Tell students that in this lesson they will compare and contrast what these two texts say about habitats.

Ask for a volunteer to describe the terms **compare** and **contrast**, and support the response.

Model

Display a Compare-and-Contrast Chart and read aloud the head for each section. Review that details that pertain only to one or the other text belong in the left and right columns—these details show how the texts are different. The ways texts are alike belong in the middle column. Think aloud about similarities and differences, and note them in the chart. If needed, model how to compare and contrast the two texts.

Sample modeling. *I know that "The Coldest Place on Earth" gives facts about Antarctica. It is an informational text. In contrast, "Postcards from Alex" is an animal fantasy. I'll note these differences in the chart.*

Sample modeling. *When I ask myself how the two texts are alike, I think about what I've learned from both of them. "The Coldest Place on Earth" describes Antarctica and one animal that lives in this habitat—the emperor penguin. "Postcards from Alex" tells about different habitats that an armadillo visits. In the "Both Texts" section of the chart, I'll list a similarity: "Give information about habitats."*

Guided Practice

Compare and contrast the text and graphic features in both texts. Pose text-dependent questions to guide students' thinking.

- *What kinds of images are in "The Coldest Place on Earth?" What kinds of images are in "Postcards from Alex?" Are the images similar or different?*
- *What do you notice about how the text is presented in "The Coldest Place on Earth?" How about "Postcards from Alex?" Is that a similarity or a difference?*

CROSS-TEXT MINI-LESSON

WEEK 1 · DAY 5

Compare and contrast the structure and other elements of both texts:

• *"The Coldest Place on Earth" gives facts and details about Antarctica. How is "Postcards from Alex" similar? How is it different?*
• *"Postcards from Alex" is organized to show what Alex does first, next, then, and last. Does "The Coldest Place on Earth" describe events in sequence, too?*
• *Who is giving readers the information in "The Coldest Place on Earth?" Who is telling the story in "Postcards from Alex?"*

If necessary, continue modeling how you think about these comparisons and contrasts. Collaborate with students to complete the chart. Encourage them to use complete sentences to share their ideas. Review class discussion rules, reminding students to listen attentively, ask questions to help a speaker explain more, and build on other speakers' ideas.

"The Coldest Place on Earth"	Both Texts	"Postcards from Alex"
• Informational text • One place: Antarctica • Talks about an animal in this habitat: emperor penguin • Map and photos with captions • Author informs and explains	• Give information about habitats • Focus on a particular animal • Show what animals need to survive • Include events told in sequence	• Animal fantasy • Different places: rain forest, mountain, city, desert • Animal: armadillo • Illustrations • Postcard messages in italic • Narrator and main character tell story

Compare-and-Contrast Chart

☑️ Show Your Knowledge

During independent time, ask students to copy these sentence starters and complete them with at least one idea from "The Coldest Place on Earth" and "Postcards from Alex."

• *Both texts are alike because . . .*
• *The texts are different because . . .*

Use students' writing to evaluate their ability to state and support a point of comparison and contrast. You may also use this sample to assess students' use of English conventions and their progress in printing legibly.

(iELD) Integrated ELD

Light Support

Review the Compare-and-Contrast Chart in Guided Practice. Discuss and compare the texts.
Use the charts below entries to prompt discussion. Provide sentence frames that will help students compare and contrast the texts.
Model and practice:
I think both stories are alike, because _____.
I think these stories are different, because _____.
"The Coldest Place on Earth" _____, but "Postcards from Alex" _____.

"The Coldest Place on Earth"	Both Texts	"Postcards from Alex"
Father penguin has a job.	Both main characters are males.	Alex is on an adventure.

Moderate Support

Present as above.

"The Coldest Place on Earth"	Both Texts	"Postcards from Alex"
Penguin has many friends.	Describes all settings	Alex has one friend.

Substantial Support

Present as above.

"The Coldest Place on Earth"	Both Texts	"Postcards from Alex"
Provides facts about real animals	Describe events in animals' lives	Describes feelings, not facts

---

RI.2.9 Compare and contrast the most important points presented by two texts on the same topic. **SL.2.1a** Follow agreed-upon rules for discussions (e.g., gaining the floor in respectful ways, listening to others with care, speaking one at a time about the topics and texts under discussion). **SL.2.1b** Build on others' talk in conversations by linking their comments to the remarks of others. **SL.2.1c** Ask for clarification and further explanation as needed about the topics and texts under discussion.

©2018 Benchmark Education Company, LLC

Grade 2 • Unit 3 • Week 1   **39**

DAY 5

WRITING TO SOURCES

Mentor Writing Prompt

Write an informative report that describes how emperor penguins survive Antarctica's harsh winters. Support your ideas with facts and definitions from "The Coldest Place on Earth" and information from "Adapting to Survive."

Student Objectives

I will be able to:
- Recognize when two simple sentences can be joined to form a compound sentence.
- Produce complete compound sentences.

Materials

Weekly Presentation: Unit 3, Week 1
- Modeling Text
- Informative Report Anchor Chart

Informative Report Anchor Chart

To write an informative report, writers…
Include facts, details, and content words
- State facts about the topic
- Include descriptive details to support the facts
- Define content words

Include an introduction, body, and conclusion
- Give background information in the introduction
- Provide facts and details in the body
- Sum up the ideas in the conclusion

Start by taking notes on source texts
- Create an organized notetaking form
- Fill in the form with information taken from the source text
- Take notes using the writer's own words

Take notes on media sources
- Create an organized notetaking form
- Watch and listen for facts and the details that support them
- Fill in the form with information learned from the media source
- Take notes using the writer's own words

Use conventions of English correctly
- Understand simple and compound sentences
- Understand that words such as *and, or, but, so,* and *because* are used to join simple sentences together to form compound sentences

---

Conventions of Language: Produce Complete Compound Sentences

(15 MIN.) L.2.1f

Focus the Learning

Explain that a sentence states a complete thought and has two parts: a subject and a verb. When you create a sentence that has two complete thoughts that are related, it is called a compound sentence. A conjunction—a word, such as **and**, **or**, **but**, **so**, or **because**—is used to join the two thoughts. Tell students that it can be fun to figure out how to put two simple sentences together to make a compound sentence.

Model

Demonstrate how compound sentences are formed and how they improve the flow of a text.

Say: *One reason that we use compound sentences when we write is because we use them when we speak. We want our writing to sound natural. If we spoke in only simple sentences, our thoughts would sound choppy, the way a robot might talk! Listen to how choppy this text sounds.*

Display Modeling Text A and read it aloud.

Say: *The text will sound much more natural if I combined the related ideas to make compound sentences. For example, I could combine the first two sentences because they are both about the physical traits of penguins: "Penguins are black and white, and they have four layers of feathers and one layer of fat."*

Explain how different conjunctions are used in compound sentences:

- **and** is used to connect similar ideas or to add new ideas
- **or** is used to state choices or give other possibilities
- **but** is used to make contrasts or tell about differences
- **so** is used to tell the reason for or result of something
- **because** is used to show cause and effect relationships

---

40   Grade 2 • Unit 3 • Week 1   ©2018 Benchmark Education Company, LLC

WEEK 1 · DAY 5

WRITING TO SOURCES

Text A
Penguins are black and white. They have four layers of feathers and one layer of fat. Penguins are fat with short wings. They cannot fly. Penguins don't walk well. Penguins are great swimmers.

Text B
Penguins are black and white, and they have four layers of feathers and one layer of fat. Penguins are fat with short wings, so they cannot fly. Penguins don't walk well, but they are great swimmers.

Modeling Text

Peer Practice

Have partners decide together about how to form two more compound sentences using the other simple sentences from Modeling Text A. Ask them to write down the sentences they produce.

Share Your Understanding

Bring students together and invite partners to share their compound sentences.

Ask: *How does using compound sentences improve your writing?*

Help students understand that using a combination of simple and compound sentences can make their text sound more natural and easier to read.

Add information about compound sentences and conjunctions to the anchor chart.

☑ Quick Write

During independent time, have students complete the following writing assignment: *Write two more simple sentences about emperor penguins that could be joined to form a compound sentence. Then write the compound sentence.* Use students' writing to evaluate their understanding of how to create compound sentences.

(iELD) Integrated ELD

Light Support
Review the conjunctions **and**, **or**, **but**, **so**, and **because**, reminding students how each one is used. Then have students use each conjunction to join two simple sentences into a compound sentence.

Moderate Support
Write and display these three conjunctions: **and**, **but**, **or**. Review how each word is used to join two simple sentences. Use each of the conjunctions in a compound sentence, then discuss with students why that particular word was used. For example, help students understand that the conjunction **but** in this sentence is used to contrast the behaviors of penguin fathers and mothers:

*Penguin fathers care for the eggs on land, **but** the mothers return to the sea.*

Substantial Support
Write and display these two conjunctions: **and**, **but**. Pronounce each conjunction, have students repeat the word, and explain how it is used in a compound sentence. Then provide two simple sentences for students to join into a compound sentence. For example:

Antarctica is an icy place. The winter days are long and dark.

Help students choose the most appropriate conjunction (**and** or **but**) to use.

L.2.1f Produce, expand, and rearrange complete simple and compound sentences (e.g., The boy watched the movie; The little boy watched the movie; The action movie was watched by the little boy).

©2018 Benchmark Education Company, LLC

Grade 2 · Unit 3 · Week 1   **41**

DAY 5

PHONICS & WORD STUDY

Texts for Close Reading, p. 14
"The Deserts of Utah"

Student Objectives

I will be able to:
- Build, read, and spell words with long **u**.
- Reread word study (decodable) text for fluency.
- Read high-frequency words.

Additional Materials

- Letter cards: **b, c, e, e, f, g, h, l, m, n, r, t, u, w**
- Long **u** frieze card
- Long **u** sound-spelling card

Weekly Presentation: Unit 3, Week 1
- Letter cards for each high-frequency word
- High-frequency word cards: **again, below, carry, does, eight, find, house, laugh, mother, school**

For additional word study/decodable practice, see:
More About Utah, Camping Out, and *The Rescue Park*.

Review and Assess Long u: ew, ue, u, u_e (20 MIN.) RF.2.3a, RF.2.3b, RF.2.3c, RF.2.3e, RF.2.3f, L.2.2d

Build Words

Model: cub, cube, cute
- Display the letter cards for **cub**. Blend the sounds: /kuuub/, **cub**.
- Add the **e** to the end and repeat with **cube**.
- Replace the **b** with **t** and repeat with **cute**.

Practice: hug, huge; few, fuel; men, menu
Use the same routine to guide student practice.

Review Multisyllabic Words

Model: man, human

Write the word **man** and ask students to identify the vowel sound. Point out that **man** is a closed syllable. It ends in a consonant and has a short vowel sound.

Write the word **human**. Model how to read the longer word. Point out the open first syllable **hu** (ends in a vowel, has a long vowel sound).

Practice: cue, rescue; cut, cute; argue, value; music, unit
Use the same routine to guide student practice.

Reread for Fluency: "The Deserts of Utah"

Have students independently whisper-read "The Deserts of Utah." Circulate and listen to their readings. Provide corrective feedback. For students having difficulty reading independently, have them read with a more skilled partner.

42 Grade 2 • Unit 3 • Week 1   ©2018 Benchmark Education Company, LLC

PHONICS & WORD STUDY

Spelling

Posttest

Use the following procedure to assess students' spelling of this week's words.

- Say each spelling word and use it in the sentence provided.
- Have students write the complete sentence on a piece of paper. Then continue with the next word. Remind students to write legibly.
- When students have finished, collect their papers and analyze any misspelled words.

1. Did you <u>use</u> that pen?
2. I need a <u>few</u> books to read.
3. That baby is so <u>cute</u>!
4. He had a <u>huge</u> problem.
5. A box is in the shape of a <u>cube</u>.
6. I like pop <u>music</u>.
7. We had to <u>rescue</u> a cat stuck in a tree.
8. May I have a <u>menu</u>?
9. We need more <u>fuel</u> for the truck.
10. <u>January</u> can be very cold.

High-Frequency Words

Review: *again, below, carry, does, eight, find, house, laugh, mother, school*

Display the high-frequency word cards. Say each word and have students repeat the word together out loud and spell it.

Place letter cards for one of the words in random order in a pocket chart. Have a volunteer beat the clock to form the word. Allow 15 seconds. Then have the rest of the class check the spelling and give a thumbs up or thumbs down.

Next have students turn to a partner and say a sentence using the word. Call on volunteers to check their sentences.

Integrated ELD

Light Support

Students echo-read "The Deserts of Utah." Emphasize fluency.

To assist with fluency, review vocabulary. Spanish cognates: **unusual/inusual; leopard/el leopard, cactus/el cactus; rescue/rescatar, animal/el animal, state/el estado.** Groups find words from the text and dictate them to you, such as: **Utah, a hard place, blood vessels, off the ground, sharp needles, keep animals away, stems.** Students echo-read.

Pairs write the words and context clues from the text and then share them with the class.

Pairs role-play, draw, or present simple phrases to show understanding of the vocabulary.

Pairs read and present their words, as above, and write and share original sentences using the words.

Moderate Support

Present the story and cognates as above.

Groups find new words, such as: **land areas, away, toes, below, lift, stay cool, rescue, roots** (*underground base of a plant*). Record responses. Students echo-read.

Assist. Students discuss meanings. Provide visual support, gestures, and context clues.

Assign groups words. Groups write words on cards. Students present their words, as above, and switch cards.

Groups use at least two words in one original sentence.

Record sentences. Students echo-read and role-play to show comprehension.

Substantial Support

Present the story and cognates as above.

Explain key vocabulary, such as: **wetlands, jackrabbit, unusual, skin, leopard, lizard, cactus, stores** (*keep, save, put away*). Use visual support, gestures, simple language, and context clues. Students act out or use simple phrases to show understanding of vocabulary. Write the words on cards. Groups practice and present their assigned words, and then switch cards.

Model presenting: *This is the word* **stores.**
Here is the word **stores.** (students point)
In this story, **stores** *means to keep, save, or to put away.*
A cactus can **store** *water in its roots.*

RF.2.3a Distinguish long and short vowels when reading regularly spelled one-syllable words. **RF.2.3b** Know spelling-sound correspondences for additional common vowel teams. **RF.2.3c** Decode regularly spelled two-syllable words with long vowels. **RF.2.3e** Identify words with inconsistent but common spelling-sound correspondences. **RF.2.3f** Recognize and read grade-appropriate irregularly spelled words. **L.2.2d** Generalize learned spelling patterns when writing words (e.g., cage → badge; boy → boil).

©2018 Benchmark Education Company, LLC

Week 2 Mini-Lessons at a Glance

	Day 1	Day 2
Reading Mini-Lessons	**Build Knowledge and Review Strategies (10 Min.), p. 46** SL.2.1a, SL.2.1b, SL.2.2, SL.2.3 **Shared Reading (10 Min.), p. 47** RF.2.3b, RF.2.4a, RF.2.4b, RF.2.4c **"Habitats Around the World": Identify the Main Topic of a Text, Part 1 (15 Min.), p. 48** RI.2.1, RI.2.2, SL.2.1a, SL.2.1b, SL.2.1c	**Shared Reading (10 Min.), p. 54** RF.2.3f, RF.2.4a, RF.2.4b, RF.2.4c **"Habitats Around the World": Identify the Main Topic of a Text, Part 2 (20 Min.), p. 56** RI.2.1, RI.2.2, SL.2.1a, SL.2.1b, SL.2.1c
Writing and Language Mini-Lessons	**Write an Informative Report: Read and Analyze the Prompt (15 Min.), p. 50** W.2.5	**Write an Informative Report: Find Facts, Definitions, and Details in a Source Text (15 Min.), p. 58** W.2.7, W.2.8
Phonics/Word Study Mini-Lessons	**r-Controlled Vowel ar (20 Min.), p. 52** RF.2.3b, RF.2.3e, RF.2.3f, L.2.2d • High-Frequency Words: *move, never, once, round, small, their, too, walk, where, year* • Weekly Spelling Words: *car, star, march, smart, hard, farm, large, shark, garden, yard*	**r-Controlled Vowel ar (15 Min.), p. 60** RF.2.3b, RF.2.3e, RF.2.3f, L.2.2d • High-Frequency Words: *move, never, once, round, small, their, too, walk, where, year*

Extended Read 1: "Habitats Around the World"

Informational Science

Quantitative	Lexile® 560L
Qualitative Analysis of Text Complexity	

Purpose and Levels of Meaning ❸
• Purpose includes detailed explanation and the interpretation of a large amount of highly detailed information.

Structure ❷
• The text is ordered in subtitled sections and uses reasoned explanation to build connections between ideas.
• Readers encounter photos and other visuals necessary to comprehension.

Language Conventionality and Clarity ❷
• Technical vocabulary such as *tropical rain forest, thaws, coral reefs,* and *Arctic tundra* are defined in context through direct definitions and strong context. Sentences are a mix of simple, complex, and compound.

Knowledge Demands ❷
• The text requires some prior knowledge of the nature of animal habitats.

Total QM: 9
Moderate Complexity*

*The texts in *Benchmark Advance* are qualitatively evaluated based on their grade-level placement in the program. Reader maturity and age appropriateness are key considerations in the subjective use of the rubrics.

44   Grade 2 • Unit 3 • Week 2   ©2018 Benchmark Education Company, LLC

Day 3	Day 4	Day 5
Shared Reading (10 Min.), p. 62 RF.2.4a, RF.2.4b, RF.2.4c	**Shared Reading (15 Min.), p. 69** RF.2.4a, RF.2.4b, RF.2.4c, L.2.2c	**Shared Reading (10 Min.), p. 75** RI.2.1, RF.2.4b, SL.2.2, SL.2.3, L.2.1e
Build Vocabulary: Determine the Meaning of Words and Phrases (10 Min.), p. 63 RI.2.4, L.2.4a, L.2.4e	**Close Reading: Use Text Evidence to Draw Inferences (20 Min.), p. 70** RI.2.1, SL.2.1a, SL.2.1b, SL.2.2, SL.2.3	**Close Reading: Compare and Contrast Key Points in Two Texts on the Same Topic to Make Connections Across Texts (15 Min.), p. 76** RI.2.1, RI.2.9, SL.2.1a, SL.2.1b, SL.2.1c, SL.2.2, SL.2.3, SL.2.6
Close Reading: Explain How Images Contribute to and Clarify a Text (10 Min.), p. 64 RI.2.1, RI.2.5, RI.2.7, SL.2.1a, SL.2.1b, SL.2.2, SL.2.3		
Write an Informative Report: Active Viewing and Notetaking from a Media Source (15 Min.), p. 66 W.2.7, W.2.8	**Write an Informative Report: Organize Your Ideas (15 Min.), p. 72** W.2.5	**Conventions of Writing: Capitalize Holidays and Geographic Names (15 Min.), p. 78** L.2.2a
r-Controlled Vowel ar (15 Min.), p. 68 RL.2.3, RF.2.3b, RF.2.3c, RF.2.3e, RF.2.3f, L.2.2d	**r-Controlled Vowel ar (15 Min.), p. 74** RF.2.3b, RF.2.3c, RF.2.3d, RF.2.3e, RF.2.3f, L.2.2d	**Review and Assess r-Controlled Vowel ar (15 Min.), p. 80** RL.2.10, RF.2.3b, RF.2.3c, RF.2.3e, RF.2.3f, L.2.2d
• High-Frequency Words: *move, never, once, round, small, their, too, walk, where, year*	• High-Frequency Words: *move, never, once, round, small, their, too, walk, where, year*	• High-Frequency Words: *move, never, once, round, small, their, too, walk, where, year*

©2018 Benchmark Education Company, LLC

Grade 2 • Unit 3 • Week 2   **45**

DAY 1

UNIT REFLECTION

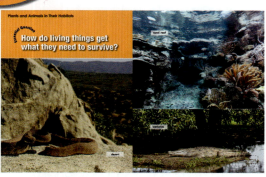

Texts for Close Reading, pp. 2–3
Unit Introduction

Student Objectives

I will be able to:
- Reflect on strategies I have learned to help me read an informational text.
- Follow three-step oral directions.

Additional Materials

Weekly Presentation: Unit 3, Week 2

iELD Integrated ELD

Light Support
Review making inferences about a text. Display "Postcards from Alex."

Say: *Let's draw inferences about Alex's habitat.* Use the information below to prompt students.

Rain Forest	City
delicious insects to eat	only garbage and a few fleas and spiders to eat

Moderate Support
Present as above.

Rain Forest	Mountains
warm	cold

Model and then have students practice making inferences using the prompts provided.

Substantial Support
Review making inferences about a text. Display and review "Postcards from Alex."

Say: *Let's draw inferences about Alex's habitat.* Model making an inference.

Say: *I can infer that Alex needs water to survive, because when there wasn't a drop of water, and the desert was dry, he was upset.*

Help students complete the following sentence frame to make an inference about the text: *I can infer that Alex needs ___ to survive, because ___, he was upset.*

Build Knowledge and Review Strategies (10 MIN.) SL.2.1a, SL.2.1b, SL.2.2, SL.2.3

Discuss the Essential Question

Display the introduction to "Plants and Animals in Their Habitats" and review the Essential Question. After students flip through the Week 1 selections, ask them to listen carefully to your three-step directions. Ask them to turn and talk to a partner about animals and their habitats:

1. Name an animal you have learned about.
2. Tell what that animal's habitat is like.
3. Ask a question about the animal's habitat.

Discuss students' ideas. Explain that in Week 2, students will learn about different kinds of habitats and the living things found in them.

Review Unit Strategies

Use Text Features to Locate Information. Remind students that during Week 1, they looked for captions that gave information about photographs. Display the first page of "The Coldest Place on Earth."

Say: *When we read "The Coldest Place on Earth," we learned in the first paragraph that Antarctica is "the iciest, windiest, and emptiest place on Earth." The caption for the map and photograph gave us more information. The caption helped us understand where Antarctica is located: "Antarctica is the frozen land around the South Pole."*

Have students find a sentence in paragraph 2 that is connected to the photo caption on that page. Ask how that caption provides more information.

Draw Inferences. Remind students that they used information directly stated in the text to figure out ideas that were not directly stated—they drew inferences.

Say: *When we read "The Coldest Place on Earth," we asked a question about what the father penguin ate while he was protecting the egg. We learned from the text that penguins eat fish in the sea and that the father penguin eats only after the mother penguin returns. We drew the inference that a father penguin doesn't eat anything while protecting the egg.*

Ask students to reread Alex's first postcard in "Postcards from Alex." Ask them to draw inferences about what armadillos need to survive.

Explain to students that thinking about captions and other text features and drawing inferences based on text evidence will help them understand the extended text they will read this week.

SL.2.1a Follow agreed-upon rules for discussions (e.g., gaining the floor in respectful ways, listening to others with care, speaking one at a time about the topics and texts under discussion). **SL.2.1b** Build on others' talk in conversations by linking their comments to the remarks of others. **SL.2.2** Recount or describe key ideas details from a text read aloud or information presented orally or through other media. **SL.2.3** Ask and answer questio about what a speaker says in order to clarify comprehension, gather additional information, or deepen understandin f a topic or issue.

46   Grade 2 • Unit 3 • Week 2   ©2018 Benchmark Education Company, LLC

Shared Reading (10 MIN.) RF.2.3b, RF.2.4a, RF.2.4b, RF.2.4c

SHARED READING — WEEK 2 • DAY 1

Introduce the Text (iELD)

Display "A City Park Habitat" and read aloud the title. Invite students to turn to a partner and infer what the text will be about. If necessary, model making an inference using the title and photos.

Sample modeling. *The title "A City Park Habitat" is the name of a place, and I learned what **habitat** means last week. The photos show three animals. I'll use the title and photos to infer that I will learn how a city park is a home for animals and other living things.*

Texts for Close Reading, p. 16 "A City Park Habitat"

Model Fluent Reading: Accuracy/Rereading

First Reading. Read aloud the text fluently and accurately. Tell students that reading accurately is reading without skipping words or saying words incorrectly. Remind them that accurate reading requires listening in order to go back and reread to fix any errors.

Second Reading. Invite students to reread the text aloud with you and monitor themselves for accuracy.

Student Objectives

I will be able to:
- Read an informational text accurately.
- Identify words with long **u** vowel team.

Additional Materials

Weekly Presentation: Unit 3, Week 2

Model Determine Text Importance

Tell students that they will be reading informational texts and an animal fantasy this week. Remind students that last week they used the reading strategy Determine Text Importance. Parts of an informational text will vary in importance, and so it is an excellent strategy to consider text importance before, during, and after reading. Model determining text importance on the first two paragraphs of "A City Park Habitat."

Sample modeling. *The first paragraph begins with a question, which is a nice, friendly way to bring readers into the topic. The next sentence defines the word **habitat**, which is in the title, so I know that this text is important. Paragraph 2 just presents facts and details about the park habitat, so I can determine that it is all important text. Now I think that the very first sentence, which was nice and interesting, really isn't so important. It doesn't provide and real information, so I won't pay as much attention to it.*

iELD Integrated ELD

Light Support
Students echo-read "A City Park Habitat." Discuss the cognate **park/parque**. Choose key vocabulary from the chart. Students echo-read.

leafy home	come up
dart	make their homes

Help groups say, read, write, and present original sentences using the key vocabulary words.

Moderate Support
Present as above.

city park	clover
underground	ponds

Students use at least two key vocabulary words in one original sentence.

Substantial Support
Students echo-read "A City Park Habitat." Discuss the cognate **park/parque**. Choose key vocabulary from the chart. Students echo-read.

park	turtles	fish
squirrels	nuts	frogs

Use the illustrations and text, and gestures and simple phrases, to discuss key vocabulary. Students role-play to show comprehension. Write the words on cards. Model presenting the word **park**.

Say: *This is the word **park**.*
Here it is in the story. (point to the word)
*A **park** is a public place outside for us to use or go to.*

Transfer Skills to Context: Long u Vowel Teams

Point to the word **you** in paragraph 1. Tell students to say it with you. Ask students to name the two vowel letters that spell the long **u** sound (**ou**). Then point to the word **few** in paragraph 3. Ask students to listen for the vowel sound, tell its name, and identify the two letters that spell the sound (**ew**).

RF.2.3b Know spelling-sound correspondences for additional common vowel teams. **RF.2.4a** Read on-level text with purpose and understanding. **RF.2.4b** Read on-level text orally with accuracy, appropriate rate, and expression on successive readings. **RF.2.4c** Use context to confirm or self-correct word recognition and understanding, rereading as necessary.

©2018 Benchmark Education Company, LLC

Grade 2 • Unit 3 • Week 2   47

DAY 1

EXTENDED READ 1 MINI-LESSON

Texts for Close Reading, pp. 18–25
"Habitats Around the World"

Student Objectives

I will be able to:
- Read an informational text.
- Identify and annotate key details in a text.
- Use key details to determine the main idea.

Additional Materials

Weekly Presentation: Unit 3, Week 2
- Key Details and Main Ideas Chart

Ways to Scaffold the First Reading

Use your observational assessment to determine the intensity of scaffolding your students need.

IF . . .	THEN consider . . .
Students are English learners who may struggle with vocabulary and language demands . . .	**Read the text TO students.** • Conduct a before-reading picture walk to introduce vocabulary and concepts. • Stop after meaningful chunks to define unfamiliar words and paraphrase difficult sentences.
Students are struggling readers who may decode with little comprehension . . .	**Read the text WITH students.** • Stop after meaningful chunks to ask **who, what, when, where, how** questions. • Work with students to define unfamiliar words and paraphrase key ideas.
Students need some support to read unfamiliar texts with comprehension . . .	**Have students PARTNER-READ.** *Partners should:* • take turns reading aloud meaningful chunks. • ask each other **who, what, when, where, how** questions about the text. • circle unfamiliar words and define them using context clues.

"Habitats Around the World": Identify the Main Topic of a Text, Part 1 (15 MIN.) RI.2.1, RI.2.2, SL.2.1a, SL.2.1b, SL.2.1c

Preview the Text

Ask students to open to "Habitats Around the World" and quickly skim the text with a partner. Students should tell a partner what they notice about the text, especially as regards headings, photos, and captions.

Read to Find Key Details

Ask students to read paragraphs 1–8 to identify key events, the main idea, and important text in each section. ("Introduction," "Welcome to the Grasslands!" and "Welcome to the Tundra!") Instruct them to annotate their text.

Give students time to read and annotate. Observe their annotations to assess their ability to identify the focus of specific paragraphs within the text.

Collaborative Conversation: Partner

Display a blank Key Details and Main Ideas Chart. Ask partners to complete the chart by selecting key details they underlined and using those details to state the main idea of the section. Point out that the second and third section heads both include a word that will help readers think about the different sections. Observe students' conversations. Use your observations to determine what kinds of support students may need in identifying the key details and main ideas.

Section	Key Details (paragraph)	Main Ideas
"Introduction"	"A habitat is a place where plants and animals live in nature." (1)	Different animals and plants around the world live in natural places called habitats.
	"different kinds of habitats around the world" (1)	
	"Different animals and plants live in different habitats." (2)	
"Welcome to the Grasslands!"	"lands covered in grass" (4)	Grasslands are large, flat areas of land covered in grass that animals eat.
	"Most grasslands are flat." (4)	
	"cover thousands of miles" (4)	
	savannas in Africa (5)	
	Animals find food in grasslands. (5)	
"Welcome to the Tundra!"	"The tundra is a habitat that gets very cold." (6)	Animals live in the cold Arctic tundra, which has plants only in summer.
	The Arctic tundra is near the North Pole. (7)	
	Plants grow in summer. (8)	
	"Polar bears, foxes, seals, and oxen" (8)	

Sample Key Details and Main Ideas Chart

48 Grade 2 • Unit 3 • Week 2   ©2018 Benchmark Education Company, LLC

EXTENDED READ 1 MINI-LESSON

WEEK 2 · DAY 1

Share

Call on partners to share the key details they noted for each section and the main ideas they formulated. Ask other students to listen carefully to note connections between the key details and the main ideas. Revisit the text as a group to answer the question, "What is this section mostly about?" in order to state a main idea.

Reinforce or Reaffirm the Strategy

If your students need support to understand the text, refer to "Ways to Scaffold the First Reading." Pose text-dependent questions to guide students' thinking. For example:

- *What's the first fact you learn about grasslands?*
- *What's the first fact you learn about the tundra?*

Choose one of the following options based on your observations during partner collaboration.

IF …	THEN …
Students need support to identify the key details and state the main ideas . . .	**Model to reinforce the strategy.** • *This section is called "Introduction." I would expect the key details in this section to explain what habitats are and why they are important.* • *The heading "Welcome to the Grasslands!" tells me the main topic of this section. The first paragraph tells that grasslands are all around the world. The next paragraph explains what grasslands are.* • *The heading "Welcome to the Tundra!" also tells me the main topic of the section. The three paragraphs in that section tell about where tundras are, what they are like, and the plant and animal life there.*
Students independently identify the key details and state the main ideas . . .	**Invite partners or small groups to reflect on their strategy use by discussing the following question:** • *How did identifying the key details help you understand what habitats are and why they are important?*

☑ Show Your Knowledge

During independent time, ask students to reread paragraph 5 and write a heading for it that tells its focus. Then ask them to use key details in the paragraph to write a statement of the main idea.

---

iELD Integrated ELD

Light Support
Preview "Habitats Around the World" Part 1. Provide visual support, cognates, and science facts: **tundra/ tundra; temperature/temperatura; savanna/sabana; mile/millas.**
Have students draw conclusions about habitats. Provide sentence frames.
The tundra is probably _____, because _____.
The grasslands might _____, because _____.

Moderate Support
Preview "Habitats Around the World" Part 1. Choose and present key vocabulary: **grasslands, flat, allow, season, thaws, Poles, cover, as cold as, North, South, rise, rainwater, thaws out.** Students act out terms to show comprehension.
Ask: *Which habitat needs to thaw out? When can the animals from the savanna drink rainwater?*

Substantial Support
Preview "Habitats Around the World" Part 1. Provide visual support, cognates, and science facts: **tundra/ tundra; temperature/temperatura; savanna/sabana; mile/millas.**
Choose and present key vocabulary: **grasslands, flat, allow, season, thaws, poles.** Students act out terms to show comprehension.
Ask: *When do the animals return to the savanna? Where can you find the flat grasslands?*

RI.2.1 Ask and answer such questions as who, what, where, when, why, and how to demonstrate understanding of key details in a text. **RI.2.2** Identify the main topic of a multiparagraph text as well as the focus of specific paragraphs within the text. **SL.2.1a** Follow agreed-upon rules for discussions (e.g., gaining the floor in respectful ways, listening to others with care, speaking one at a time about the topics and texts under discussion). **SL.2.1b** Build on others' talk in conversations by linking their comments to the remarks of others. **SL.2.1c** Ask for clarification and further explanation as needed about the topics and texts under discussion.

©2018 Benchmark Education Company, LLC

Grade 2 · Unit 3 · Week 2   49

DAY 1

WRITING TO SOURCES

Write an Informative Report: Read and Analyze the Prompt (15 MIN.) W.2.5

Student Writing Prompt

In an informative report, describe grasslands and the plants and animals that live in them. Support your ideas with facts and definitions from "Habitats Around the World" and information from "Plant Life of the Australian Savanna."

Student Objectives

I will be able to:
- Read and analyze a writing prompt and checklist to plan for my writing.
- Describe the features of an informative report.

Materials

Weekly Presentation: Unit 3, Week 2
- Informative Report Anchor Chart
- Student Writing Prompt
- Informative Report Checklist

Informative Report Anchor Chart

To write an informative report, writers…

Include facts, details, and content words
- State facts about the topic
- Include descriptive details to support the facts
- Define content words

Include an introduction, body, and conclusion
- Give background information in the introduction
- Provide facts and details in the body
- Sum up the ideas in the conclusion

Start by taking notes on source texts
- Create an organized notetaking form
- Fill in the form with information taken from the source text
- Take notes using the writer's own words

Take notes on media sources
- Create an organized notetaking form
- Watch and listen for facts and the details that support them
- Fill in the form with information learned from the media source
- Take notes using the writer's own words

Use conventions of English correctly
- Understand simple and compound sentences
- Understand that words such as *and, or, but, so,* and *because* are used to join simple sentences together to form compound sentences

---

Engage Thinking

Remind students that last week they analyzed a mentor informative report on the topic of how emperor penguins survive the harsh winters in Antarctica. Tell them that this week they will plan their own informative report on a different topic using information from two sources: "Habitats Around the World" and "Plant Life of the Australian Savanna."

Review the Anchor Chart

Display the completed anchor chart from last week and review the key points about writing an informative report.

Read the Writing Prompt and Checklist

Display and distribute copies of the writing prompt and informative report checklist. Read aloud the prompt, then use a think-aloud to model how you analyze it.

Sample think-aloud. *This prompt reminds me of the one we read last week. I need to use two sources to find information about grasslands and the plants and animals that live there. I must be sure to include facts, descriptive details, and special content word definitions.*

Call students' attention to the checklist. Explain that it includes the important points on the anchor chart. Read aloud each item on the checklist and find that point on the anchor chart. Then tell students they will refer to their checklist as they plan, draft, revise, and edit their report. Point out that the bulleted items on the checklist should serve as a reminder to use that strategy if they haven't done so. Emphasize to students that using the checklist as a guide can help them write a strong informative report.

Partner Role-Play. Have partners role-play how they might use the checklist when doing a peer review of each other's work. Encourage them to think of positive comments they might make about a peer's text that reflect a "Yes" response to a checklist item.

WRITING TO SOURCES

WEEK 2 · DAY 1

Share Your Understanding

Bring students together and invite partners to share their ideas.

Ask: *How is using a checklist helpful in writing a strong informative report?*

Help students understand that the checklist is like a guide.

☑ Quick Write

During independent time, have students answer the following question: *As you write an informative report, what tools can you use to make your report as good as possible?* Use students' writing to evaluate their understanding of the tools they can use to write a strong report.

---

iELD Integrated ELD

Light Support
Provide students with a format for exchanging comments in the partner role-play. For example, a student gives his or her partner a positive statement based on the first item on the checklist, then the partner affirms the statement:
Student: *You will give facts and details in your report?*
Partner: *Yes, I will use facts and details from the two sources.*

Moderate Support
During the partner role-play, guide students to affirm their partner's positive comments by restating the comment. Echoing the positive comments about their work can help build students' confidence. For example:
Student: *Your writing will have many details to support the facts?*
Partner: *I will work hard to include details to support the facts in my writing.*

Substantial Support
For the partner role-play, help students break down each item on the checklist into several points. For example, item 1 could be separated into three individual points:
I will state facts.
I will use descriptive details.
I will define content words.
Have students use one point at a time when commenting on their partners' text.

W.2.5 With guidance and support from adults and peers, focus on a topic and strengthen writing as needed by revising and editing.

©2018 Benchmark Education Company, LLC

Grade 2 • Unit 3 • Week 2   51

DAY 1

PHONICS & WORD STUDY

r-Controlled *a* Frieze Card and r-controlled vowel /är/ Sound-Spelling Card

Student Objectives

I will be able to:
- Identify, blend, and spell words with r-controlled **a**.
- Learn high-frequency words.
- Review high-frequency words.

Additional Materials

- Letter cards: **a, c, d, h, r, t**

Weekly Presentation: Unit 3, Week 2
- r-controlled **a** frieze card
- r-controlled vowel /är/ sound-spelling card
- High-frequency word cards: **move, never, once, round, small, their, too, walk, where, year**
- Review high-frequency word cards: **again, below, carry, does, eight, find, house, laugh, mother, school**

For additional word study/decodable practice, see: *Shark Teeth.*

r-Controlled Vowel ar (20 MIN.) RF.2.3b, RF.2.3e, RF.2.3f, L.2.2d

Spelling-Sound Correspondences

Introduce: r-Controlled Vowel ar
Display the r-controlled **a** frieze card.

Say: *These sounds are /är/. The /är/ sounds are spelled* **ar**.

Model: ar
Point to the spelling on the card and provide a sample word: **ar** as in **car**. Write the sample word and underline the r-controlled **a** spelling.

Say: *Look at the word I wrote:* **c-a-r**. *I see the r-controlled* **a** *spelling* **ar**. *Listen and watch as I sound out the word:* /kär/, **car**.

Run your hand under the word as you sound it out.

Practice: car
Repeat the r-controlled **a** word. Ask students to write the word and underline the r-controlled **a** spelling.

Blend Words

Model: r-Controlled Vowel ar
Display the letter cards for **cat**. Model how to blend the sounds together as you run your hand under each letter.

Say: *This is the letter* **c**. *It stands for* /k/. *This is the letter* **a**. *It stands for* /a/. *Listen as I blend these sounds together:* /kaaa/. *This is the letter* **t**. *It stands for* /t/. *Now listen as I blend all three sounds together:* /kaaat/, **cat**. *Say the word with me:* **cat**.

Model adding an **r** after the **a** to make the word **cart**.

Say: *I can add an* **r** *after the* **a** *to make the* **r-**controlled vowel spelling **ar**. *The* **ar** *spelling stands for the* /är/ *sounds. Listen as I blend the new word:* /kärt/. *Say the word with me:* **cart**.

Continue modeling the words **had, hard**.

Practice: start, farm, march, jar, arm, art
Write each word. Have students read together to blend the sounds. Provide corrective feedback, as needed.

52 Grade 2 • Unit 3 • Week 2 ©2018 Benchmark Education Company, LLC

PHONICS & WORD STUDY

WEEK **2** · DAY **1**

Spelling

Pretest

Say each spelling word. Read the sentence and say the word again. After the pretest, write each word as you say the letter names. Have students check their work.

car	Mr. Sanchez bought a new **car**.
star	Can you see the brightest **star** in the night sky?
march	It was fun to **march** to the lunchroom.
smart	It is **smart** to do your homework on time.
hard	Is school sometimes a little **hard**?
farm	The **farm** had pigs, chickens, and horses.
large	I need a **large** glass of water.
shark	Be careful! There's a **shark** in the water.
garden	We grew roses in our **garden**.
yard	Dad cut the grass in our **yard**.

High-Frequency Words (iELD)

Introduce: *move, never, once, round, small, their, too, walk, where, year*

Use the following routine: Write simple sentences using each high-frequency word. Underline the word and discuss important features about it. Say the word and have students repeat. Then spell the word with students as you point to each letter. Finally have students write the word as they spell it aloud.

Practice

Display the high-frequency word cards. Have students work with a partner to write sentences using the words. Then have volunteers read a sentence and identify the high-frequency word.

Review: *again, below, carry, does, eight, find, house, laugh, mother, school*

Review last week's words using the high-frequency word cards. Mix and display one word card at a time as students repeat each word together.

(iELD) Integrated ELD

Light Support

Ask students to echo-read the high-frequency words below.

move	once	small	too	where
never	round	their	walk	year

Write the words on cards. Hold up a card. Volunteers read the word aloud.

Pairs alternate dictating the high-frequency words to each other, and self-check their work using the word bank.

Moderate Support

Ask students to echo-read the high-frequency words below.

move	once	small	too	where
never	round	their	walk	year

Dictate the words, students repeat after you and spell the words orally. Students self-check their work using the word bank.

Substantial Support

Ask students to echo-read the high-frequency words below.

move	once	small	too	where
never	round	their	walk	year

Students say, spell, and write the words with you. Model using the words in sentences with *because* clauses.

Say: *There is a round water hole that small animals never walk to, because _____.*

Pairs orally present original sentences using the target words.

RF.2.3b Know spelling-sound correspondences for additional common vowel teams. **RF.2.3e** Identify words with inconsistent but common spelling-sound correspondences. **RF.2.3f** Recognize and read grade-appropriate irregularly spelled words. **L.2.2d** Generalize learned spelling patterns when writing words (e.g., cage → badge; boy → boil).

©2018 Benchmark Education Company, LLC

Grade 2 • Unit 3 • Week 2   **53**

DAY 2

SHARED READING

Texts for Close Reading, p. 16
"A City Park Habitat"

Student Objectives

I will be able to:
- Read an informational text about a city park habitat.
- Read words with r-controlled /är/ syllable pattern.
- Recognize words I know in different texts.

Additional Materials

Weekly Presentation: Unit 3, Week 2

Shared Reading (10 MIN.) RF.2.3f, RF.2.4a, RF.2.4b, RF.2.4c

Reread for Fluency: Accuracy/Rereading to Self-Correct

Partner Reading. Tell partners to alternate reading the paragraphs of "A City Park Habitat" and then switch roles. Remind students to aim for an accurate reading. They should listen for any words that don't seem to fit in the context and go back and check the words and then reread so that the sentences make sense.

Collaborative Conversation: Determine Text Importance

Recall for students that you showed them how you used the Determine Text Importance reading strategy on the first two paragraphs of "A City Park Habitat." Tell them that today partners will practice the strategy reading paragraphs 3 and 4. Stress that they should think about what text and text features are important as opposed to those that are merely interesting. In this way they can separate what they need to read carefully from what they can pay less attention to. If necessary, guide partners with questions. For example:

- *Is any of the text friendly and engaging but not telling any factual details?*
- *How can you tell what the animals are in the pictures?*

Transfer Skills to Context: Annotate Key Details

Remind students that underlining key details will help them think about the most important ideas and information. Model how you think about the topic as you read to identify and underline key details in the text. For example:

Sample modeling. *I can ask myself questions about the topic of the text. I'll ask, "What is a city park habitat?" I'll find and underline the answer: A habitat is a special place where animals live. Here's another question: "What are some habitats in a city park?" I'll underline answers: trees, underground, ponds.*

Ask students to underline details that answer the question, "What animals live in city park habitats?"

54 Grade 2 • Unit 3 • Week 2

©2018 Benchmark Education Company, LLC

SHARED READING

Transfer Skills to Context: r-Controlled /är/ Syllable Pattern

Point to the words **parks** and **dart** in paragraph 2. Ask students to read each word aloud. Ask what is similar about the spelling and sounds in both words. Guide them to identify the letters **ar** and the same r-controlled vowel sound, /är/.

Transfer Skills to Context: Review High-Frequency Words *where, their*

Tell students that this text includes words they have learned. Point to the previously taught word **where** in paragraph 3, and tell partners to turn to each other and say the word. Repeat for the word **their** in the same sentence. Remind students to look for words they know when they read a new text.

iELD Integrated ELD

Light Support
Display and review "A City Park Habitat." Assist as pairs take turns asking and answering questions about key words and facts from the text.
Pairs take turns reading meaningful chunks and role-playing to show comprehension.

Moderate Support
Display and review "A City Park Habitat." Have students echo-read. Ask questions about key facts.
Ask: *What different animals/habitats are described in the story? What words describe the habitats? What do the animals do/eat?*
Students can use photos from the text, and gestures or simple phrases to respond.
Invite a student to role-play one of the animals. Have other students identify the animal, its habitat, and what it does/eats.

Substantial Support
Display and review "A City Park Habitat." Have students echo-read. Ask questions to discuss key facts.
Ask: *What different animals/habitats are described in the story? What words describe the habitats? What do the animals do/eat?*
Students can use photos from the text, and gestures or simple phrases, to respond.

RF.2.3f Recognize and read grade-appropriate irregularly spelled words. **RF.2.4a** Read on-level text with purpose and understanding. **RF.2.4b** Read on-level text orally with accuracy, appropriate rate, and expression on successive readings. **RF.2.4c** Use context to confirm or self-correct word recognition and understanding, rereading as necessary.

DAY 2

EXTENDED READ 1 MINI-LESSON

Texts for Close Reading, pp. 18–25
"Habitats Around the World"

Student Objectives

I will be able to:
- Read an informational text.
- Identify key details that support a main idea.
- Share my thinking with peers.

Additional Materials

Weekly Presentation: Unit 3, Week 2
- Key Details and Main Ideas Chart

Ways to Scaffold the First Reading

Use your observational assessment to determine the intensity of scaffolding your students need.

IF ...	THEN consider ...
Students are English learners who may struggle with vocabulary and language demands . . .	**Read the text TO students.** • Conduct a before-reading picture walk to introduce vocabulary and concepts. • Stop after meaningful chunks to define unfamiliar words and paraphrase difficult sentences.
Students are struggling readers who may decode with little comprehension . . .	**Read the text WITH students.** • Stop after meaningful chunks to ask *who, what, when, where, how* questions. • Work with students to define unfamiliar words and paraphrase key ideas.
Students need some support to read unfamiliar texts with comprehension . . .	**Have students PARTNER-READ.** Partners should: • take turns reading aloud meaningful chunks. • ask each other *who, what, when, where, how* questions about the text. • circle unfamiliar words and define them using context clues.

"Habitats Around the World": Identify the Main Topic of a Text, Part 2 (20 MIN.) RI.2.1, RI.2.2, SL.2.1a, SL.2.1b, SL.2.1c

Preview the Text

Remind students that they have already read the first part of "Habitats Around the World." Tell partners to scan the whole text again and to think about how Part 2 will be similar to and different from Part 1.

Read to Find Key Details

Ask students to read paragraphs 9–11 to identify key details and the main idea in each section. ("Welcome to the Rain Forest!", "Welcome to the Coral Reef!" and "Conclusion") Ask them to underline the key details.

Give students time to read and annotate. Observe their annotations to assess their ability to identify the focus of each paragraph.

After students have finished reading the text, tell them you want them to distinguish between what text is important and what text is not as important.

Sample modeling. *In paragraph 9, I read that there are many different kinds of forests. A tropical rain forest is hot and rainy. The important information is a tropical rain forest is hot and rainy. I will underline that. The fact that there are other kinds of forests is less important to understanding this informational text. I will not underline that.*

 ## Collaborative Conversation: Partner

Sample modeling. *It is important that I listen carefully when being spoken to.*

Display and distribute a blank Key Details and Main Ideas Chart. Direct partners to complete the chart by discussing the key details they underlined and deciding on a main-idea statement based on the details in each section.

Section	Key Details	Main Idea
"Welcome to the Rain Forest!"	"A tropical rain forest is hot and rainy." (9)	Trees and other plants stay green all year in a hot, rainy tropical rain forest.
	"Trees and other plants stay green all year long." (9)	
"Welcome to the Coral Reef!"	"A coral reef is a place in the ocean." (10)	Tiny ocean animals called corals form hilly reefs that are home to other living things.
	made of hundreds of thousands of tiny animals called corals (10)	
	Other plants and animals live at a coral reef. (10)	
"Conclusion"	"four habitats" (11)	What is your opinion of the four habitats?
	"what you like" "what you don't like" (11)	
	grasslands, tundra, rain forest, coral reef (captions)	

Sample Key Details and Main Ideas Chart

56 Grade 2 • Unit 3 • Week 2

©2018 Benchmark Education Company, LLC

Share (iELD)

Invite volunteers to share the key details they found in a particular section and the main idea they formulated. Ask other students to listen carefully for connections between the key details and the main ideas. Revisit the text as needed.

Reinforce or Reaffirm the Strategy

If your students need support to understand the text, refer to "Ways to Scaffold the First Reading." Provide directive and/or corrective feedback as needed: For example:

- *What's the first fact you learn about forest habitats?*
- *What's the first fact you learn about coral reefs?*

Choose one of the following options based on your observations during partner collaboration.

IF …	THEN …
Students need support to identify the key details and state the main ideas …	**Model to reinforce the strategy.** • The heading "Welcome to the Rain Forest!" tells me that I am reading about a rain forest. What is most important to understand about rain forests? The focus of this paragraph is tropical rain forests. The details tell what tropical rain forests are like and what lives in them. • The heading "Welcome to the Coral Reef!" tells me that this section will be about coral reefs. What is most important to understand about coral reefs? Details in the paragraph answer the questions, "Where?", "What are they made of?" and "What lives in them?" • The heading "Conclusion" tells me that the information in the text will be summed up. The sentences ask questions to get me thinking about the four habitats.
Students independently identify the key details and state the main ideas …	Invite partners or small groups to reflect on their strategy use by discussing the following question: • How do you use a title and headings to guide your thinking about the main ideas?

✓ Show Your Knowledge

During independent time, ask students to think about the title of the text and use it to write a sentence that states the main idea of the whole text.

Challenge Activity. Have students read paragraphs 10 and 11 and find one part of the text that isn't important to understanding the informational text.

> **iELD Integrated ELD**
>
> **Light Support**
> Observe, assess, and evaluate pairs as they share key details with peers.
> Based on your answers, plan future mini-lessons to support speaking skills.
> Do pairs:
> - pose and respond to questions to clarify information?
> - support their partners as they both participate?
> - retell key facts with accuracy?
> - choose appropriate key facts to share?
>
> **Moderate Support**
> Evaluate as above. Include the following assessments:
> - build on the comments of others appropriately?
> - ask appropriate questions using language and vocabulary related to the topic?
> - respond to questions appropriately?
>
> **Substantial Support**
> Evaluate as above. Include the following assessments:
> - stay on topic throughout the discussion?
> - use background knowledge and language they know?
> - use key vocabulary and language they have learned so far?
> - listen and wait respectfully?

RI.2.1 Ask and answer such questions as who, what, where, when, why, and how to demonstrate understanding of key details in a text. **RI.2.2** Identify the main topic of a multiparagraph text as well as the focus of specific paragraphs within the text. **SL.2.1.a** Follow agreed-upon rules for discussions (e.g., gaining the floor in respectful ways, listening to others with care, speaking one at a time about the topics and texts under discussion). **SL.2.1.b** Build on others' talk in conversations by linking their comments to the remarks of others. **SL.2.1.c** Ask for clarification and further explanation as needed about the topics and texts under discussion.

DAY 2

WRITING TO SOURCES

Student Writing Prompt

In an informative report, describe grasslands and the plants and animals that live in them. Support your ideas with facts and definitions from "Habitats Around the World" and information from "Plant Life of the Australian Savanna."

Student Objectives

I will be able to:
- Take notes while reading a print source.
- Write questions about additional information I need to learn about the topic.

Materials

Weekly Presentation: Unit 3, Week 2
- Student Writing Prompt
- Source Text Notetaking Chart

Write an Informative Report: Find Facts, Definitions, and Details in a Source Text (15 MIN.) W.2.7, W.2.8

Engage Thinking

Reread the writing prompt with students. Then tell them that they will have two sources to use in finding the facts, details, and definitions to include in their report. Explain that today they will read and take notes from the printed source text.

Model

Display and distribute fresh copies of the notetaking form for the source text. Use a think-aloud to model how to fill out the first three sections of the form.

Sample think-aloud. *I know I can fill in the top part of the form based on what the prompt tells me. The prompt says I need to focus on the plants and animals that live in the grasslands, so the big idea is "Plants and animals live in the grasslands." The print source I will use is "Habitats Around the World."*

Model filling in the first two sections on the notetaking form. Have students fill in the same sections on their form. Then display "Habitats Around the World" and have students turn to this selection in their Texts for Close Reading. Direct them to the section titled "Welcome to the Grasslands!" Continue your think-aloud.

Sample think-aloud. *When I think about the background I need to provide in my report, I come up with two questions: "What are grasslands?" and "Where are grasslands found?" I notice that the first paragraph of the source text says grasslands are found everywhere except the South Pole. That answers one of my background questions. I can write a note that answers this question in the background section of my form.*

Write the note on your form and have students add a similar note to their form, reminding them to use their own words.

Peer Practice

Have students work in pairs to answer the other background question and to add notes to that section of their form, using their own words. Remind them that their notes should include facts about grasslands, descriptive details that support those facts, and the definitions of any words that will help readers. Instruct them to continue taking notes to fill in the other sections of their form and stress that they use their own words.

58 Grade 2 • Unit 3 • Week 2   ©2018 Benchmark Education Company, LLC

Share Your Understanding (iELD)

Bring students together and invite partners to share their notes. Using the input from students, model filling in information about the grasslands on the rest of your notetaking form.

☑ Quick Write

During independent time, have students respond to the following: *Compare your notes to the prompt. What information do you still need to learn? Write the questions you need to answer.* Use students' writing to evaluate their understanding of the kind of information they need to include in their report.

(iELD) Integrated ELD

Light Support
Encourage partners to share facts and details about grassland plants and animals that they learned from the source text. Ask them to identify the information they would choose to include in their informative report. Have them fill in those facts and details on their notetaking form, using their own words to write the notes.

Moderate Support
Provide sentence frames to help students come up with their own words to restate facts and details from the source text. For example:
Source: *Grasslands are covered with grass, flat, and cover thousands of miles.*
Student: *Grasslands are ____ and ____ places.*
Source: *Many plants and flowers grow in grasslands but only a few bushes and trees.*
Student: *Plants in the grasslands include ____ and ____.*

Substantial Support
Help students choose words and phrases from the second paragraph of the source text that describe grasslands (**covered with grass, flat, cover thousands of miles**). Have them share those words and/or phrases with a partner. Then discuss each word or phrase and offer suggestions on ways to restate that idea. Provide sentence frames students can use to fill the information on their notetaking form. For example:
Grasslands have a lot of _____. (**grass, plants**)
The ground is _____. (**flat, low, even**)
They take up ____ areas of land. (**big, huge**)

W.2.7 Participate in shared research and writing projects (e.g., read a number of books on a single topic to produce a report; record science observations). **W.2.8** Recall information from experiences or gather information from provided sources to answer a question.

DAY 2

PHONICS & WORD STUDY

r-Controlled Vowel ar (15 MIN.) RF.2.3b, RF.2.3e, RF.2.3f, L.2.2d

Review r-Controlled Vowel ar

Display the r-controlled **a** frieze card. Review the r-controlled **a** spelling **ar** as in **car**. Point to the spelling.

Ask: *What are the letters? What sounds do they stand for?*

Blend Words

Model: star
Display letter cards for **star**. Model blending.

Say: *This is the letter **s**. It stands for /s/. This is the letter **t**. It stands for /t/. These are the letters **ar**. They stand for /är/. Listen as I blend these sounds together: /stär/, **star**. Say the word with me: **star**.*

Practice: sharp, barn, park, yarn, arm
Use the same routine to guide student practice.

Build Words

Model: tar, star, start, smart
Display the letter cards for **tar**. Blend the sounds: /tär/, **tar**.

- Add the **s** and repeat with **star**.
- Add the **t** and repeat with **start**.
- Replace the first **t** with **m** and repeat with **smart**.

Practice: art, ark, bark, shark; car, cart, card
Use the same routine to guide student practice.

r-Controlled *a* Frieze Card and r-controlled vowel /är/Sound-Spelling Card

Student Objectives

I will be able to:
- Blend, build, and spell words with r-controlled **a**.
- Practice high-frequency words: **move, never, once, round, small, their, too, walk, where, year**.
- Read words with inflectional endings –**ed**, –**ing** (no spelling changes).

Additional Materials

- Letter cards: **a, b, c, d, h, k, m, n, p, r, s, t, t, y**

Weekly Presentation: Unit 3, Week 2
- r-controlled **a** frieze card
- r-controlled vowel /**är**/ sound-spelling card
- High-frequency word cards: **move, never, once, round, small, their, too, walk, where, year**

For additional word study/decodable practice, see: *Shark Teeth*.

PHONICS & WORD STUDY

WEEK 2 • DAY 2

Spelling

Word Families: *car, star, march, smart, hard, farm, large, shark, garden, yard*

Write and display each word on an index card. Ask students to read together and spell each word. Then have students write other words that belong to each word family (e.g., **car/star: bar, far, jar, tar, scar**).

Ask students to write each word family in a separate column on the board. When completed, have students read and spell the words together in each column.

High-Frequency Words

Review: *move, never, once, round, small, their, too, walk, where, year*

Display the high-frequency word cards. Ask students to read and spell each word. Focus on the spellings and meanings of homophones **too/to/two** and **their/there/they're**. Have students generate sentences for each word.

Inflectional Endings –ed, –ing (iELD)

Introduce: Inflectional Endings

Introduce verbs that end in –**ed** to show past tense. Explain that to show the past tense for most regular verbs that end with a consonant, students must add the inflectional ending –**ed**. The inflectional ending –**ing** is added to the verb to show the present tense.

Practice: show, showed, showing; call, called, calling

Use the same routine to guide student practice.

(iELD) Integrated ELD

Light Support

Review verbs that end in –**ed,** and the three ending sounds: **/ed/, /d/, /t/.** Draw the blank chart below on the board. Have students write the chart headings: **–ed, –d, –t.**

Write words on cards: **barked, farmed, started, leaked, sailed, seated.** Assist as students choose a card, read it, write the word in the correct column of the chart, and use the word in an original sentence.

Moderate Support

Review verbs that end in –**ed,** and the three ending sounds: **/ed/, /d/, /t/.** Draw the chart below on the board.

–ed	–d	–t

Write words on cards: **barked, farmed, started, picked, called, heated.** Students choose a card, say the word, and place the card in the correct column of the chart. Model using the word **called** in a sentence. **Say:** *I called Mom on my cell phone yesterday.* Challenge students to use the words in original sentences.

Substantial Support

Review verbs that end in –**ed,** and the three ending sounds: **/ed/, /d/, /t/.** Draw the chart below on the board.

–ed	–d	–t

Write words on cards: **barked, farmed, started.** Students echo-read. Hold up a card. Students repeat the word after you and place the card in the correct column of the chart. As a group, practice using each word in sentences that show simple past.

RF.2.3b Know spelling-sound correspondences for additional common vowel teams. **RF.2.3e** Identify words with inconsistent but common spelling-sound correspondences. **RF.2.3f** Recognize and read grade-appropriate irregularly spelled words. **L.2.2d** Generalize learned spelling patterns when writing words (e.g., cage → badge; boy → boil).

©2018 Benchmark Education Company, LLC

Grade 2 • Unit 3 • Week 2   61

DAY 3

SHARED READING

Texts for Close Reading, p. 17
"A New Home for Margie"

Student Objectives

I will be able to:
- Read an animal fantasy.
- Read a story aloud accurately.

Additional Materials

Weekly Presentation: Unit 3, Week 2

---

iELD Integrated ELD

Light Support
Have students echo-read "A New Home for Margie" and find unfamiliar words and phrases, such as **hermit crab, shell, hard popcorn, conch shell, scampered, Icky sticky, no answer, Anyone home.** Record words and phrases on cards. Have students form groups of three and give each group a card. Help groups write an original sentence using the word or phrase, and then present the word or phrase.

Moderate Support
Have students echo-read "A New Home for Margie" and find unfamiliar words and phrases, such as **beach, crawled out, crawled into, bottom, spotted.** Have students form groups of three and give each group a card. Model presenting the word **shell**. Help groups form an original sentence using the word or phrase, and then present the word or phrase.

Substantial Support
Students echo-read "A New Home for Margie" and find unfamiliar words and phrases, such as **hermit crab, shell, hard popcorn, conch shell.** Record words and phrases on cards. Hold up a card. Students echo-read. Have students form groups of three and give each group a card. Groups present words, and then switch cards. Model presenting the word shell. Say: This is the word *shell*. Here it is in the story. (point to the word) A **shell** can be covering for a crab. I found a crab **shell**.

Shared Reading (10 MIN.) RF.2.4a, RF.2.4b, RF.2.4c

Introduce the Text

Display "A New Home for Margie," and read aloud the title. Tell students that this is a literary text—an animal fantasy. Invite students to turn to a partner and infer what the story will be about. If necessary, model how you preview a text.

Sample modeling. *The title "A New Home for Margie" makes me wonder who Margie is. The illustration shows a cartoon crab. I think that the main character is a crab named Margie, and the story will be about her new home. If I'm right, text related to Margie finding a new home will be important text.*

Model Fluent Reading: Accuracy/Rereading

First Reading. Read the text aloud fluently and accurately. Remind students that in order to read accurately, readers listen for meaning and go back and reread to correct any mistakes.

Second Reading. Have students whisper-read the story aloud with you. Remind them to self-correct and reread as needed.

Model Determine Text Importance

Tell students that the reading strategy Determine Text Importance can be used when reading literary texts as well as informational texts. Explain that authors want readers to pay attention to the main events of their stories and also details that introduce characters and the setting. Model determining text importance for the first half of "A New Home for Margie."

Sample modeling. *I know that titles are always important text. This title tells me that a character named Margie is going to get a new home. I'll circle "New Home for Margie" and read on. Okay—Margie saying that her old shell is too small and that she needs a new home is certainly important. It is the problem Margie faces and what the story will be about. I'll underline it. But I don't think that Margie crying "This won't do!" at the beginning is so important. It's funny, but it isn't a big part of the plot.*

Transfer Skills to Context: Annotate Genre Features

Tell students that an animal fantasy is an imaginative story in which animals think and talk like people. Model annotating features that characterize an animal fantasy.

Sample modeling. *The first sentence of this story shows me the main character is a hermit crab named Margie, who speaks like a person. I'll underline Margie's words and jot a note in the margin:* **animal fantasy**.

Ask volunteers for other examples showing that this story is an animal fantasy.

RF.2.4a Read on-level text with purpose and understanding. **RF.2.4b** Read on-level te... ally with accuracy, appropriate rate, and expression on successive readings. **RF.2.4c** Use context to confirm or self-corre... word recognition and understanding, rereading as necessary.

---

62   Grade 2 • Unit 3 • Week 2   ©2018 Benchmark Education Company, LLC

Build Vocabulary: Determine the Meaning of Words and Phrases

(10 MIN.) RI.2.4, L.2.4a, L.2.4e

EXTENDED READ 1 MINI-LESSON

WEEK 2 · DAY 3

Engage Thinking

Say: *Sometimes when we're reading, we come across a word we've never seen before. We may be pretty sure that we're pronouncing it correctly, but we're not sure of what the word means. What are some things we can do to understand a new word?*

Invite students' suggestions and emphasize that readers can use context clues and a dictionary to figure out a new word's meaning.

Texts for Close Reading, pp. 18–25
"Habitats Around the World"

Model

Read aloud paragraph 1 of "Habitats Around the World." Model noting the meaning of the word **habitat.**

Sample modeling (paragraph 1). *The word **habitat** is new to me. But I see the author has included a definition in the first sentence: "A **habitat** is a place where plants and animals live in nature." Whenever I read an informational text that has new terms in it, I try to look for definitions right in the context. I will highlight that word in the text.*

Model using a print or digital dictionary to check the meaning of **habitat.**

Student Objectives

I will be able to:
- Find definitions for new words in context.
- Check definitions in a dictionary.

Additional Materials

Weekly Presentation: Unit 3, Week 2
- Word Meaning Chart

Guided Practice (iELD)

Ask students to reread paragraphs 3 and 4. Discuss where in the text the author has defined the term **grasslands.** Tell students to underline the definition: <u>lands covered in grass</u>. Ask volunteers to demonstrate looking up **grasslands** in a print or digital dictionary and reading aloud the meaning. Display the words **prairie**, **savanna**, **blubber**, **tundra**. Ask students to find and check definitions of each word. Create a chart to note definitions in context.

Word	Definition in Context (paragraph)
habitat	"a place where plants and animals live in nature" (1)
grasslands	"lands covered in grass" (4)
prairie	"Grasslands in the United States and Canada are called prairies." (caption)
savanna	"Grasslands in Africa are called savannas." (5)
blubber	"a thick layer of fat called blubber" (caption)
tundra	"a habitat that gets very cold" . . . "located near or at the North and South Poles" (6)

Word Meaning Chart

iELD Integrated ELD

Light Support
Review "Habitats Around the World." Ask students to reread the Word Meaning Chart. Have students complete the following sentence frame to add the word **thaws** to the chart: *Since I saw _____, and I read _____, I can infer that the word _____ means _____.*

Moderate Support
Review "Habitats Around the World." Ask students to echo-read the Word Meaning Chart. Have students complete the following sentence frame to add the phrase **rainy season** to the chart: *I can guess that _____ means _____, because I read _____.*

Substantial Support

Word and Paragraph	Context Clue	Conclusion
dry season (5)	animals leave home to find water	a time when there is no water

Review "Habitats Around the World." Ask students to echo-read the Word Meaning Chart. Have students complete the following sentence frame to add the phrase **dry season** to the chart. Use the cues above if necessary. *I read that _____, so the word _____ probably means _____.*

Show Your Knowledge

During independent time, ask students to find a definition for the word **coral** in paragraph 10 and explain how knowing the meaning helps them understand what a coral reef is.

RI.2.4 Determine the meaning of words and phrases in a text relevant to a grade 2 topic or subject area. **L.2.4a** Use sentence-level context as a clue to the meaning of a word or phrase. **L.2.4e** Use glossaries and beginning dictionaries, both print and digital, to determine or clarify the meaning of words and phrases.

©2018 Benchmark Education Company, LLC

Grade 2 • Unit 3 • Week 2   63

DAY 3

EXTENDED READ 1 MINI-LESSON

Close Reading: Explain How Images Contribute to and Clarify a Text (10 MIN.)

RI.2.1, RI.2.5, RI.2.7, SL.2.1a, SL.2.1b, SL.2.2, SL.2.3

Engage Thinking

We just looked at context clues in "Habitats Around the World." Now we will look at text features in the informational text. Remind students that informational texts may have maps in them. Review that a map is a special drawing that shows all or part of Earth's surface.

Model

Display and read aloud the close reading prompt and annotation instructions. Think aloud about the prompt.

> **Close Reading Prompt:** Examine the map on page 20. How does the map relate to the information in paragraph 5?
> **Annotate!** Underline the text evidence and jot down notes in the margin.

Display page 20, and tell students that the text on the page gives information about savannas. Point out that there is also a map on the same page. Ask students to jot notes in the margin about how the map helps them understand information in the paragraph. Have students underline the words in the paragraph that help them understand the map.

Display a Close Reading Chart. Read aloud paragraph 5 as students follow along. Then model how the map helps them understand information about savannas.

Sample modeling. *The text in paragraph 5 tells me that savannas are grasslands in Africa. The map helps me understand where in Africa the savannas are, and how big they are. The map shows me the whole continent of Africa. The map key shows that green represents savannas. I'll jot down notes in the margin about what I notice in the map that helps me learn about savannas. I will also underline parts of the text that refer to the map.*

What the Text Describes	What the Map Shows
Savannas are grasslands in Africa.	Savannas stretch east-west across the widest part of Africa.
	Savannas spread across the southern part of Africa.
	Savannas are vast!

Sample Close Reading Chart

Texts for Close Reading, pp. 18–25
"Habitats Around the World"

Student Objectives

I will be able to:
- Explain how photos and captions help me understand a text.
- Share my thinking with peers.

Additional Materials

Weekly Presentation: Unit 3, Week 2
- Close Reading Chart

Observation Checklist for Productive Engagement

Is the Productive Engagement Productive?

As groups discuss the relationship between photographs, captions, and text, look for evidence that they are truly engaged in the task.

Partners are engaged productively if . . .
- ❏ they ask questions and use feedback to address the task.
- ❏ they demonstrate engagement and motivation.
- ❏ they apply strategies with some success.

If the discussion is productive, continue the task. If the discussion is unproductive, end the task and provide support.

64 Grade 2 • Unit 3 • Week 2 ©2018 Benchmark Education Company, LLC

EXTENDED READ 1 MINI-LESSON

WEEK 2 • DAY 3

⚙️ Productive Engagement: Peer Group

Organize students into groups of three or four. Each group should designate specific students to be the group's discussion facilitator, scribe, timekeeper, and encourager. Display and read aloud a second close reading prompt.

Close Reading Prompt: Read paragraphs 6–8 that describe the tundra. Tell them the author uses a caption and a photograph on page 21 to provide additional information about polar bears. How do the photo and caption relate to the information in the paragraphs?

Annotate! Underline the text evidence and jot down notes in the margin.

Ask students to reread the section about the tundra and annotate the text. They should write notes in the margin that explain the connections between the photo and the text on pages 21 and 22. Observe students' notes to determine if they need additional modeling or directive feedback.

Share (iELD)

Call on students to share their responses to the close reading prompt. Use this opportunity to provide additional modeling, corrective feedback, or validation based on students' responses.

☑️ Show Your Knowledge

During independent time, have students look closely at the photo and caption accompanying paragraph 10. Have them write one or two sentences explaining how the photo and caption are connected to what they read in the text. They may note, for example, what "other kinds of animals" are shown in the photo, and give ideas about why those animals might come to a coral reef.

---

iELD Integrated ELD

Light Support

Observe, assess, evaluate, and plan for ELLs' reading, language, and conversation needs as they share key details with peers.

Can students . . .

- *support partners as they ask and answer questions?*
- *retell key facts about the savanna with accuracy?*
- *share appropriate key facts about the savanna?*

Moderate Support

Observe, assess, evaluate, and plan for ELLs' reading, language, and conversation needs as they share key details with peers.

Can pairs . . .

- *build on comments of peers as they discuss facts about the savanna?*
- *ask appropriate questions about the savanna using vocabulary and language from the text?*
- *ask and answer questions about the text using key vocabulary?*

Substantial Support

Observe, assess, evaluate, and plan for ELLs' reading, language, and conversation needs as they share key details with peers.

Can group members . . .

- *talk about savannas throughout the discussion?*
- *use vocabulary and language from the first reading in their discussion?*
- *listen and wait respectfully as peers contribute to conversation?*

RI.2.1 Ask and answer such questions as who, what, where, when, why, and how to demonstrate understanding of key details in a text. **RI.2.5** Know and use various text features (e.g., captions, bold print, subheadings, glossaries, indexes, electronic menus, icons) to locate key facts or information in a text efficiently. **RI.2.7** Explain how specific images (e.g., a diagram showing how a machine works) contribute to and clarify a text. **SL.2.1a** Follow agreed-upon rules for discussions (e.g., gaining the floor in respectful ways, listening to others with care, speaking one at a time about the topics and texts under discussion). **SL.2.1b** Build on others' talk in conversations by linking their comments to the remarks of others. **SL.2.2** Recount or describe key ideas or details from a text read aloud or information presented orally or through other media. **SL.2.3** Ask and answer questions about what a speaker says in order to clarify comprehension, gather additional information, or deepen understanding of a topic or issue.

©2018 Benchmark Education Company, LLC

Grade 2 • Unit 3 • Week 2 **65**

DAY 3

WRITING TO SOURCES

Student Writing Prompt

In an informative report, describe grasslands and the plants and animals that live in them. Support your ideas with facts and definitions from "Habitats Around the World" and information from "Plant Life of the Australian Savanna."

Student Objectives

I will be able to:
- Take notes while viewing a media source.
- Write about what it means to actively view a media source.

Materials

Weekly Presentation: Unit 3, Week 2
- Take Organized Notes from a Media Source
- "Plant Life of the Australian Savanna" Media Source

Write an Informative Report: Active Viewing and Notetaking from a Media Source (15 MIN.) W..2.7, W.2.8

Engage Thinking

Remind students that yesterday they took notes on a source text. They recorded facts, descriptive details, and content word definitions on a notetaking form. Tell them that today they will view a media source and take notes on it.

Model iELD

Display and distribute fresh copies of the notetaking form for a media source. Review the sections of the form and have students fill in the top two rows.

Then play "Plant Life of the Australian Savanna." Model how to pause and take notes on what you see and hear.

Say: *The narrator says that many kinds of grasses and shrubs grow in the Australian savanna. That is the first fact I will write on my notetaking form. Then I will look and listen for descriptive details that support that fact.*

Continue playing the media source. Pause as needed to record details, such as the names of trees and animals, and what happens during the wet and dry seasons.

Peer Practice

Have students work with a partner to take notes from the media source. Remind them to listen and watch for important facts and the details that support the facts. Encourage students to use their own words when writing their notes.

Facts and Details I See	Facts and Details I Hear
open, wide, and flat area with grasses	Not many trees grow in the Australian savanna.
a plant burning	The Australian savanna can get so dry that plants catch on fire.

Sample Take Organized Notes from a Media Source

WRITING TO SOURCES

WEEK 2 • DAY 3

Share Your Understanding

Bring students together and invite partners to share their notes.

Ask: *What is the topic of your report and what kind of information did you include in your notes?*

Confirm that students now have enough facts and details to fully answer the writing prompt.

**Quick Write**

During independent time, have students answer this question: *What does it mean to actively view a media source?* Use students' writing to evaluate their understanding that to actively view something means they watch and listen attentively to that source.

**Integrated ELD**

Light Support

Have students work with a partner to take notes from the media source. Remind them to listen and watch for important facts and the details that support the facts. Encourage students to use their own words when writing their notes.

Moderate Support

Bring students together and invite partners to share their notes.

Ask: *What is the topic of your report and what kind of information did you include in your notes?*
Confirm that students now have enough facts and details to fully answer the writing prompt.

Substantial Support

Have students independently answer this question: *What does it mean to actively view a media source?* Use students' writing to evaluate their understanding that to actively view something means they watch and listen attentively to that source.

W.2.7 Participate in shared research and writing projects (e.g., read a number of books on a single topic to produce a report; record science observations). **W.2.8** Recall information from experiences or gather information from provided sources to answer a question.

©2018 Benchmark Education Company, LLC

DAY 3

PHONICS & WORD STUDY

Texts for Close Reading, p. 26
"An Ocean Visit"

Student Objectives

I will be able to:
- Blend and spell words with r-controlled **a**.
- Read word study (decodable) text.
- Practice high-frequency words.

Additional Materials

- Letter cards: **a, b, c, d, h, k, n, p, r, s, y**
- r-controlled **a** frieze card
- r-controlled vowel /är/ sound-spelling card

Weekly Presentation: Unit 3, Week 2
- *High-frequency word cards:* **move, never, once, round, small, their, too, walk, where, year**
- *Review high-frequency word cards:* **again, below, carry, does, eight, find, house, laugh, mother, school**

For additional word study/decodable practice, see: *Shark Teeth*.

Monitor Student Reading of Word Study (Decodable) Text

As students read the word study (decodable) text and answer questions, ask yourself these questions:

Are students able to . . .
☐ blend and read r-controlled vowel words in the text?
☐ read new high-frequency words with automaticity?
☐ demonstrate comprehension of the text by answering text-based questions?

Based on your observations, you may wish to support students' fluency, automaticity, and comprehension with additional decodable reading practice during intervention time.

r-Controlled Vowel ar (15 MIN.) RL.2.3, RF.2.3b, RF.2.3c, RF.2.3e, RF.2.3f, L.2.2d

Blend Words

Practice: yarn, barn, hard, sharp, spark, arch
Display pocket chart letter cards for the word **yard**. Model how to blend the sounds to say the word. Use the same routine with other r-controlled **a** words to guide practice.

Read Word Study (Decodable) Text

Introduce the Text
Read the title "An Ocean Visit" aloud. Pronounce the irregular word **Ocean** and have students repeat. Model how to divide the word **Visit** into two closed syllables to read it.

Read the Text
Ask students to read the text. If students need modeling, guide them to blend decodable words and read high-frequency words. You may wish to conduct a second reading, having partners read to each other while you circulate and monitor the reading.

Connect Phonics to Comprehension
Ask some or all of the following questions:

- *When does the family go to the ocean each year?*
- *How is the ocean different from where the family lives?*
- *What does the family do at the ocean?*

Spelling

Word Clues
Write the word **clues**. Have students write the spelling word that goes with each clue.

1. has a barn and fields (**farm**)
2. something you can ride in (**car**)
3. knows a lot about something (**smart**)
4. big (**large**)

High-Frequency Words

Practice: *move, never, once, round, small, their, too, walk, where, year*
Draw a ladder with ten rungs. Write a high-frequency word on each rung. Have students take turns climbing the ladder by reading the words.

Review: *again, below, carry, does, eight, find, house, laugh, mother, school*

RL.2.3 Describe how characters in a story respond to major events and challenges. **RF.2.3b** Know spelling-sound correspondences for additional common vowel teams. **RF.2.3c** Decode regularly spelled two-syllable words with long vowels. **RF.2.3e** Identify words with inconsistent but common spelling-sound correspondences. **RF.2.3f** Recognize and read grade-appropriate irregularly spelled words. **L.2.2d** Generalize learned spelling patterns when writing words (e.g., cage → badge; boy → boil).

Shared Reading (15 MIN.) RF.2.4a, RF.2.4b, RF.2.4c, L.2.2c

Reread for Fluency: Accuracy/Rereading

Partner Reading. Assign partners to reread "A New Home for Margie" to each other. They may take turns reading the paragraphs and then switch roles. Remind them to go back and reread to correct any errors they hear.

Collaborative Conversation: Determine Text Importance

Remind students that you showed them how to begin determining text importance in the story yesterday. Tell students that today they will read the story with a partner and practice determining and annotating important text. Remind them that for literary texts, authors want readers to pay close attention to the main events of their stories and also to details that introduce characters and the setting. Some dialogue and detailed description may not be as important. Guide students with questions if necessary. For example:

- *How is the first sentence of paragraph 2 important?*
- *Do you have to know that Margie thinks it could be fun to live in the popcorn box to understand the story?*
- *What do hermit crabs need to survive?*

Transfer Skills to Context: Annotate Dialogue

Model identifying and underlining dialogue in a story.

Sample modeling (paragraph 1). *I can tell that the first words of the story are spoken because of the quotation marks around them. The exclamation point at the end and the word **cried** show me how Margie sounds as she speaks. I'll underline her exact words and jot a note in the margin about how she says them: with strong feeling.*

Read aloud paragraph 1, expressing how Margie feels as she speaks. Then tell students to find and underline another example of Margie's spoken words and jot a note in the margin to tell how she says them.

Transfer Skills to Context: Contractions

Point to the word **won't** in paragraph 1 and ask students to read it aloud. Identify it as a contraction, and ask students to tell what two words make up the contraction **won't** (**will not**). Ask what letter the punctuation mark replaces in the word **not** (**o**). Repeat a similar process for the word **didn't** in paragraph 2.

RF.2.4a Read on-level text with purpose and understanding. **RF.2.4b** Read on-level text orally with accuracy, appropriate rate, and expression on successive readings. **RF.2.4c** Use context to confirm or self-correct word recognition and understanding, rereading as necessary. **L.2.2c** Use an apostrophe to form contractions and frequently occurring possessives.

©2018 Benchmark Education Company, LLC

SHARED READING

Texts for Close Reading, p. 17
"A New Home for Margie"

Student Objectives

I will be able to:
- Read an animal fantasy.
- Identify dialogue in a story.
- Explain how contractions are formed.

Additional Materials

Weekly Presentation: Unit 3, Week 2

Integrated ELD

Light Support
Draw on the board an outline of the chart below. Display a list of words and contractions.
he is/he's, will not/won't
Pairs fill in the headings of the chart and categorize the words and contractions on the list. Have students use the words in original sentences and then replace the words with the contraction.

Two Words	Contractions
that is	(that's)
it is	(it's)

Moderate Support
Draw on the board an outline of the chart above. Display a list of words and contractions.
did not/didn't, do not/don't.
Make cards for the two words and the two contractions, mix them up, and have students match the pairs. Volunteers use the words in original sentences and then replace the words with the contraction.

Substantial Support
Draw on the board an outline of the chart above. Display a list of words and contractions.
that is/that's, it is/it's.
Students echo-read column 1. Elicit and write the contractions. Students echo-read.
Ask: How did you form the contraction?
Model sentences like the following:
That is a wildebeest. _____ a wildebeest.
It is called the tundra. _____ called the tundra.

Grade 2 • Unit 3 • Week 2

DAY 4
EXTENDED READ 1 MINI-LESSON

Texts for Close Reading, pp. 18–25
"Habitats Around the World"

Student Objectives

I will be able to:
- Read an informational text.
- Identify and annotate text evidence.
- Draw inferences using information in the text.

Additional Materials

Weekly Presentation: Unit 3, Week 2
- Inferences Chart

Close Reading: Use Text Evidence to Draw Inferences (20 MIN.) RI.2.1, SL.2.1a, SL.2.1b, SL.2.2, SL.2.3

Engage Thinking

Say: *We just reread "A New Home for Margie." Now, we will read particular paragraphs of "Habitats Around the World."*

Explain that students will be making inferences—using what is directly stated in a text to think about what is not stated.

Model

Display and read aloud the close reading prompt and annotation instructions. Think aloud about the prompt.

> **Close Reading Prompt:** What can you infer about the South Pole when the author says in paragraph 3, "Grasslands are found all over the world. Only the South Pole does not have one?"
> **Annotate!** Circle any other references to grasslands or the South Pole in the text. Use this information to support your inference.

Sample modeling. *This question asks me what I can "infer about the South Pole" given that grasslands are found everywhere in the world except the South Pole. To answer that I need to reread the text to understand more about grasslands and what the South Pole is like. I need to think about what is directly stated in the text to draw an inference.*

Display and distribute an Inferences Chart. Model how to draw an inference about the South Pole.

Sample modeling. *I ask myself, "Why aren't there grasslands in the South Pole?" I'll reread paragraph 3 and circle the sentence about the South Pole. Next, I'll scan the text to find other evidence about the South Pole. Paragraph 6 describes the tundra and the South Pole. I'll circle paragraph 6. I know that grass doesn't grow where the land is always frozen and covered with snow. I can make the inference that it is too cold and snowy at the South Pole for grasslands to grow there.*

What I Read	What I Know	What I Infer
Only the South Pole does not have grasslands. (1) Tundra is at the South Pole. (6) The South Pole is one of the coldest places on Earth. (6)	The South Pole is covered with snow and ice. Grass needs soil and water to grow.	The South Pole doesn't have grasslands because it is too cold and snow-covered there.

Sample Inferences Chart

70 Grade 2 • Unit 3 • Week 2 ©2018 Benchmark Education Company, LLC

EXTENDED READ 1 MINI-LESSON

WEEK 2 • DAY 4

⚙️ Productive Engagement: Peer Group

Organize students into groups of three or four. Each group should designate specific students to be the group's discussion facilitator, scribe, timekeeper, and encourager. Display and read aloud a second close reading prompt.

> **Close Reading Prompt:** Reread paragraph 8. It tells that "Polar bears, foxes, seals, and oxen live on the Arctic tundra." Use evidence from the text to tell what inference you can make about all these animals.
> **Annotate!** Ask students to circle text evidence throughout "Habitats Around the World" that supports their inference.

Have students begin by circling the sentence in paragraph 8 that names the Arctic animals. Advise them to look for details that tell about habitats, any of the listed animals, and the Arctic tundra. Ask students to fill out a three-column chart to show "What I Read," "What I Know," and "What I Infer."

Share

Call on students to share their answers to the close reading prompt. Use this opportunity to provide additional modeling, corrective feedback, or validation based on students' responses. Students should have found text evidence supporting inferences about the animals' physical traits that help them stay warm, foods the animals are able to find, methods of getting around, and methods of hunting or grazing.

✅ Show Your Knowledge

During independent time, have students reread paragraph 9 and draw an inference about why "trees and other plants stay green all year long." Ask them to explain how they drew their inference.

Challenge Activity. Have students read paragraphs 4 (Grasslands) and 6 (Tundra) of "Habitats Around the World," and then write brief answers to the following questions: *Would Alex be happy living in grasslands? Why or why not? Would he be happy living in tundra? Why or why not?*

---

iELD Integrated ELD

Light Support
Have students echo-read the Inferences Chart. Ask students to complete this sentence frame to add a new chart entry: *I read that _____, and I know that _____, so I can infer that _____.*

What I Read	What I Know	What I Infer
Animals on the savanna leave during the dry season.	Animals need water and food to survive.	The animals must find food and water in another place in Africa during the savanna's dry season.

Moderate Support
Present as above.

What I Read	What I Know	What I Infer
Polar bears have blubber to keep them warm.	Other animals live on the tundra.	The other animals must have a way to stay warm, or they wouldn't survive.

Substantial Support
Present as above.

What I Read	What I Know	What I Infer
The Arctic is cold and has a short summer.	Plants need warm weather, sun, and water to grow.	There aren't many plants there because the summer is too short.

RI.2.1 Ask and answer such questions as who, what, where, when, why, and how to demonstrate understanding of key details in a text. **SL.2.1a** Follow agreed-upon rules for discussions (e.g., gaining the floor in respectful ways, listening to others with care, speaking one at a time about the topics and texts under discussion). **SL.2.1b** Build on others' talk in conversations by linking their comments to the remarks of others. **SL.2.2** Recount or describe key ideas or details from a text read aloud or information presented orally or through other media. **SL.2.3** Ask and answer questions about what a speaker says in order to clarify comprehension, gather additional information, or deepen understanding of a topic or issue.

DAY 4

WRITING TO SOURCES

Write an Informative Report: Organize Your Ideas (15 MIN.) W.2.5

Engage Thinking

Remind students that they have taken notes from two sources. Ask them to have those two notetaking forms in front of them. Then tell students that they will organize their notes today by deciding on the order in which they will present the facts and details that they want to include in their report.

Model

Display the Informative Text Structure Diagram. Then use a think-aloud to model how to begin organizing your notes for writing.

INTRODUCTION →	BODY →	CONCLUSION

Informative Text Structure

Sample think-aloud. *I remember that an informative text has an introduction, a body, and a conclusion, as this diagram shows. So I should think about what to put in each of the three sections. I believe an outline would be the most helpful way for me to do this.*

Display and distribute the Informative Report Outline. Explain how the outline is set up and review the purpose of each of the three main parts of an informative report (introduction, body, and conclusion).

Say: *You can use the background information from your source text notes to fill in the Introduction section of the outline. For the Body section, you will use the facts and details sections of both notetaking forms. Then you will think of two good concluding statements to sum it all up for the Conclusion. You can find and circle the content words in your notes and then jot down those definitions at the bottom of the outline.*

Point out that the Introduction will be one paragraph, the Body will be two or three paragraphs, and the Conclusion will be one paragraph.

Student Writing Prompt

In an informative report, describe grasslands and the plants and animals that live in them. Support your ideas with facts and definitions from "Habitats Around the World" and information from "Plant Life of the Australian Savanna."

Student Objectives

I will be able to:
- Use an outline to organize my notes.
- Write about the need for a step between taking notes and writing a text.

Materials

Weekly Presentations: Unit 3, Week 2

- Students' completed notetaking forms (Source Text, Media Source)
- Informative Text Structure Diagram
- Informative Report Outline

72   Grade 2 • Unit 3 • Week 2   ©2018 Benchmark Education Company, LLC

WRITING TO SOURCES

WEEK 2 • DAY 4

Peer Practice

Have partners work together to fill in their Informative Report Outline. Remind students to use the information from their notes. Encourage them to include the most relevant and interesting facts and details in the outline.

Share Your Understanding

Bring students together and invite partners to share their ideas about the helpfulness of the outline as a tool for organizing their notes.

☑ Quick Write

During independent time, have students answer this question: *Why do you need a step between taking notes and writing your informative report?* Use students' writing to evaluate their understanding that an outline helps them organize their notes into a format that they can follow when writing their report.

Integrated ELD

Light Support
Have students find and pronounce at least two content words in their notes. Guide partners to talk about the meaning of each word they chose and write the meanings at the bottom of their outlines.

Moderate Support
Help students identify content words in their outline. Say each word they select and have them repeat the pronunciation.
Ask: *What does _____ mean?*
Help students define the word.

Substantial Support
Have students point to content words in their outlines. Say the words they find and have students mimic your pronunciation. Together, discuss the meaning of each word. Then provide a sentence frame for students to complete for each word. For example:
The word _____ means _____.

W.2.5 With guidance and support from adults and peers, focus on a topic and strengthen writing as needed by revising and editing.

©2018 Benchmark Education Company, LLC

Grade 2 • Unit 3 • Week 2   73

DAY 4

PHONICS & WORD STUDY

Student Objectives

I will be able to:
- Blend multisyllabic words with r-controlled **a.**
- Spell words with r-controlled **a.**
- Read high-frequency words.

Additional Materials

- r-controlled **a** frieze card
- r-controlled vowel /är/ sound-spelling card

Weekly Presentation: Unit 3, Week 2
- High-frequency word cards: **move, never, once, round, small, their, too, walk, where, year**

For additional word study/decodable practice, see: *Shark Teeth*.

r-Controlled Vowel ar (15 MIN.) RF.2.3b, RF.2.3c, RF.2.3d, RF.2.3e, RF.2.3f, L.2.2d

Read Multisyllabic Words

Model: garden
Explain that when a vowel is followed by **r**, it acts as a team and must remain in the same syllable in a longer word. Model using the word **garden**.

- Write **gar** and point out the r-controlled vowel spelling **ar**.
- Add **den**. Point out that it's a closed syllable.
- Circle the vowel spellings **ar** and **e**. Tell students you will divide the word after **ar**: gar/den.
- Blend the syllables to read the word.

Practice: marching, smarter, artist, barnyard, party, starlight
Use the same routine to guide student practice.

Spelling

Categories
Write the groups of words. Read the words, and ask students to complete each category with a spelling word. Ask students to come up with other category word groups for the other spelling words.

1. fish, dolphin, whale, _____ (**shark**)
2. barn, cows, field, _____ (**farm**)
3. big, huge, gigantic, _____ (**large**)
4. January, April, June, _____ (**March**)

High-Frequency Words

Review: *move, never, once, round, small, their, too, walk, where, year*
Display the high-frequency word cards. Read each word and have students repeat the word together and spell it. Have students sit in a circle. Pass the cards, one at a time. Each student reads the word and uses it in a sentence before passing the card.

RF.2.3b Know spelling-sound correspondences for additional common vowel teams. **RF.2.3c** Decode regularly spelled two-syllable words with long vowels. **RF.2.3d** Decode words with common prefixes and suffixes. **RF.2.3e** Identify words with inconsistent but common spelling-sound correspondences. **RF.2.3f** Recognize and read grade-appropriate irregularly spelled words. **L.2.2d** Generalize learned spelling patterns when writing words (e.g., cage → badge; boy → boil).

74 Grade 2 • Unit 3 • Week 2

©2018 Benchmark Education Company, LLC

Shared Reading (10 MIN.) RI.2.1, RF.2.4b, SL.2.2, SL.2.3, L.2.1e

Determine Text Importance

Review with students that they have been determining text importance all week on a number of texts. Stress that it is important to identify big ideas, themes, and key details when they read. To do that, they must distinguish less important text from the more important text. By doing so, readers are able to determine what text they must read more carefully and use to support their answers to questions.

Remind students that "A City Park Habitat" and "A New Home for Margie" are very different types of writing: one is an informational text and the other is an animal fantasy. Then, model how to think about the way you used the Determine Text Importance strategy this week.

Sample modeling: *In the beginning of the week, we determined the text importance of different sentences in "A City Park Habitat." Most of the text in that informational article was important. But we decided that the first and last sentence are really just meant to engage readers, and they don't provide any important information on the topic. We also decided that the picture captions were important text. For the literary text "A New Home for Margie" it was more important to look for text the author used to convey details about setting, character, and events. Some of the dialogue the author used was funny and interesting, but it didn't tell anything much about the important events. So that text was less important.*

Reread for Fluency: Accuracy/Rereading (iELD)

Partner Reading. Assign partners to take turns reading aloud "A City Park Habitat," dividing the text as they wish. Remind them to listen for any errors and to reread to correct them.

Transfer Skills to Context: Adjectives (iELD)

Remind students that an adjective is a describing word that may answer the question "How many?" Ask students to reread the last sentence in paragraph 3 of "A City Park Habitat" and to find the adjectives by answering these questions:

Ask: *How many parks have ponds?* (**a few**) *How many fish, frogs, and turtles make their home in ponds?* (**many**) *What adjective in paragraph 2 tells how many parks have trees?* (**most**)

Build and Reflect

During independent time, tell students to think about the Week 2 selections, and ask them to complete the "Build, Reflect, and Write" activity on page 27 to help them think more about why different plants and animals live in different habitats.

RI.2.1 Ask and answer such questions as who, what, where, when, why, and how to demonstrate understanding of key details in a text. **RF.2.4b** Read on-level text orally with accuracy, appropriate rate, and expression on successive readings. **SL.2.2** Recount or describe key ideas or details from a text read aloud or information presented orally or through other media. **SL.2.3** Ask and answer questions about what a speaker says in order to clarify comprehension, gather additional information, or deepen understanding of a topic or issue. **L.2.1e** Use adjectives and adverbs, and choose between them depending on what is to be modified.

©2018 Benchmark Education Company, LLC

SHARED READING

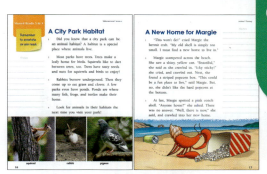

Texts for Close Reading, p. 16–17 "A City Park Habitat" and "A New Home for Margie"

Student Objectives

I will be able to:
- Reread an informational text to determine text importance.
- Identify adjectives that tell how many.

Additional Materials

Weekly Presentation: Unit 3, Week 2

iELD Integrated ELD

Light Support

If . . .	Then . . .
ELLs need support with understanding, and accuracy . . .	**Students review with a partner and:** • take turns reading aloud meaningful chunks; use context clues to assist with vocabulary: **special place, burrow, the next time.** • monitor their accuracy and self-correct.

Moderate Support

If . . .	Then . . .
ELLs have difficulty with understanding and accuracy . . .	**Read with students.** • Stop after meaningful chunks; discuss vocabulary and language: **squirrels, frogs, turtles, park.** • Model reading with accuracy and self-correction.

Substantial Support

If . . .	Then . . .
ELLs struggle with understanding and accuracy . . .	**Read to students.** • Conduct a pre-reading picture-walk; review vocabulary and context: **city park, ponds, underground, clover.** • Model reading with accuracy. • Students echo-read.

Grade 2 • Unit 3 • Week 2

DAY 5

CROSS-TEXT MINI-LESSON

Texts for Close Reading, pp. 10–13 "Postcards from Alex" and pp. 18–25 "Habitats Around the World"

Student Objectives

I will be able to:
- Use text evidence to make connections between texts.
- Share my ideas through collaborative conversation.
- Write to respond to a question about two texts.

Additional Materials

Weekly Presentation: Unit 3, Week 2
- Making Connections Chart

Close Reading: Compare and Contrast Key Points in Two Texts on the Same Topic To Make Connections Across Texts (15 MIN.) RI.2.1, RI.2.9, SL.2.1a, SL.2.1b, SL.2.1c, SL.2.2, SL.2.3, SL.2.6

Engage Thinking

Display "Habitats Around the World" and "Postcards from Alex." Remind students that last week they compared key points in two texts, and tell them they will do so again.

Introduce the Prompt

Display and read aloud the prompt. Tell students that in this lesson, they will think about how the author of each text gives information on rain forests.

> **Close Reading Prompt:** Reread "Postcards from Alex" and paragraph 9 from "Habitats Around the World." What key details about rain forests are provided in both texts? What details are provided only in one text?
> **Annotate!** Underline the text evidence and jot down notes in the margin.

Reread to Find Text Evidence

Before students reread, remind them to keep in mind that they are looking for details about rain forests from the two texts to compare and contrast. Give students time to reread and annotate the texts.

Collaborative Conversation: Peer Group

Sample modeling. *When I am the discussion facilitator, I make sure all members of the group have a chance to speak.*

Display a blank Making Connections Chart. Give groups of students time to jot ideas on the chart by sharing and comparing their annotations from both texts. Ensure that each group has a discussion facilitator whose job it is to make sure that all students participate in the conversation and that students support each other. Observe students' conversations. Use your observations to determine the level of Gradual Release instruction your students may need.

Details only in "Postcards from Alex"	Details in Both Texts	Details only in "Habitats Around the World"
• A rain forest has many insects.	• Rain forests are hot and wet.	• The temperature averages about 23°C (73°F). • A tropical rain forest can have up to 1,016 centimeters (400 inches) of rain in a year. • Trees and other plants stay green all year long.

Making Connections Chart

76 Grade 2 • Unit 3 • Week 2   ©2018 Benchmark Education Company, LLC

CROSS-TEXT MINI-LESSON

WEEK 2 · DAY 5

Share

Call on several groups to share their answers to the close reading question. Invite students to ask questions as needed to clarify what speakers say. Remind students to follow your classroom's agreed-upon rules for discussions and to link their ideas to previous comments.

Reinforce or Reaffirm the Strategy

Provide modeling and/or engage students in self-reflection to build metacognitive awareness.

IF ...	THEN ...
Students need support to identify text evidence on a shared topic . . .	**Model to reinforce the strategy.** • *In both of these texts, the author has provided information about rain forests. In "Habitats Around the World," the author gives several facts about rain forests. In "Postcards from Alex," the author has the characters in the story talk about rain forests.*
Students independently identify text evidence on a shared topic . . .	**Invite partners or small groups to reflect on or extend their connections by discussing another question:** • *If Alex were to visit a new habitat, described in "Habitats Around the World," how might the author give information about that habitat?*

☑ Show Your Knowledge

During independent time, tell students to write two or three sentences about life in a rain forest, using information from both "Habitats Around the World" and "Postcards from Alex." Use their writing to help you assess their ability to identify text evidence from two texts.

(iELD) Integrated ELD

Light Support
Have students echo-read the Making Connections Chart.
Ask: *What is the purpose of the chart? How does the chart organize information?*
Encourage students to use the chart to complete sentence frames and compare the texts.
_____ *talks about* _____, *and so does* _____.
_____ *talks about* _____, *while* _____ *talks about* _____.

Moderate Support
Have students echo-read the Making Connections Chart.
Ask: *What is the purpose of the chart? How does the chart organize information?*
Encourage students to use the chart to complete sentence frames and compare the texts.
Both _____ *and* _____ *discuss* _____.
Only _____ *talks about* _____.

Substantial Support
Have students echo-read the Making Connections Chart.
Ask: *What is the purpose of the chart? How does the chart organize information?*
Model how to use the chart to form sentences that compare the two stories.
Say: *Both texts talk about places that have grass. Both texts discuss cold habitats, the mountains in Chile, and the Arctic.*
Encourage students to use the chart to complete sentence frames and compare and contrast the texts.
Both stories talk about _____.
Only _____ *talks about* _____.

RI.2.1 Ask and answer such questions as who, what, where, when, why, and how to demonstrate understanding of key details in a text. **RI.2.9** Compare and contrast the most important points presented by two texts on the same topic. **SL.2.1a** Follow agreed-upon rules for discussions (e.g., gaining the floor in respectful ways, listening to others with care, speaking one at a time about the topics and texts under discussion). **SL.2.1b** Build on others' talk in conversations by linking their comments to the remarks of others. **SL.2.1c** Ask for clarification and further explanation as needed about the topics and texts under discussion. **SL.2.2** Recount or describe key ideas or details from a text read aloud or information presented orally or through other media. **SL.2.3** Ask and answer questions about what a speaker says in order to clarify comprehension, gather additional information, or deepen understanding of a topic or issue. **SL.2.6** Produce complete sentences when appropriate to task and situation in order to provide requested detail or clarification.

©2018 Benchmark Education Company, LLC

Grade 2 • Unit 3 • Week 2   **77**

DAY 5

WRITING TO SOURCES

Student Writing Prompt

In an informative report, describe grasslands and the plants and animals that live in them. Support your ideas with facts and definitions from "Habitats Around the World" and information from "Plant Life of the Australian Savanna."

Student Objectives

I will be able to:
- Correctly capitalize holiday names, product names, and geographic names.
- Explain how to use an informative report writing rubric.

Materials

Unit 3 Week 2 Weekly presentations:
- Capitalization Modeling Text
- Writing Rubric: Informative Report
- Informative Report Anchor Chart
- Informative Report Rubric

Informative Report Anchor Chart

To write an informative report, writers…
Include facts, details, and content words
- State facts about the topic
- Include descriptive details to support the facts
- Define content words

Include an introduction, body, and conclusion
- Give background information in the introduction
- Provide facts and details in the body
- Sum up the ideas in the conclusion

Start by taking notes on source texts
- Create an organized notetaking form
- Fill in the form with information taken from the source text
- Take notes using the writer's own words

Take notes on media sources
- Create an organized notetaking form
- Watch and listen for facts and the details that support them
- Fill in the form with information learned from the media source
- Take notes using the writer's own words

Use conventions of English correctly
- Understand simple and compound sentences
- Understand that words such as *and, or, but, so,* and *because* are used to join simple sentences together to form compound sentences
- Capitalize holidays and geographic names

Conventions of Writing: Capitalize Holidays and Geographic Names

(15 MIN.) L.2.2a

Focus the Learning

Tell students that they already know a lot about when to use capital letters. For example, they know to start the first word of every sentence with a capital letter. They also know that people's names and the pronoun "I" is always capitalized.

Model

Introduce students to other types of words that need to be capitalized. For each category introduced (names of holidays, product names, and geographic names), write down the examples that you provide and point out the capital letters in the names.

Say: *Other words that are always capitalized are the names of holidays, product names, and geographic names. Examples of holiday names are "New Year's Day" and "Fourth of July." Product names are the names of things you buy, like "Super Crunch Cereal" or the "Awful Aliens" video game. And geographic names are the names of places you might see on a map, such as continents, countries, states, cities, and bodies of water. You've seen names like these in the sources you used for your informative report. For example, "Australia" is the name of a place that has grasslands. Can you think of other geographic names to add to our list?*

Display Text A and read the first sentence aloud.

Say: *I see a product name that should be capitalized here. The last word in the sentence is the name of the tennis shoe brand. For this sentence to be correctly written, the word "Blastoffs" should be capitalized.*

Text A
1. My favorite brand of tennis shoes is blastoffs.
2. We always make our own cards for valentine's day.
3. Many parts of the united states have grasslands.
4. Two states with grasslands are texas and iowa.
5. Many dads like to play golf on father's day.

Text B
1. My favorite brand of tennis shoes is Blastoffs.
2. We always make our own cards for Valentine's Day.
3. Many parts of the United States have grasslands.
4. Two states with grasslands are Texas and Iowa.
5. Many dads like to play golf on Father's Day.

Capitalization Modeling Text

---

78 Grade 2 • Unit 3 • Week 2 ©2018 Benchmark Education Company, LLC

WRITING TO SOURCES

WEEK 2 · DAY 5

Peer Practice

Have students work with a partner to correct sentences 2, 3, 4, and 5. Have them write the complete sentences correctly.

Share Your Understanding

Bring the students pairs together.

Ask: *Which words did you capitalize? Why?*

Then display Text B for students to use as a reference to check their work. Point out that for two-word names in these categories, both words must be capitalized.

Introduce the Rubric (iELD)

Inform students that next week, they will write their informative report about the grasslands and hand in a final copy. Explain that you will grade their report using a rubric. Display the Informative Report Rubric and review how to use it. Point out that the rubric reflects the key points on the Informative Report Anchor Chart and writing checklist, and it provides a scoring system to evaluate each area. Tell students that they will use the rubric to grade their own writing before turning in their report. This will help them reflect on their writing and identify areas in which their text is strong or needs more work.

☑ Quick Write

During independent time, have students complete the following writing assignment: *Write three sentences in which you use capitalization correctly. One sentence should include a holiday name, one a product name, and one a geographic name.* Use students' writing to evaluate their understanding of the use of capitalization.

(iELD) Integrated ELD

Light Support

Have students choose something from their outline that they would like to "bring to life" in their writing. Help them brainstorm words and phrases they might use to achieve the effect they desire. Encourage students to consider their word choices for other items in their outline.

Moderate Support

Encourage partners to identify and talk about words from their outline that might be replaced to help readers visualize what they are saying.

Substantial Support

Guide students to understand that their word choice helps to show their voice. Encourage them to think about different words they might use in the sentences they write. To practice, have students tell you which word they would use in each of these sentences:

Grassland areas are **big/gigantic**.

Some **lovely/nice** flowers grow in the grasslands.

New grass is **good/delicious** to the grazing animals.

Informative Report Rubric

The informative report...	4	3	2	1
	My report...	My report...	My report...	My report...
includes facts, details, and content words	states all facts clearly, includes descriptive details about each fact, and defines all content words	states most facts clearly, includes details about several facts, and defines only a few content words	states some facts clearly, includes details about one or two facts, and defines one or two content words	does not state facts clearly or support them with details, and does not define content words
includes an introduction, a body, and a conclusion	includes interesting information in the introduction, gives plenty of strong facts and details in the body, and provides an excellent summary in the conclusion	includes information in the introduction, gives adequate facts and details in the body, and provides a good summary in the conclusion	includes little information in the introduction, presents just a few facts and details in the body, and to provide an adequate summary in the conclusion	is disorganized, or includes inadequate information
is based on organized notes taken in writers' own words from text and media sources	presents information from two different sources that is well-organized and written clearly in my own words	presents acceptable information from two sources that is organized and written in my own words	presents some information from two sources that is somewhat organized but not always clearly written in my own words	presents little information from one or two sources, and the information might not be organized clearly and written in my own words
includes compound sentences as well as simple sentences	includes several compound sentences that are correctly written with different conjunctions	includes compound sentences that are correctly written but does not use various conjunctions	includes one or two compound sentences but might not write them correctly	does not write compounds sentences correctly or use them at all
uses capitalization correctly	correctly capitalizes all words that should be capitalized, including several geographic names	correctly capitalizes most words that should be capitalized, including one or two geographic names	does not capitalize several words that should be capitalized	does not follow capitalization rules most of the time

Key: 4–exemplary 3–accomplished 2–developing 1–beginning

Informative Report Rubric

L.2.2a Capitalize holidays, product names, and geographic names.

©2018 Benchmark Education Company, LLC

Grade 2 • Unit 3 • Week 2   **79**

DAY 5

PHONICS & WORD STUDY

Review and Assess r-Controlled Vowel ar (15 MIN.) RF.2.3b, RF.2.3c, RF.2.3e, RF.2.3f, L.2.2d

Build Words

Model: car, cart, chart

Display the letter cards for **car**. Blend the sounds: /kär/, **car**.

- Add the **t** and repeat with **cart**.
- Add the **h** and repeat with **chart**.

Practice: far, farm, harm; yarn, yard, hard

Use the same routine to guide student practice.

Review Long u (ew, u, ue, u_e)

Model: few

Write the word **few** and ask students to identify the vowel sound. Point out the long **u** spelling **ew**.

Repeat with **unit**, **fuel**, and **cube**. Point out the open first syllable **u** in **unit**.

Practice: cute, use, music, huge, human, menu

Use the same routine to guide student practice.

Reread for Fluency: "An Ocean Visit"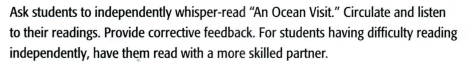

Ask students to independently whisper-read "An Ocean Visit." Circulate and listen to their readings. Provide corrective feedback. For students having difficulty reading independently, have them read with a more skilled partner.

Texts for Close Reading, p. 26
"An Ocean Visit"

Student Objectives

I will be able to:
- Build, reread, and spell words with r-controlled **a**.
- Reread word study (decodable) text for fluency.
- Read high-frequency words.

Additional Materials

- Letter cards: **a, b, c, d, f, h, k, m, n, r, t, y**
- r-controlled **a** frieze card
- r-controlled vowel /är/ sound-spelling card

Weekly Presentation: Unit 3, Week 2
- Letter cards for each high-frequency word
- High-frequency word cards: **move, never, once, round, small, their, too, walk, where, year**

For additional word study/decodable practice, see: *Shark Teeth*.

PHONICS & WORD STUDY

Spelling

Posttest

Use the following procedure to assess students' spelling of this week's words.

- Say each spelling word and use it in the sentence provided.
- Have students write the complete sentence on a piece of paper. Then continue with the next word.
- When students have finished, collect their papers and analyze any misspelled words.

1. I have a green car.
2. The star shines in the night sky.
3. We like to march in a line.
4. Ann is a very smart girl.
5. It is hard to jump on one leg.
6. The farm has a big truck.
7. I ate a large meal.
8. The shark has sharp teeth.
9. We planted roses in the garden.
10. I helped Dad clean the yard.

High-Frequency Words

Review: *move, never, once, round, small, their, too, walk, where, year*

Display the high-frequency word cards. Say each word and have students repeat the word and spell it out loud together.

Place letter cards for one of the words in random order in a pocket chart. Have a volunteer beat the clock to form the word. Allow 15 seconds. Then have the rest of the class check the spelling and give a thumbs up or thumbs down.

Next have students turn to a partner and say a sentence using the word. Call on volunteers to check their sentences.

Integrated ELD

Light Support
Display "An Ocean Visit." Ask partners to identify punctuation marks in the text and explain what to do at each mark. Have students take turns reading paragraphs aloud, focusing on fluency and accuracy.

Moderate Support
Display "An Ocean Visit." Put students into pairs. Ask partners to identify punctuation marks in the text and explain what to do at each mark.
Model reading the text with fluency and accuracy. Have partners take turns reading paragraphs, focusing on fluency and accuracy. Students can use context clues to read unfamiliar words.

Substantial Support
Display "An Ocean Visit." Have students identify punctuation marks in the text. Model pausing briefly after a comma and coming to a full stop at a period. Model reading the text line by line, using context clues to read unfamiliar words. Emphasize fluency. Partners take turns reading sentences fluently and accurately. Assist as needed.

RF.2.3b Know spelling-sound correspondences for additional common vowel teams. **RF.2.3c** Decode regularly spelled two-syllable words with long vowels. **RF.2.3e** Identify words with inconsistent but common spelling-sound correspondences. **RF.2.3f** Recognize and read grade-appropriate irregularly spelled words. **L.2.2d** Generalize learned spelling patterns when writing words (e.g., cage → badge; boy → boil).

Week 3 Mini-Lessons at a Glance

	Day 1	Day 2
Reading Mini-Lessons	Build Knowledge and Review Strategies (10 Min.), p. 84 SL.2.1a, SL.2.1b, SL.2.2, SL.2.3 Shared Reading (10 Min.), p. 85 RF.2.4a, RF.2.4b, RF.2.4c "Lost in the Desert": Recount Story Events, Part 1 (15 Min.), p. 86 RL.2.1, RL.2.5, SL.2.2, SL.2.3, SL.2.6	Shared Reading (10 Min.), p. 92 RF.2.3f, RF.2.4a, RF.2.4b, RF.2.4c "Lost in the Desert": Recount Story Events, Part 2 (20 Min.), p. 94 RL.2.1, RL.2.5, SL.2.2, SL.2.3, SL.2.6
Writing and Language Mini-Lessons	Write an Informative Report: Introduce Your Topic (15 Min.), p. 88 W.2.2	Write an Informative Report: Draft and Develop Your Points and Include a Conclusion (15 Min.), p. 96 W.2.2
Phonics/Word Study Mini-Lessons	r-Controlled Vowels er, ir, ur (20 Min.), p. 90 RF.2.3b, RF.2.3e, RF.2.3f, L.2.2d • High-Frequency Words: *all, away, better, by, change, done, even, found, learn, only* • Weekly Spelling Words: *bird, hurt, her, nurse, girl, shirt, burn, third, never, winter*	r-Controlled Vowels er, ir, ur (15 Min.), p. 98 RF.2.3b, RF.2.3e, RF.2.3f, L.2.2d • High-Frequency Words: *all, away, better, by, change, done, even, found, learn, only*

Extended Read 2: "Lost in the Desert"

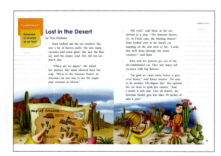

Realistic Fiction

Quantitative	Lexile® 450L

Qualitative Analysis of Text Complexity

Purpose and Levels of Meaning ❷
• Story has a dual purpose—explicitly to tell the tale of a family trip, implicitly to describe conditions in the Sonoran Desert.

Structure ❸
• The story has a chronological structure with a major shift in narrative point of view.
• Specific details about the desert will make this feel like a nonfiction travelogue, as well.

Language Conventionality and Clarity ❷
• Sentences are mostly simple, but there are domain-specific terms related to life and conditions in the desert, such as *kangaroo rat, organ pipe cactuses,* and *Sonoran Desert.*

Knowledge Demands ❷
• Prior knowledge of deserts will help students grasp the conditions that drive the narrative.

Total QM: 9
Moderate Complexity*

*The texts in *Benchmark Advance* are qualitatively evaluated based on their grade-level placement in the program. Reader maturity and age appropriateness are key considerations in the subjective use of the rubrics.

Day 3	Day 4	Day 5
Shared Reading (10 Min.), p. 100 RF.2.4a, RF.2.4b, RF.2.4c	**Shared Reading (10 Min.), p. 107** RF.2.4a, RF.2.4b, RF.2.4c, L.2.2a	**Shared Reading (10 Min.), p. 113** RL.2.1, RF.2.4b, SL.2.2, SL.2.3, L.2.4d
Build Vocabulary: Distinguish Shades of Meaning Among Related Adjectives (10 Min.), p. 101 RL.2.4, L.2.5b	**Close Reading: Compare and Contrast Key Points in Two Texts on the Same Topic (20 Min.), p. 108** RI.2.1, RI.2.9, SL.2.1a, SL.2.1b	**Reflect on Unit Concepts (20 Min.), p. 118** W.2.6, SL.2.1a, SL.2.1b, SL.2.1c, SL.2.2, SL.2.3, SL.2.5, SL.2.6
Close Reading: Describe the Overall Structure of a Story (15 Min.), p. 102 RL.2.1, RL.2.5, RL.2.7, SL.2.1a, SL.2.1b, SL.2.1c, SL.2.2, SL.2.3		
Write an Informative Report: Revise to Improve Sentence Fluency by Creating Compound Sentences (15 Min.), p. 104 L.2.1f	**Write an Informative Report: Check and Correct Capitalization (15 Min.), p. 110** L.2.2a	**Evaluate and Reflect on Writing (15 Min.), p. 114** W.2.2a
r-Controlled Vowels er, ir, ur (10 Min.), p. 106 RL.2.3, RL.2.10, RF.2.3b, RF.2.3c, RF.2.3e, RF.2.3f, L.2.2d	**r-Controlled Vowels er, ir, ur (20 Min.), p. 112** RF.2.3b, RF.2.3c, RF.2.3d, RF.2.3e, RF.2.3f, L.2.2d	**Review and Assess r-Controlled Vowels er, ir, ur (15 Min.), p. 116** RL.2.10, RF.2.3b, RF.2.3c, RF.2.3d, RF.2.3e, RF.2.3f, L.2.2d
• High-Frequency Words: *all, away, better, by, change, done, even, found, learn, only*	• High-Frequency Words: *all, away, better, by, change, done, even, found, learn, only*	• High-Frequency Words: *all, away, better, by, change, done, even, found, learn, only*

©2018 Benchmark Education Company, LLC

Grade 2 • Unit 3 • Week 3

DAY 1

UNIT REFLECTION

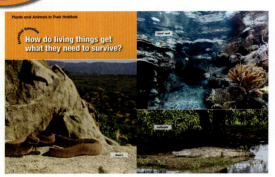

Texts for Close Reading, pp. 2–3
Unit Introduction

Student Objectives

I will be able to:
- Reflect on strategies I have learned to help me read a text.
- Follow three-step oral directions.

Additional Materials

Weekly Presentation: Unit 3, Week 3

iELD Integrated ELD

Light Support
Review "Postcards From Alex." Discuss how to distinguish shades of meaning among adjectives. Elicit adjectives from the text. For example:

| damp | wet | rainy |

Students can use visual support, role-playing, gestures, and sentence frames to explain word meanings.
I don't like a _____ rain forest.
When the rain forest was _____, I was upset.
I left when the rain forest was _____.

Moderate Support
Present as above.

| big | large | huge |

I looked at the armadillo's _____ claws.
I was surprised that the armadillo had really _____ claws.
When I saw the armadillo's _____ claws, I was _____.

Substantial Support
Review "Postcards From Alex." Discuss how to distinguish shades of meaning among adjectives. Elicit adjectives from the text. For example:

| good | nice | greatest |

Model using each adjective in a sentence.
Say: *This rain forest has **nice** insects.*
*This rain forest has **good** insects.*
*This rain forest has the **greatest** insects.*

Build Knowledge and Review Strategies (10 MIN.) SL.2.1a, SL.2.1b, SL.2.2, SL.2.3

Discuss the Essential Question

Display the introduction to "Plants and Animals in Their Habitats." Review the Essential Question and the selections for Weeks 1 and 2. Ask partners to listen carefully to follow these three-step directions:

1. Share a fact you learned about habitats.
2. Name something that animals need in all habitats.
3. Ask a question about what living things need to survive.

As partnerships share their ideas with the class, remind them to follow discussion rules. Explain that this week, students will continue to investigate the Essential Question using selections about animals and habitats.

Review Unit Strategies

Analyze Story Structure. Remind students that they have been identifying elements of literary stories so they understand stories better and remember what happens in them.

Say: *When we read the animal fantasy "Postcards from Alex," we identified these story elements: the main character, settings, problem, events, and solution. The main character was Alex the armadillo. The settings were his home in the rain forest and the different habitats he visited. His problem was that he didn't like the rain forest. The key events were his three attempts to find better places to live. What was the solution at the end? He learned that the best place for him was the rain forest.*

Ask students how they figure out who the main character is and why the story problem is especially important.

Distinguish Shades of Meaning Among Adjectives. Remind students that they have thought about the different shades of meaning of adjectives.

Say: *When we read "Postcards from Alex," we found the adjectives **cold**, **chilly**, and **freezing**. These adjectives are synonyms because they have similar meanings. We decided that a chilly day was probably not quite as cold as a cold day and that a freezing day was the coldest of all. Each synonym has a different shade of meaning.*

Ask students to distinguish the shades of meaning in these two statements:

1. I swam in **cool** water.
2. I swam in **chilly** water.

Tell students that understanding story elements and thinking about shades of meaning will help them understand the extended text they will read this week.

SL.2.1a Follow agreed-upon rules for discussions (e.g., gaining the floor in respectful ways, listening to others with care, speaking one at a time about the topics and texts under discussion). **SL.2.1b** Build on others' talk in conversations by linking their comments to the remarks of others. **SL.2.2** Recount or describe key ideas or details from a text read aloud or information presented orally or through other media. **SL.2.3** Ask and answer questions about what a speaker says in order to clarify comprehension, gather additional information, or deepen understanding of a topic or issue.

84 Grade 2 • Unit 3 • Week 3   ©2018 Benchmark Education Company, LLC

Shared Reading (10 MIN.) RF.2.4a, RF.2.4b, RF.2.4c

Introduce the Text

Display "Burt the Sea Turtle" and read aloud the story title. Invite students to turn to a partner and infer what the text will be about. As needed, model how to preview the text.

Sample modeling. *The title helps me infer who the main character will be—a sea turtle named Burt. I think that this story will be an animal fantasy because the illustration shows a cartoon sea turtle in a city instead of in the sea. I think that the story will be about what happens to Burt when he leaves the sea for the city. If I'm right, these ideas will be important text in the story.*

Model Fluent Reading: Prosody/Intonation

Read the text aloud fluently with appropriate rising and falling pitch. Tell students that reading to show meaning requires emphasizing certain words and making the voice go up and down naturally. Provide an example by choosing one sentence to read in a monotone and then reread naturally.

Model Determine Text Importance

Remind students that they have been practicing the Determine Text Importance reading strategy for the last two weeks. Then remind them how determining text importance was different when reading literary texts from when reading informational texts. An animal fantasy like "Burt the Sea Turtle" is meant to be fun and entertaining. However, it is still important to determine the text that tells about character, setting, and story events—as well as the unit theme of animals and their habitats. Model the strategy on the first two paragraphs.

Sample modeling. *The first sentence tells about the setting, and that is important. The next two sentences tell about story events, but I don't think they are important in terms of Burt and his habitat. Then in paragraph 2, I read that Burt lived for eighty years in the same place, and that he decided to leave his ocean habitat to see the rest of the world. I will circle that whole paragraph because it has important story events and it is clearly about animal habitats.*

Transfer Skills to Context: r-Controlled /âr/ Syllable Pattern

Point to the word **hard** in paragraph 3 and ask students to read it aloud. Ask students what vowel sound they hear in **hard**. Then ask them to find another word with the same sound. (**cars**)

SHARED READING

WEEK 3 • DAY 1

Texts for Close Reading, p. 28 "Burt the Sea Turtle"

Student Objectives

I will be able to:
- Read an animal fantasy.
- Read with fluency and appropriate intonation.
- Identify words with r-controlled /âr/ syllable pattern.

Additional Materials

Weekly Presentation: Unit 3, Week 3

iELD Integrated ELD

Light Support
Display "Burt the Sea Turtle." Point out key vocabulary such as **Atlantic, been outside the ocean, seen enough, away from home, soon found himself, crawled out**.
Ask students to use each word or phrase from the chart in an original sentence.

Moderate Support
Display "Burt the Sea Turtle." Students tell what they see. Choose and place key vocabulary in a chart. Write words and phrases from the chart on cards. Have students form small groups, and assign a card to each group. Ask students to use each word or phrase from the chart in an original sentence.

laid	once hatched	hurried
outside the ocean	rushed by	stepped over

Substantial Support
Display "Burt the Sea Turtle." Students tell what they see. Choose and place key vocabulary in a chart.

turtle	sand	eighty
crawled	rushed by	best place

Write words and phrases from the chart on cards. Have students form small groups, and assign a card to each group. Ask students to use each word or phrase from the chart in an original sentence.

RF.2.4a Read on-level text with purpose and understanding. **RF.2.4b** Read on-level text orally with accuracy, appropriate rate, and expression on successive readings. **RF.2.4c** Use context to confirm or self-correct word recognition and understanding, rereading as necessary.

DAY 1

EXTENDED READ 2 MINI-LESSON

"Lost in the Desert": Recount Story Events, Part 1 (15 MIN.) RL.2.1, RL.2.5, SL.2.2, SL.2.3, SL.2.6

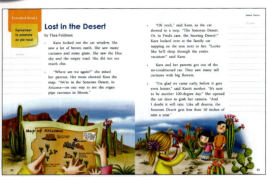

Texts for Close Reading, pp. 30–37
"Lost in the Desert"

Student Objectives

I will be able to:
- Read an animal fantasy.
- Identify and annotate key story events.
- Share my thinking with my peers.

Additional Materials

Weekly Presentation: Unit 3, Week 3
- Flow Chart

Ways to Scaffold the First Reading

Use your observational assessment to determine the intensity of scaffolding your students need.

IF …	THEN consider …
Students are English learners who may struggle with vocabulary and language demands …	**Read the text TO students.** • Conduct a before-reading picture walk to introduce vocabulary and concepts. • Stop after meaningful chunks to define unfamiliar words and paraphrase difficult sentences.
Students are struggling readers who may decode with little comprehension …	**Read the text WITH students.** • Stop after meaningful chunks to ask *who, what, when, where, how* questions. • Work with students to define unfamiliar words and paraphrase key ideas.
Students need some support to read unfamiliar texts with comprehension …	**Have students PARTNER-READ.** Partners should: • take turns reading aloud meaningful chunks. • ask each other *who, what, when, where, how* questions about the text. • circle unfamiliar words and define them using context clues.

Preview the Text (iELD)

Display and ask students to open to "Lost in the Desert." Guide students to preview the text and illustrations and then turn to a partner to discuss what they see. As needed, prompt them to notice what the title and illustrations suggest about the type of text it seems to be.

Read to Identify Key Story Events

Have students read paragraphs 1–10 to identify key story events. Have them determine text importance by making notes and drawings in the margin to help them remember what they read. Have them underline key story events.

Give students time to read and annotate. Observe their annotations to assess their ability to recognize key story events.

Collaborative Conversation: Partner

Ask: *What type of story is "Lost in the Desert"?*

Confirm that they recognize it as an animal fantasy, because Fred the cat thinks like a person. Display and distribute a blank Flow Chart. Ask partners to complete the chart by identifying key story events. Remind students that partners should take turns speaking and build on each other's ideas. Use your observations to determine if students need support to identify the key story events.

Paragraphs 1–3	Paragraphs 4–6	Paragraphs 7–8	Paragraphs 9–10
Kara and her family are visiting the Sonoran Desert while their cat Fred naps in the car.	Kara and her parents leave the car to see the cactus flowers, and they don't see Fred slip out into the warm desert air.	Fred chases a kangaroo rat into its hole.	As Fred begins to feel hot, he hears the car doors slam. He runs toward the car, but it drives off without him.

Sample Flow Chart

Tell students that they will continue to identify key events when they read Part 2 of the story.

Share

Invite partnerships to share their statements about the key events in the story. Encourage group discussion of the statements, including whether enough, or too many, details have been included. Remind students to connect their comments to what they have heard from previous speakers.

86 Grade 2 • Unit 3 • Week 3

©2018 Benchmark Education Company, LLC

EXTENDED READ 2 MINI-LESSON

WEEK 3 · DAY 1

Reinforce or Reaffirm the Strategy

If your students need support to understand the text, refer to "Ways to Scaffold the First Reading." Pose text-dependent questions to guide students' thinking. For example:

- *Why does Fred leave the car?*
- *What's the first thing that changes for Fred when he is in the desert alone?*

Choose one of the following options based on your observations during partner collaboration.

IF ...	THEN ...
Students need support to identify story events . . .	**Model to reinforce the strategy.** • *As I read, I think about what is most important to pay attention to in order to keep track of what is happening in a story–the key events.* • *In paragraphs 1–3, I learn that Kara and her family are on a road trip to the Sonoran Desert in Arizona while Fred the cat naps in the car.* • *In paragraphs 4–6, I ask myself what is most important to understand. The answer is that while the family gets out to view the cactus flowers, they don't see Fred slip out of the car into the desert.*
Students independently identify key story events . . .	**Invite partners to reflect on their strategy use by discussing the following question:** • *How did you decide which details to include when identifying the key events?*

☑ Show Your Knowledge

During independent time, ask students to reread paragraph 7 and write a sentence that summarizes the key event.

Challenge Activity. Have students reread paragraph 7. Ask them whether they think the first sentence describes a key event in the story and have them explain their reasons.

(iELD) Integrated ELD

Light Support
Preview the text. Provide visual support and cognates: **cactus/cactos; desert/desierto; vacation/vacaciones; rat/rata; disappeared/desaparecido; air conditioned/airecondicionado, doubt, slipped outside, strolled around, peered, brush, chased, bloom.**

Have students complete sentence frames to draw conclusions about **the habitat, the family, and the cat.**

The _____ must be _____, because _____.
Since _____, the _____ must have _____.
It looks like _____.

Moderate Support
Preview the text. Provide visual support and cognates: **cactus/cactos; desert/desierto; vacation/vacaciones; rat/rata; disappeared/desaparecido; air conditioned/airecondicionado, brush, chased, bloom.**

Ask: *Why did Kara call it the "Snoring Desert"?*
What did the characters say about the desert habitat?
What happened to Fred?

Substantial Support
Preview the text. Provide visual support and cognates: **cactus/cactos; desert/desierto; vacation/vacaciones; rat/rata; disappeared/desaparecido; air conditioned/ airecondicionado.**

Have students act out the following terms to show comprehension: **organ pipe cactuses, notice, kangaroo rat, hole, stretched.**

Help students ask simple questions about the text.

Where is the _____?
What was _____ doing?
What does _____ look like?
What happened to _____?

RL.2.1 Ask and answer such questions as who, what, where, when, why, and how to demonstrate understanding of key details in a text. **RL.2.5** Describe the overall structure of a story, including describing how the beginning introduces the story and the ending concludes the action. **SL.2.2** Recount or describe key ideas or details from a text read aloud or information presented orally or through other media. **SL.2.3** Ask and answer questions about what a speaker says in order to clarify comprehension, gather additional information, or deepen understanding of a topic or issue. **SL.2.6** Produce complete sentences when appropriate to task and situation in order to provide requested detail or clarification.

©2018 Benchmark Education Company, LLC

Grade 2 • Unit 3 • Week 3

DAY 1

WRITING TO SOURCES

Student Writing Prompt

In an informative report, describe grasslands and the plants and animals that live in them. Support your ideas with facts and definitions from "Habitats Around the World" and information from "Plant Life of the Australian Savanna."

Student Objectives

I will be able to:
- Write an effective opening paragraph.
- Share my ideas in collaborative conversation and in writing.

*Materials

Weekly Presentation: Unit 3, Week 3
- Sample Opening Paragraph
- Mentor Informative Report
- Informative Report Anchor Chart
- Informative Report Checklist
- Informative Report Rubric

Write an Informative Report: Introduce Your Topic (15 MIN.) W.2.2

Engage Thinking

Explain that the opening paragraph of an informative report is very important. A well-constructed opening paragraph gets readers interested and helps them understand what the text will be about.

Say: *Today I'm going to show you how I think about and write my introductory paragraph.*

Model

Reread the writing prompt. Then display and read aloud the sample opening paragraph. Use think-alouds to analyze how you developed this paragraph.

> Grasslands, also known as savannas or prairies, are vast areas of land where grass, low shrubs, and wildflowers grow. Grasslands are found all over the world—except at the South Pole! Many animals, such as bison, zebras, and wildebeests, live in these habitats. The plants and animals that live in the grasslands have special characteristics that help them survive.

Sample Opening Paragraph

Sample think-aloud (sentences 1 and 2). *I wanted my readers to understand what a grassland is, so I stated this in my first sentence. I wrote "grasslands or prairies" in case some readers don't know that they are the same thing. I got my information from "Habitats Around the World." In the second sentence, I wanted readers to know where grasslands are found, and I thought it would interest them to know that the only place you don't find them is at the South Pole.*

Sample think-aloud (sentence 3). *My report needs to talk about the plants and animals in grasslands, so in this sentence, I let readers know that is what I will talk about. I give them examples of animals I saw in the illustrations, but these are only some of the animals I might talk about in my text.*

Peer Practice

Tell students to team up with a partner, read the last sentence in your opening paragraph, and discuss why you included it.

88 Grade 2 • Unit 3 • Week 3   ©2018 Benchmark Education Company, LLC

WRITING TO SOURCES

WEEK 3 • DAY 1

Share Your Understanding

Bring students together and invite the partners to explain what purpose the last sentence in your opening paragraph serves. As necessary, reinforce that this paragraph lets readers know that your report will explain the special characteristics, or features, that help grassland plants and animals survive.

Independent Writing

During independent time, ask students to begin drafting their informative reports by focusing on the introductory paragraph. Remind them to refer to the tools they have: mentor text, anchor chart, writer's checklist and rubric, notes, outlines, and source materials.

✓ Confer and Monitor

As you monitor students' independent writing, provide feedback, as needed. For example:

Directive Feedback: *Reread the writing prompt. What does your report need to focus on? Now think of a sentence to introduce that focus. Go back to your sources for information if you need to.*

Self-Monitoring and Reflection: *What sentence could you start with that would introduce the topic? If you were reading this informative report, what interesting facts would make you want to keep reading?*

Validating and Confirming: *You told me what your topic is. You introduced the ideas you will develop within your report, and you made your topic seem interesting.*

---

iELD Integrated ELD

Light Support
Have partners share their draft ideas with each other. Encourage students to provide constructive feedback about ways to make the paragraph more focused or interesting.

Moderate Support
Ask partners to share their ideas for an opening paragraph. Provide sentence frames to help students expand their ideas. For example:
I will include _____ and _____ to help readers _____.
I will make my paragraph about grasslands more interesting by _____ and _____.

Substantial Support
Talk with students about their draft ideas. Help them focus on the information they should include in their introductory paragraph by presenting them with sentence frames. For example:
One thing I can say about grasslands is _____.

W.2.2 Write informative/explanatory texts in which they introduce a topic, use facts and definitions to develop points, and provide a concluding statement or section.

©2018 Benchmark Education Company, LLC

Grade 2 • Unit 3 • Week 3   89

DAY 1

PHONICS & WORD STUDY

r-Controlled *e, i, u* Frieze Card and r-controlled vowel /ur/ Sound-Spelling Card

Student Objectives

I will be able to:
- Identify, blend, and spell words with r-controlled **e, i, u**.
- Learn high-frequency words.
- Review high-frequency words.

Additional Materials

- Letter cards: **b, h, n, r, t, u**

Weekly Presentation: Unit 3, Week 3
- r-controlled **e, i, u** frieze card
- r-controlled /ur/ sound-spelling card
- High-frequency word cards: **all, away, better, by, change, done, even, found, learn, only**
- Review high-frequency word cards: **move, never, once, round, small, their, too, walk, where, year**

For additional word study/decodable practice, see: *Everglades, Visit the Everglades,* and *The Hurt Turtle.*

r-Controlled Vowels er, ir, ur (20 MIN.) RF.2.3b, RF.2.3e, RF.2.3f, L.2.2d

Spelling-Sound Correspondences

Introduce: r-Controlled Vowels er, ir, ur
Display the r-controlled **e, i, u** frieze card.

Say: *These sounds are /ûr/. The /ûr/ sounds are spelled many ways:* **er, ir, ur.**

Model: er, ir, ur
Point to each spelling on the card and provide a sample word: **er** as in **her**, **ir** as in **girl**, **ur** as in **turn**. Write each sample word and underline the r-controlled **e, i, u** spelling.

Say: *Look at the first word I wrote:* **h-e-r.** *I see the r-controlled e spelling* **er.** *Listen and watch as I sound out the word:* /hûr/, **her.**

Run your hand under the word as you sound it out.

Practice: her, girl, turn
Repeat the r-controlled **e, i, u** words one at a time. Ask students to write each word and underline the r-controlled **e, i, u** spellings.

Blend Words

Model: r-Controlled Vowels er, ir, ur
Display the letter cards for **bun**. Model how to blend the sounds together as you run your hand under each letter.

Say: *This is the letter* **b.** *It stands for /b/. This is the letter* **u.** *It stands for /u/. Listen as I blend these sounds together: /buuu/. This is the letter* **n.** *It stands for /n/. Now listen as I blend all three sounds together: /buuun/,* **bun.** *Say the word with me:* **bun.**

Model adding an **r** after the **u** to make the word **burn**.

Say: *I can add an* **r** *after the* **u** *to make the r-controlled vowel spelling* **ur.** *The* **ur** *spelling stands for the /ûr/ sounds. Listen as I blend the new word: /bûrn/. Say the word with me:* **burn.**

Continue modeling the words **hut, hurt**.

Practice: dirt, shirt, third, fern, verb, fur, nurse
Write each word. Have students read together and blend the sounds. Provide corrective feedback, as needed.

90 Grade 2 • Unit 3 • Week 3 ©2018 Benchmark Education Company, LLC

PHONICS & WORD STUDY

WEEK 3 • DAY 1

Spelling

Pretest

Say each spelling word. Read the sentence and say the word again. After the pretest, write each word as you say the letter names. Have students check their work.

bird	The **bird** has two eggs in its nest.
hurt	Did that boy **hurt** his arm when he fell?
her	Please tell **her** that she can come to the party.
nurse	The **nurse** made sure the patient took his medicine.
girl	The **girl** wore pink shoes at her dance recital.
shirt	My **shirt** has a big stain on it from lunch.
burn	We needed to **burn** all the logs in the fireplace.
third	He is the **third** boy to win a prize.
never	I will **never** jump out of a plane.
winter	We had three blizzards last **winter**.

High-Frequency Words (iELD)

Introduce: *all, away, better, by, change, done, even, found, learn, only*

Use the following routine: Write simple sentences using each high-frequency word. Underline the word and discuss important features about it. Say the word and have students repeat. Then spell the word with students as you point to each letter. Finally, have students write the word as they spell it aloud.

Practice

Display the high-frequency word cards. Have students work with a partner to write sentences using the words. Then have volunteers read a sentence and identify the high-frequency word.

Review: *move, never, once, round, small, their, too, walk, where, year*

Review last week's words using the high-frequency word cards. Mix and display one word card at a time as students say each word aloud together.

(iELD) Integrated ELD

Light Support

Have students echo-read the word bank below with the high-frequency words.

| all | away | better | by | change |
| done | even | found | learn | only |

Pairs alternate dictating the high-frequency words to each other, and self-check their work using the word bank.

Moderate Support

Have students echo-read the word bank below with the high-frequency words.

| all | away | better | by | change |
| done | even | found | learn | only |

Dictate the words. Volunteers point to the word in the word bank and read it aloud. Students self-check their work using the word bank.

Substantial Support

Have students echo-read the word bank below with the high-frequency words.

| all | away | better | by | change |
| done | even | found | learn | only |

Write the words on cards. Hold up a card. Students choral-read. Volunteers point to the word in the word bank and read it aloud.

Students read aloud, spell, and write the words with you. Model using the words in sentences with **so**.

Say: *We found a better cactus, **so** we took more pictures.*

*We were done taking pictures, **so** we went back to the car.*

Have students use each word from the work bank in a sentence using the sentence frame,

We _____, so _____.

RF.2.3b Know spelling-sound correspondences for additional common vowel teams. **RF.2.3e** Identify words with inconsistent but common spelling-sound correspondences. **RF.2.3f** Recognize and read grade-appropriate irregularly spelled words. **L.2.2d** Generalize learned spelling patterns when writing words (e.g., cage → badge; boy → boil).

©2018 Benchmark Education Company, LLC

Grade 2 • Unit 3 • Week 3   91

DAY 2

SHARED READING

Texts for Close Reading, p. 28
"Burt the Sea Turtle"

Student Objectives

I will be able to:
- Read an animal fantasy about a sea turtle's habitat.
- Read with appropriate intonation.
- Recognize words I know in different texts.

Additional Materials

Weekly Presentation: Unit 3, Week 3

Shared Reading (10 MIN.) RF.2.3f, RF.2.4a, RF.2.4b, RF.2.4c

Reread for Fluency: Prosody/Intonation

Partner reading. Tell partners to share the rereading of "Burt the Sea Turtle" by alternating paragraphs and then switching roles. Remind them to show meaning and feeling by varying the pitch of their voice and stressing particular words, as if speaking naturally.

Collaborative Conversation: Determine Text Importance

Remind students that yesterday you showed them how you used the Determine Text Importance reading strategy as you read the start of "Burt the Turtle." Tell them that today partners will practice the strategy as they read the rest of the story. Stress how important it is that they determine what text relates directly to key story events as opposed to text that is merely interesting. By doing that, readers can distinguish between what they need to read carefully and what they may pay less attention to. If necessary, guide partners with questions. For example:

- *How do events in this story relate to the unit theme about animals in their habitats?*
- *How does the sea turtle's habitat meet Burt's needs?*
- *What is Burt's experience when he leaves his habitat?*

Transfer Skills to Context: Annotate Key Details

Model underlining key details that help you summarize a story.

Sample modeling (paragraphs 1–2). *I'll ask myself what is most important to understand about the beginning of this story. I'll underline the first sentence because it answers the questions **who** and **where**. In paragraph 2, I'll underline "eighty years later" and "wanted to learn about life outside the ocean" because those details answer the questions **when** and **what**. I can summarize the beginning of the story: "For eighty years, Burt the Sea Turtle has lived in the ocean, but now he wants to learn about life on land."*

Guide students to underline other details that help them summarize the middle and end of the story.

SHARED READING

Transfer Skills to Context: r-Controlled /ûr/ Syllable Patterns

Remind students that the consonant **r** can change the sound of a vowel that comes before it. Point to the name **Burt** in the title, and tell students to listen for **/ûr/** as they say the name. Then ask them to find another word in the title with the same r-controlled sound (**Turtle**). Tell them to look in paragraph 2 for three words with that same vowel sound but different spellings. They should find, say, and spell **later**, **never**, and **learn.**

Transfer Skills to Context: High-Frequency Words
away, learn, learned, found

As you point to each of these previously taught words in paragraphs 2 and 3, tell partners to say the words to each other: **away**, **learn**, **found**, **learned**. Remind students to look for words they know when they read a new text.

Integrated ELD

Light Support
Display and review "Burt the Sea Turtle." Review key vocabulary. Then assist as pairs take turns asking and answering questions about the story. Questions should focus on key word use, descriptive language, and key events.
Pairs take turns reading meaningful chunks, role-playing, and paraphrasing to show comprehension.

Moderate Support
Pairs use the text and picture, and take turns asking and answering questions about key story events. Assist if needed.
Then have students role-play events, while other students try to identify the event using complete sentences.

Substantial Support
Display and review "Burt the Sea Turtle." Review key vocabulary. Students echo-read. Ask questions about key events.
Ask: *What is Burt's habitat?*
Why did Burt want to see a new habitat?
What did Burt decide about his original habitat?

RF.2.3f Recognize and read grade-appropriate irregularly spelled words. **RF.2.4a** Read on-level text with purpose and understanding. **RF.2.4b** Read on-level text orally with accuracy, appropriate rate, and expression on successive readings.
RF.2.4c Use context to confirm or self-correct word recognition and understanding, rereading as necessary.

DAY 2

EXTENDED READ 2 MINI-LESSON

"Lost in the Desert": Recount Story Events, Part 2 (20 MIN.) RL.2.1, RL.2.5, SL.2.2, SL.2.3, SL.2.6

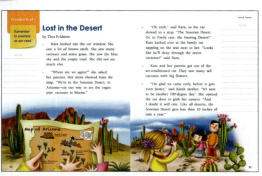

Texts for Close Reading, pp. 30–37
"Lost in the Desert"

Student Objectives

I will be able to:
- Read an animal fantasy.
- Identify and annotate key story events.
- Work cooperatively with a partner to summarize key events.

Additional Materials

Weekly Presentation: Unit 3, Week 3
- Flow Chart

Ways to Scaffold the First Reading

Use your observational assessment to determine the intensity of scaffolding your students need.

IF …	THEN consider …
Students are English learners who may struggle with vocabulary and language demands …	**Read the text TO students.** • Conduct a before-reading picture walk to introduce vocabulary and concepts. • Stop after meaningful chunks to define unfamiliar words and paraphrase difficult sentences.
Students are struggling readers who may decode with little comprehension…	**Read the text WITH students.** • Stop after meaningful chunks to ask *who*, *what*, *when*, *where*, *how* questions. • Work with students to define unfamiliar words and paraphrase key ideas.
Students need some support to read unfamiliar texts with comprehension …	**Have students PARTNER-READ.** *Partners should:* • take turns reading aloud meaningful chunks. • ask each other *who*, *what*, *when*, *where*, *how* questions about the text. • circle unfamiliar words and define them using context clues.

Preview the Text

Remind students that they have already read the first part of "Lost in the Desert." Tell partners to scan the whole text again and discuss what might happen to Fred the cat in Part 2 of the story.

Read to Find Key Details

Have students read paragraphs 11–19 to identify key story events. Have them determine text importance by making notes and drawings in the margin to help them remember what they read. Have them underline key story events.

Give students time to read and annotate. Observe their annotations to assess their ability to recognize key story events.

💬 Collaborative Conversation: Partner

Sample modeling. *When I am discussing a story with another person, I listen to all their ideas and I share my own.*

Display a blank Flow Chart. Ask partners to write the key story event or events in each section noted in the chart. Have them discuss the details they underlined as they decide how to identify each event. Use your observations to determine if students need support in the form of guiding questions.

Paragraphs 11–12	Paragraphs 13–15	Paragraphs 16–17	Paragraphs 18–19
Fred stops chasing the car. He is very thirsty but doesn't see any water. He knows he must find some shade to get out of the hot sun.	Fred is scared when he sees a sidewinder snake. He is hungry. As he rests in the shade, he hopes his family will return.	When he sees a growling bobcat, Fred freezes in terror. At that moment, he hears his family calling him.	Fred runs to the car, where Kara gives him water and food. Fred agrees with her comment that "a house cat doesn't belong in the desert."

Sample Flow Chart

Share

Invite partnerships to share their key story events and their notes and drawings with the class. Ask listeners to decide if the most important events are included and to offer comments in respectful ways. Ask questions to confirm students' comprehension of the story and deepen their understanding.

94 Grade 2 • Unit 3 • Week 3 ©2018 Benchmark Education Company, LLC

EXTENDED READ 2 MINI-LESSON

WEEK 3 • DAY 2

Reinforce or Reaffirm the Strategy

If your students need support to understand the text, refer to "Ways to Scaffold the First Reading." Pose text-dependent questions to guide their thinking. For example:

- *Why can't Fred catch the car?*
- *What happens to Fred when he licks himself? Why?*

Choose one of the following options based on your observations during partner collaboration.

IF …	THEN …
Students need support to identify key story events …	Model to reinforce the strategy. • In paragraph 11, I read interesting information about how desert plants and animals get water. The most important details in paragraph 11 are, "Fred ran after the car, he was thirsty, and he did not see a single drop of water." • In paragraph 12, I read that most desert animals rest underground or in the shade during the day. That fact is interesting, but the most important details are about Fred: "needed to get out of the hot sun, hoping he would find shade." • I can use the important details I found in paragraphs 11 and 12 to summarize key story events: "Fred stops chasing the car. He is very thirsty but doesn't see any water. He knows he must find some shade to get out of the hot sun."
Students identify key story events …	Invite partners or small groups to reflect on their strategy use by discussing the following question: • What are some questions readers can ask to decide on key story events?

✓ Show Your Knowledge

During independent time, display this sentence starter for students to copy and complete: *At the end of "Lost in the Desert," Fred the cat …*

Challenge Activity. Ask students to summarize the entire story in just three or four sentences.

iELD Integrated ELD

Light Support
Have students draw conclusions about what happened to Fred in the story. Provide sentence frames.
Fred was probably _____, because _____.
Fred's family might _____, because _____.

Moderate Support
Review "Lost in the Desert" Part 1. Present Part 2. Choose key vocabulary. Provide visual support and cognates: **stomach/estomago; realized/realizado; calm/calma; terror/terror; rocky/rocoso.**
Students can act out key vocabulary to show comprehension: **thirsty, store, wondered, snakes, hungry, got dark, froze, bobcat, trap, shade, sidewinder, missing, belong, drove off.**
Ask: *Why do desert plants trap rainwater? Did Fred's family know he was missing? In what habitat does Fred belong?*

Substantial Support
Review "Lost in the Desert" Part 1. Present Part 2. Choose key vocabulary. Provide visual support and cognates: **stomach/estomago; realized/realizado; calm/calma; terror/terror; rocky/rocoso.**
Students can act out key vocabulary to show comprehension: **thirsty, store, wondered, snakes, hungry, got dark, froze, bobcat.**
Ask: *What did Fred do when he saw the snake? How did Fred feel when he froze? Was Fred thirsty after Kara gave him water?*

RL.2.1 Ask and answer such questions as who, what, where, when, why, and how to demonstrate understanding of key details in a text. **RL.2.5** Describe the overall structure of a story, including describing how the beginning introduces the story and the ending concludes the action. **SL.2.2** Recount or describe key ideas or details from a text read aloud or information presented orally or through other media. **SL.2.3** Ask and answer questions about what a speaker says in order to clarify comprehension, gather additional information, or deepen understanding of a topic or issue. **SL.2.6** Produce complete sentences when appropriate to task and situation in order to provide requested detail or clarification.

DAY 2

WRITING TO SOURCES

Write an Informative Report: Draft and Develop Your Points and Include a Conclusion (15 MIN.) W.2.2

Student Writing Prompt

In an informative report, describe grasslands and the plants and animals that live in them. Support your ideas with facts and definitions from "Habitats Around the World" and information from "Plant Life of the Australian Savanna."

Student Objectives

I will be able to:
- Use details and definitions to support facts in my body paragraphs.
- Write a strong closing paragraph.

Materials

Weekly Presentation: Unit 3, Week 3
- Informative Text Body Paragraph
- Informative Text Closing Paragraph
- Mentor Informative Report
- Informative Report Anchor Chart
- Informative Report Checklist
- Informative Report Rubric

Engage Thinking

Point to and read aloud the first section of the Informative Report Anchor Chart. Remind students that people read informative reports to learn about a topic. The details and definitions included in the text help readers understand the facts that are presented.

Say: *Today I'm going to show you how I use details and definitions in the body of my informative report.*

Model

Explain that the body paragraphs of an informative report provide facts and details about the topic. Display and read aloud Paragraph A, which does not include details and definitions.

Sample think-aloud. *The writing prompt tells me to include facts and definitions in my report. I did give several facts, but I did not provide many details to support those facts. Also, I notice that I used the word "predators," but did not explain its meaning. A reader might not know what predators are.*

Display and read Paragraph B. Then continue your think-aloud, underlining the places in the text where you made changes or additions.

Sample think-aloud, continued. *I looked back at my notes and saw that I could give more information about where grasslands are and how they look. I added these details. I also included information to help the reader understand why grassland animals run so fast. Finally, I added a sentence that explained the word "predators." The new details and definition in this paragraph make the facts easier to understand.*

Paragraph A
Grasslands share common features. That means the animals that live there are similar. Many of the animals eat the grasses. Few animals have places to hide. So most of them are fast runners. They have to get away from predators.

Paragraph B
Grasslands <u>around the world</u> share common features. That means the animals that live in grasslands are similar <u>from continent to continent</u>. Many of the animals eat the grasses. Few animals have places to hide, <u>since the grasslands are huge and flat</u>. That means most of the animals are fast runners, <u>so they can get away from predators. Predators are the animals that might eat them.</u>

Informative Text Body Paragraph

Tell students that after writing their body paragraphs, they will need to draft a closing for their report.

96 Grade 2 • Unit 3 • Week 3

©2018 Benchmark Education Company, LLC

WRITING TO SOURCES

WEEK 3 • DAY 2

Say: *The final paragraph in an informative report sums up the ideas, but it also keeps readers thinking about the topic. For example, I learned from the media source that certain plants in the Australian savanna have actually adapted to withstand heat and fire. I think I'll end my report with this interesting fact, and then state that grasslands are worth protecting.*

Display and read aloud the closing paragraph.

> Grasslands are found all around the world. They have many unique plants and animals. For instance, the Australian Pandanus palms have adapted to be fire resistant because fires are so common in the grasslands there. Grasslands and the fascinating plants and animals that live in them are certainly worth preserving.

Informative Text Closing Paragraph

Peer Practice

Have partners discuss the closing paragraph, sharing what they think is strong about the conclusion and what they might change to make it more interesting.

Share Your Understanding

Bring students together and have partners share their ideas about the closing paragraph with the class. Then ask students to explain the difference between a body paragraph in an informative report and a closing paragraph.

Independent Writing

During independent time, have students draft the body paragraphs and conclusion for their informative report. Remind them to refer to the tools they have: mentor text, anchor chart, writer's checklist and rubric, notes, outlines, and source materials.

Confer and Monitor

As you monitor students' independent writing, provide feedback, as needed. For example:

Directive Feedback: *Go back to your outline and look at the facts you have listed. These are the main ideas that you might include in your body paragraph. Now think about which details you could use to support those facts and to keep readers interested.*

Self-Monitoring and Reflection: *What are some main facts about grassland animals that you can share? What details about these facts could you include to make your body paragraphs interesting and informative?*

Validating and Confirming: *You included interesting facts about your topic and used details to give more information about the facts.*

---

iELD Integrated ELD

Light Support
Have partners share their drafts, then discuss additional details that could be added to their body paragraphs that would answer a question the reader might have.

Moderate Support
Guide students to come up with questions that the details in their body paragraphs might answer. For example:
What do grassland animals eat? Why are most animals fast runners?

Substantial Support
Help students understand that details can be used to answer what, where, and why questions. Use information from their drafts to formulate questions for students to answer. For example: *Where are grasslands found? Why can't grassland animals hide? What are predators?* Then encourage students to ask a question that they would like to have answered. Help them add the detail that answers their question to their draft.

W.2.2 Write informative/explanatory texts in which they introduce a topic, use facts and definitions to develop points, and provide a concluding statement or section.

Grade 2 • Unit 3 • Week 3

DAY 2
PHONICS & WORD STUDY

r-Controlled Vowels er, ir, ur (15 MIN.) RF.2.3b,
RF.2.3e, RF.2.3f, L.2.2d

r-Controlled *e, i, u* Frieze Card and r-controlled vowel /ur/ Sound-Spelling Card

Student Objectives

I will be able to:
- Blend, build, and spell words with r-controlled **e, i, u**.
- Practice high-frequency words.
- Read r-controlled vowel **ar**.

Additional Materials

- Letter cards: **b, d, e, f, h, i, j, k, n, p, r, r, s, t, t, u**

Weekly Presentation: Unit 3, Week 3
- r-controlled **e, i, u** frieze card
- r-controlled **/ur/** sound-spelling card
- High-frequency word cards: **all, away, better, by, change, done, even, found, learn, only**

For additional word study/decodable practice, see: *Everglades, Visit the Everglades,* and *The Hurt Turtle.*

Review r-Controlled Vowels er, ir, ur

Display the r-controlled **e, i, u** frieze cards. Review the r-controlled vowel sounds spelled **er** as in **her**, **ir** as in **girl**, and **ur** as in **turn**. Point to each spelling sound.

Say: *What are the letters? What sounds do they stand for?*

Blend Words

Model: dirt

Display letter cards for **dirt**. Model blending.

Say: *This is the letter* **d***. It stands for* **/d/***. These are the letters* **ir***. They stand for* **/ûr/***. This is the letter* **t***. It stands for* **/t/***. Listen as I blend these sounds together:* **/dûrt/***, dirt. Say the word with me:* **dirt***.*

Practice: first, third, jerk, fur, purse

Use the same routine to guide student practice.

Build Words

Model: dirt, skirt, shirt, squirt

Display the letter cards for **dirt**. Have a volunteer blend the sounds: **/dûrt/, dirt**.

- Replace the **d** with **sk** and repeat with **skirt**.
- Replace the **k** with **h** and repeat with **shirt**.
- Replace the **h** with **qu** and repeat with **squirt**.

Practice: fit, first, thirst; burn, turn, return

Use the same routine to guide student practice.

Spelling

Closed Sort: bird, hurt, her, nurse, girl, shirt, burn, third, never, winter

Write and display each word on an index card. Ask students to read and spell each word aloud together. Then make a three-column chart. Place a card for **er** on the top of column 1, **ir** on the top of column 2, and **ur** on the top of column 3.

Have students place each card in the correct column. When completed, have students read and spell aloud together the words in each column. Ask students what they notice about the r-controlled vowel spellings (e.g., **er** at the end of a multisyllabic word).

98 Grade 2 • Unit 3 • Week 3   ©2018 Benchmark Education Company, LLC

PHONICS & WORD STUDY

WEEK 3 · DAY 2

High-Frequency Words

Review: *all, away, better, by, change, done, even, found, learn, only*
Display the high-frequency word cards. Have students read and spell each word. Focus on common spelling patterns, such as the **er** in **better**. Point out that when a multisyllabic word has two consonants in the middle, we usually divide the word between the consonants to read it syllable by syllable (**bet-ter**).

Review r-Controlled Vowel ar

Model: barn, barnyard
Write the word **barn** and ask students to identify the vowel sound and spelling. Point out that the vowel spelling **ar** acts as a team and must stay in the same syllable in a longer word.

Write the word **barnyard**. Underline each vowel spelling. Have a volunteer divide the word into syllables. Then have students use the syllables to read the word.

Practice: start, starting, march, marching, star, starlight
Use the same routine to guide student practice.

Integrated ELD

Light Support
Review the spelling words and the Closed Sorting Chart. Emphasize the target sounds, letters, and different spellings. Assign each pair 3–4 spelling words. Pairs write two sentences using as many spelling words as possible in each sentence. Students use gestures or simple drawings about their sentences to show comprehension.

Moderate Support
Present as above.
Pairs write one sentence using at least two spelling words. Students act out the sentence to show comprehension.
Example:
I never saw her wear that shirt in the winter.

Substantial Support
Review the spelling words and the Closed Sorting Chart. Emphasize the target sounds, letters, and different spellings. Assign students to groups, and assign each group 3–4 spelling words. Groups write the words on separate cards and present them.
Model orally presenting the words:
*One of our words is **girl**, g-i-r-l.*
*In the word **girl**, the letters -ir make the /ur/ sound.*
*The third **girl** is wearing a blue shirt.*

RF.2.3b Know spelling-sound correspondences for additional common vowel teams. **RF.2.3e** Identify words with inconsistent but common spelling-sound correspondences. **RF.2.3f** Recognize and read grade-appropriate irregularly spelled words. **L.2.2d** Generalize learned spelling patterns when writing words (e.g., cage → badge; boy → boil).

©2018 Benchmark Education Company, LLC   Grade 2 • Unit 3 • Week 3

DAY 3

SHARED READING

Texts for Close Reading, p. 29
"The Monarchs' Journey"

Student Objectives

I will be able to:
- Read an informational text about monarch butterflies and their habitat.
- Read a text with appropriate intonation.
- Identify words with r-controlled /ûr/ syllable patterns.

Integrated ELD

Light Support
Display "The Monarchs' Journey." Have students use sentence frames while they preview the text:
Since these butterflies ____, I think ____.
____ know ____, because ____.

Moderate Support
Preview "The Monarchs' Journey." Discuss cognates: **explain/explique; exciting/excitacion; mysteries/misterios; scientists/cientificos; miles/millas.**
Choose and present key vocabulary: **monarch butterfly, fly, nature's, bright colors, Mexico, Keep away, warning, take flight, the way, predator, poisonous, each fall.**
Ask questions, such as:
What kind of warning do these butterflies have?
Where do these butterflies fly each fall?

Substantial Support
Preview "The Monarchs' Journey." Discuss cognates: **explain/explique; exciting/excitacion; mysteries/misterios; scientists/cientificos; miles/millas.**
Choose and present key vocabulary: **monarch butterfly, fly, nature's, bright colors, Mexico, Keep away.**
Ask simple questions to check students' understanding, such as:
What do the bright colors of a monarch butterfly mean?
Why do birds keep away from these butterflies?
Where do these butterflies fly?

Shared Reading (10 MIN.) RF.2.4a, RF.2.4b, RF.2.4c

Introduce the Text (iELD)

Display "The Monarchs' Journey" and read aloud the title of this informational text. Ask students to turn to a partner and discuss what the text will be about. As needed, model previewing and inferences.

Sample modeling. *The word **journey** in the title suggests a long trip. The photo shows butterflies gathering on a tree. I think that I will learn about the butterflies called monarchs and the trip they take. If I'm right, ideas related to this will be important text.*

Model Fluent Reading: Prosody/Intonation

First Reading. Read the text aloud fluently with appropriate intonation. Point out that you raised and lowered your pitch and stressed certain words to express the meaning of sentences.

Second Reading. Ask students to read the text aloud with you. Remind them to use their voices to express meaning and to pay attention to end punctuation as they read.

Model Determine Text Importance

Remind students that for the last two days they have been practicing the reading strategy Determine Text Importance on an animal fantasy story. Tell them that today you will work with them on an informational text. Determining important text is different for informational texts. For these, readers must determine the central idea of the text, and then identify only the important ideas that support it. Stress that students should question whether amusing or interesting bits of text truly support the central idea. Model reading paragraph 1.

Sample modeling. *In paragraph 1, the first sentence states an opinion. I think I agree with the opinion, but I don't think it tells much about monarch butterflies themselves, which is the author's topic. But the next two sentences have information about the butterflies that seems very important—monarchs are poisonous to eat, and their pretty colors are a warning to other creatures. I'll underline these sentences and read on.*

Transfer Skills to Context: r-Controlled /ûr/ Syllable Patterns

Point to the word **butterfly** in paragraph 1, and tell students to listen for /ûr/ as they read the word. Explain that the letters **er** spell /ûr/ in **butterfly**. Ask students to identify other words in the text that have the /ûr/ sound. (**predator, bird, colors, northern, journey, nature's, mysteries**)

RF.2.4a Read on-level text with purpose and understanding. **RF.2.4b** Read on-level text orally with accuracy, appropriate rate, and expression on successive readings. **RF.2.4c** Use context to confirm or self-correct word recognition and understanding, rereading as necessary.

Grade 2 • Unit 3 • Week 3 ©2018 Benchmark Education Company, LLC

Build Vocabulary: Distinguish Shades of Meaning Among Related Adjectives (10 MIN.) RL.2.4, L.2.5b

EXTENDED READ 2 MINI-LESSON

WEEK 3 • DAY 3

Texts for Close Reading, pp. 30–37
"Lost in the Desert"

Engage Thinking

Remind students that some words have similar meanings but one meaning may be stronger than another. Ask for students' ideas about the different meanings of the adjectives in the phrases "a **loud** shout" and "an **earsplitting** shout." Use the discussion to point out that when writers choose an adjective to describe something, they think about which word best expresses their idea. Explain that in this mini-lesson, students will think about the adjectives used in "Lost in the Desert."

Model

Read aloud paragraph 6. Model how a word that has a stronger or slightly different meaning can change the meaning of a sentence.

Sample modeling. *The writer says that "At the same time, in the cool car, Fred woke up." The word **freezing** would change the meaning of the sentence. When Fred was cool, he was somewhat cold. But if Fred were described as being **freezing**, he would have been uncomfortably cold. Being cool means almost the same thing, but it does not have as strong a meaning. By using the word **cool**, the writer wants the reader to know that Fred was only slightly uncomfortable.*

Guided Practice

Ask students to read the first sentence of paragraph 12. Ask them to identify the adjective that describes the desert (**quiet**). Guide them to substitute each of these synonyms in the sentence and offer ideas about how the sentence meaning changes: **silent**, **hushed**, and **peaceful**. Students may suggest that a **silent** desert has no sounds at all, a **hushed** desert has low sounds, and a **peaceful** desert is calm and restful.

Continue drawing attention to each of these adjectives in the paragraph noted. Display a synonym, and ask students for ideas about how the meanings of the two adjectives differ.

- (paragraph 14) Then he realized he was **hungry** now too. (**starving**)
- (paragraph 15) . . . was **happy** to see some shade. (**delighted**)
- (paragraph 15) . . . was **afraid** of what he might see. (**terrified**)
- (paragraph 19) "**Silly** Fred," she said. . . (**Goofy**)

✓ Show Your Knowledge

During independent time, ask students to read paragraph 10 and find the adjective that describes the ground (**hot**). Ask them to rewrite the sentence using a synonym for **hot** and have them explain how the sentence meanings differ.

RL.2.4 Describe how words and phrases (e.g., regular beats, alliteration, rhymes, repeated lines) supply rhythm and meaning in a story, poem, or song. **L.2.5b** Distinguish shades of meaning among closely related verbs (e.g., toss, throw, hurl) and closely related adjectives (e.g., thin, slender, skinny, scrawny).

Student Objectives

I will be able to:
- Distinguish shades of meaning among related adjectives.

Additional Materials

Weekly Presentation: Unit 3, Week 3

iELD Integrated ELD

Light Support

Review and discuss "Lost in the Desert." Create a chart and have students echo-read the first adjective. Elicit and record an adjective that has a stronger meaning in column 2. Use visual support, role-playing, or gestures to explain word meanings.

Adjective	Stronger Adjective
hungry	(starving)

Model and practice sentences, such as:
At first _____ thought _____, but after a while, _____ realized _____.
Continue the activity. Use "The Monarchs' Journey."
interesting/amazing.

Moderate Support

Present and create chart as above.

Adjective	Stronger Adjective
good	(wonderful)

Model and Practice:
The water tasted _____, because _____ was so thirsty.
"The Monarchs' Journey": **poisonous/deadly**.
Birds know that monarch butterflies are _____, so they keep away!

Substantial Support

Present and create chart as above.

Adjective	Stronger Adjective
all of	(entire)

Model and practice sentences, such as:
Kara thought Fred was going to sleep through _____ vacation.
Continue the activity. Use "The Monarch's Journey."
fun/exciting.

©2018 Benchmark Education Company, LLC

Grade 2 • Unit 3 • Week 3   101

DAY 3

EXTENDED READ 2 MINI-LESSON

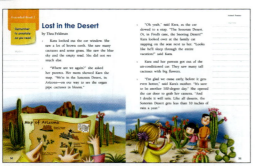

Texts for Close Reading, pp. 30–37
"Lost in the Desert"

Student Objectives

I will be able to:
- Identify a story problem and its solution.
- Work cooperatively in a group to discuss a story.

Additional Materials

Weekly Presentation: Unit 3, Week 3
- Problem/Solution Chart

Observation Checklist for Productive Engagement

Is the Productive Engagement Productive?

As peer groups discuss the structure of the story, look for evidence that they are truly engaged in the task.

Partners are engaged productively if . . .
- ❏ they ask questions and use feedback to address the task.
- ❏ they demonstrate engagement and motivation.
- ❏ they apply strategies with some success.

If the discussion is productive, continue the task. If the discussion is unproductive, end the task and provide support.

Close Reading: Describe the Overall Structure of a Story (15 MIN.) RL.2.1, RL.2.5, RL.2.7, SL.2.1a, SL.2.1b, SL.2.1c, SL.2.2, SL.2.3

Engage Thinking

We just learned about words that have almost the same meaning. Now, we are going to talk about certain terms that belong together.

Say: *Listen as I say some terms that often belong together. Can you think of why they belong together?*

Name these terms: **events**, **characters**, **setting**, **problem**, **solution**. Use students' responses to review that many literary texts share these elements, and that thinking about story elements helps readers understand and remember stories.

Model

Display and read aloud the close reading prompt and annotation instructions. Model how you think about the prompt.

> **Close Reading Prompt:** In paragraph 1, Kara describes the setting of the story by describing what she sees outside. How does the illustration at the bottom of page 30 describe the setting?
> **Annotate!** Underline details and jot down notes in the margin.

Reread paragraph 1 as students follow along.

Sample modeling. *The prompt tells me to think about the setting of this story. The setting is where and when a story takes place. Paragraph 1 describes what Kara sees:* **brown earth, many cactuses, some grass, blue sky,** *and* **empty road**. *The illustration gives me more information about the setting. I can see the green cactuses with their sharp spines. I see one flowering cactus. I see brown hills and sandy soil. A map helps me understand where the story takes place. I'll jot down a note in the margin: "The setting is a desert in Arizona."*

EXTENDED READ 2 MINI-LESSON

WEEK 3 • DAY 3

⚙️ Productive Engagement: Peer Group

Organize students into groups of three or four. Each group should designate specific students to be the group's discussion facilitator, scribe, timekeeper, and encourager. Display and read aloud a second close reading prompt.

> **Close Reading Prompt:** In paragraphs 9 and 10, the narrator explains Fred's problem. What is Fred's problem, and how is it solved?
> **Annotate!** Underline details in the paragraphs, and jot down notes in the margin.

Ask students to respond to the prompt by rereading paragraphs 9 and 10 to identify the problem. They should also look ahead to the paragraphs that describe the solution. Tell them to underline details and write notes in the margin.

Observe students' notes to determine if they need additional modeling or directive feedback. Ask students to fill out a Problem/Solution Chart.

Story Problem (paragraph)	Story Solution (paragraph)
Fred's family leaves him in the hot desert because they think he is still in the car with them. (10)	Fred's family comes back for him, and he runs to safety in their car. (17, 18)

Problem/Solution Chart

Share

Call on students to share their answers to the close reading question. Guide a discussion of why being left in the desert alone is a problem for Fred. Remind students to listen carefully to each speaker and to ask questions if they need further explanation. Provide additional modeling, corrective feedback, or validation based on students' responses.

☑ Show Your Knowledge

During independent time, ask students to reread paragraphs 12 and 15 in order to write a sentence about Fred's problem and its solution.

Challenge Activity. Provide a blank story map for students to fill out showing the elements of setting, characters, problem, events, and solution.

RL.2.1 Ask and answer such questions as who, what, where, when, why, and how to demonstrate understanding of key details in a text. **RL.2.5** Describe the overall structure of a story, including describing how the beginning introduces the story and the ending concludes the action. **RL.2.7** Use information gained from the illustrations and words in a print or digital text to demonstrate understanding of its characters, setting, or plot. **SL.2.1a** Follow agreed-upon rules for discussions (e.g., gaining the floor in respectful ways, listening to others with care, speaking one at a time about the topics and texts under discussion). **SL.2.1b** Build on others' talk in conversations by linking their comments to the remarks of others., **SL.2.1c** Ask for clarification and further explanation as needed about the topics and texts under discussion. **SL.2.2** Recount or describe key ideas or details from a text read aloud or information presented orally or through other media. **SL.2.3** Ask and answer questions about what a speaker says in order to clarify comprehension, gather additional information, or deepen understanding of a topic or issue.

©2018 Benchmark Education Company, LLC

🟠 iELD Integrated ELD

Light Support
Have pairs ask and answer questions about the story using *wh-* question words, such as:
What is/are _____?
Who is/are _____?
When _____?
Where _____?
Students discuss each element in the story.
Record observations for future mini-lessons.

Moderate Support
Groups work cooperatively to create a Story Element Chart for a literary text so they can discuss a text. Provide chart and headings.

Story Element	Definition

Elicit and record story elements and definitions. Students discuss the story elements and the text. Model and practice:
The _____ for "Lost in the Desert" is _____.
Record observations for future mini-lessons.

Substantial Support
Groups work cooperatively to create a Story Element Chart for a literary text so they can discuss a text. Provide elements. Elicit and record definitions. Monitor students as they discuss.

Story Element	Definition
events	what happens in the story
characters	people or animals, who do things in a story
setting	where and when a story happens
problem	something that goes wrong
solution	answer that fixes the problem

Students cooperatively discuss the story elements in "Lost in the Desert."

DAY 3

WRITING TO SOURCES

Student Writing Prompt

In an informative report, describe grasslands and the plants and animals that live in them. Support your ideas with facts and definitions from "Habitats Around the World" and information from "Plant Life of the Australian Savanna."

Student Objectives

I will be able to:
- Revise my writing to include compound sentences.
- Share my ideas in collaborative conversation and in writing.

Materials

Weekly Presentation: Unit 3, Week 3
- Body Paragraph Draft and Revision
- Mentor Informative Report
- Informative Report Anchor Chart
- Informative Report Checklist
- Informative Report Rubric

Write an Informative Report: Revise to Improve Sentence Fluency by Creating Compound Sentences (15 MIN.) L.2.1f

Engage Thinking

Explain to students that a paragraph that includes both simple and compound sentences not only flows better, but is easier to understand. Tell them that today you will model how to revise a paragraph by looking for sentences with related ideas that can be combined to make compound sentences.

Model

Display and read aloud Paragraph A. Point out that the text includes a main idea and supporting details. But, all of the sentences are simple sentences. This makes the writing seem choppy.

Say: *I'm going to look for places to combine simple sentences about related ideas into compound sentences. I see two opportunities.*

Display and read aloud Paragraph B, emphasizing and underlining the conjunctions in the first two sentences.

Paragraph A
The soil is rich in grasslands. Many plants can grow. The most common plants are grasses. Some grasses grow more than a foot tall. There are not as many shrubs or trees. There are wildflowers. You might see sunflowers or asters blooming in warm grasslands.

Paragraph B
The soil is rich in grasslands, **so** many plants can grow. The most common plants are grasses, **and** some grow more than a foot tall. There are not as many shrubs or trees. There are wildflowers. You might see sunflowers or asters blooming in warm grasslands.

Body Paragraph Draft and Revision

Peer Practice

Ask partners to look for another opportunity in Paragraph A to combine two remaining sentences with related ideas into a compound sentence. Have them test several conjunctions in their new sentence to determine which word works best.

104 Grade 2 • Unit 3 • Week 3   ©2018 Benchmark Education Company, LLC

WRITING TO SOURCES

Share Your Understanding

Bring students together and invite the partners to share their compound sentences with the class. Remind students that compound sentences include a comma and a joining conjunction that makes sense when combining two related thoughts.

Independent Writing (iELD)

During independent time, have students look for opportunities to combine simple sentences with related ideas into compound sentences as they revise their body paragraphs. Remind them to refer to the tools they have: mentor text, anchor chart, writer's checklist and rubric, notes, outlines, and source materials.

✓ Confer and Monitor

As you monitor students' independent writing, provide feedback as needed. For example:

Directive Feedback: *Read your text aloud, listening for short sentences that make it sound choppy. Try to find two simple sentences that you can combine into a compound sentence.*

Self-Monitoring and Reflection: *Reread your paragraphs. Are there other simple sentences you could combine? Are there other conjunctions you might use?*

Validating and Confirming: *You included several compound sentences, and they express two connected ideas very well. This makes your text sound natural.*

(iELD) Integrated ELD

Light Support
Lead students to see that when they combine two simple sentences, they can add variety by using **Because** at the beginning of a sentence that shows cause and effect. Encourage students to look for opportunities in their own writing to begin a compound sentence in this way. Or have them write new sentences using this format. For example: *Because the soil is rich in grasslands, many plants can grow there.*

Moderate Support
Review two additional conjunctions that students might use: **since** (instead of **because**), **yet** (instead of **but**). Provide examples of sentence pairs that can be joined with these conjunctions, then help students form compound sentences with them.

Substantial Support
List and say **and, but, or, so**, and **because**, having students mimic your pronunciation of each conjunction. Keep the list on display as students work on their drafts. Encourage them to refer to the list to choose the best conjunction when combining different sentences.

L.2.1f Produce, expand, and rearrange complete simple and compound sentences (e.g., The boy watched the movie; The little boy watched the movie; The action movie was watched by the little boy).

©2018 Benchmark Education Company, LLC   Grade 2 • Unit 3 • Week 3

DAY 3

PHONICS & WORD STUDY

Texts for Close Reading, p. 38
"Kurt's Big Trip"

Student Objectives

I will be able to:
- Blend, read, and spell words with r-controlled **e, i, u.**
- Read word study (decodable) text.
- Practice high-frequency words.

Additional Materials

- Letter cards: **b, d, e, e, h, i, k, n, r, t, u, v, y**
- r-controlled **e, i, u** frieze card
- r-controlled **/ur/** sound-spelling card

Weekly Presentation: Unit 3, Week 3
- High-frequency word cards: **all, away, better, by, change, done, even, found, learn, only**
- Review high-frequency word cards: **move, never, once, round, small, their, too, walk, where, year**

For additional word study/decodable practice, see: *Everglades, Visit the Everglades,* and *The Hurt Turtle*

Monitor Student Reading of Word Study (Decodable) Text

As students read the word study text and answer questions, ask yourself these questions:

Are students able to . . .
- ❏ blend and read r-controlled vowel **er, ir, ur** words in the text?
- ❏ read new high-frequency words with automaticity?
- ❏ demonstrate comprehension of the text by answering text-based questions?

Based on your observations, you may wish to support students' fluency, automaticity, and comprehension with additional decodable reading practice during intervention time.

r-Controlled Vowels er, ir, ur (10 MIN.) RL.2.3, RF.2.3b, RF.2.3c, RF.2.3e, RF.2.3f, L.2.2d

Blend Words

Practice: bird, hurt, third, never, turkey
Display pocket chart letter cards for the word **bird**. Model how to blend the sounds to say the word. Use the same routine with other r-controlled **e, i, u** words.

Read Word Study (Decodable) Text

Introduce the Text
Read the title "Kurt's Big Trip" aloud. Repeat the word **Kurt**. Point out the r-controlled vowel spelling **ur**.

Read the Text
Ask students to read the text. If students need modeling, guide them to blend decodable words and read high-frequency words. You may wish to conduct a second reading, having partners read to each other while you circulate and monitor the reading.

Connect Phonics to Comprehension
Ask some or all of the following questions:

- *Where did Kurt and his dad go on their big trip?*
- *What fish did Kurt find? What did it look like?*
- *What problems has the lionfish caused? Why?*

Spelling

Word Clues
Write the word clues. Have students write the spelling word that goes with each clue.

1. not a boy (**girl**)
2. has wings and can fly (**bird**)
3. a piece of clothing (**shirt**)
4. a season (**winter**)

High-Frequency Words

Practice: *all, away, better, by, change, done, even, found, learn, only*
Draw a ladder with ten rungs. Write a high-frequency word on each rung. Have students take turns climbing the ladder by reading the words.

Review: *move, never, once, round, small, their, too, walk, where, year*

RL.2.3 Describe how characters in a story respond to major events and challenges. **RF.2.3b** Know spelling-sound correspondences for additional common vowel teams. **RF.2.3c** Decode regularly spelled two-syllable words with long vowels. **RF.2.3e** Identify words with inconsistent but common spelling-sound correspondences. **RF.2.3f** Recognize and read grade-appropriate irregularly spelled words. **L.2.2d** Generalize learned spelling patterns when writing words (e.g., cage → badge; boy → boil).

Shared Reading (10 MIN.) RF.2.4a, RF.2.4b, RF.2.4c, L.2.2a

Reread for Fluency: Prosody/Intonation (iELD)

Partner Reading. Assign partners to reread "The Monarchs' Journey," alternating paragraphs and then switching roles. Remind them to listen for natural-sounding changes in intonation as they read.

Collaborative Conversation: Determine Text Importance

Recall for students that yesterday you showed them how you determined text importance reading the first paragraph of "The Monarchs' Journey." Tell them that today they will work together in pairs practicing the reading strategy on the rest of the text. Remind them that in paragraph 1 the important text told about the monarchs being poisonous to predators and that their bright coloring was a warning of that. Guide them as they work on paragraph 2 with leading questions. For example:

- *Where is the monarchs' habitat?*
- *Do they live in a single place? What text explains this information?*
- *What do butterflies have to do to meet their needs?*
- *Is the question the author asks important or just engaging?*

Transfer Skills to Context: Annotate Context Clues

Model identifying and underlining a clue to an unfamiliar term. Emphasize **predator** as you read.

Sample modeling (paragraph 1). *At first, I'm not sure of the meaning of **predator**, but a context clue helps me understand it. The clue is an example, introduced by the words **such as**. I'll underline the clue: **such as a bird**. I know that birds eat butterflies, so a predator must be an animal that eats other animals.*

Guide students to identify and underline the context clue that helps them understand the meaning of **warning**.

Transfer Skills to Context: Capitalize Geographical Names

Point out **North America** in paragraph 2 and ask students to read it aloud. Ask students to explain why these words are capitalized. Ask them to identify other geographical names in the text. (**Canada**, **United States**, **Mexico**)

SHARED READING

Texts for Close Reading, p. 29
"The Monarchs' Journey"

Student Objectives

I will be able to:
- Read an informational text.
- Identify context clues that help me understand word meaning.
- Identify geographical names that should be capitalized.

Additional Materials

Weekly Presentation: Unit 3, Week 3

(iELD) Integrated ELD

Light Support
Have students review with a partner and take turns reading aloud meaningful chunks; use context clues to paraphrase the text.
Monitor their pitch and fluency; adjust their voices to show meaning. Model as needed.

Moderate Support
Read with students. Stop after meaningful chunks; discuss vocabulary and language.
Model reading with correct pitch; emphasize reading with expression to show meaning; model fluency. Have students read aloud together.

Substantial Support
Read with students. Display the text; students tell what they see; review vocabulary and context.
Model reading with correct pitch; adjust your voice to express meaning; model fluency.
Students echo-read.

RF.2.4a Read on-level text with purpose and understanding. **RF.2.4b** Read on-level text orally with accuracy, appropriate rate, and expression on successive readings. **RF.2.4c** Use context to confirm or self-correct word recognition and understanding, rereading as necessary. **L.2.2a** Capitalize holidays, product names, and geographic names.

DAY 4
CROSS-TEXT MINI-LESSON

Texts for Close Reading, pp. 18–25 "Habitats Around the World" and pp. 30–37 "Lost in the Desert"

Student Objectives

I will be able to:
- Compare and contrast habitats in two texts.
- Speak and listen cooperatively in a discussion with my peers.

Additional Materials

Weekly Presentation: Unit 3, Week 3
- Compare-and-Contrast Chart

Close Reading: Compare and Contrast Key Points in Two Texts on the Same Topic (20 MIN.) RI.2.1, RI.2.9, SL.2.1a, SL.2.1b

Engage Thinking

Display "Habitats Around the World" and "Lost in the Desert." Explain that students are going to compare and contrast the texts. Remind them that "Habitats Around the World" is an informational text about four different habitats. "Lost in the Desert" is a literary text, but it includes factual information about a desert habitat. Explain that in this lesson students will think about how these different texts present similar ideas and information.

Model

Display and read aloud the close reading prompt and annotation instructions. Model analyzing the prompt and responding to it.

> **Close Reading Prompt:** The topic of this unit is plant and animal habitats. Compare and contrast the habitats presented in "Habitats Around the World" and "Lost in the Desert."
> **Annotate!** Be sure to mark evidence in both texts that supports your response.

Sample modeling. *The prompt asks me to compare and contrast habitats in two texts. "Habitats Around the World" is an informational text about four different habitats. "Lost in the Desert" is a literary story, but it includes factual information about a desert habitat. I will look for details about the habitats in each text.*

Display a blank Compare-and-Contrast Chart. Read aloud the column heads. Explain that in the far left and right columns you will list the ways that a habitat in each text is different. In the middle column, you will list the ways a habitat in each text is alike. Model how to compare and contrast two habitats from the texts.

Sample modeling. *First, I'll review "Habitats Around the World." Of the four habitats, I'll choose the African savanna to compare with the desert in "Lost in the Desert." In paragraph 5, I learn that the savanna is covered with grasses during the rainy season, and dry and hot the rest of the year.*

Sample modeling. *Now, I'll look for details about plants and the climate of the Sonoran Desert in "Lost in the Desert." In paragraph 2, I learn that cactuses grow here. That is one way the habitats are different. Paragraph 3 has facts about the desert heat and lack of rain—"less than ten inches a year." That is similar to the African savanna. Both climates are dry and have hot temperatures. I'll write these details on the chart.*

Savanna in "Habitats Around the World"	Both Habitats	Sonoran Desert in "Lost in the Desert"
grasses	dry for at least part of the year	cactuses
Climate: dry season and rainy season	hot temperatures	Climate: little rainfall all year

Sample Compare-and-Contrast Chart

WEEK 3 · DAY 4

CROSS-TEXT MINI-LESSON

Guided Practice

Display and read aloud a second reading prompt.

> **Close Reading Prompt:** Choose an animal from "Habitats Around the World."
> Compare and contrast that animal with a Sonoran Desert animal in "Lost in the Desert."
> What traits does each animal have? How do those traits help it survive in its habitat?
> **Annotate!** Jot down notes in the margin and underline details.

Invite students to annotate the text to respond to the prompt. Tell students to choose two animals to compare and contrast. Observe students' annotations to determine if they need additional modeling or directive feedback.

Share

Ask students to share their answers to the close reading prompt. Remind students that attentive listeners think about the ideas they hear and do not interrupt speakers. Use this opportunity to provide additional modeling, corrective feedback, or validation based on students' responses. Students should express their understanding that an animal's body and behavior help it survive in its natural habitat. A polar bear, for example, has fur and blubber to keep it warm in the Arctic tundra, and its coloring helps it hide in the snow as it hunts.

✓ Show Your Knowledge

During independent time, ask students to choose another animal from "Habitats Around the World" and from "Lost in the Desert." Have them write one sentence about how the animals are alike, and one sentence about how they are different.

Challenge Activity. Tell students to imagine that Fred the cat is lost in one of the habitats in "Habitats Around the World" other than the African savanna. Assign partners to write a paragraph from a new story, "Lost in the (Habitat)," to describe what problems Fred encounters.

(iELD) Integrated ELD

Light Support

Students echo-read the Compare-and-Contrast Chart. Use sentence frames that allow students to discuss the similarities and differences presented in the chart, such as:

Both habitats are similar, because _____.

The savanna _____, while the Sonoran Desert _____.

Pairs use the texts to find additional information to add to the chart. Elicit and record responses and then have students echo-read. Students use the sentence frames above to continue comparing and contrasting the habitats and animals:

Savanna	Both Habitats	Sonoran Desert
a lot of grass	not a good habitat for a house cat—too hot and too dry	only a little grass

Moderate Support
Present as above.

Savanna	Both Habitats	Sonoran Desert
animals drink rainwater from the rainy season	both have a dry season	plants store water for the dry season

Ask: *Is the savanna a good habitat for a house cat? Why? Why not?*
Is the Sonoran Desert a good habitat for a house cat? Why? Why not?

Substantial Support
Present as above.

Savanna	Both Habitats	Sonoran Desert
found in Africa	don't have trees	found in the U.S.

Ask: *Did Fred like the Sonoran Desert? Why? Why not?*
Do you think Fred would like the savanna? Why? Why not?

RI.2.1 Ask and answer such questions as who, what, where, when, why, and how to demonstrate understanding of key details in a text. **RI.2.9** Compare and contrast the most important points presented by two texts on the same topic. **SL.2.1a** Follow agreed-upon rules for discussions (e.g., gaining the floor in respectful ways, listening to others with care, speaking one at a time about the topics and texts under discussion). **SL.2.1b** Build on others' talk in conversations by linking their comments to the remarks of others.

©2018 Benchmark Education Company, LLC

Grade 2 • Unit 3 • Week 3   **109**

DAY 4
WRITING TO SOURCES

Write an Informative Report: Check and Correct Capitalization (15 MIN.) L.2.2a

Engage Thinking

Remind students that in this unit they have learned some new capitalization rules. They have learned that the names of holidays, product names, and geographical names must be capitalized. Tell that today you will show them how you edit your writing for the specific purpose of checking that you have capitalized correctly.

Model

Display and read aloud Text A, which contains purposely embedded capitalization errors for you to demonstrate and correct. Use a think-aloud to model how you read and edit. **Say**: *First, I will check to be sure each sentence starts with a capital letter. That looks good. Now I'm going to look for specific words that need to start with capital letters. I remember that geographic names are capitalized, and I have used many of those! The first one is "United States." I see that I capitalized the first word but not the second. I need to fix that. I notice that "prairies" is capitalized. That is a name, but it is not the name of a specific place, so it should not be capitalized.*

Text A
Grasslands in the United states are called Prairies. They are found in many states in the middle of north america. For example, prairies stretch from North Dakota all the way down to texas.

Text B
Grasslands in the United States are called prairies. They are found in many states in the middle of North America. For example, prairies stretch from North Dakota all the way down to Texas.

Capitalization Modeling Text

Peer Practice

Ask partners to identify the geographic names in the remaining two sentences of Text A and write down any words that need to be capitalized.

Share Your Understanding

Bring students together and invite the partners to tell the class which additional geographic names in Text A needed to be capitalized. Then display Text B and reread it with students, pointing out the capital letters in all of the geographic names. Reinforce students' understanding that names of specific places need to be capitalized.

Student Writing Prompt

In an informative report, describe grasslands and the plants and animals that live in them. Support your ideas with facts and definitions from "Habitats Around the World" and information from "Plant Life of the Australian Savanna."

Student Objectives

I will be able to:
- Edit a text for correct capitalization.
- Share my ideas in collaborative conversation and in writing.

Materials

Weekly Presentation: Unit 3, Week 3
- Capitalization Modeling Text
- Mentor Informative Report
- Informative Report Anchor Chart
- Informative Report Checklist
- Informative Report Rubric

WRITING TO SOURCES

WEEK 3 • DAY 4

Independent Writing (iELD)

During independent time, instruct students to pay attention to capitalization as they edit their drafts. Have them refer to the writing checklist and rubric for guidance in the types of words that should be capitalized. Remind them to refer to the tools they have: mentor text, anchor chart, writer's checklist and rubric, notes, outlines, and source materials.

☑ Confer and Monitor

As you monitor students' independent writing, provide feedback as needed. For example:

Directive Feedback: *Look at each of your sentences to be sure you started it with a capital letter.*

Self-Monitoring and Reflection: *Did you remember to check that you used a capital letter for specific geographic names?*

Validating and Confirming: *You corrected some capitalization errors that would have distracted readers.*

(iELD) Integrated ELD

Light Support
Have students edit their own writing for capitalization. Then encourage them to share their work with a partner to discuss the edits and find any additional capitalization errors to correct.

Moderate Support
Encourage students to do one whole editing pass to focus on capitalizing proper nouns correctly. Have the more proficient student point to trouble areas and encourage his or her partner to identify and explain why the word needs to be capitalized.

Substantial Support
Ask students to focus on checking that all of their sentences begin with a capital letter. Have their partner also check and point out any capitalization errors that need to be corrected.

L.2.2a Capitalize holidays, product names, and geographic names.

©2018 Benchmark Education Company, LLC

Grade 2 • Unit 3 • Week 3   **111**

DAY 4

PHONICS & WORD STUDY

Student Objectives

I will be able to:
- Blend multisyllabic words with r-controlled **e**, **i**, **u**.
- Spell words with r-controlled **e**, **i**, **u**.
- Read high-frequency words.

Additional Materials
- r-controlled **e, i, u** frieze card
- r-controlled /ur/ sound-spelling card

Weekly Presentation: Unit 3, Week 3
- High-frequency word cards: **all, away, better, by, change, done, even, found, learn, only**

For additional word study/decodable practice, see: *Everglades*, *Visit the Everglades*, and *The Hurt Turtle*.

r-Controlled Vowels er, ir, ur (20 MIN.) RF.2.3b, RF.2.3c, RF.2.3d, RF.2.3e, RF.2.3f, L.2.2d

Read Multisyllabic Words

Model: disturb
Explain that when an r-controlled vowel spelling such as **er**, **ir**, or **ur** appears in a long word, the spelling acts as a team and must remain in the same syllable. Model using the word **disturb**.

- Write **dis** and point out that it's a closed syllable (short vowel sound).
- Add **turb**. Point out the r-controlled vowel spelling **ur**.
- Circle the vowel spellings **i** and **ur**. Tell students you will divide the word between the two consonants in the middle: **dis/turb**.
- Blend the syllables to read the word. Explain its meaning.

Practice: return, blackbird, twirling, thirsty, burning, sunburn
Use the same routine to guide student practice.

Spelling

Categories
Write the groups of words. Read the words, and ask students to complete each category with a spelling word. Ask students to come up with other category word groups for the spelling words.

1. pants, socks, _____ (**shirt**)
2. first, second, _____ (**third**)
3. woman, lady, _____ (**girl**)
4. doctor, surgeon, _____ (**nurse**)

High-Frequency Words

Review: *all, away, better, by, change, done, even, found, learn, only*
Display the high-frequency word cards. Read each word and have students repeat the word and spell it aloud together. Have students sit in a circle. Pass the cards, one at a time. Each student reads the word and uses it in a sentence before passing the card.

RF.2.3b Know spelling-sound correspondences for additional common vowel teams. **RF.2.3c** Decode regularly spelled two-syllable words with long vowels. **RF.2.3d** Decode words with common prefixes and suffixes. **RF.2.3e** Identify words with inconsistent but common spelling-sound correspondences. **RF.2.3f** Recognize and read grade-appropriate irregularly spelled words. **L.2.2d** Generalize learned spelling patterns when writing words (e.g., cage → badge; boy → boil).

Shared Reading (10 MIN.) RL.2.1, RF.2.4b, SL.2.2, SL.2.3, L.2.4d

Determine Text Importance

Tell students that it is time to review the Determine Text Importance reading strategy. Stress that it is important to identify big ideas, themes, and key details when they read. To do that, readers must distinguish less important text from the more important text. This way they can determine what text they should pay more attention to and what text is just interesting or entertaining. Point out that "Burt the Sea Turtle" and "The Monarchs' Journey" are very different types of writing: one is an informational text and the other is an animal fantasy. Model how to think about the way you used the Determine Text Importance strategy this week.

Sample modeling. *Once we established that "Burt the Sea Turtle" is a literary text, we knew how to go about determining the more important text. We identified the text the author used to tell about the setting, the characters, and the important story events, including the problem Burt encountered. We decided that some of the dialogue in the story was more for entertainment. "The Monarchs' Journey," on the other hand, is an informational text. Therefore we sorted out the important text that tells about animal habitats from the text that was less important. The less important text is included just to engage readers or finish the text in a fun way.*

Transfer Skills to Context: Annotate Inferences

Ask students whether they think that adult sea turtles ever come out of the sea. Ask them to identify the sentence in paragraph 1 that offers a clue; underline the sentence, which tells about female turtles laying eggs in the sand. Then ask whether adult male sea turtles ever leave the sea; prompt students to find text evidence that supports their inference.

Transfer Skills to Context: Review Compound Words

Point to the word **outside** in paragraph 2, and ask students to identify the two smaller words in the compound word. Ask them what "outside the ocean" means. Have them identify another compound word with **side** in paragraph 3 (**sidewalk**) and use both smaller words to define it.

Build and Reflect

During independent time, tell students to think about the Unit 3 selections, and ask them to complete the "Build, Reflect, and Write" activity on page 39 to help them think more about how living things survive in different habitats.

RL.2.1 Ask and answer such questions as who, what, where, when, why, and how to demonstrate understanding of key details in a text. **RF.2.4b** Read on-level text orally with accuracy, appropriate rate, and expression on successive readings. **SL.2.2** Recount or describe key ideas or details from a text read aloud or information presented orally or through other media. **SL.2.3** Ask and answer questions about what a speaker says in order to clarify comprehension, gather additional information, or deepen understanding of a topic or issue. **L.2.4d** Use knowledge of the meaning of individual words to predict the meaning of compound words (e.g., birdhouse, lighthouse, housefly; bookshelf, notebook, bookmark).

©2018 Benchmark Education Company, LLC

SHARED READING

Texts for Close Reading, p. 28–29 "Burt the Sea Turtle" and "The Monarchs' Journey"

Student Objectives

I will be able to:
- Use story details to draw inferences.
- Define a compound word by using both words in it.

Additional Materials

Weekly Presentation: Unit 3, Week 3

iELD Integrated ELD

Light Support
Review drawing inferences. Elicit inferences and story details. Present them in a chart. Have students echo-read the chart, and use sentence frames to discuss the inferences.

I read that _____, so I can infer that _____.

Story Details	Inference
Burt crawled into the sea 80 years ago.	Burt didn't leave home for a long time, 80 years, and wanted an adventure.

Pairs write their inferences and present them to the class.

Moderate Support
Present as above, but write:

Story Details	Inference
Burt said, "I've seen enough."	Burt probably won't visit the city again.

Groups role-play story details and present inferences.

Substantial Support
Present as above, but write:

Story Details	Inference
Burt hurried home.	Burt probably didn't like the city.

Students role-play story details and inferences to show comprehension.

DAY 5

WRITING TO SOURCES

Evaluate and Reflect on Writing

(15 MIN.) W.2.2

Engage Thinking

Tell students that today they will have an opportunity to evaluate their final draft and decide if they are ready to turn it in. Explain that, first, you will model how you use the writing rubric to evaluate an informative text.

Model

Display the Mentor Informative Report from Week 1 and have students take out their copies of the same text. Reread the text aloud.

Display the rubric evaluation form and read the criteria with students. Also review the scoring key. Remind students that the rubric aligns to the anchor chart and checklist they have used throughout the unit. Then use think-alouds to model how you evaluate three of the criterion.

Student Writing Prompt

In an informative report, describe grasslands and the plants and animals that live in them. Support your ideas with facts and definitions from "Habitats Around the World" and information from "Plant Life of the Australian Savanna."

Student Objectives

I will be able to:
- Evaluate my informative report using a rubric.
- Share my ideas in collaborative conversation and in writing.

Materials

Weekly Presentation: Unit 3, Week 3
- Mentor Informative Report
- Informative Report Anchor Chart
- Informative Report Checklist
- Informative Report Rubric

Rubric Criteria	Sample Think-Alouds	Sample Score
Include facts, details, and content words	As I look through the paragraphs, I see that I have stated many facts. They are supported well with details. I have also introduced two content words, "blubber" and "huddle," and given good definitions for readers.	4
Include an introduction, a body, and a conclusion	I do have an introductory paragraph, body paragraphs, and a concluding paragraph. **Introduction:** My opening paragraph gives the background information about Antarctica that readers need. I think I presented that information in an interesting way. **Body paragraphs:** I have already talked about how well-developed my facts and details are throughout the text. **Conclusion:** I like the way I restated how harsh winters are in Antarctica and the fact that emperor penguins and their babies know how to survive it.	4
Uses capitalization correctly	Antarctica is a geographic name, and I did remember to capitalize it every time. I also capitalized Earth and made sure to begin each sentence with a capital letter.	4

114   Grade 2 • Unit 3 • Week 3   ©2018 Benchmark Education Company, LLC

WRITING TO SOURCES

WEEK 3 • DAY 5

Peer Practice

Ask students to independently evaluate and score their writing for one of the criteria on the chart. Have them discuss their evaluation with a partner.

Share Your Understanding

Ask students to complete their evaluation using the rubric and then share their evaluation with a partner. Have them decide if they are prepared to turn in their final draft or if, based on their self-evaluation, they would like to revise or edit their writing further before turning it in.

✔ Quick Write

During independent time, have students respond to the following: *What was the most challenging part of writing your informative report? What did you do to help overcome that challenge?* Use students' writing to evaluate their ability to review and reflect on their own writing.

Note: Each student should save a copy of their informative report to keep in a writing portfolio. They will have a chance to reflect on their writing portfolios at the end of the writing program.

---

iELD Integrated ELD

Light Support
Ask students questions about the topic that you know they can answer by providing more details in their report. Encourage them to take the details from their notetaking forms or outlines and add them to their writing.

Moderate Support
Point out areas in students' reports that could use more details. Work with them to find appropriate details from their notes to add to their report.

Substantial Support
Read aloud each fact and related details in a student's report. Talk about if and how the details support the facts. Determine where more details are needed. Then point out specific details from the student's notes or outline that he or she can use in the report.

W.2.2 Write informative/explanatory texts in which they introduce a topic, use facts and definitions to develop points, and provide a concluding statement or section.

DAY 5

PHONICS & WORD STUDY

Texts for Close Reading, p. 38
"Kurt's Big Trip"

Student Objectives

I will be able to:
- Build words with r-controlled **e**, **i**, **u**.
- Read multisyllabic words with r-controlled **e**, **i**, **u**.
- Reread word study (decodable) text for fluency.
- Spell words with r-controlled **e**, **i**, **u**.
- Read high-frequency words.

Additional Materials

- Letter cards: **b, d, f, h, i, k, r, s, t, t, y**
- r-controlled **e, i, u** frieze card
- r-controlled **/ur/** sound-spelling card

Weekly Presentation: Unit 3, Week 3
- Letter cards for each high-frequency word
- High-frequency word cards: **all, away, better, by, change, done, even, found, learn, only**

For additional word study/decodable practice, see:
Everglades, *Visit the Everglades*, and *The Hurt Turtle*.

Review and Assess r-Controlled Vowels er, ir, ur (15 MIN.) RF.2.3b, RF.2.3c, RF.2.3d, RF.2.3e, RF.2.3f, L.2.2d

Build Words

Model: skit, skirt, shirt
Display the letter cards for **skit**. Blend the sounds: **/skiiit/**, **skit**.

- Add the **r** after **i** and repeat with **skirt**.
- Replace the **k** with **h** and repeat with **shirt**.

Practice: bid, bird, third; fist, first, thirst, thirsty
Use the same routine to guide student practice.

Review Multisyllabic Words

Model: hurt, hurting
Write the word **hurt** and ask students to identify the vowel sound and spelling. Point out the letters **ur** act as a team, which means they must stay in the same syllable.

Write the word **hurting**. Model how to read the longer word. Point out the added syllable (**ing**) is a suffix.

Practice: burn, burning; twirl, twirling; curl, curling; chirp, chirping
Use the same routine to guide student practice.

Reread for Fluency: "Kurt's Big Trip"

Ask students to independently whisper-read "Kurt's Big Trip." Circulate and listen to their readings. Provide corrective feedback. For students having difficulty reading independently, have them read with a more skilled partner.

PHONICS & WORD STUDY

Spelling

Posttest

Use the following procedure to assess students' spelling of this week's words.

- Say each spelling word and use it in the sentence provided.
- Have students write the complete sentence on a piece of paper. Then continue with the next word.
- When students have finished, collect their papers and analyze any misspelled words.

1. The <u>bird</u> has five eggs in its nest.
2. I <u>hurt</u> my leg when I fell.
3. Tell <u>her</u> to come to our house at six.
4. The <u>nurse</u> helped me feel better.
5. Which <u>girl</u> read the most books this week?
6. Do you like my <u>shirt</u>?
7. Did the fire <u>burn</u> all day?
8. Are you in the <u>third</u> grade?
9. A friend will <u>never</u> hurt you.
10. It is cold in the <u>winter</u>.

High-Frequency Words

Review: *all, away, better, by, change, done, even, found, learn, only*

Display the high-frequency word cards. Say each word and have students repeat the word and spell it aloud together.

Place letter cards for one of the words in random order in a pocket chart. Have a volunteer beat the clock to form the word. Allow 15 seconds. Then have the rest of the class check the spelling and give a thumbs up or thumbs down.

Next have students turn to a partner and say a sentence using the word. Call on volunteers to check their sentences.

Integrated ELD

Light Support
Display and review "Kurt's Big Trip." Model reading fluently. Students echo-read, line-by-line, as you read line-by-line.
Students then take a few minutes to find difficult or new vocabulary, such as: **trip, plane, engine, beautiful, sting, rented, took off, spines, aquariums.** Record the words, and have students echo-read.
Students take turns reading paragraphs aloud, focusing on fluency, accuracy, and understanding. They switch paragraphs and repeat. Observe, assess, and assist as needed.

Moderate Support
Present as above, only including some vocabulary, such as: **rented, took off, spines, aquariums.**
Partners identify punctuation and how to read it. Then have partners take turns reading complete paragraphs, focusing on fluency, accuracy, and understanding. Observe, assess, and assist as needed.

Substantial Support
Present as above, only including some vocabulary, such as: **trip, plane, engine, beautiful, sting.** Record the words, and have students echo-read.
With students, discuss meanings using gestures, visual support, and simple phrases. Students role-play meanings to show comprehension.
Explain that when we read aloud, we should make it sound as if we are talking.
Remind students that when we read fluently, we should:
- identify punctuation and pause briefly after a comma; come to a full stop at a period
- use context clues to read new and unfamiliar words

Then have partners take turns reading sentences fluently and accurately.

RF.2.3b Know spelling-sound correspondences for additional common vowel teams. **RF.2.3c** Decode regularly spelled two-syllable words with long vowels. **RF.2.3d** Decode words with common prefixes and suffixes. **RF.2.3e** Identify words with inconsistent but common spelling-sound correspondences. **RF.2.3f** Recognize and read grade-appropriate irregularly spelled words. **L.2.2d** Generalize learned spelling patterns when writing words (e.g., cage → badge; boy → boil).

DAY 5

UNIT REFLECTION

Texts for Close Reading, pp. 2–3
Unit Introduction

Student Objectives

I will be able to:
- Find information from several texts to support my ideas.
- Ask and answer questions about living things and habitats.
- Create an audio recording to present ideas.

Additional Materials

Weekly Presentation: Unit 3, Week 3
- Unit 3 Video
- Essential Question and Answer Chart

Reflect on Unit Concepts (20 MIN.) W.2.6, SL.2.1a, SL.2.1b, SL.2.1c, SL.2.2, SL.2.3, SL.2.5, SL.2.6

Engage Thinking

Say: *The unit we are completing is called "Plants and Animals in Their Habitats." We have read informational and literary texts about habitats around the world. What are some interesting facts and ideas you learned about habitats and living things from different places?*

Display the titles from the unit as you encourage varied responses to the question. Then display the introduction to *Plants and Animals in Their Habitats* and read aloud the Essential Question.

> **How do living things get what they need to survive?**

Say: *By reading about habitats, we can think about how plants and animals are different depending on where they live, and why those differences are important. In this lesson, we will continue to share ideas about our learning.*

View Multimedia

Remind students that they watched a short video at the beginning of the unit before they read any of the selections. Show the video to students again. Prompt students to discuss how the video fits with the unit and the Essential Question. Ask them to share how their second viewing experience was different from the first viewing.

Collaborative Conversation: Peer Group

Assign students to peer groups. Guide the groups as they select a facilitator, a scribe, a timekeeper, and an encourager. Tell them that they will collaborate to develop a group answer to the Essential Question. Present the steps for groups to follow during their conversation.

Say: *We have three directions to follow for our conversation today:*

1. Choose one person to begin the conversation.
2. Raise your hand after a speaker has finished when you want the facilitator to give you a turn to speak.
3. Add to the speaker's ideas. Include details and ideas from the texts you have read to support your ideas.

Make sure that all students understand the directions. Ask a volunteer from each group to restate the directions in his or her own words. Monitor their conversations to ensure that they follow the directions and that all students have a chance to participate.

118 Grade 2 • Unit 3 • Week 3 ©2018 Benchmark Education Company, LLC

Share

Give students about five minutes to share their ideas and develop their answer. Then bring the class together. Call on the scribe from each group to share the group's answer to the Essential Question.

Review directions for participation as the groups share their ideas:

- The scribe tells the group's answer to the Essential Question.
- Classmates listen attentively.
- Anyone with a follow-up question or comment raises a hand.

Capture each group's ideas in a chart. At the end of the unit, post the chart in your classroom.

How do living things get what they need to survive?
1. Plants use rainwater to grow.
2. Grazing animals travel to find grasses and other plants.
3. Some animals eat seeds and nuts made by plants.
4. Animals hunt other animals in their habitat.
5. Predators have traits that help them catch their food.
6. Animals' bodies are made to keep them warm in cold habitats.
7. Animals find shade or stay underground in hot habitats.
8. Some animals stay safe by hiding in burrows.
9. Some animals stay safe by warning away predators.

Sample Essential Question and Answer Chart

Use Digital Media

Ask each group to choose one animal or plant from a selection they have read and develop a short script about how it gets what it needs to survive. Then they can assign roles and use the script to make an audio recording.

Observe and Assess

As students reflect on unit concepts and present ideas, use the following questions to informally assess their understanding:

- Do students understand what a habitat is?
- Do students understand that a living thing's physical traits and behaviors help it survive?
- Are students able to explain and support their ideas?

W.2.6 With guidance and support from adults, use a variety of digital tools to produce and publish writing, including in collaboration with peers. **SL.2.1a** Follow agreed-upon rules for discussions (e.g., gaining the floor in respectful ways, listening to others with care, speaking one at a time about the topics and texts under discussion). **SL.2.1b** Build on others' talk in conversations by linking their comments to the remarks of others. **SL.2.1c** Ask for clarification and further explanation as needed about the topics and texts under discussion. **SL.2.2** Recount or describe key ideas or details from a text read aloud or information presented orally or through other media. **SL.2.3** Ask and answer questions about what a speaker says in order to clarify comprehension, gather additional information, or deepen understanding of a topic or issue. **SL.2.5** Create audio recordings of stories or poems; add drawings or other visual displays to stories or recounts of experiences when appropriate to clarify ideas, thoughts, and feelings. **SL.2.6** Produce complete sentences when appropriate to task and situation in order to provide requested detail or clarification.

©2018 Benchmark Education Company, LLC

iELD Integrated ELD

Light Support
Write, present, and have students echo-read and explain key words, such as: **habitat, grasslands, tundra, savanna, rain forest, mountains, city, desert, arctic, the poles, the sea, dry, hot, freezing, warm, cold, winter, summer, ocean, plants,** and other words students suggest.

Pairs use the key words to discuss, write, and draw about how living things survive in their habitats by getting what they need.

Moderate Support
Ask and model:
Ask: *Can all animals survive in the same habitats? Why? Why not?*
Let's give an example:
Fred's habitat was a house. Fred got his food and water from his family. When Fred got lost in the desert, he was finding it hard to survive, because it was too hot and dry for him, and he couldn't find food.
Help students organize their thoughts and remember text evidence by prompting with more questions.

Substantial Support
Provide support before students engage in answering the Essential Question. Display the texts from this unit for students to use as a reference. Help them organize their thoughts and remember text evidence by prompting them with questions, such as:
Ask: *What habitats did we read about?*
We read about _____.
Ask: *What do animals and plants have in their habitats that help them survive? What do plants and animals do so that they can survive in their habitats?*
Habitats have _____, which help(s) the animals and plants survive.
Animals _____ so they can survive.
Plants _____ so they can survive.
Say: *Let's put it all together.*
There are many habitats in the world. We read about a lot of them. Animals and plants that live in a habitat can usually find _____ so they can survive. Animals and plants also _____ so they can survive.

Grade 2 • Unit 3 • Week 3   119

UNIT 4

Many Characters, Many Points of View

Essential Question

How can a story change depending on who tells it?

Enduring Understanding:

Different characters in a story have different points of view about story events.

In this unit, students read and compare selections with varying points of view and analyze how point of view affects the reader's understanding of a story.

Unit Strategies and Skills

Unit 4

	WEEK 1	WEEK 2	WEEK 3	
Metacognitive	Make Inferences/Predictions →	Make Inferences/Predictions →	Make Inferences/Predictions	
Reading	Recount Story Events →	Recount Story Events →	Recount Story Events	☑
	Describe the Overall Structure of a Story →	Describe the Overall Structure of a Story		☑
	Acknowledge Differences in the Points of View of Characters →		Acknowledge Differences in the Points of View of Characters	☑
	Describe How Characters Respond to Major Events and Challenges →	Describe How Characters Respond to Major Events and Challenges		☑
	Compare and Contrast Two Folktales			
		Compare and Contrast the Central Message in Two Stories		
			Compare and Contrast Two Versions of the Same Story	☑
Vocabulary	Describe How Words and Phrases Supply Rhythm and Meaning in a Story →		Describe How Words and Phrases Supply Rhythm and Meaning in a Story	☑
		Identify Real-Life Connections Between Words and Their Uses		☑

	WEEK 1	WEEK 2	WEEK 3	
Writing	Writing to Sources: Opinion Essay	Writing to Sources: Opinion Essay	Writing to Sources: Opinion Essay	☑
Conventions of English	Use Adjectives Correctly	Form and Use Contractions	Descriptive Words Correct Use of Contractions	☑
Phonics/Word Study	**r**-Controlled Vowel **or, oar, ore**	**r**-Controlled Vowels **ear, eer, ere**	**r**-Controlled Vowels **air, are, ear, ere**	☑
Fluency	Read on-level text with purpose and understanding.	Read on-level text with purpose and understanding.	Inflection and Intonation: Pitch* Expression: Dramatic Expression*	
Speaking and Listening	Participate in Collaborative Conversations Recount or Describe Key Details Ask and Answer Questions to Gather Information or to Clarify			

☑ = Strategies and skills are assessed on the Unit Assessment. Skills with no check mark are *not* assessed in this unit.

* See Reader's Theater Teacher's Handbook

UNIT 4 Differentiated Instruction Planner Meeting t

Small-Group Reading Instruction Options:

☐ Unit-Specific Leveled Texts for Differentiated Instruction

Group students by instructional level to support their reading development.
Use the lesson-specific Teacher's Guide and Text Evidence Question Card for each title.

| 310L H/14 | 370L H/13 | 500L I/16 | 530L J/18 | 380L J/18 | 540L L/24 | 440L N |

☐ Close Reading of Complex Text

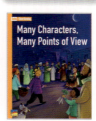

Reread complex texts in the unit's *Texts for Close Reading*. Use the text-evidence questions aligned to DOK levels provided online.

☐ Reader's Theater

Group students heterogeneously for multi-leveled reader's theater experiences that build fluency and comprehension. Use the 5-day lesson plans provided, pages 44–55.

☐ Literature Circles

Select trade books for groups based on their interests and reading abilities. See the Unit 4 Recommended Trade Books on page AR83.

☐ Reading Strategy Instruction

Group students for additional modeling and guided practice with specific strategies from the unit. See Small-Group Texts for Reteaching Strategies and Skills on pages AR18–AR25.

☐ English Language Development

Preview or review the unit selections with amplified visual support, and build English language skills based on the readings.

☐ Intervention

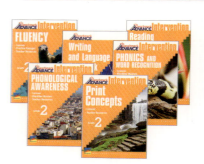

Select appropriate intervention lessons based on data from your weekly, unit, and interim assessments as well as informal assessments.

Many Characters, Many Points of View

Essential Question
How can a story change depending on who tells it?

K 2 | WEEK 3

- The Basket Weaver, Part 2
- Good Sports

Part 1

Shared Read 3:
"A Good Switch!," p. 16
Fable, 420L

Shared Read 4:
"Ira and Jeb," p. 17
Fable, 680L

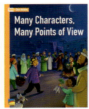

Shared Read 5:
"Why Owls Are Wise," p. 28
Pouquoi Tale, 710L

Shared Read 6:
"Wind and Sun," p. 29
Fable, 550L

Extended Read 1:
"Stone Soup," pp. 18–25
Folktale, 440L

Extended Read 2:
"The Stone Garden," pp. 30–37
Fractured Folktale, 520L

 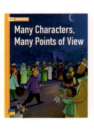 

- G/11–12
- H/13–14
- I/15–16
- J/18
- K/20

- F/9–10
- G/11–12
- H/13–14
- I/15–16
- J/18
- K/20
- L/24
- M/28

Reader's Theater
Teacher's Handbook

and Text Evidence
for each title

: Opinion Essay

Develop Your Reasons
ils to Support Your Opinion
Your Opinion Essay
riting
tractions

Writing to Sources: Opinion Essay
- Draft an Effective Opening for Your Essay
- Draft Body Paragraphs That Support Your Opinion
- Revise to Include More Descriptive Words
- Edit to Correct Use of Contractions
- Review and Reflect

dy Read:
se and Country Mouse," p. 26
L

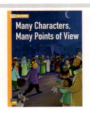 

Word Study Read:
"Goldilocks and the Three Bears," p. 38
Fairy Tale, 540L

onal practice, see:
Cat," "King Grisly Beard, "Here or There?"

For additional practice, see:
"Two Boys, One Day" "Manners in Tales,"
"Tell the Tale"

Quick Checks
Monitor students' progress using focused informal assessments.

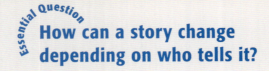

Digital Learning Portal
Interactive Resources & Instruction for the Entire Program

E-Planner
Plan & Manage Student Groups

Video
Multimedia to Reinforce Unit Topic

Weekly Presentations
Collected Resources for Whole-Group Instruction

E-Books
Whole-Group and Small-Group Texts

Home to School
Take-Home Letter and Activities

Online Assessments
Test-Taking Environment for Students
Reporting Platform for Teachers

Components at a Glance

			WEEK 1	WEEK 2
Interactive Read-Aloud	10 MINUTES PER LESSON		**Metacognitive Strategy:** Make Inferences/Predictions Conduct an interactive read-aloud at any point in your literacy block. Over the course of the unit, you may choose a recommended trade book or from these selections provided in the Read-Aloud Handbook:	• Dog Talk • Dad's Big News • The Basket Weaver,
Shared Reading	10 MINUTES PER LESSON		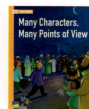  **Shared Read 1:** "The Boy Who Cried Wolf," p. 4 Fable, 440L **Shared Read 2:** "Ferdinand Frog and the Flea," p. 5 End-Rhyme Poem, NP	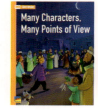 
Reading Mini-Lessons	10 MINUTES PER LESSON		 **Short Read 1:** "The Blind Men and the Elephant," pp. 6–9 Folktale, 660L **Short Read 2:** "How the Beetle Got Its Gorgeous Coat," pp. 10–13 Pourquoi Tale, 580L	 
Small-Group Reading	15–20 MINUTES PER GROUP		 310L H/14 370L H/13 500L I/16 530L J/18 380L J/18 540L L/24 440L N	 Teacher's Guid Question Card
Writing and Language Mini-Lessons	10 MINUTES PER LESSON		 **Writing to Sources: Opinion Essay** • Read a Mentor Opinion Essay • Analyze an Author's Reasons • Note Supporting Facts and Details • Analyze the Author's Concluding Statement **Conventions of Language** • Use Adjectives Correctly	 **Writing to Source** • Plan the Writing • Reread the Text to • Use Facts and Det • Plan and Organize **Conventions of W** • Form and Use Co
Phonics/Word Study Mini-Lessons	15–20 MINUTES PER LESSON		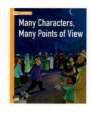 **Word Study Read:** "How Deer Got Its Horns," p. 14 Pourquoi Tale, 570L **For additional practice, see:** "'Why' Stories," "Pecos Bill's Tornado," "That's How I Saw It!"	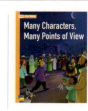 **Word Str** "City Mou Fable, 34 **For addi** "Fox and
Assessment			 **Week 1**, p. 95 **Week 2**, p. 101 **Unit 4**, p. 117	 **Informal Assessments** Conduct and document meaningful, ongoing observations using informal assessments.	 **Foundational Skills Screeners** Assess students' proficien in Print Concepts, Phonological Awareness, Phonics, and Fluency.

the Needs of All Learners

Independent and Collaborative Activity Options:

Read Independently

Make a range of informational and literary texts available for students to self-select based on their interests including:
- previously read leveled texts and e-books.
- books and magazines related to Many Characters, Many Points of View.
- trade fiction and nonfiction titles.

Confer with individuals or groups to support their reading development.

Read Collaboratively

Engage students in one or more of the following fluency-building activities, including:
- partner reading of previously read leveled texts.
- partner or trio listening and reading along to an e-book.
- small-group rehearsal of Unit 4 Reader's Theater scripts.

Write Independently

Have students complete the Independent Writing tasks specified at the end of each day's writing mini-lesson. Look for the ✓

Conduct Research

Assign groups of students one of the unit-related Connect Across Disciplines Inquiry Projects to complete during the three-week unit (see pages AR4–AR5).
- Create a Family History Map
- Create a Then-and-Now Collage
- Keep an Ice Cube Cool (Challenge Project)

Apply Understanding

Assign an informal assessment activity to help you evaluate students' mastery of targeted strategies and skills. Look for the ✓

Answer Questions Using Text Evidence

Assign questions from the Text Evidence Question Card to individuals or partners based on the leveled texts they have read.

Skill Practice

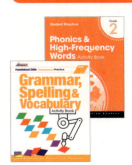

Assign pages from the Grammar, Spelling, and Vocabulary Activity Book.

Assign pages from the Phonics and High-Frequency Words Activity Book.

Build, Reflect, Write

At the end of each week, ask students to reflect on their understanding of the weekly selections and their ideas related to the unit Essential Question by completing the "Build Knowledge" and "Reflect" sections of the Build, Reflect, Write page.

Unit 4 Writing & Vocabulary

Writing to Sources: Opinion Text

In Week 1, teachers guide students through an analysis of a Mentor Opinion Text and how to apply that analysis to their writing. In Week 2, teachers guide students through the prewriting steps in the writing process: brainstorm, evaluate ideas, and plan. In Week 3, teachers guide students to draft, revise, and edit their opinion text.

Week	Focus	Daily Writing Mini-Lesson	Page
1	Analyze the Text Type	Read a Mentor Opinion Text	130
		Analyze an Author's Reasons	138
		Note Supporting Facts and Details	146
		Analyze the Author's Concluding Statement	154
		Conventions of Language: Use Adjectives Correctly	160
2	Organize Ideas	Plan the Writing	170
		Reread the Text to Develop Your Reasons	178
		Use Facts and Details to Support Your Opinion	186
		Plan and Organize Your Opinion Essay	192
		Conventions of Writing: Form and Use Contractions	198
3	Draft, Revise, and Edit	Draft an Effective Opening for Your Essay	208
		Draft Body Paragraphs That Support Your Opinion	216
		Revise to Include More Descriptive Words	224
		Edit to Correct Use of Contractions	230
		Review and Reflect	234

Vocabulary Instruction

Build students' vocabulary related to the unit topic using explicit vocabulary mini-lessons and vocabulary routines.

Week	Lesson Type	Vocabulary Words from *Texts for Close Reading*	Instruction
1	Build Vocabulary	**"Ferdinand Frog and the Flea":** happily (p. 5) **"How the Beetle Got Its Gorgeous Coat":** happily (p. 10), suddenly (p. 10), quickly (p. 11), probably (p. 11)	**Day 4:** Describe How Words and Phrases Supply Rhythm and Meaning in a Story, p. 150
	Phonics & Word Study	fork, born, more, store, oars, roar, horn, before, sports, wore	**Days 1–5:** r-Controlled Vowel **or, oar, ore**, pp. 132–133, 140–141, 148, 156, 162–163 *Word Study vocabulary words are also the week's spelling words.*
	Making Meaning with Words	**"How the Beetle Got Its Gorgeous Coat":** admire (p. 10), boasted (p. 11), unique (p. 12)	Use the routine on pp. AR13–AR14 to introduce these words. Have students complete the "Making Meaning with Words" glossary on the inside back cover of the *Texts for Close Reading*.
2	Build Vocabulary	**"How the Beetle Got Its Gorgeous Coat":** whispered (p. 13) **"Stone Soup":** share (pp. 18, 19, 21, 25), smell (p. 23), dropped (pp. 20, 22), whispered (p. 20), rubbed (p. 20), tasty (pp. 21, 23), delicious (p. 24), begged (p. 25) **Related Words:** stir, mix, swirl, sniff, breathe in, taste, sample, sip, beg	**Day 3:** Identify Real-Life Connections Between Words and Their Uses, p. 183
	Phonics & Word Study	year, deer, near, clear, here, cheer, fear, ears, hear, steer	**Days 1–5:** r-Controlled Vowels **ear, eer, ere**, pp. 172–173, 180–181, 188, 194, 200–201 *Word Study vocabulary words are also the week's spelling words.*
	Making Meaning with Words	**"Stone Soup":** feast (p. 22), spare (p. 24), begged (p. 25)	Use the routine on pp. AR13–AR14 to introduce these words. Have students complete the "Making Meaning with Words" glossary on the inside back cover of the *Texts for Close Reading*.
3	Build Vocabulary	**"The Blind Men and the Elephant":** side (p. 8) **"The Stone Garden":** side (p. 30), lot (pp. 30, 31), rose (p. 31), plus (p. 34), sign (pp. 32, 35, 37), direction (p. 35), deal (p. 34)	**Day 3:** Describe How Words and Phrases Supply Rhythm and Meaning in a Story, p. 221
	Phonics & Word Study	where, hair, pear, care, share, stairs, square, bear, wear, chair	**Days 1–5:** r-Controlled Vowels **air, are, ear, ere**, pp. 210–211, 218–219, 226, 232, 236–237 *Word Study vocabulary words are also the week's spelling words.*
	Making Meaning with Words	**"The Stone Garden":** encouragement (p. 35), insulted, (p. 32), rubble (p. 32), tidy (p. 30)	Use the routine on pp. AR13–AR14 to introduce these words. Have students complete the "Making Meaning with Words" glossary on the inside back cover of the *Texts for Close Reading*.

©2018 Benchmark Education Company, LLC

Week 1 Mini-Lessons at a Glance

	Day 1	Day 2
Reading Mini-Lessons	Introduce Unit 4: Many Characters, Many Points of View (10 Min.), p. 124 RL.2.1, SL.2.1a, SL.2.1b, SL.2.2, SL.2.3, L.2.4 Shared Reading (10 Min.), p. 126 RF.2.4a, RF.2.4b, RF.2.4c "The Blind Men and the Elephant": Recount Story Events (15 Min.), p. 128 RL.2.1, RL.2.5, SL.2.2, SL.2.3	Shared Reading (10 Min.), p. 134 RF.2.3f, RF.2.4a, RF.2.4b, RF.2.4c Describe the Overall Structure of a Story (10 Min.), p. 135 RL.2.5, SL.2.1a, SL.2.1b, SL.2.1c, SL.2.2 Acknowledge Differences in the Points of View of Characters (15 Min.), p. 136 RL.2.6, SL.2.1a, SL.2.1b, SL.2.1c, SL.2.2
Writing and Language Mini-Lessons	Write an Opinion Essay: Read a Mentor Opinion Essay (15 Min.), p. 130 W.2.5	Write an Opinion Essay: Analyze an Author's Reasons (15 Min.), p. 138 W.2.5
Phonics/Word Study Mini-Lessons	r-Controlled Vowels or, oar, ore (15 Min.), p. 132 RF.2.3b, RF.2.3e, RF.2.3f, L.2.2d • High-Frequency Words: *long, now, our, some, them, through, upon, was, when, work* • Weekly Spelling Words: *fork, born, more, store, oars, roar, horn, before, sports, wore*	r-Controlled Vowel or, oar, ore (15 Min.), p. 140 RF.2.3b, RF.2.3c, RF.2.3e, RF.2.3f, L.2.2d • High-Frequency Words: *long, now, our, some, them, through, upon, was, when, work*

Short Read 1: "The Blind Men and the Elephant"

Folktale

Quantitative	Lexile® 660L

Qualitative Analysis of Text Complexity

Purpose and Levels of Meaning ②
• This tale has a simple purpose: to explain that people experience things differently, but it requires interpretation.

Structure ①
• Narrative structure is sequential and straightforward.

Language Conventionality and Clarity ②
• Sentences are almost all simple, but there is a culturally specific term that is important to understanding: rajah's palace.

Knowledge Demands ②
• For full comprehension, readers will benefit from familiarity with similar tales.

Total QM: 7
Moderate Complexity*

*The texts in *Benchmark Advance* are qualitatively evaluated based on their grade-level placement in the program. Reader maturity and age appropriateness are key considerations in the subjective use of the rubrics.

Day 3	Day 4	Day 5
Shared Reading (10 Min.), p. 142 RF.2.3b, RF.2.4a, RF.2.4b, RF.2.4c	Shared Reading (10 Min.), p. 149 RL.2.4, RF.2.4a, RF.2.4b, RF.2.4c, L.2.1e	Shared Reading (10 Min.), p. 157 RL.2.1, RF.2.4b, SL.2.2, SL.2.3
"How the Beetle Got Its Gorgeous Coat": Recount Story Events (15 Min.), p. 144 RL.2.1, RL.2.5, SL.2.2, SL.2.3	Build Vocabulary: Describe How Words and Phrases Supply Rhythm and Meaning in a Story (10 Min.), p. 150 RL.2.4 Describe How Characters Respond to Major Events and Challenges (15 Min.) p. 152 RL.2.3, SL.2.1a, SL.2.1b, SL.2.1c, SL.2.2	Compare and Contrast Two Folktales (20 Min.), p. 158 RL.2.1, RL.2.2, RL.2.3, RL.2.5, RL.2.9, SL.2.2, SL.2.3
Write an Opinion Essay: Note Supporting Facts and Details (15 Min.), p. 146 W.2.7, W.2.8	Write an Opinion Essay: Analyze the Author's Concluding Statement (15 Min.), p. 154 W.2.5	Conventions of Language: Use Adjectives Correctly (15 Min.), p. 160 L.2.1e, L.2.6
r-Controlled Vowel or, oar, ore (15 Min.), p. 148 RF.2.3b, RF.2.3c, RF.2.3e, RF.2.3f, L.2.2d • High-Frequency Words: *long, now, our, some, them, through, upon, was, when, work*	r-Controlled Vowel or, oar, ore (20 Min.), p. 156 RF.2.3b, RF.2.3c, RF.2.3d, RF.2.3e, RF.2.3f, L.2.2 • High-Frequency Words: *long, now, our, some, them, through, upon, was, when, work*	Review and Assess r-Controlled Vowel or, oar, ore (15 Min.), p. 162 RF.2.3b, RF.2.3c, RF.2.3d, RF.2.3e, RF.2.3f, L.2.2d • High-Frequency Words: *long, now, our, some, them, through, upon, was, when, work*

Short Read 2: "How the Beetle Got Its Gorgeous Coat"

Pourquoi Tale

Quantitative	Lexile® 580L
Qualitative Analysis of Text Complexity	

Purpose and Levels of Meaning ❷
• This animal myth expresses two levels of meaning: explicitly how the beetle got its coat, implicitly that humility has its rewards.

Structure ❸
• This pourquoi tale has anthropomorphic characters and is told in a straightforward way.
• Readers must pay close attention to interpret an implicit theme.

Language Conventionality and Clarity ❷
• Language is entirely common usage, with some rich description; sentences are for the most part simple.

Knowledge Demands ❷
• Prior knowledge of animal origin stories will help readers grasp the basic concept here.

Total QM: 9
Moderate Complexity*

DAY 1

UNIT INTRODUCTION

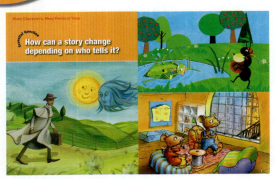

Texts for Close Reading, pp. 2–3
Unit Introduction

Student Objectives

I will be able to:
- Share what I know about the Essential Question.
- Ask and answer questions about classmates' ideas.
- Follow our rules for discussion.

Additional Materials

Weekly Presentation: Unit 4, Week 1
- Unit 4 Video
- Guiding Questions/Initial Ideas Chart

✓ Observation Checklist for Collaborative Conversation

As peer groups discuss the Essential Question, use the questions below to evaluate how effectively students communicate with each other. Based on your answers, you may wish to plan future core lessons to support the collaborative conversation process.

Do peer groups . . .
- ❏ stay on topic throughout the discussion?
- ❏ listen respectfully?
- ❏ build on the comments of others appropriately?
- ❏ pose or respond to questions to clarify information?
- ❏ support their partners to participate?

Introduce Unit 4: Many Characters, Many Points of View (10 MIN.) RL.2.1, SL.2.1a, SL.2.1b, SL.2.2, SL.2.3, L.2.4

Pose Essential Question

Ask students to access the introduction of *Many Characters, Many Points of View* in their texts or on their devices. Explain that as students read *Many Characters, Many Points of View*, they will find ideas that help to answer the question under the title. Invite a volunteer to read aloud the Essential Question:

> **How can a story change depending on who tells it?**

Explain to students that over the next three weeks, they will read literary texts that show how different characters have different points of view.

▶ View Multimedia and Build Vocabulary

Display or have students access the Unit 4 Video on their devices. Pause the video periodically to allow students to sketch ideas or jot questions that the images suggest to them.

Ask students what they especially noticed about the images in the video. Add new ideas to your class list. Write the domain-specific vocabulary words **character**, **narrator**, and **point of view** on the board. Replay the video and ask students to use audio and video clues to determine the meaning of these words.

💬 Collaborative Conversation: Peer Group

Sample modeling. *When I serve as scribe for a group conversation, I take careful notes, and I write as neatly as I can.*

To guide their thinking as they begin Unit 4, ask peer groups to generate questions about characters in the same story who may have different points of view. Explain that they should try to ask questions that can be answered in more than one way. You may wish to have each group designate a discussion facilitator, scribe, timekeeper, and encourager. Ask them to start thinking about possible answers and to jot down some initial ideas.

Share Your Understanding

Call on the scribe from each peer group to share a guiding question their group generated. Call on the discussion facilitator to share the group's initial responses to the question. Capture the questions and ideas on a class Guiding Questions/Initial Ideas Chart like the one shown. Invite members of other groups to add their own ideas based on questions they hear. As needed, provide modeling to review or reinforce classroom rules for discussion. For example:

Say: Your group's question really gets me thinking! I'll try to remember some stories with characters who disagree about something.

I see that everyone waited for [Name] to finish speaking before raising hands. That showed that everyone was listening attentively to [Name's] ideas.

Use the brief conversation to help you benchmark students' knowledge around the unit topic and to build their interest.

Light Support
Explain and discuss key vocabulary and concepts, such as **point of view, different ideas, think differently, different lessons**.

As students participate in the discussion and answer questions about the Essential Question, observe, monitor, assess, and evaluate.

Use the information to plan lessons that support conversation skills.

Do students . . .
- show understanding of the question and how to answer it?
- support peers, even if they have a different opinion?
- choose appropriate information to share?

Moderate Support
Do students . . .
- build appropriately on the comments of others?
- ask appropriate questions using language and vocabulary related to the topic?
- respond to questions appropriately?

Substantial Support
Do students . . .
- stay on topic?
- use background knowledge?
- use vocabulary and language they know?
- listen and wait respectfully?

Guiding Questions	Initial Ideas
Why do some story characters disagree with each other?	They have different ideas about how to do something. They don't want to share something. They think they are stronger or better than each other.
How do characters show their different points of view?	They argue. One character might trick another or teach a lesson. They describe the same thing differently.
Which characters from the same story show different points of view?	the tortoise and the hare Troll and Great Billy Goat Gruff the wolf and the three little pigs

Sample Guiding Questions/Initial Ideas Chart

RL.2.1 Ask and answer such questions as who, what, where, when, why, and how to demonstrate understanding of key details in a text. **SL.2.1a** Follow agreed-upon rules for discussions (e.g., gaining the floor in respectful ways, listening to others with care, speaking one at a time about the topics and texts under discussion). **SL.2.1b** Build on others' talk in conversations by linking their comments to the remarks of others. **SL.2.2** Recount or describe key ideas or details from a text read aloud or information presented orally or through other media. **SL.2.3** Ask and answer questions about what a speaker says in order to clarify comprehension, gather additional information, or deepen understanding of a topic or issue. **L.2.4** Determine or clarify the meaning of unknown and multiple-meaning words and phrases based on grade 2 reading and content, choosing flexibly from an array of strategies.

©2018 Benchmark Education Company, LLC

DAY 1

SHARED READING

Texts for Close Reading, p. 4
"The Boy Who Cried Wolf"

Student Objectives

I will be able to:
- Read a fable to find key events.
- Read aloud at the best rate to show meaning.
- Read words with /ûr/.

Additional Materials

Weekly Presentation: Unit 4, Week 1

Shared Reading (10 MIN.) RF.2.4a, RF.2.4b, RF.2.4c

Introduce the Text

Display "The Boy Who Cried Wolf." Read aloud the title of the fable as you point under the words. Invite students to turn to a partner to make inferences about what the story will be about.

Model Make Inferences and Predictions

Explain to students that readers make inferences when they use clues and information in a text to figure something out that the author isn't directly telling them. Readers also make predictions about what a story will be about, or what will happen before and during their reading. Readers make inferences before, during, and after they read. Readers make inferences by: using story clues to figure out what is happening or why it is happening; using clues about characters (their actions, words, thoughts) to figure out what they are like and what they might do next; and using clues to figure out the book's themes, or "big ideas." Model inferencing by looking closely at the illustration and reading the title of the selection.

Sample modeling. The title tells me that the story will be about a boy who cried wolf. I'm not sure what it means to "cry wolf," but the illustrations show the boy, a sheep, and a wolf. I know that wolves eat sheep. I can infer that the story is about a boy who cries out about the wolf coming to eat the sheep.

Model Fluent Reading: Rate/Pacing

Echo-Reading. Read aloud the text fluently at an appropriate rate. Explain that the best rate for reading aloud is neither too fast nor too slow, but just right for showing meaning. Choose a sentence to read aloud word by word, and then fluently. Ask students why the fluent reading was better. Then invite students to read the story aloud together with you. Remind them to think about the best rate to show meaning.

SHARED READING

WEEK 1 • DAY 1

Transfer Skills to Context: Annotate Story Structure

Remind students that many stories begin with a main character who has a problem. Readers want to find out what the character does to try to solve the problem. Model underlining details about the character and his problem.

Sample modeling (paragraph 1). *I ask myself, "Who is the main character?" I'll underline* **boy**. *Then I ask myself, "What is the main character's problem?" I'll underline* **bored** *and wanted some excitement.*

Ask students to identify details about what the main character does to solve his problem and what happens as a result.

Transfer Skills to Context: r-Controlled /ûr/ Syllable Patterns

Remind students that the consonant **r** can change the sound of a vowel that comes before it. Point to the words **villagers** and **shepherd** in paragraph 2, and tell students to listen for /ûr/ as they say each word. Ask them to name the letters that spell /ûr/ in both words. Then tell them to look in paragraph 4 to find and say a word with a different spelling for /ûr/ (**third**).

iELD Integrated ELD

Light Support
Display "The Boy Who Cried Wolf." Conduct a pre-reading picture walk. Discuss story events. Choose and preview key vocabulary, such as **job, watch, sheep, villagers, lied, help**.

Ask: *Why did the shepherd want some excitement? What happened when the boy tricked the villagers the first time? The last time?*
What appeared and began to stalk the sheep on the third day? What happened?

Moderate Support
Display "The Boy Who Cried Wolf." Conduct a pre-reading picture walk. Discuss story events. Choose and preview key vocabulary, such as **grazed, bored, arrived, no one, shepherd**.

Ask: *What did the shepherd do as the sheep grazed? What happened when no one arrived?*

Substantial Support
Display "The Boy Who Cried Wolf." Conduct a pre-reading picture walk. Discuss story events. Choose and preview key vocabulary, such as **job, watch, sheep, villagers, lied, help**.
Students act out terms to show comprehension.
Ask simple questions to check for understanding.

Ask: *What was the boy's job?*
What did the villagers do when the boy lied?
When didn't the villagers help the boy?

RF.2.4a Read on-level text with purpose and understanding. **RF.2.4b** Read on-level text orally with accuracy, appropriate rate, and expression on successive readings., **RF.2.4c** Use context to confirm or self-correct word recognition and understanding, rereading as necessary.

©2018 Benchmark Education Company, LLC

DAY 1

SHORT READ 1 MINI-LESSON

Texts for Close Reading, pp. 6–9
"The Blind Men and the Elephant"

Student Objectives

I will be able to:
- Read a folktale to identify and annotate key events.
- Participate in a class discussion by listening and speaking.

Additional Materials

Weekly Presentation: Unit 4, Week 1
- Story Events Chart

Ways to Scaffold the First Reading

Use your observational assessment to determine the intensity of scaffolding your students need.

IF...	THEN consider...
Students are English learners who may struggle with vocabulary and language demands...	**Read the Text TO students.** • Conduct a before-reading picture walk to introduce vocabulary and concepts. • Stop after meaningful chunks to define unfamiliar words and paraphrase difficult sentences.
Students are struggling readers who may decode with little comprehension...	**Read the Text WITH students.** • Stop after meaningful chunks to ask **who, what, when, where, how** questions. • Work with students to define unfamiliar words and paraphrase key ideas.
Students need some support to read unfamiliar texts with comprehension...	**Have students PARTNER-READ.** *Partners should:* • take turns reading aloud meaningful chunks. • ask each other **who, what, when, where, how** questions about the text. • circle unfamiliar words and define them using context clues.

"The Blind Men and the Elephant": Recount Story Events (15 MIN.) RL.2.1, RL.2.5, SL.2.2, SL.2.3

Preview the Text

Display and ask students to open to "The Blind Men and the Elephant." Tell students that this folktale is based on an ancient story from India. Remind students that before they read, they should preview the story and make inferences about what might happen in it. Ask students to preview the story and then tell a partner one inference they have made. Ask a few students to share their inferences with the class.

Sample modeling. As I read the title and look at the illustrations, I know that there are five men and an elephant, and after thinking about the title, I am going to make the inference that those men are blind, and that the elephant will have an important role in the folktale.

Model

Ask students to follow along as you read paragraphs 1–3 to identify key story events. Underline key details and events as you read.

Say: *Whenever we think about what happens first, next, and last in a story, we are thinking about the key events. We can use the details in a story to summarize the key events in sequence.*

Sample modeling (paragraphs 1–2). As the story begins, I learn when and where it takes place, so I'll underline those details. I also learn who the main characters are, so I'll underline **five blind men***. I learn that the men are curious about elephants. I'll keep reading to see what happens first.*

Sample modeling (paragraph 3). In paragraph 3, I learn what happens. They go to the rajah's palace, where the wise ruler encourages them to examine the elephant. I'll underline **took the five men to the rajah's palace** *and* **encouraged the men to examine the elephant.** *I can use what I've underlined to summarize the first key event: In India long ago, five blind men want to learn what an elephant is like. The rajah encourages the men to examine his elephant.*

---

128 Grade 2 • Unit 4 • Week 1   ©2018 Benchmark Education Company, LLC

SHORT READ 1 MINI-LESSON

WEEK 1 · DAY 1

Guided Practice

Ask students to read paragraphs 4–9 with a partner to identify key story events. Ask them to underline key story events as they read.

Give students time to read and annotate. Observe their annotations to assess their ability to identify the key story events. Pose text-dependent questions to guide their learning. For example:

- *According to the text, why do the villagers take the men to the rajah's palace?*
- *Why do the men touch the elephant? Use evidence from the text to support your reasoning.*
- *According to the text, what does the first blind man touch?*
- *What does the first blind man think about the elephant? How do you know?*
- *What happens next? Use evidence from the text to support your answer.*
- *What do the blind men do after they all touch the elephant? Find it in the text.*

Collaborate with students to summarize the key story events.

Beginning	Middle	End
In India long ago, five blind men want to learn what an elephant is like. The rajah encourages the men to examine his elephant.	• The first man touches the trunk and says the elephant is like a snake. • The second man touches the side and says the elephant is like a wall. • The third man feels the tusk and says the elephant is like a spear. • The fourth man feels the ear and says the elephant is like a fan. • The fifth man feels the tail and says the elephant is like a rope.	The men argue about who is right until the rajah explains that they must put their knowledge together.

Story Events Chart

Show Your Knowledge

During independent time, ask students to write a summary of the story. Remind them to include the key events. Use their work to evaluate their strategy development and to help you make instructional decisions.

---

iELD Integrated ELD

Light Support
Conduct a pre-reading picture walk for "The Blind Men and the Elephant." Discuss the story. Choose and preview key vocabulary, such as **wise ruler, encouraged, was kept, proclaimed, announced, exclaimed, explained**.
Students complete sentence frames to draw conclusions about the men's experiences.
Each man proclaimed something different, because ____.
The rajah was a wise ruler, because ____.

Moderate Support
Conduct a pre-reading picture walk for "The Blind Men and the Elephant." Discuss the story. Choose and preview key vocabulary, such as **since birth, side, hard wall, sharp as a spear, together**.
Ask: What information do the men need to put together?

Substantial Support
Conduct a pre-reading picture walk for "The Blind Men and the Elephant." Discuss the story. Choose and preview key vocabulary, such as **blind, parts, rely, examine, trunk, tusk, rope**.
Provide cognates, such as **gigantic/gigantesco; elephant/elefante; curious/curioso; senses/sentidos; interrupted/interrumpido; especially/especialmente**.
Ask simple questions.
Ask: *What happened when the men examined the elephant?*

RL.2.1 Ask and answer such questions as who, what, where, when, why, and how to demonstrate understanding of key details in a text. **RL.2.5** Describe the overall structure of a story, including describing how the beginning introduces the story and the ending concludes the action. **SL.2.2** Recount or describe key ideas or details from a text read aloud or information presented orally or through other media. **SL.2.3** Ask and answer questions about what a speaker says in order to clarify comprehension, gather additional information, or deepen understanding of a topic or issue.

DAY 1

WRITING TO SOURCES

Mentor Writing Prompt

Is "The Blind Men and the Elephant" a story you would recommend to your friends? Why or why not? State your opinion in an essay. Supply reasons, based on details from the story, to support your opinion.

Student Objectives

I will be able to:
- Read and analyze a writing prompt.
- Read and analyze an opinion essay.
- Share my ideas in collaborative conversation and in writing.

Materials

Weekly Presentation: Unit 4, Week 1
- Mentor Writing Prompt
- Mentor Opinion Essay
- Opinion Essay Anchor Chart

Opinion Essay Anchor Chart

To write an informative report, writers…
State their opinion
- Clearly state their opinion in the first paragraph.
- Use a first-person point of view with pronouns such as I and my.
- Give reasons for their opinion.
- Include a conclusion.

Write an Opinion Essay: Read a Mentor Opinion Essay (15 MIN.) W.2.5

Engage Thinking

Tell students that in this unit, they will be writing an opinion essay. Explain that in opinion essays, writers express what they think or believe about a subject and give reasons for their opinion. A writer's opinion is neither right nor wrong, but it could affect the way a reader thinks about the subject.

Read and Analyze the Prompt

Display and/or distribute the writing prompt, then read it aloud. Use a think-aloud to analyze the prompt.

Sample think-aloud. *This prompt asks me to give my opinion. First, I need to think about the story and decide if I would recommend it to my friends. Then I need to state my opinion and give reasons for it, using details from the story. Since my essay will be about what I think, I'll use words such as **I** and **my** in my writing.*

Read the Mentor Text

Display and/or distribute the Mentor Opinion Essay, explaining that this was written in response to the prompt. Ask students to listen and follow along as you read it aloud.

Are you looking for a good story to read? If so, I recommend "The Blind Men and the Elephant." I tell my friends to read this story because it makes you think about things in a different way. It also teaches about putting thoughts together to understand the big idea.

The story takes place in India. I think people should learn about other places, like India, and the people that live there. Another reason I recommend the story is that the main characters don't have the sense of sight. Reading the story helps you imagine what it would be like to be blind. It's good for us to think about how others live.

Because the men in the story couldn't see, they didn't know what an elephant looked like. One day, people brought the men to a real elephant. Each man touched a different part of the animal. For example, one man touched only the elephant's long trunk. He said, "The elephant is like a large snake!" Another man touched the elephant's tail. He said, "The elephant is like a rope!" We know that an elephant doesn't look like a snake or a rope. That's because we can see the whole animal. I think it's interesting to read what each blind man thought about the elephant by touching just one part of the animal.

Read "The Blind Men and the Elephant." It's a good story to read because it helps you think about things from a different point of view. I believe it also has an important moral, which is that you should put together as much information as you can before reaching a conclusion.

Mentor Opinion Essay

---

130 Grade 2 • Unit 4 • Week 1

©2018 Benchmark Education Company, LLC

WRITING TO SOURCES

WEEK 1 · DAY 1

Analyze the Mentor Text

Explain that the mentor text includes the following features of an opinion essay: clearly states an opinion using a first-person point of view, gives reasons for that opinion, and includes a conclusion. Create an anchor chart (like the sample provided) listing these features. Then reread the first paragraph and highlight the second sentence.

Say: *This sentence states my opinion. Notice that I use the word **I** because the opinion reflects what I think or feel.*

Share Your Understanding

Bring students together and invite partners to share their dialogues with the class. Discuss how the differing opinions might affect a listener's view.

During independent time, have students answer the following question: *What are the features of an opinion essay?* Use students' writing to evaluate their understanding of the genre.

---

iELD Integrated ELD

Light Support
Write a list of words and phrases that students can use to elaborate on their opinions, such as **because**, **for example**, and **first**. Demonstrate the use of one of these words: *I think the movie was exciting **because** it kept me wondering what would happen next.* Have students form sentences using words and phrases from the list to state their opinion.

Moderate Support
Remind students that an opinion is not right or wrong, and that it is okay to have a different opinion from someone else. Provide expanded sentence frames to help students give their opinion respectfully. For example:
I agree with you about ____, but I think ____.

Substantial Support
As partners engage in the role-play, provide sentence frames to help them state their opinion about the story. For example:
I liked/didn't like ____.

W.2.5 With guidance and support from adults and peers, focus on a topic and strengthen writing as needed by revising and editing.

DAY 1

PHONICS & WORD STUDY

r-Controlled Vowels or, oar, ore (15 MIN.)

RF.2.3b, RF.2.3e, RF.2.3f, L.2.2d

r-Controlled *o* Frieze Card and Sound-Spelling card ôr

Student Objectives

I will be able to:
- Identify words with r-controlled **o**.
- Blend and spell words with r-controlled **o**.
- Read high-frequency words.

Additional Materials

- Letter cards: **h, o, p, r, s, t**

Weekly Presentation: Unit 4, Week 1
- r-controlled **o** frieze card
- Sound-spelling card **ôr**
- High-frequency word cards: **long, now, our, some, them, through, upon, was, when, work**
- Review high-frequency word cards: **all, away, better, by, change, done, even, found, learn, only**

For additional word study/decodable practice, see: *"Why" Stories, Pecos Bill's Tornado,* and *That's How I Saw It!*

Spelling-Sound Correspondences

Introduce: r-Controlled Vowels or, oar, ore

Display the r-controlled o frieze card.

Say: *These sounds are /ôr/. The /ôr/ sounds are spelled many ways: **or, oar, ore.***

Model: or, oar, ore

Point to each spelling on the card and provide a sample word: **or** as in **corn**, **oar** as in **roar**, **ore** as in **more**. Write each sample word and underline the r-controlled **o** spelling.

Say: *Look at the first word I wrote: **c-o-r-n**. I see the r-controlled **o** spelling **or**. Listen and watch as I sound out the word: /kôrn/, **corn**.*

Run your hand under the word as you sound it out.

Practice: corn, roar, more

Repeat the r-controlled o words one at a time. Ask students to write each word and underline the r-controlled **o** spellings.

Blend Words

Model: r-Controlled Vowel or, oar, ore

Display the letter cards for **pot**. Model how to blend the sounds together as you run your hand under each letter.

Say: *This is the letter **p**. It stands for /p/. This is the letter **o**. It stands for /o/. Listen as I blend these sounds together: /pooo/. **This is the letter t**. It stands for /t/. Now listen as I blend all three sounds together: /pooot/, **pot**. Say the word with me: **pot**.*

Model adding an **r** after the **o** to make the word **port**.

Say: *I can add an **r** after the **o** to make the r-controlled vowel spelling **or**. The **or** spelling stands for the /ôr/ sounds. Listen as I blend the new word: /pôrt/. Say the word with me: **port**.*

Continue modeling the words **shot, short**.

Practice: born, horse, porch, store, wore, oar

Write each word. Have students blend the sounds aloud together. Provide corrective

132 Grade 2 • Unit 4 • Week 1   ©2018 Benchmark Education Company, LLC

PHONICS & WORD STUDY

WEEK 1 • DAY 1

feedback, as needed.

Spelling

Pretest

Say each spelling word. Read the sentence and say the word again. After the pretest, write each word as you say the letter names. Have students check their work.

fork	You can use a **fork**, knife, and spoon to eat.
born	In what month were you **born**?
more	Do you want **more** juice to drink?
store	We went to the **store** to buy groceries.
oars	Dan lost one of the boat's **oars** in the river.
roar	The lion's **roar** scared away the rabbit.
horn	He made a loud noise when he blew his **horn**.
before	You need to study **before** the big spelling test.
sports	Olivia and Sarah like to play **sports**.
wore	She **wore** a long white dress at her wedding.

High-Frequency Words (iELD)

Introduce: *long, now, our, some, them, through, upon, was, when, work*

Use the following routine: Write simple sentences using each high-frequency word. Underline the word and discuss important features about it. Say the word and have students repeat. Then spell the word with students as you point to each letter. Finally have students write the word as they spell it aloud.

Practice

Display the high-frequency word cards. Have students work with a partner to write sentences using the words. Then have volunteers read a sentence and identify the high-frequency word.

Review: *all, away, better, by, change, done, even, found, learn, only*

Review last week's words using the high-frequency word cards. Mix and display one word card at a time as students read each word aloud together.

(iELD) Integrated ELD

Light Support

Display a word bank with the high-frequency words.

| long | our | them | upon | when |
| now | some | through | was | work |

Pairs alternate dictating the high-frequency words to each other, and self-check their work using the word bank. Pairs write sentences using high-frequency words.
***When was** our **work** supposed to be ready?*

Moderate Support

Read aloud the word bank below. Have students repeat after you.

| long | our | them | upon | when |
| now | some | through | was | work |

Pairs alternate dictating the high-frequency words, and self-check their work using the word bank. Model using the high-frequency words in sentences and then have pairs compose original sentences using the words.
***When** we looked **through** the books, I found **some**_ that I wanted to read.*

Substantial Support

Students echo-read the word bank below with the high-frequency words.

| long | our | them | upon | when |
| now | some | through | was | work |

Write the words on cards. Hold up a card. Have students read aloud together. Volunteers point to the word in the word bank and read it aloud.

Show each card. Students repeat, spell, and write the words with you.

Model using the words in sentences. Include the high-frequency word **when** in each sentence.

*I will help **them work** on their research papers **when** our teacher takes us to the library.*

RF.2.3b Know spelling-sound correspondences for additional common vowel teams. **RF.2.3e** Identify words with inconsistent but common spelling-sound correspondences. **RF.2.3f** Recognize and read grade-appropriate irregularly spelled words. **L.2.2d** Generalize learned spelling patterns when writing words (e.g., cage → badge; boy → boil).

©2018 Benchmark Education Company, LLC

Grade 2 • Unit 4 • Week 1   **133**

DAY 2
SHARED READING

Texts for Close Reading, p. 4
"The Boy Who Cried Wolf"

Student Objectives

I will be able to:
- Read a fable about characters with different points of view.
- Read and identify words with r-controlled /ôr/ syllable patterns.

Additional Materials

Weekly Presentation: Unit 4, Week 1

iELD Integrated ELD

Light Support
Assist as pairs take turns asking and answering questions. Questions should focus on key words, descriptive language, and key story events.
Pairs take turns reading meaningful chunks of the text, role-playing, and paraphrasing to show comprehension.

Moderate Support
Review the text using the illustrations.
Ask: *What did the shepherd do first? Next? Last? How do you think the villagers/shepherd felt about lying?*
Pairs take turns asking and answering the questions about the illustrations. Help students record their answers using simple phrases or drawings.

Substantial Support
Review the text. Use the illustrations. Students echo-read the text. List key words and phrases:
whose, no one came, too many times.
Help students role-play and use simple phrases to discuss meanings.
Ask: *What did the shepherd do first? Next? Last? How do you think the villagers/shepherd felt about lying?*

Shared Reading (10 MIN.) RF.2.3f, RF.2.4a, RF.2.4b, RF.2.4c

Reread for Fluency: Rate/Pacing

Partner Reading. Assign partners to read aloud "The Boy Who Cried Wolf" to each other. Each may read a paragraph and then switch roles. Remind them to read at the best rate of speed to show meaning.

Collaborative Conversation: Make Inferences and Predictions

Remind students that yesterday you demonstrated making inferences before reading—while you were previewing the story. Share that the reading strategy of making inferences is important for all literary and informational texts, but can be especially helpful when reading fables, which are often used to teach a larger lesson. Model making inferences as you read the text.

Sample modeling. *In paragraph 1, I read that the shepherd boy was bored by his job, and wanted some excitement. In paragraph 2, I see that he lies in order to create some excitement, but when the villagers come to his aid, they found out that he has lied and is not in trouble. Yesterday, I wasn't sure what "to cry wolf" meant exactly. While I am reading, I can infer that "to cry wolf" means to pretend to be in trouble. I can also predict that the villagers may not trust him in the future if he keeps "crying wolf."*

Invite students to use sentence frames to help them make inferences.

- *While reading, I can make an inference about _____.*
- *The words _____ help me infer that _____.*

Transfer Skills to Context: Annotate Key Events

Remind students that many stories have a beginning, middle, and end. Readers can use details to summarize the key events in a story. Model how to identify and underline details in a story.

Sample modeling (paragraph 2). *In paragraph 2, the first sentence tells me an important detail: "One day he cried, "Wolf! A wolf is eating the sheep!" I'll underline* **One day** *and continue reading to summarize the first key event. I learn that the villagers run to help the shepherd but discover that he lied to them. That's the first key event and I will write it in the annotation column.*

Ask students to identify and underline details in paragraphs 3 and 4 that help them summarize more key events in the fable.

RF.2.3f Recognize and read grade-appropriate irregularly spelled words. **RF.2.4a** Read on-level text with purpose and understanding. **RF.2.4b** Read on-level text orally with accuracy, appropriate rate, and expression on successive readings. **RF.2.4c** Use context to confirm or self-correct word recognition and understanding, rereading as necessary.

Describe the Overall Structure of a Story (10 MIN.) RL.2.5, SL.2.1a, SL.2.1b, SL.2.1c, SL.2.2

SHORT READ 1 MINI LESSON

WEEK 1 • DAY 2

Engage Thinking

We just reread "The Boy Who Cried Wolf." Now we will reread "The Blind Men and the Elephant" to complete a story map. Display "The Blind Men and the Elephant" along with the Story Map chart.

Model

Sample modeling. *As I start reading the story, I look for where and when it takes place. The first sentence names the setting: a village in India long ago. The first sentence also tells me that the characters are five blind men. In paragraph 3, I learn about another character, the rajah. Characters and setting are often introduced in the beginning of a story.*

Sample modeling. In many stories, the problem is a goal—something that the characters want to achieve. In paragraph 2, I learn that the blind men want to know what an elephant is like. The problem in a story is often stated at or near the beginning. The key events in the middle of the story tell me what the men do to learn about an elephant. In paragraph 9, the rajah solves the problem. The solution comes at the end of a story.

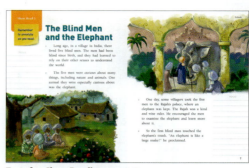

Texts for Close Reading, pp. 6–9
"The Blind Men and the Elephant"

Student Objectives

I will be able to:
- Identify the elements in a story.
- Explain a story problem and solution.

Additional Materials

Weekly Presentation: Unit 4, Week 1
- Story Map

Guided Practice (iELD)

Display a Story Map and work with students to identify story elements.

Story Title: "The Blind Men and the Elephant"	
Setting (Where and When): in a village in India long ago	**Characters (Who):** five blind men, the Rajah
Problem: The blind men want to learn what an elephant is like.	
Key Events: 1. The rajah invites the men to examine his elephant. 2. Each man touches one part of the elephant and says that is what the whole animal is like. 3. The men argue about who is right.	
How the Problem Is Solved: The rajah explains that everyone must combine their ideas to get the whole picture of an elephant.	

Sample Story Map

Reflect on the Strategy

Ask students to turn to a partner and answer this question: *When readers come to the part of the story where they learn what the problem is, what do they want to find out?*

 Show Your Knowledge

During independent time, ask students to think about the story problem and solution. Have them write two or more sentences to identify the problem the characters want to solve, and how they solve it.

RL.2.5 Describe the overall structure of a story, including describing how the beginning introduces the story and the ending concludes the action. **SL.2.1a** Follow agreed-upon rules for discussions (e.g., gaining the floor in respectful ways, listening to others with care, speaking one at a time about the topics and texts under discussion). **SL.2.1b** Build on others' talk in conversations by linking their comments to the remarks of others. **SL.2.1c** Ask for clarification and further explanation as needed about the topics and texts under discussion. **SL.2.2** Recount or describe key ideas or details from a text read aloud or information presented orally or through other media.

iELD Integrated ELD

Light Support
Pairs ask and answer **wh-** questions about the text and story elements. Assist as needed.
What is/are _____.
Who is/are _____?
When _____?
Where _____?

Moderate Support
Elicit and record story elements and definitions. Students use the illustrations and role-playing to discuss the story elements and the text.
The _____ for this story is/are _____.

Substantial Support

Story Element	Definition
setting	
characters	
problem	
solution	

Display the chart and write simple definitions for each story element on sentence strips. Students echo-read the chart and the sentence strips. Help students place each sentence strip on the chart next to the correct story element.

©2018 Benchmark Education Company, LLC

Grade 2 • Unit 4 • Week 1

DAY 2

SHORT READ 1 MINI-LESSON

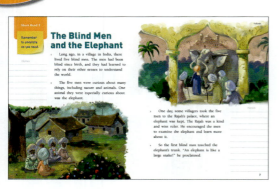

Texts for Close Reading, pp. 6–9
"The Blind Men and the Elephant"

Student Objectives

I will be able to:
- Look for text evidence that shows a character's point of view.
- Read aloud to express characters' points of view.
- Share my ideas respectfully with a group.

Additional Materials

Weekly Presentation: Unit 4, Week 1
- Point of View Chart

Acknowledge Differences in the Points of View of Characters (15 MIN.) RL.2.6, SL.2.1a, SL.2.1b, SL.2.1c, SL.2.2

Engage Thinking

We will continue reading and working with "The Blind Men and the Elephant." Remind students that a character's exact words are set between quotation marks. Ask for ideas about what readers look for to help them imagine how a character sounds while speaking. Use the brief discussion to review the concept of point of view.

Say: *A character has a point of view—a way of looking at things. A character's words and the way they are spoken show what the character believes and feels.*

Model

Give an expressive rereading of paragraphs 4 and 5 of "The Blind Men and the Elephant" as students follow along. Think aloud about how the voices of the first and second men reflect their point of view.

*Sample modeling (paragraphs 4 and 5). In paragraph 4, I learn what the first blind man thinks as he touches the elephant's trunk. The word **proclaimed** shows that he is sure that the elephant is like a large snake. In paragraph 5, I learn that the second blind man touches the elephant's side and thinks that the elephant is like a hard wall. The word **announced** shows that he, too, speaks with confidence. I'll reread to make the characters sound firm and sure as they speak.*

Guided Practice

Guide students to explore the points of view of the other characters in the story. Encourage students to reread each character's words as he might say them. Ask them to point out words that show how the characters sound. Complete the class Point of View Chart. Pose text-dependent questions to guide their learning:

- *How is the point of view of all five men the same? How are the points of view of all five men different? Use evidence from the text to support your answer.*
- *According to the text, why do the five men argue?*
- *How is the Rajah's point of view different from those of the men? Find the place in the text where this information appears.*

Character	Point of View	Text Evidence (paragraph)
Man 1	is sure that an elephant is like a snake	"proclaimed" (4)
Man 2	is sure that it's like a wall	"announced" (5)
Man 3	is sure that it's like a spear	"exclaimed" (6)
Man 4	is sure that it's like a gigantic fan	"announced" (7)
Man 5	is sure that it's like a rope	"declared" (8)
Rajah	believes that everyone must put ideas together	"a kind and wise ruler" (3) "explained" (9)

Sample Point of View Chart

SHORT READ 1 MINI-LESSON

WEEK 1 • DAY 2

Reflect on the Strategy

Ask partners to reflect on point of view by answering this question: *When characters in a story have an argument, what can you tell about their points of view?*

Show Your Knowledge

During independent time, ask partners to take turns giving an expressive rereading of paragraph 9. Ask them to explain how they decided how the rajah should sound.

Challenge Activity. Ask students to write a paragraph or two rewriting the story. The five men will meet a different animal. How would it feel if they met a giraffe, a rhinoceros, or a puppy?

iELD Integrated ELD

Light Support
List verbs from the text that show characters' points of view. Present cognates.

proclaimed/proclamado; announced/anunciado; declared/declarado; explained/explicado; interrumpido/interrumpido

Display the following chart:

Paragraph - Verb Meaning	Character	Verb
9 - said	rajah	interrupted
5 - said	rajah	explained

Students paraphrase the text to explain characters' points of view.

Moderate Support
Elicit verbs from the text that show characters' points of view. Present cognates.

proclaimed/proclamado; announced/anunciado; declared/declarado; explained/explicado; interrumpido/interrumpido

Students echo-read the following chart:

Paragraph - Verb Meaning	Character	Verb
6 - said	Third Man	exclaimed
5 - said	Fifth Man	declared

Students read the paragraphs, find the sentences with the verbs, and paraphrase the text to explain characters' points of view.

Substantial Support
Elicit, discuss, and list verbs from the text that show characters' points of view. Present cognates.

proclaimed/proclamado; announced/anunciado; declared/declarado; explained/explicado; interrumpido/interrumpido

Students echo-read the following chart:

Paragraph - Verb Meaning	Character	Verb
4 - said	First Man	proclaimed
5 - said	Blind Man	announced

Students echo-read the paragraphs, find the sentences with the verbs, read aloud the verbs together, and role-play verb meanings to show characters' points of view.

RL.2.6 Acknowledge differences in the points of view of characters, including by speaking in a different voice for each character when reading dialogue aloud. **SL.2.1a** Follow agreed-upon rules for discussions (e.g., gaining the floor in respectful ways, listening to others with care, speaking one at a time about the topics and texts under discussion). **SL.2.1b** Build on others' talk in conversations by linking their comments to the remarks of others. **SL.2.1c** Ask for clarification and further explanation as needed about the topics and texts under discussion. **SL.2.2** Recount or describe key ideas or details from a text read aloud or information presented orally or through other media.

©2018 Benchmark Education Company, LLC

Grade 2 • Unit 4 • Week 1

DAY 2

WRITING TO SOURCES

Mentor Writing Prompt

Is "The Blind Men and the Elephant" a story you would recommend to your friends? Why or why not? State your opinion in an essay. Supply reasons, based on details from the story, to support your opinion.

Student Objectives

I will be able to:
- Identify details from a source text that are used in an opinion essay.
- Identify how a writer uses those details to formulate and support an opinion.

Materials

Unit 4 Week 1 Weekly Presentations
- Analyze the Author's Reasons
- Opinion Essay Anchor Chart

Opinion Essay Anchor Chart

To write an informative report, writers…
State their opinion
- Clearly state their opinion in the first paragraph.
- Use a first-person point of view with pronouns such as *I* and *my*.
- Give reasons for their opinion.
- Include a conclusion.

Use facts and details from a source text
- Determine their opinion about the source text.
- Identify reasons for the opinion.
- Include facts and details from the source text to support their reasons.

Write an Opinion Essay: Analyze an Author's Reasons (15 MIN.) W.2.5

Engage Thinking

Remind students that yesterday you read them a writing prompt and an opinion essay written in response to that prompt. Then you analyzed the features of an opinion essay. Explain that today you will show students how you used facts and details from the story to form your opinion and support the reasons for it.

Model

Display "Analyze the Author's Reasons" and distribute copies to students. Read aloud the first excerpt. Then model how you used facts and details from the story to form your opinion.

Say: *In my opening, I stated my opinion that I would recommend the story. Next, I needed to give reasons for my opinion, basing them on facts and details from the story. I reread the story to determine the reasons for my opinion. I wrote one of my reasons at the beginning of the second paragraph, and I included a detail from the story to support that reason. Let's read the source text to find that detail.*

Read aloud Source Text Excerpt 1 and highlight the detail. Point out that you feel it is important to learn about other countries and cultures. The fact that this story takes place in India helped you form your opinion.

Mentor Opinion Essay Excerpts	Source Text Excerpts: "The Blind Men and the Elephant"
1. The story takes place in India. I think people should learn about other places, like India, and the people that live there.	1. Long ago, in a village in India, there lived five blind men.

Analyze the Author's Reasons, Excerpt 1

Peer Practice

Ask students to work in pairs to compare the remaining excerpts of the mentor and source texts. Have them find additional reasons that are given for the author's opinion and then highlight the facts and/or details from the story that support those reasons.

138 Grade 2 • Unit 4 • Week 1   ©2018 Benchmark Education Company, LLC

WRITING TO SOURCES

WEEK 1 • DAY 2

Share Your Understanding

Bring students together and invite partners to share their findings. Help students understand that authors include reasons for their opinion and provide facts and details from a source text that support their opinions.

Add these points to the anchor chart you started yesterday.

✓ Quick Write

During independent time, have students answer the following question: *What facts and details were included in the mentor text to support the author's opinion?* Use students' writing to evaluate their understanding of the genre.

---

iELD Integrated ELD

Light Support
Ask students to identify one of the reasons the author gives for recommending "The Blind Men and the Elephant." Have them locate facts and/or details from the story that support that reason. Then ask students to explain how they think the author arrived at the opinion stated in the opening.

Moderate Support
Help students understand that the author arrived at the opinion stated in the opening by using facts and details from the story. Provide sentence frames that help students make that connection. For example: *The author believes _____ because the story says _____.*

Substantial Support
Provide sentence frames to help students identify the reasons for the opinion the author gives. For example: *One reason the author recommends the story is _____.* Then have students find and talk about the supporting fact or detail from the text.

W.2.5 With guidance and support from adults and peers, focus on a topic and strengthen writing as needed by revising and editing.

DAY 2

PHONICS & WORD STUDY

r-Controlled *o* Frieze Card and Sound-Spelling card ôr

Student Objectives

I will be able to:
- Blend, build, and spell words with r-controlled **o**.
- Practice high-frequency words.
- Read r-controlled vowels **er, ir, ur**.

Additional Materials

- Letter cards: **a, c, e, f, h, k, m, n, o, p, r, s, t, w**

Weekly Presentation: Unit 4, Week 1
- r-controlled **o** frieze card
- Sound-spelling card **ôr**
- High-frequency word cards: **long, now, our, some, them, through, upon, was, when, work**

For additional word study/decodable practice, see: *"Why" Stories, Pecos Bill's Tornado*, and *That's How I Saw It!*

r-Controlled Vowel or, oar, ore (15 MIN.)

RF.2.3b, RF.2.3c, RF.2.3e, RF.2.3f, L.2.2d

Review r-Controlled Vowel or, oar, ore

Display the r-controlled **o** frieze card. Review the r-controlled **o** sound spelled **or** as in **corn**, **oar** as in **roar**, and **ore** as in **more**. Point to each spelling-sound.

Say: *What are the letters? What sounds do they stand for?*

Blend Words

Model: store

***Display letter cards for* store.** Model blending.

Say: *This is the letter* **s**. *It stands for* /s/. *This is the letter* **t**. *It stands for* /t/. *These are the letters* **ore**. *They stand for* /ôr/. *Listen as I blend these sounds together:* /**stôr**/, **store**. *Say the word with me:* **store**.

Practice: short, storm, fork, soar, score

Use the same routine to guide student practice.

Build Words

Model: for, fork, cork, corn

Display the letter cards for for. Blend the sounds: /fôr/, **for**.

- Add the **k** and repeat with **fork**.
- Replace the **f** with **c** and repeat with **cork**.
- Replace the **k** with **n** and repeat with **corn**.

Practice: tore, torn, worn, wore, more, sore, sort, shore, short, sport, spot

Use the same routine to guide student practice.

140 Grade 2 • Unit 4 • Week 1 ©2018 Benchmark Education Company, LLC

PHONICS & WORD STUDY

WEEK 1 • DAY 2

Spelling

Closed Sort: *fork, born, more, store, oars, roar, horn, before, sports, wore*

Write and display each word on an index card. Ask students to read aloud and spell each word together. Then make a three-column chart. Place a card for **or** on the top of column 1, **oar** on the top of column 2, and **ore** on the top of column 3.

Have students place each card in the correct column. When completed, have students read aloud and spell the words in each column together. Ask students what they notice about the r-controlled vowel spellings (e.g., other words with the same spelling patterns).

High-Frequency Words

Review: *long, now, our, some, them, through, upon, was, when, work*

Display the high-frequency word cards. Have students read and spell each word. Focus on common spelling patterns, such as the /ou/ sound in **now** and **our**. Then compare the common spelling pattern in **some** and **come**.

Review r-Controlled Vowels er, ir, ur

Model: burn, burning

Write the word **burn** and ask students to identify the vowel sound and spelling. Point out that the r-controlled vowel spelling **ur** acts as a team, which means it must stay in the same syllable in a longer word.

Write the word **burning**. Underline each vowel spelling. Have a volunteer divide the word into syllables. Then have students use the syllables to read the word.

Practice: turning, girl, first, never, under

Use the same routine to guide student practice.

---

iELD Integrated ELD

Light Support
Read aloud each minimal pair below.
port/part; born/barn; store/star; pork/park; cord/card; lord/lard
Students repeat and determine one of the two sounds as the target sound by showing thumbs up.
Pairs write two sentences using the target words and use gestures or simple drawings about the sentences to show comprehension.

Moderate Support
Read aloud each minimal pair below.
or/are; for/far; spork/spark
Pairs choose one of the target words, write a sentence, and act it out to show comprehension.

Substantial Support
List words with the target sound on the board.
for, lord, port, spork
Students echo-read and underline the letters that make the target sound.
Use visual support. Students orally practice composing short phrases or simple sentences using the words listed.

RF.2.3b Know spelling-sound correspondences for additional common vowel teams. RF.2.3c Decode regularly spelled two-syllable words with long vowels. RF.2.3e Identify words with inconsistent but common spelling-sound correspondences. RF.2.3f Recognize and read grade-appropriate irregularly spelled words. L.2.2d Generalize learned spelling patterns when writing words (e.g., cage → badge; boy → boil).

©2018 Benchmark Education Company, LLC

Grade 2 • Unit 4 • Week 1 **141**

DAY 3

SHARED READING

Texts for Close Reading, p. 5
"Ferdinand Frog and the Flea"

Student Objectives

I will be able to:
- Read and annotate a poem.
- Read a poem fluently.
- Identify words with long **e** vowel teams.

Additional Materials

Weekly Presentation: Unit 4, Week 1

Shared Reading (10 MIN.) RF.2.3b, RF.2.4a, RF.2.4b, RF.2.4c

Preview the Text

Display "Ferdinand Frog and the Flea." Read aloud the title of the poem as you point under the words. Invite students to turn to a partner and describe what they think the poem will be about.

Invite a few students to share their observations and inferences with the class.

Model Make Inferences and Predictions

Explain to students that they use a number of strategies when they read. Remind them that they learned about the Make Inferences strategy when they read the fable "The Boy Who Cried Wolf." Making inferences when reading a poem is very similar. Students should make inferences before they read, when they preview the poem. They should also make inferences during and after reading. Model making inferences and predictions about the poem for students.

Sample modeling. *The title names two characters who are in this poem: a frog named Ferdinand and a flea. The illustration shows a cartoon frog and a flea talking. I can infer that the poem will be about their silly conversation. Looking at the picture, I can tell the frog is surprised. Perhaps the frog is startled by the flea?*

Reread for Fluency: Rate/Pacing

First Reading. Read the poem aloud at an appropriate rate. Demonstrate reading at a rate that makes the dialogue clear to listeners.

Read Aloud. Invite students to read the poem aloud with you. Remind them to read at a rate that sounds like a conversation.

SHARED READING

Transfer Skills to Context: Annotate Rhyming Words

Model identifying and annotating rhyming words.

Sample modeling. *When I say the first five lines of the poem, I hear rhymes at the ends of four lines:* **flee/cheerfully/see/me**. *All of those words end with the same long* **e** *sound. I'll underline those words. In the next line of the poem, I hear long* **e** *rhymes:* **Flee/flea/be/thee**. *I'll underline those words, too.*

Guide students to find and underline more words that end with the long **e** sound, along with one pair of rhyming words that have a different ending sound. Help them to recognize that the repeated ending sounds make the poem sound silly and playful.

Transfer Skills to Context: Long e Vowel Teams

Point to the word **Flea** in the title of the poem. Ask students to read it aloud with you. Ask them to identify the letters that stand for the sound /ē/. Then ask students to find other examples of words with long **e** spelled **ea** and **ee**.

Integrated ELD

Light Support
Preview "Ferdinand Frog and the Flea." Review rhyming words. Write on the board the following rhyming words in random order: **flea, cheerfully, hog, see, me, thee, knee, happily, dog**. Pairs write words on cards, match and say each set of rhyming words, and create a two-line verse with rhyming words at the end.

Moderate Support
Preview "Ferdinand Frog and the Flea." Review rhyming words. Write on the board the following rhyming words in random order: **me, thee, see, flea, dog, hog**. Pairs write words on cards, say and match all of the long **e** rhyming words, and then match **dog/hog**. Groups write pairs of sentences that end with rhyming words.

Substantial Support
Preview "Ferdinand Frog and the Flea." Review rhyming words. Write each set of rhyming words below on cards, with one card for each word, and have students echo-read.
flea/see
me/thee
dog/hog
Display the cards. Read one word at a time. With students, say, find, and read the correct rhyming word. Mix up the cards. Pairs take turns finding and saying sets of rhyming words, and using them in sentences.

RF.2.3b Know spelling-sound correspondences for additional common vowel teams. **RF.2.4a** Read on-level text with purpose and understanding. **RF.2.4b** Read on-level text orally with accuracy, appropriate rate, and expression on successive readings. **RF.2.4c** Use context to confirm or self-correct word recognition and understanding, rereading as necessary.

©2018 Benchmark Education Company, LLC

DAY 3

SHORT READ 2 MINI-LESSON

"How the Beetle Got Its Gorgeous Coat": Recount Story Events (15 MIN.) RL.2.1, RL.2.5, SL.2.2, SL.2.3

Texts for Close Reading, pp. 10–13
"How the Beetle Got Its Gorgeous Coat"

Student Objectives

I will be able to:
- Read a pourquoi tale about characters with different points of view.
- Identify and annotate key details and events.
- Participate in collaborative conversations.

Additional Materials

Weekly Presentation: Unit 4, Week 1
- Story Events Chart

Ways to Scaffold the First Reading

Use your observational assessment to determine the intensity of scaffolding your students need.

IF...	THEN consider...
Students are English learners who may struggle with vocabulary and language demands...	**Read the Text TO students.** • Conduct a before-reading picture walk to introduce vocabulary and concepts. • Stop after meaningful chunks to define unfamiliar words and paraphrase difficult sentences.
Students are struggling readers who may decode with little comprehension...	**Read the Text WITH students.** • Stop after meaningful chunks to ask **who, what, when, where, how** questions. • Work with students to define unfamiliar words and paraphrase key ideas.
Students need some support to read unfamiliar texts with comprehension...	**Have students PARTNER-READ.** Partners should: • take turns reading aloud meaningful chunks. • ask each other **who, what, when, where, how** questions about the text. • circle unfamiliar words and define them using context clues.

Preview the Text

Display and ask students to open to "How the Beetle Got Its Gorgeous Coat."

Say: *This kind of folktale is often called a pourquoi tale. The word* pourquoi *is French for "why," and a pourquoi tale gives an imaginative explanation of why something came to be.*

Ask students to use your explanation, along with the title and illustrations, to infer what might happen in the story. Invite a few students to share their inferences with the class. Remind students that we can infer things about the text by using what we already know about a subject.

Sample modeling. *After reading the title, I can infer that there will be a beetle in this story, and the beetle will be a major character. As I scan the pages, I see an illustration of a parrot holding a trumpet. I know that trumpets are used for announcing events. I can also make an inference that there is going to be some kind of ceremony or major event in the story. I will write my inference in the margin, and I will continue reading to see if I am right.*

Model

Read paragraphs 1–7 as students follow along. Tell them you will underline key details and events as you read.

Model annotating the key events.

Say: *Key story details and events are the most important things that happen. We can use the details in a story to summarize the key events.*

Sample modeling (paragraph 1). The story begins with the narrator explaining that beetles of Brazil were not always as colorful as they are today. I'll underline the detail about their plain brown coats because it's important to know what the beetles used to look like.

Sample modeling (paragraphs 2–7). In paragraphs 2 and 3, I learn that a gray rat runs over to the crawling beetle and boasts about how fast he is. I'll underline the rat's boastful words and the beetle's polite reply, because they show that the two characters have a disagreement. In paragraph 5, the parrot's idea seems important, so I'll underline **have a race**. *In paragraphs 6 and 7, I learn that the prize is a brightly colored coat. I'll underline* **Both wanted a colorful coat**, *because that sentence tells me what the story problem is.*

144 Grade 2 • Unit 4 • Week 1 ©2018 Benchmark Education Company, LLC

SHORT READ 2 MINI-LESSON

WEEK 1 • DAY 3

Guided Practice

If your students need support to understand the text, refer to "Ways to Scaffold the First Reading." Pose text-dependent questions to guide their thinking: For example:

- *According to this text, how did the beetle get its "gorgeous coat"?*
- *What details from the text help to describe the beetle?*
- *What details from the text help to describe the rat?*

Ask students to read paragraphs 8–12 to identify the key story events. Ask them to underline the key details and events as they read.

Give students time to read and annotate. Observe their annotations to assess their ability to identify details about key events. Pose text-dependent questions to guide their thinking. For example:

- *What does the rat think as the race begins? Where does it say this in the text?*
- *According to the text, why is the rat surprised?*
- *Who wins the race, and why? Use evidence from the text to support your answer.*

Collaborate with students to summarize key story events.

Beginning	Middle	End
A gray rat boasts to a brown beetle about how fast he runs, but the beetle says she doesn't envy his speed. When a parrot offers a prize of a colorful coat to whoever wins a race, both the beetle and the rat want it.	The gray rat runs fast and is sure the beetle "can't possibly win." He is surprised to see the beetle at the finish line. He didn't know that she could fly.	The beetle chooses the "gorgeous green and gold coat" that beetles still wear today.

Sample Story Events Chart

Show Your Knowledge

During independent time, ask students to turn the title of the story into a question. Have them use what they learned from the story to answer the question in just one or two written sentences. Review their work to evaluate their strategy development and help you make instructional decisions.

> **iELD Integrated ELD**
>
> **Light Support**
> Before reading, conduct a pre-reading picture walk. Choose and preview key vocabulary: **speed, politely, overheard, your choice, proudly**.
> Students complete sentence frames to draw conclusions.
> *Since the beetle took her prize politely and proudly, I think she is _____.*
> *I don't think the beetle envied the rat's speed, because _____.*
>
> **Moderate Support**
> Before reading, conduct a pre-reading picture walk. Choose and preview key vocabulary: **excited, swiftly, reached, boasted, receive, change**.
> **Ask:** *Who boasted that he could run swiftly?*
> *Who reached the finish line first? Why?*
>
> **Substantial Support**
> Before reading, conduct a pre-reading picture walk. Choose and preview key vocabulary: **gorgeous, coats, prize, quickly, jealous, winner, finish line**.
> Provide cognates, such as: **rat/rata; envy/envidia; surprise/sopresa; admired/admirado; special/especial; probably/problemente; unique/unico**.
> Ask simple questions.
> **Ask:** *Why did the beetle win the prize at the finish line?*
> *Why didn't the rat win a gorgeous coat?*

RL.2.1 Ask and answer such questions as who, what, where, when, why, and how to demonstrate understanding of key details in a text. **RL.2.5** Describe the overall structure of a story, including describing how the beginning introduces the story and the ending concludes the action. **SL.2.2** Recount or describe key ideas or details from a text read aloud or information presented orally or through other media. **SL.2.3** Ask and answer questions about what a speaker says in order to clarify comprehension, gather additional information, or deepen understanding of a topic or issue.

DAY 3

WRITING TO SOURCES

Write an Opinion Essay: Note Supporting Facts and Details (15 MIN.) W.2.7, W.2.8

Mentor Writing Prompt

Is "The Blind Men and the Elephant" a story you would recommend to your friends? Why or why not? State your opinion in an essay. Supply reasons, based on details from the story, to support your opinion.

Student Objectives

I will be able to:
- Identify how notes taken by a writer match the information in a source text.
- Take organized notes from a source.
- Share my ideas in collaborative conversation and in writing.

Materials

Weekly Presentation: Unit 4, Week 1
- Opinion Essay Notes from a Source Text
- Mentor Opinion Essay
- Opinion Essay Anchor Chart

Opinion Essay Anchor Chart

To write an informative report, writers…
State their opinion
- Clearly state their opinion in the first paragraph.
- Use a first-person point of view with pronouns such as I and my.
- Give reasons for their opinion.
- Include a conclusion.

Use facts and details from a source text
- Determine their opinion about the source text.
- Identify reasons for the opinion.
- Include facts and details from the source text to support their reasons.

Take notes on the source text
- Create an organized notetaking form.
- Record their opinion.
- Take notes in their own words about the facts and details.
- Note character dialogue that supports the opinion and reasons.

Engage Thinking

Recall with students that yesterday you showed them how to use facts and details from the "The Blind Men and the Elephant" to support your opinion that you would recommend the story to friends. Tell them that today you will demonstrate how you took notes from the story to support your opinion and the reasons for it.

Model

Display and distribute "Opinion Essay Notes from a Source Text."

Say: *Before I began writing, I read the prompt carefully to learn exactly what I needed to include in my opinion essay. Then I made a notetaking form I could use. I wrote the title of the source text at the top. I knew that I would need to state my opinion, so I added a section for this statement. And I would need to give reasons for my opinion. I created a section for each reason and allowed space in that section to take notes on the facts and details that I would use from the story.*

Display "The Blind Men and the Elephant" and have students turn to this selection in their Texts for Close Reading.

Say: *Next, I reviewed the story and thought about the reasons I would recommend it to my friends. I wrote this note as one reason for my opinion: "The story makes you think about things in a different way." I also thought about what details and facts in the story supported my reason. I noted: "The men couldn't see, so they had to use other senses. That is different from how most people learn about things." Then I added this note: "Each man touched a different part of the elephant to learn about it. This makes me think about how I would learn if I were blind."*

Model writing these notes on the notetaking form. Point out how you use your own words to take notes. Have students fill in their forms using their own words.

Peer Practice

Read aloud the last sentence of the first paragraph and explain that this tells another reason you would recommend the story. Have students work with a partner to take notes about the facts and details from the story that support this reason. Encourage them to use their own words unless they are including the exact words that a character in the story speaks. In that case, students should put quotation marks around the character's words, as in, "The elephant is like a large snake!" (See the third paragraph in the Mentor Opinion Essay.)

146 Grade 2 • Unit 4 • Week 1 ©2018 Benchmark Education Company, LLC

WRITING TO SOURCES

WEEK 1 • DAY 3

Share Your Understanding

Bring students together and invite partners to share their notes. Use the supporting evidence that students identified to fill in information about the second reason on your notetaking form. Guide students to understand that creating a notetaking form, using it to record facts and details that support their opinion, and taking notes in their own words (except when quoting a character's words) are strategies that will help them take organized, relevant notes for their essay.

Add these points to the anchor chart you've been creating.

**Quick Write**

During independent time, have students answer the following question: *How does a notetaking form help you organize your thoughts to write an opinion essay?* Use students' writing to evaluate their understanding.

---

iELD Integrated ELD

Light Support
Talk with students about ways they might expand their notes to include more details that support the reasons for their opinion. Ask leading questions, as needed, and guide students' responses.

Moderate Support
As students take notes, use sentence frames and questions to help them express reasons for the opinion and explain how facts or details from the story support those reasons. For example:
One reason to recommend the story is that _____.
Why is this important?
Something in the story that makes me give that reason is _____.
Guide student responses, as needed.

Substantial Support
Provide sentence frames to help students take notes about relevant facts and details from the story that support a particular reason. For example:
One of the blind men said the elephant was like a _____.
Another said it was like a _____.
Each blind man had a different _____ about the elephant.
The rajah told them that they had to _____ to know the elephant.

W.2.7 Participate in shared research and writing projects (e.g., read a number of books on a single topic to produce a report; record science observations). **W.2.8** Recall information from experiences or gather information from provided sources to answer a question.

DAY 3

PHONICS & WORD STUDY

Texts for Close Reading, p. 14
"How Deer Got Its Horns"

Student Objectives

I will be able to:
- Blend and read words with r-controlled **o**.
- Read word study (decodable) text.
- Practice high-frequency words.

Additional Materials

- Letter cards: **a, b, e, h, k, m, n, o, p, r, s, t**
- r-controlled **o** frieze card
- Sound-spelling card **ôr**

Weekly Presentation: Unit 4, Week 1
- **High-frequency word cards:** long, now, our, some, them, through, upon, was, when, work
- Review high-frequency word cards: **all, away, better, by, change, done, even, found, learn, only**

For additional word study/decodable practice, see: *"Why" Stories*, *Pecos Bill's Tornado*, and *That's How I Saw It!*

Monitor Student Reading of Word Study (Decodable) Text

As students read the word study (decodable) text and answer questions, ask yourself these questions:

Are students able to . . .
- ❏ blend and read r-controlled vowel **or, oar, ore** words in the text?
- ❏ read new high-frequency words with automaticity?
- ❏ demonstrate comprehension of the text by answering text-based questions?

Based on your observations, you may wish to support students' fluency, automaticity, and comprehension with additional word study reading practice during intervention time.

r-Controlled Vowel or, oar, ore (15 MIN.)

RF.2.3b, RF.2.3c, RF.2.3e, RF.2.3f, L.2.2d

Blend Words

Practice: soar, shore, pork, storm, born
Display pocket chart letter cards for the word **soar**. Model how to blend the sounds to say the word. Use the same routine with other r-controlled **o** words to guide student practice. Discuss the homophones **soar/sore**.

Read Word Study (Decodable) Text

Introduce the Text
Read the title "How Deer Got Its Horns" aloud. Stop when you come to the word **Horns**. Point out the r-controlled vowel spelling **or**.

Read the Text
Ask students to read the text. If students need modeling, guide them to blend decodable words and read high-frequency words. You may wish to conduct a second reading, having partners read to each other while you circulate and monitor.

Connect Phonics to Comprehension
Ask some or all of the following questions:

- *What special skills were Deer and Rabbit born with?*
- *Why did the animals want to have a race?*
- *Who won the race? Why?*

Spelling

Write the word clues. Have students write the spelling word that goes with each one.

1. something you can play on teams (**sports**)
2. used to eat with (**fork**)
3. used to row a boat (**oars**)
4. place where you buy things (**store**)

High-Frequency Words

Practice: *long, now, our, some, them, through, upon, was, when, work*
Draw a ladder with ten rungs. Write a high-frequency word on each rung. Have students take turns climbing the ladder by reading the words.

Review: *all, away, better, by, change, done, even, found, learn, only*

RF.2.3b Know spelling-sound correspondences for additional common vowel teams. **RF.2.3c** Decode regularly spelled two-syllable words with long vowels. **RF.2.3e** Identify words with inconsistent but common spelling-sound correspondences. **RF.2.3f** Recognize and read grade-appropriate irregularly spelled words. **L.2.2d** Generalize learned spelling patterns when writing words (e.g., cage → badge; boy → boil).

Shared Reading (10 MIN.) RL.2.4, RF.2.4a, RF.2.4b, RF.2.4c, L.2.1e

Reread for Fluency: Rate/Pacing

Partner Reading. Ask partners to read "Ferdinand Frog and the Flea" aloud to each other. They may divide the poem into lines 1–6 and 7–14 and take turns reading each section. Remind them to read at a rate that sounds like a conversation.

Collaborative Conversation: Make Inferences and Predictions

Remind students that you demonstrated making inferences and predicting before reading—while you were previewing the story. Share that the reading strategy of making inferences and predictions is important for all literary and informational texts, but can be especially helpful when reading poems, which often use less language than a story or informational text. Model making inferences as you read the text.

Sample modeling. When I read this poem, I can tell that Ferdinand is surprised to have a flea. I know this because he says: "Frogs don't get fleas! This should never happen to me." I can also tell that the flea is an unwanted guest, because the frog says, "Flee little flea. Be away with thee." In other words, he is saying "Go away!" From this I can infer fleas are annoying pests.

Transfer Skills to Context: Annotate Alliteration

Explain to students that many words in the poem begin with the sound /f/. Read and underline lines 1–2. Explain the sound-meaning connection.

Sample modeling (lines 1–2). Almost every word in these lines begins with /f/. Even the word **cheerfully** has a syllable beginning with /f/. I think the poet repeated the sounds to make the poem sound silly and funny.

Guide students to note additional examples of lines with alliteration.

Transfer Skills to Context: Review Adverbs

Point out that the word **cheerfully** in line 2 has the suffix **-ly**. Explain that the word **cheerful** is an adjective and the added suffix turns it into an adverb, a word that describes how something is done. Ask students why **cheerfully**, and not **cheerful**, belongs in the sentence. Then ask them to explain why **happily**, and not **happy**, is the correct word to use in the last line of the poem.

RL.2.4 Describe how words and phrases (e.g., regular beats, alliteration, rhymes, repeated lines) supply rhythm and meaning in a story, poem, or song. **RF.2.4a** Read on-level text with purpose and understanding. **RF.2.4b** Read on-level text orally with accuracy, appropriate rate, and expression on successive readings. **RF.2.4c** Use context to confirm or self-correct word recognition and understanding, rereading as necessary. **L.2.1e** Use adjectives and adverbs, and choose between them depending on what is to be modified.

©2018 Benchmark Education Company, LLC

SHARED READING

Texts for Close Reading, p. 5
"Ferdinand Frog and the Flea"

Student Objectives

I will be able to:
- Read a poem at a rate that shows meaning.
- Recognize repeated sounds in a poem.
- Distinguish among adverbs and adjectives.

Additional Materials

Weekly Presentation: Unit 4, Week 1

iELD Integrated ELD

Light Support
Review adjectives and adverbs.
Write pairs of adjectives and adverbs on cards: **gentle, gently; nice, nicely; perfect, perfectly; help, helpfully.**
Partners explain when to use adjectives and adverbs, write sentences using the target words, and act out sentences.

Moderate Support
Review adjectives and adverbs.
Write pairs of adjectives and adverbs on cards: **happy, happily; possible, possibly; curious, curiously.**
Students orally compose sentences, act them out, and identify the adjectives and adverbs.

Substantial Support
Review adjectives and adverbs.
Write pairs of adjectives and adverbs on cards: **sad, sadly; cheer, cheerfully; quick, quickly.**
Students practice using the adjective and adverb in separate sentences.
This is a **quick** rat.
The rat ran **quickly** up the stairs.
Ask: When do we use adjectives? Adverbs?
Draw the following chart on the board:

Adjective	Adverb

Students choose a card, say the word, and place it in the correct column of the chart.

DAY 4

SHORT READ 2 MINI-LESSON

Texts for Close Reading, pp. 10–13
"How the Beetle Got Its Gorgeous Coat"

Student Objectives

I will be able to:
- Describe how words and phrases supply rhythm in a story.
- Describe how words and phrases supply meaning in a story.

Additional Materials

Weekly Presentation: Unit 4, Week 1

Build Vocabulary: Describe How Words and Phrases Supply Rhythm and Meaning in a Story (10 MIN.) RL.2.4

Engage Thinking

We just reread "Ferdinand Frog and the Flea." Now, we are going to reread "How the Beetle Got Its Gorgeous Coat."

Say: *In poems and stories, words and phrases can supply rhythm as well as meaning to the text.*

Model

Display and read aloud the title "How the Beetle Got Its Gorgeous Coat."

*Sample modeling (paragraph 2). In paragraph 2, I read that "A brown beetle was **happily** crawling along a wall. **Suddenly**, a large gray rat ran to her and laughed." The word **happily** tells me how the beetle felt. The word **suddenly** tells me how the rat moved. These two words also add rhythm to this part of the story.*

Guided Practice

Direct students to reread paragraphs 3 and 4. Tell them to underline the repeated rhythms in each paragraph.

("<u>See how quickly I run</u>!" the rat boasted. / "<u>I'm not jealous of you</u>," the beetle replied.)

Help students count the syllables in each phrase, and then have them echo-read the lines after you stress the iambic pentameter as you read aloud. Explain how the matching rhythms make the phrases easy to read aloud, and show that they create a musical, pleasing effect for listeners.

150 Grade 2 • Unit 4 • Week 1 ©2018 Benchmark Education Company, LLC

SHORT READ 2 MINI-LESSON

WEEK 1 • DAY 4

Reflect on the Strategy

Ask students to turn to a partner and answer this question: *What is another example of words and phrases supplying rhythm and meaning in a story or poem?*

✓ Show Your Knowledge

Tell students to find an example of the rhythm they found in paragraphs 3 and 4 repeated in paragraph 5. Who is speaking in this paragraph?

Challenge Activity. Have students write 2–3 sentences that use words and phrases to supply rhythm and meaning to the beginning of an original story.

---

iELD Integrated ELD

Light Support
Use "How the Beetle Got Its Gorgeous Coat." Review Guided Practice, and have students discuss the rhythm and meaning supplied by the words and phrases in paragraphs 3 and 4.

Moderate Support
Add paragraph 5.
Ask: *Which words supply meaning?*

Substantial Support
Add paragraph 5.
Ask: *Which words supply meaning? Which words or phrases supply rhythm?*

RL.2.4 Describe how words and phrases (e.g., regular beats, alliteration, rhymes, repeated lines) supply rhythm and meaning in a story, poem, or song.

©2018 Benchmark Education Company, LLC

Grade 2 • Unit 4 • Week 1   **151**

DAY 4

SHORT READ 2 MINI-LESSON

Texts for Close Reading, pp. 10–13
"How the Beetle Got Its Gorgeous Coat"

Student Objectives

I will be able to:
- Use details in the story to support my ideas about characters.
- Explain how characters in a story respond to major events and challenges.
- Share ideas respectfully in a class discussion.

Additional Materials

Weekly Presentation: Unit 4, Week 1
- Analyze Character Chart

Describe How Characters Respond to Major Events and Challenges (15 MIN.) RL.2.3, SL.2.1a, SL.2.1b, SL.2.1c, SL.2.2

Engage Thinking

Now, we will continue reading "How the Beetle Got Its Gorgeous Coat."

Say: In many folktales, the characters face a challenge or must respond to an event. The challenge or event is often stated at the beginning of the story.

Point out that being able to describe how characters respond to challenges and events is an important part of understanding a story. Explain that in this lesson students will describe how characters in "How the Beetle Got Its Gorgeous Coat" respond to the events in the story.

Model

Read aloud paragraphs 1–4 of "How the Beetle Got Its Gorgeous Coat." Then think aloud about the event described and the beetle's response.

Sample modeling. In paragraphs 2 and 3, I see an event. The rat runs to the beetle and laughs at her. In paragraph 4, I see how the beetle responds. She is polite to the rat.

Guided Practice

Ask students to read paragraph 5 of "How the Beetle Got Its Gorgeous Coat" and underline details that show how another character responds to this event. Pose text-dependent questions to guide students' thinking:

- *According to the text, how does the rat respond to the idea of having a race? Why?*
- *How does the beetle respond to the idea of having a race? Why?*
- *How does the rat respond to the race when it begins? Why?*
- *How does the rat respond to what happens at the end of the race?*
- *How does the beetle respond to what happens at the end of the race?*

Use students' ideas to complete a class Analyze Character Chart:

Rat	Beetle
Responds to the idea of having a race with excitement. Wants a colorful coat. When race begins, is confident he will win. Believes the beetle is too slow to win. At end of race, is amazed that he has lost.	Responds to the idea of having a race with excitement. Wants a colorful coat. At end of race, is polite about winning.

Sample Analyze Character Chart

152 Grade 2 • Unit 4 • Week 1

©2018 Benchmark Education Company, LLC

SHORT READ 2 MINI-LESSON

WEEK 1 • DAY 4

Reflect on the Strategy

Ask partners to discuss varied answers to this question: *Why do characters sometimes respond differently to the same event or challenge?*

After discussion, call on partnerships to share their ideas with the class.

Show Your Knowledge

Point out that paragraphs 10 and 12 tell how the beetle responded to winning the race. Tell students to write at least one sentence that could come at the end of the story and tell how the rat responded to losing the race. Use students' responses to evaluate their strategy development and to help you make instructional decisions.

iELD Integrated ELD

Light Support

Display "How the Beetle Got Its Gorgeous Coat." Review using details from the story to support ideas about characters.

Ask: *What words can you use to describe the rat? The beetle? What made you think this?*

Create a chart with students' responses.

Character	Detail	Conclusion
The rat Paragraph 8	The rat liked to brag.	The rat is arrogant; proud.
The beetle Paragraph 10	The beetle replied quietly.	The beetle is gentle.

When I read that _____, I decided that _____ was _____.

Moderate Support

Display and review "How the Beetle Got Its Gorgeous Coat." Review using details from the story to support ideas about characters.

Ask: *What words can you use to describe the beetle? What made you think this?*

Create a chart with students' responses.

Character	Detail	Conclusion
The beetle Paragraph 4	The beetle replied politely.	The beetle is humble.

In my opinion, the beetle showed she was _____ when _____.

Substantial Support

Display and review "How the Beetle Got Its Gorgeous Coat." Review using details from the story to support ideas about characters.

Ask: *What words can you use to describe the rat? What made you think this?*

Create a chart with students' responses.

Character	Detail	Conclusion
The rat Paragraph 3	The rat boasted.	The rat is a show-off.

I think the rat is _____, because _____.

RL.2.3 Describe how characters in a story respond to major events and challenges. **SL.2.1a** Follow agreed-upon rules for discussions (e.g., gaining the floor in respectful ways, listening to others with care, speaking one at a time about the topics and texts under discussion). **SL.2.1b** Build on others' talk in conversations by linking their comments to the remarks of others. **SL.2.1c** Ask for clarification and further explanation as needed about the topics and texts under discussion. **SL.2.2** Recount or describe key ideas or details from a text read aloud or information presented orally or through other media.

©2018 Benchmark Education Company, LLC

DAY 4

WRITING TO SOURCES

Mentor Writing Prompt

Is "The Blind Men and the Elephant" a story you would recommend to your friends? Why or why not? State your opinion in an essay. Supply reasons, based on details from the story, to support your opinion.

Student Objectives

I will be able to:
- Analyze a concluding statement.
- Restate an opinion statement.
- Share my ideas in collaborative conversation and in writing.

Materials

Weekly Presentation: Unit 4, Week 1
- Opinion and Concluding Statements
- Opinion Essay Anchor Chart

Opinion Essay Anchor Chart

To write an informative report, writers...

State their opinion
- Clearly state their opinion in the first paragraph.
- Use a first-person point of view with pronouns such as *I* and *my*.
- Give reasons for their opinion.
- Include a conclusion.

Use facts and details from a source text
- Determine their opinion about the source text.
- Identify reasons for the opinion.
- Include facts and details from the source text to support their reasons.

Take notes on the source text
- Create an organized notetaking form.
- Record their opinion.
- Take notes in their own words about the facts and details.
- Note character dialogue that supports the opinion and reasons.

Provide a concluding statement
- Include key words and phrases from the opinion statement.
- Restate, but do not repeat, the opinion statement.
- Summarize, without adding new information.

Write an Opinion Essay: Analyze the Author's Concluding Statement

(15 MIN.) W.2.5

Engage Thinking

Tell students that so far in this unit, they have learned about the features of an opinion essay and identified an opinion statement. They have also analyzed reasons for the opinion and taken notes on the facts and details from a story that support the opinion and reasons. Explain that today you will model how to write the concluding statement of an opinion essay.

Model

Display Opinion and Concluding Statements and distribute copies to students. Point out the first pair of opinion and concluding statements on the chart. Then use a think-aloud to model how you restate an opinion statement.

Sample think-aloud. *In the first paragraph of my essay, I wrote the opinion statement shown here. To end my essay, I needed to write a concluding statement that would reinforce my original opinion, but not repeat it word-for-word–this would make my writing boring. So I needed to restate the opinion, or say it another way. I decided to write, "It's a good story to read because you learn to think from a different point of view."*

Opinion statement: I tell my friends to read the story because it makes you think about things in a different way.	
Concluding statement: It's a good story to read because it helps you learn to think about things from a different point of view.	
Opinion statement: It also teaches about putting thoughts together to understand the big idea.	
Concluding statement:	
Opinion statement: I think people should learn about other places, like India, and the people that live there.	
Concluding statement:	

Sample Opinion and Concluding Statements

Peer Practice

Point out the last two sets of the opinion/concluding statements on the chart. Have partners work together on the second set to find the concluding opinion in the mentor opinion essay, write it on their chart, and talk about how it compares to the corresponding opinion statement. Then challenge students to write a concluding statement for the last set, reminding them that it should express the same ideas as in the opinion but be stated in a different way.

154 Grade 2 • Unit 4 • Week 1 ©2018 Benchmark Education Company, LLC

WRITING TO SOURCES

WEEK 1 · DAY 4

Share Your Understanding

Bring students together and invite partners to share the concluding statements from their chart. Point out that when writing a concluding statement, authors might use some of the key words from their original opinion, but they do not copy the statement exactly as it is.

Add these points to the anchor chart.

 **Quick Write**

During independent time, have students respond to the following: *Choose one of the opinion statements from the body of the opinion essay and restate it.* Use students' writing to evaluate their understanding of how to restate an opinion.

---

iELD Integrated ELD

Light Support
Provide a two-column chart to help students identify similar language in the opinion and concluding statements. Have students use the chart to describe how the language supports the author's opinion.

Words in Both Statements	How the Word Supports the Opinion

Moderate Support
Help students note similarities and differences in the opinion and concluding statements. Use sentence frames for students to complete to make their comparisons. For example:
In the original opinion, the author said the story makes you _____.
In the concluding statement, the author said the story helps you _____.

Substantial Support
Circle the words and phrases that appear in both the opinion and concluding statements of each set on the chart (such as "think about things" and "different" in the first set). Then look with students at how the two statements differ. Help them understand that by using some of the same terms, the author is able to communicate the same idea without repeating the exact words of the opinion.

W.2.5 With guidance and support from adults and peers, focus on a topic and strengthen writing as needed by revising and editing.

DAY 4

PHONICS & WORD STUDY

r-Controlled Vowel or, oar, ore (20 MIN.)

RF.2.3b, RF.2.3c, RF.2.3d, RF.2.3e, RF.2.3f, L.2.2

Read Multisyllabic Words

Model: before

Explain that when an r-controlled vowel spelling such as **or**, **oar**, or **ore** appears in a long word, the spelling must remain in the same syllable. Model using the word **before**.

- Write the word **be** and point out that it's an open syllable.
- Add **fore**. Point out the r-controlled vowel spelling **ore**.
- Circle the vowel spellings **e** and **ore**. Tell students you will divide the word before the one consonant between them: **be/fore**.
- Blend the syllables to read the word.

Practice: report, popcorn, perform, snowstorm, explore

Use the same routine to guide student practice.

Spelling

Write the groups of words. Read the words, and ask students to complete each group with a related spelling word. Ask students to come up with other word groups for the spelling words.

1. knife, spoon, _____ (**fork**)
2. baseball, soccer, hockey_____ (**sports**)
3. bark, meow, howl, _____ (**roar**)
4. trumpet, trombone, tuba, _____ (**horn**)

High-Frequency Words

Review: long, now, our, some, them, through, upon, was, when, work

Display the high-frequency word cards. Read each word and have students repeat the word aloud and spell it together. Have students sit in a circle. Pass the cards, one at a time. Each student reads the word and uses it in a sentence before passing the card.

Student Objectives

I will be able to:
- Blend multisyllabic words with r-controlled **o**.
- Spell words with r-controlled **o**.
- Read high-frequency words.

Additional Materials

- r-controlled **o** frieze card
- Sound-spelling card **ôr**

Weekly Presentation: Unit 4, Week 1
- High-frequency word cards: **long, now, our, some, them, through, upon, was, when, work**

For additional word study/decodable practice, see: *"Why" Stories, Pecos Bill's Tornado,* and *That's How I Saw It!*

RF.2.3b Know spelling-sound correspondences for additional common vowel teams. **RF.2.3c** Decode regularly spelled two-syllable words with long vowels. **RF.2.3d** Decode words with common prefixes and suffixes. **RF.2.3e** Identify words with inconsistent but common spelling-sound correspondences. **RF.2.3f** Recognize and read grade-appropriate irregularly spelled words. **L.2.2** Demonstrate command of the conventions of standard English capitalization, punctuation, and spelling when writing.

Shared Reading (10 MIN.) RL.2.1, RF.2.4b, SL.2.2, SL.2.3

Reread for Fluency: Rate/Pacing (iELD)

Partner Reading. Ask partners to take turns reading "Ferdinand Frog and the Flea" aloud. One partner may read the words of the narrator and the frog, and the other may read the flea's words. Remind them to read at a rate that helps listeners follow the conversation.

Make Inferences and Predictions

Remind students that you showed them how you made inferences and predictions before and during reading. Students also practiced making inferences and predictions while they read the story. Tell them that today you will reread the poem and students will make inferences and predictions after they read.

Sample think-aloud. *In this poem, the frog wants the flea to go away, but the flea demands that the frog find the flea a dog or a hog to live with instead. From this information in the poem, I can infer that the flea prefers furry animals to frogs. I can also infer that the flea is not going anywhere without the help of the frog. I predict that the frog will find this flea a dog or a hog in order to get rid of the flea. Based on the poem, what do you think will happen next?*

Transfer Skills to Context: Imagery

Have the students listen as you read the first sentence aloud.

Sample modeling. Poets use vivid language to help readers form a picture in their minds. When I read "a flip-flopping flea frolicking cheerfully," I picture a flea bouncing around happily. What picture was in your mind as I read?

Build and Reflect

During independent time, tell students to think about the Week 1 selections, and ask them to complete the "Build, Reflect, and Write" activity on page 15 to help them think more about how a story told from different points of view can change.

RL.2.1 Ask and answer such questions as who, what, where, when, why, and how to demonstrate understanding of key details in a text. **RF.2.4b** Read on-level text orally with accuracy, appropriate rate, and expression on successive readings. **SL.2.2** Recount or describe key ideas or details from a text read aloud or information presented orally or through other media. **SL.2.3** Ask and answer questions about what a speaker says in order to clarify comprehension, gather additional information, or deepen understanding of a topic or issue.

©2018 Benchmark Education Company, LLC

SHARED READING

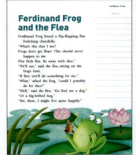

Texts for Close Reading, p. 5
"Ferdinand Frog and the Flea"

Student Objectives

I will be able to:
- Read a poem.
- Recognize contractions and possessive nouns.

Additional Materials

Weekly Presentation: Unit 4, Week 1

iELD Integrated ELD

Light Support

If . . .	Then . . .
ELLs need support with rate and fluency . . .	• Students review with a partner and point out, discuss, and take turns reading chunks that rhyme and have alliteration. • Focus on self-monitoring rate and fluency.

Moderate Support

If . . .	Then . . .
ELLs have difficulty with rate, fluency, and understanding . . .	• Read with students. • After modeling meaningful chunks with alliteration and rhyming, such as: *Flee little Flea. Be away with thee*, stop and discuss meaning. • Then model rate and fluency. • Students read aloud together.

Substantial Support

If . . .	Then . . .
ELLs struggle with rate and fluency . . .	• Model rate and read aloud with understanding. • Review reading as if it is a conversation. • Model and practice chunks with alliteration and rhyming, such as: *flip-flopping flea frolicking cheerfully; flea/me.* • Students echo-read.

WEEK 1 • DAY 5

Grade 2 • Unit 4 • Week 1

DAY 5

CROSS-TEXT MINI-LESSON

Texts for Close Reading, pp. 6–13 "The Blind Men and the Elephant" and "How the Beetle Got Its Gorgeous Coat"

Student Objectives

I will be able to:
- Ask and answer questions about elements in folktales.
- Compare and contrast two folktales.
- Participate in collaborative conversations.

Additional Materials

Weekly Presentation: Unit 4, Week 1
- Compare-and-Contrast Chart

Compare and Contrast Two Folktales

(20 MIN.) RL.2.1, RL.2.2, RL.2.3, RL.2.5, RL.2.9, SL.2.2, SL.2.3

Engage Thinking

We just read a few different stories. Now, we will compare and contrast two of them.

Display "The Blind Men and the Elephant" and "How the Beetle Got Its Gorgeous Coat." Remind students that both stories are folktales that people have told and retold for a long time. Explain that many folktales teach lessons about how to behave.

Ask: *What lessons do you think these folktales teach?*

Model

Display a three-column Compare-and-Contrast Chart, as shown. Explain that in the far left and right columns you will list ways the two selections are different. In the middle column, you will list ways in which the two selections are similar. Think aloud to model how to make comparisons and contrasts.

Sample modeling. In both folktales, the characters have a goal. That is one way the folktales are alike, so I'll write a similarity in the middle column of the chart. However, the characters' goals are different in each tale. The men in "The Blind Men and the Elephant" want to learn about an elephant. The rat and the beetle in "How the Beetle Got Its Gorgeous Coat" want to win a race and a prize. I'll write these differences in the left and right columns of the chart.

Sample modeling. I can ask myself, "What other similarities and differences are in these folktales?" One similarity I can think of is that both folktales have characters who are sure they are right, even though they're not. But the characters' ideas are different in the two folktales. I'll write these notes in the chart, too.

Guided Practice

Pose text-dependent questions to guide students' thinking as they compare and contrast elements and features in both folktales:

- *How are the settings alike and different? Use details from the text to support your answer.*
- *What do characters learn in each folktale? How do you know?*
- *What does each folktale help people understand? Use evidence from the text to help support your answer.*

Collaborate with students to complete the chart. Encourage them to use complete sentences to share their ideas, along with signal words such as **both, like, different, similar,** and **unlike**.

CROSS-TEXT MINI-LESSON

WEEK 1 · DAY 5

"The Blind Men and the Elephant"	Both Folktales	"How the Beetle Got Its Gorgeous Coat"
The men want to learn about an elephant.	Characters have goals.	The rat and the beetle want to win a race and the prize.
Each man is sure that his description of the elephant is correct, but he knows only one part of the elephant.	Characters are sure they are right, but they're wrong.	The rat is sure that he will be faster than the crawling beetle, but he doesn't know she can fly.
India	The folktales take place long ago in foreign lands.	Brazil
The men learn that a part of an elephant is not the whole elephant.	Characters learn that things are not always what they seem to be.	The rat learns that the beetle is not as slow as she seems.
Put your ideas together with other people's ideas to get the whole picture.	The folktales teach lessons.	It is not wise to boast about yourself or be overly-confident.

Sample Compare-and-Contrast Chart

☑ Show Your Knowledge

During independent time, ask students to reread paragraph 3 of "The Blind Men and the Elephant" and paragraph 5 of "How the Beetle Got Its Gorgeous Coat." Have them write a sentence about a similarity between the rajah and the parrot and a sentence about a difference. Use students' writing to evaluate their ability to state and support a point of comparison or contrast. You may also use this and other writing samples to assess students' use of English conventions and their need for support to print legibly.

(iELD) Integrated ELD

Light Support

Students echo-read the Compare-and-Contrast Chart. Have students use the chart to form sentences that compare and contrast the texts.

Even though both stories have characters with goals, the goals are different.

Even though both stories take place in foreign places, the places are different.

Moderate Support

Students echo-read the Compare-and-Contrast Chart. Discuss how to use the chart to form sentences that compare and contrast the texts.

Ask: *Why do we use Compare-and-Contrast Charts?* Check students' understanding of the chart and terms. Model and then have students practice sentence frames.

Both _____ and _____ are/have _____.

The _____ has/is _____, but the _____ has/is _____, so they are different.

Substantial Support

Students echo-read the Compare-and-Contrast Chart. Discuss how to use the chart to form sentences that compare and contrast the texts. Model sentence frames and then have students complete sentence frames.

They are similar, because both stories have characters that have goals.

The stories are different, because the men want to learn something, while the beetle and the rat want to win something.

They are similar, because both stories _____.

The stories are different, because _____, while _____.

RL.2.1 Ask and answer such questions as who, what, where, when, why, and how to demonstrate understanding of key details in a text. **RL.2.2** Recount stories, including fables and folktales from diverse cultures, and determine their central message, lesson, or moral. **RL.2.3** Describe how characters in a story respond to major events and challenges. **RL.2.5** Describe the overall structure of a story, including describing how the beginning introduces the story and the ending concludes the action. **RL.2.9** Compare and contrast two or more versions of the same story (e.g., Cinderella stories) by different authors or from different cultures. **SL.2.2** Recount or describe key ideas or details from a text read aloud or information presented orally or through other media. **SL.2.3** Ask and answer questions about what a speaker says in order to clarify comprehension, gather additional information, or deepen understanding of a topic or issue.

©2018 Benchmark Education Company, LLC

Grade 2 · Unit 4 · Week 1 **159**

DAY 5

WRITING TO SOURCES

Conventions of Language: Use Adjectives Correctly (15 MIN.) L.2.1e, L.2.6

Focus The Learning

Explain that adjectives are words that describe a noun—a person, animal, place, thing, or idea. They can help readers imagine how something might look, feel, smell, taste, or sound. Tell students that today they will learn how to use adjectives to make their writing more interesting.

Model

Display and distribute copies of the Adjectives Chart. Then think aloud to help students understand adjectives and how they are used.

Sample think-aloud. *I know an adjective is a describing word that tells about a noun. It can tell about the color, size, amount, shape, sound, smell, or feel of something. An adjective might describe a person's feelings or the day's weather. I can fill in this chart with adjectives that will help me describe different nouns. I'll start with the category "Colors" and fill in these colors: red, yellow, blue, green.*

Have students follow along by filling in their charts with the same words. Then together brainstorm a few adjectives to write under each category on the chart. Tell students they can continue to add to the chart on their own and will use it later when writing an opinion essay.

Color	Size	Number
red	big	one
yellow	small	ten
blue	long	many
green	huge	few
Shape	**Sound**	**Smell**
round	loud	sour
square	roaring	stinky
oval	high-pitched	sweet
triangular	quiet	fresh
Feel	**Feelings**	**Weather**
soft	happy	sunny
hard	mad	rainy
dry	sad	windy
slimy	angry	cloudy

Adjectives Chart

Mentor Writing Prompt

Is "The Blind Men and the Elephant" a story you would recommend to your friends? Why or why not? State your opinion in an essay. Supply reasons, based on details from the story, to support your opinion.

Student Objectives

I will be able to:
- Identify adjectives.
- Use adjectives in writing.

Materials

Weekly Presentation: Unit 4, Week 1
- Adjectives Chart
- Opinion Essay Anchor Chart

Opinion Essay Anchor Chart

To write an informative report, writers…

State their opinion
- Clearly state their opinion in the first paragraph.
- Use a first-person point of view with pronouns such as *I* and *my*.
- Give reasons for their opinion.
- Include a conclusion.

Use facts and details from a source text
- Determine their opinion about the source text.
- Identify reasons for the opinion.
- Include facts and details from the source text to support their reasons.

Take notes on the source text
- Create an organized notetaking form.
- Record their opinion.
- Take notes in their own words about the facts and details.
- Note character dialogue that supports the opinion and reasons.

Provide a concluding statement
- Include key words and phrases from the opinion statement.
- Restate, but do not repeat, the opinion statement.
- Summarize, without adding new information.

Use conventions of English correctly
- Use adjectives to describe nouns.

WRITING TO SOURCES

Sample think-aloud, continued. *Now I'm going to use some adjectives from my chart. First, I'll write this sentence from the story: "One man touched the elephant's trunk." I'm going to underline the nouns,* **man** *and* **trunk***, then I'll use an adjective from my chart to describe each of those nouns. Here's how my new sentence looks: "One* **quiet man** *touched the elephant's* **long trunk***." I used the adjective* **quiet** *to describe the man and the adjective* **long** *to describe the elephant's trunk.*

Peer Practice

Write and display these two sentences: "One man touched the elephant's tail. He thought the elephant was like a rope." Have partners work together to identify nouns in the sentences and then add appropriate adjectives to describe at least one noun in each sentence. Ask them to write their sentences then talk about other adjectives they might have used.

Share Your Understanding

Bring students together and invite partners to share their sentences.

Ask: *How did adding adjectives help improve the sentences?*

Help students understand that adjectives provide descriptive detail and help readers form a better idea about the nouns they describe.

Add information about adjectives to the anchor chart.

Quick Write

During independent time, have students respond to the following: *Choose five adjectives from the chart and use each one in a sentence.* Use students' writing to evaluate their understanding of adjectives and how they are used.

Integrated ELD

Light Support
Write and display simple noun phrases, such as "the kitten." Ask students to expand the phrase by adding one or more adjectives that describes the noun, for example, "the tiny, wet kitten." Then have students use the expanded noun phrase in a sentence.

Moderate Support
Show students a picture and have them name something in it, such as a kitten. Explain that the word they named is a noun. Then have them tell more about the noun by adding an adjective to it. Use the noun in a sentence frame, leaving the adjective open so that students can complete the sentence with the adjective of their choice. For example:
The _____ kitten climbed up the tree.

Substantial Support
Display a picture of a person, animal, place, or thing. Ask students to identify the picture, explaining that the word they use is a noun. Then help them come up with adjectives that can be used to tell more about that noun, such as "fluffy kitten" or "tall tree." Finally, help students use the descriptive phrase in a sentence. For example:
The fluffy kitten purred.
The tall tree blocked the sun.

L.2.1e Use adjectives and adverbs, and choose between them depending on what is to be modified. **L.2.6** Use words and phrases acquired through conversations, reading and being read to, and responding to texts, including using adjectives and adverbs to describe (e.g., *When other kids are happy that makes me happy*).

DAY 5
PHONICS & WORD STUDY

Review and Assess r-Controlled Vowel or, oar, ore (15 MIN.) RF.2.3b, RF.2.3c, RF.2.3d, RF.2.3e, RF.2.3f, L.2.2d

Texts for Close Reading, p. 14
"How Deer Got Its Horns"

Student Objectives

I will be able to:
- Build, read, and spell words with r-controlled **o**.
- Reread word study (decodable) text for fluency.
- Read high-frequency words.

Additional Materials

- Letter cards: **c, e, f, h, k, o, p, r, s, t**
- r-controlled **o** frieze card
- Sound-spelling card **ôr**

Weekly Presentation: Unit 4, Week 1
- Letter cards for each high-frequency word
- High-frequency word cards: **long, now, our, some, them, through, upon, was, when, work**

For additional word study/decodable practice, see: *"Why" Stories, Pecos Bill's Tornado,* and *That's How I Saw It!*

Build Words

Model: sore, score, store
Display the letter cards for sore. Blend the sounds: /sôr/, sore.

- Add the **c** after **s** and repeat with **score**.
- Replace the **c** with **t** and repeat with **store**.

Practice: sort, short, shot, spot, sport, for, fort, port, pork, porch
Use the same routine to guide student practice.

Review Multisyllabic Words

Model: sort, sorting
Write the word **sort** and ask students to identify the vowel sound and spelling. Point out that the r-controlled vowel spelling **or** acts as a team, which means it must stay in the same syllable.

Write the word **sorting**. Model how to read the longer word. Point out the added syllable –**ing** is a suffix.

Practice: record, ignore, shore, shoreline, more, anymore, storm, brainstorm, port, seaport
Use the same routine to guide student practice.

Reread for Fluency: "How Deer Got Its Horns"

Have students independently whisper-read "How Deer Got Its Horns." Circulate and listen to their readings. Provide corrective feedback. For students having difficulty reading independently, have them read with a more skilled partner.

162 Grade 2 • Unit 4 • Week 1

©2018 Benchmark Education Company, LLC

PHONICS & WORD STUDY

WEEK 1 · DAY 5

Spelling

Posttest

Use the following procedure to assess students' spelling of this week's words.

- Say each spelling word and use it in the sentence provided.
- Have students write the complete sentence on a piece of paper. Then continue with the next word. Remind students to write legibly.
- When students have finished, collect their papers and analyze any misspelled words.

1. Do you eat pizza with a **fork**?
2. I was **born** in March.
3. I need **more** books to read.
4. We went to the **store** to get milk.
5. Dad lost one of the boat's **oars**.
6. Can a cat **roar**?
7. Go blow your **horn** to wake them up.
8. I brush my teeth **before** I wash my face.
9. We like to play **sports** after school.
10. She **wore** a big red hat.

High-Frequency Words

Review: *long, now, our, some, them, through, upon, was, when, work*

Display the high-frequency word cards. Say each word and have students repeat the word aloud and spell it together.

Place letter cards, in random order, for one of the words in a pocket chart. Have a volunteer beat the clock to form the word. Allow 15 seconds. Then have the rest of the class check the spelling and give a thumbs up or thumbs down.

Next have students turn to a partner and say a sentence using the word. Call on volunteers to check their sentences.

iELD Integrated ELD

Light Support

If ELLs have trouble reading independently, with fluency, scaffold pre-reading lessons for "How Deer Got Its Horns." Then assess their needs for future lessons as they read independently.

Review confusing language, such as **come back, come out, on top of, to check on, no longer, with pride, ever since, on top of**.

Partners read meaningful chunks and discuss the text, vocabulary, and language.

Moderate Support

Review key vocabulary, such as **runner, jumper, farther, thick, chewing a path, tore**.

Students role-play key events and vocabulary to show understanding.

Students echo-read key passages and partner-read.

Substantial Support

Discuss key events and vocabulary, such as **horns, deer, born, turn around, owl, spotted, cheater**.

Students role-play to show comprehension.

Model reading key chunks, and have students echo-read.

RF.2.3b Know spelling-sound correspondences for additional common vowel teams. **RF.2.3c** Decode regularly spelled two-syllable words with long vowels. **RF.2.3d** Decode words with common prefixes and suffixes. **RF.2.3e** Identify words with inconsistent but common spelling-sound correspondences. **RF.2.3f** Recognize and read grade-appropriate irregularly spelled words. **L.2.2d** Generalize learned spelling patterns when writing words (e.g., cage →badge; boy → boil).

©2018 Benchmark Education Company, LLC

Grade 2 • Unit 4 • Week 1   **163**

Week 2 Mini-Lessons at a Glance

	Day 1	Day 2
Reading Mini-Lessons	**Build Knowledge and Review Strategies (10 Min.), p. 166** SL.2.1a, SL.2.1b, SL.2.2, SL.2.3 **Shared Reading (10 Min.), p. 167** RF.2.4a, RF.2.4b, RF.2.4c **"Stone Soup":** **Recount Story Events, Part 1 (15 Min.), p. 168** RL.2.1, RL.2.5, SL.2.1a, SL.2.1b, SL.2.1c	**Shared Reading (15 Min.), p. 174** RF.2.3f, RF.2.4a, RF.2.4b, RF.2.4c **"Stone Soup":** **Recount Story Events, Part 2 (15 Min.), p. 176** RL.2.1, RL.2.5, SL.2.1a, SL.2.1b, SL.2.1c
Writing and Language Mini-Lessons	**Write an Opinion Essay: Plan the Writing (15 Min.), p. 170** W.2.5	**Write an Opinion Essay: Reread the Text to Develop Your Reasons (15 Min.), p. 178** W.2.8
Phonics/Word Study Mini-Lessons	**r-Controlled Vowels ear, eer, ere (20 Min.), p. 172** RF.2.3b, RF.2.3e, RF.2.3f, L.2.2 • High-Frequency Words: *always, any, blue, buy, city, draw, four, great, how, live* • Weekly Spelling Words: *year, deer, near, clear, here, cheer, fear, ears, hear, steer*	**r-Controlled Vowels ear, eer, ere (20 Min.), p. 180** RF.2.3b, RF.2.3e, RF.2.3f, L.2.2d • High-Frequency Words: *always, any, blue, buy, city, draw, four, great, how, live*

Extended Read 1: "Stone Soup"

Folktale

Quantitative	Lexile® 440L

Qualitative Analysis of Text Complexity

Purpose and Levels of Meaning ❶
- This familiar folk tale has a simple moral: when people share, they will always have enough.

Structure ❷
- The narrative is chronologically structured but with multiple characters and an implicit connection between events.

Language Conventionality and Clarity ❷
- Sentence structure involves a few complex sentences, but there is no unfamiliar vocabulary.

Knowledge Demands ❶
- The basic story will be familiar to most readers and requires no prior knowledge.

Total QM: 6
Moderate Complexity*

*The texts in *Benchmark Advance* are qualitatively evaluated based on their grade-level placement in the program.
Reader maturity and age appropriateness are key considerations in the subjective use of the rubrics.

Day 3	Day 4	Day 5
Shared Reading (10 Min.), p. 182 RF.2.4a, RF.2.4b, RF.2.4c	**Shared Reading (10 Min.), p. 189** RF.2.3b, RF.2.4a, RF.2.4b, RF.2.4c	**Shared Reading (10 Min.), p. 195** RL.2.1, RF.2.4b, L.2.1e, L.2.6
Build Vocabulary: Identify Real-Life Connections Between Words and Their Uses (10 Min.), p. 183 RL.2.4, L.2.5a **Close Reading: Describe the Overall Structure of a Story (15 Min.), p. 184** RL.2.1, RL.2.5, SL.2.1a, SL.2.1b, SL.2.1c, SL.2.2	**Close Reading: Describe How Characters Respond to Major Events and Challenges (15 Min.), p. 190** RL.2.1, RL.2.3, SL.2.1a, SL.2.1b, SL.2.1c	**Close Reading: Compare and Contrast the Central Message in Two Stories (15 Min.), p. 196** RL.2.1, RL.2.2, SL.2.1a, SL.2.1b, SL.2.1c, SL.2.2, SL.2.3
Write an Opinion Essay: Use Facts and Details to Support Your Opinion (15 Min.), p. 186 W.2.5	**Write an Opinion Essay: Plan and Organize Your Opinion Essay (15 Min.), p. 192** W.2.5	**Conventions of Writing: Form and Use Contractions (15 Min.), p. 198** L.2.2c, L.2.3a
r-Controlled Vowels ear, eer, ere (10 Min.), p. 188 RL.2.3, RF.2.3b, RF.2.3c, RF.2.3e, RF.2.3f, L.2.2d • High-Frequency Words: *always, any, blue, buy, city, draw, four, great, how, live*	**r-Controlled Vowels ear, eer, ere (20 Min.), p. 194** RF.2.3b, RF.2.3c, RF.2.3d, RF.2.3e, RF.2.3f, L.2.2d • High-Frequency Words: *always, any, blue, buy, city, draw, four, great, how, live*	**Review and Assess r-Controlled Vowels ear, eer, ere (20 Min.), p. 200** RF.2.3b, RF.2.3c, RF.2.3d, RF.2.3e, RF.2.3f, L.2.2d • High-Frequency Words: *always, any, blue, buy, city, draw, four, great, how, live*

©2018 Benchmark Education Company, LLC

Grade 2 • Unit 4 • Week 2

DAY 1

UNIT REFLECTION

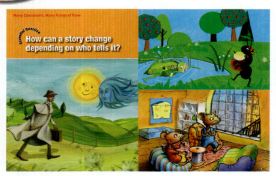

Texts for Close Reading, pp. 2–3
Unit Introduction

Student Objectives

I will be able to:
- Listen and speak cooperatively in a group discussion.
- Follow three-step oral directions.
- Show my understanding of strategies for reading.

Additional Materials

Weekly Presentation: Unit 4, Week 2

iELD Integrated ELD

Light Support
Display "How the Beetle Got Its Gorgeous Coat."
Ask: *Which character do you like best? Why?*
Students review the text with a partner and then present their answer and text evidence that supports their answer. Provide sentence frames.
When I read _____ in the story, I realized that the _____ was _____. That's when I decided _____ was my favorite character in this story.

Moderate Support
Display "How the Beetle Got Its Gorgeous Coat."
Ask: *What words best describe the beetle/rat?*
Students review the text with a partner and then present their answer. Provide a sentence frame.
I think the rat was _____, because he _____.

Substantial Support
Display "How the Beetle Got Its Gorgeous Coat."
Review key words, such as **boastful, bragger, polite, humble, gentle, proud, arrogant, show off, quiet.**
Ask: *How would you describe the beetle/rat?*
Help students review the text and find text evidence to support their answers. Model completing the sentence frame below.
I think the beetle is _____, because she _____.

Build Knowledge and Review Strategies (10 MIN.) SL.2.1a, SL.2.1b, SL.2.2, SL.2.3

Discuss the Essential Question

Display the introduction to *Many Characters, Many Points of View* and review the Essential Question. After students flip through the Week 1 selections, ask them to listen carefully to your three-step directions. Tell them to turn and talk to a partner about points of view in stories:

- Name a character from a story you read.
- Tell what that character believed.
- Give your opinion about that character's point of view.

Discuss students' ideas. Explain that in Week 2, students will continue to think about characters' points of view as they read more folktales.

Review Unit Strategies

Analyze Story Structure. Remind students that during Week 1, they thought about the beginning, middle, and end of a story and the elements that readers find in many stories.

Say: *When we read "The Blind Men and the Elephant," we looked for elements found in many stories: the setting, the characters, the problem, what characters do to solve the problem, and the solution. We found that the setting is long ago in India, and the characters are five blind men who want to learn about an elephant. The men try to figure out what an elephant is like. Only at the end do we learn what the solution is– they must put their ideas together to form a picture of a whole elephant.*

Ask volunteers to identify story elements as they summarize the folktale "How the Beetle Got Its Gorgeous Coat."

Analyze Characters. Remind students that they used descriptions of story characters, along with the characters' words and actions, to decide what the characters were like. Students also described characters based on what they did and said, and how they responded to events and challenges.

Say: *When we read "How the Beetle Got Its Gorgeous Coat," we described the rat as boastful and overconfident, and we described the beetle as polite.*

Have students look at "How the Beetle Got Its Gorgeous Coat" to suggest answers to these questions: *When the rat laughs at her for crawling slowly, how does the beetle react? Why doesn't she tell the rat that she knows how to fly?*

Tell students that thinking about how stories are set up and how characters react to story events will help them understand the extended text they will read this week.

SL.2.1a Follow agreed-upon rules for discussions (e.g., gaining the floor in respectful ways, listening to others with care, speaking one at a time about the topics and texts under discussion). **SL.2.1b** Build on others' talk in conversations by linking their comments to the remarks of others. **SL.2.2** Recount or describe key ideas or details from a text read aloud or information presented orally or through other media. **SL.2.3** Ask and answer questions about what a speaker says in order to clarify comprehension, gather additional information, or deepen understanding of a topic or issue.

Shared Reading (10 MIN.) RF.2.4a, RF.2.4b, RF.2.4c

Introduce the Text (iELD)

Display "A Good Switch!" Read aloud the title of the story as you point under the words. Explain that this a fable. A fable is a very short story that often includes talking animals and that usually has a moral or teaches a lesson.

Model Make Inferences and Predictions

Explain to students that readers use various strategies when they read, including making inferences and predictions. Remind them that they practiced making inferences and predictions last week before, during, and after reading. Today they will make inferences and predictions before they read while previewing the text. Model making inferences and predictions for students.

Sample modeling (title/illustrations). *The title makes me wonder what a good switch is. I know that when two people make a switch, they trade something. Each illustration shows a cartoon rat. One rat is running in a train tunnel, and the other is running under horses' hooves. I can infer from the title and illustrations that these two animals are the main characters. I can predict that these rats will switch places or make a trade in this fable.*

Model Fluent Reading: Accuracy/Self-Correct

First Reading. Read the story aloud fluently and accurately. Tell students that readers may mispronounce a word, or say a word that doesn't make sense, or skip words. Explain that in order to read accurately, readers listen to themselves and go back to correct errors.

Read aloud together. Invite students to reread the text with you. Tell them to listen for any errors and correct themselves.

Transfer Skills to Context: Review or, ore, oar/ôr/

Point to the word **enormous** in paragraph 2. After students read it aloud, ask them to name the letters that spell /ôr/ in the second syllable. Circle **or** in the word. Then display the words **chore** and **board**, and follow a similar procedure with each.

RF.2.4a Read on-level text with purpose and understanding. RF.2.4b Read on-level text orally with accuracy, appropriate rate, and expression on successive readings. RF.2.4c Use context to confirm or self-correct word recognition and understanding, rereading as necessary.

©2018 Benchmark Education Company, LLC

SHARED READING

WEEK 2 • DAY 1

Texts for Close Reading, p. 16 "A Good Switch!"

Student Objectives

I will be able to:
- Read a fable about characters with different points of view.
- Read a story accurately and listen for mistakes in order to self-correct.
- Read words with /ôr/.

Additional Materials

Weekly Presentation: Unit 4, Week 2

iELD Integrated ELD

Light Support
Display "A Good Switch." Conduct a pre-reading picture walk. Discuss story events. Choose and preview key vocabulary, such as **speeding, city life, neighed, switch places, a good switch.**
Ask: *Why did Ralph want to switch places? Why did Max like city life? Why was it a good switch?*

Moderate Support
Display "A Good Switch." Conduct a pre-reading picture walk. Discuss story events. Choose and preview key vocabulary, such as **enormous, subway, scraps, cousin, dodged.**
Ask: *Why did both cousins want to switch homes? Who dodged horses? Who dodged trains? Why?*

Substantial Support
Display "A Good Switch." Conduct a pre-reading picture walk. Discuss story events. Choose and preview key vocabulary, such as **prowled, switch, tunnels, trains, horses, barn.**
Students act out terms to show understanding. Ask simple questions to check for comprehension.
Ask: *Why didn't Ralph and Max like where they prowled for food? Why did Ralph and Max want to switch places?*

DAY 1

EXTENDED READ 1 MINI-LESSON

"Stone Soup": Recount Story Events, Part 1 (15 MIN.) RL.2.1, RL.2.5, SL.2.1a, SL.2.1b, SL.2.1c

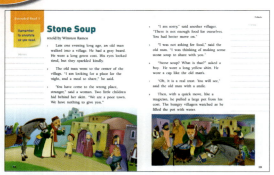

Texts for Close Reading, pp. 18–25
"Stone Soup"

Student Objectives

I will be able to:
- Read a folktale about characters with different points of view.
- Use the details to summarize key story events.
- Work cooperatively with a partner.

Additional Materials

Weekly Presentation: Unit 4, Week 2
- Details and Story Events Chart

Ways to Scaffold the First Reading

Use your observational assessment to determine the intensity of scaffolding your students need.

IF...	THEN consider...
Students are English learners who may struggle with vocabulary and language demands...	**Read the Text TO students.** • Conduct a before-reading picture walk to introduce vocabulary and concepts. • Stop after meaningful chunks to define unfamiliar words and paraphrase difficult sentences.
Students are struggling readers who may decode with little comprehension...	**Read the Text WITH students.** • Stop after meaningful chunks to ask **who, what, when, where, how** questions. • Work with students to define unfamiliar words and paraphrase key ideas.
Students need some support to read unfamiliar texts with comprehension...	**Have students PARTNER-READ.** *Partners should:* • take turns reading aloud meaningful chunks. • ask each other **who, what, when, where, how** questions about the text. • circle unfamiliar words and define them using context clues.

Preview the Text

Display and ask students to open to "Stone Soup." Guide students to preview the text and then turn to a partner to predict what it will be about. As needed, prompt them to notice what the title and illustrations suggest about the type of text it might be. Remind students that we make inferences about the text by using what we already know about a subject. Have students share their inferences and predictions with the class.

Read to Identify Key Story Events

Have students read paragraphs 1–18 to identify key story events. Ask them to underline important details about the events. Give students time to read and annotate. Observe their annotations to assess their ability to connect details in the text with key story events.

Confirm Predictions

Remind students of their predictions and ask them to confirm if their predictions were correct.

💬 Collaborative Conversation: Partner

Ask students for their ideas about the kind of story "Stone Soup" is. Confirm that they recognize it as a folktale. Explain that versions of this folktale have been told and retold in many different countries. Display the Details and Story Events Chart. Direct partners to compare the details they underlined and use them to fill out the chart by summarizing the key events for each section of the story. Remind students that partners take turns speaking and listening, and that listeners build on the ideas of speakers. Use your observations to determine if students need support in the form of guiding questions about "key events—the most important things that happen."

Paragraphs	Details (paragraph)	Story Events
Paragraphs 1–4	"an old man walked into a village" (1) "looking for a place for the night, and a meal to share" (2) "poor town … nothing to give you" (3)	An old man walks into a village, asks for a place to stay and a meal to share. Two villagers tell him that they can't help him because their village is too poor.
Paragraphs 5–10	"not asking for food … thinking of making some stone soup to share" (5) "pulled a large pot from his coat … filled the pot with water." (8) "You will see." (10)	The old man says that he just wants to share the stone soup he is making. He pulls a large pot from his coat and fills it with water. He tells the villagers, "You will see."
Paragraphs 11–14	"dropped the stone into the pot" (11) "whispers grew louder" (14)	He takes a large stone from his coat and drops it into the boiling water. The villagers whisper about stone soup.
Paragraphs 15–18	Stone soup "for anyone who wants it." (16) "villagers gathered … stone soup with cabbage is even better!" (18)	More villagers come. The old man says that the soup will taste even better with cabbage in it.

Sample Details and Story Events Chart

Tell students they will continue to summarize key events when they read Part 2.

---

168 Grade 2 • Unit 4 • Week 2 ©2018 Benchmark Education Company, LLC

EXTENDED READ 1 MINI-LESSON

WEEK 2 · DAY 1

Share

Invite partners to share their statements about key events. Encourage group discussion of the summarizing statements and whether enough, or too many, details have been included. Remind students to connect their comments to what they have heard from previous speakers.

Reinforce or Reaffirm the Strategy

Choose one of the following options based on your observations during partner collaboration.

IF . . .	THEN . . .
Students need support to identify the most important details and make summarizing statements about key events . . .	**Model to reinforce the strategy.** • *As I read, I decide what I must pay attention to so that I can keep track of what is happening in a story–the key events.* • *In paragraphs 1 and 2, I learn that the story takes place in a village one evening. An old man arrives and asks the villagers for "a place for the night, and a meal to share."* • *In paragraphs 3 and 4, two villagers answer him. I ask myself what is most important to understand about what they say. My answer is that both villagers tell him they have nothing to share with him because they are too poor.*
Students identify important details and make statements of key events . . .	Invite partners to reflect on the strategy use by discussing the following question: • *How did you decide whether or not to include details about clothing when summarizing the key events?*

☑ Show Your Knowledge

During independent time ask students to reread paragraphs 11–13 and summarize the key event in one sentence.

Challenge Activity. Have students reread paragraph 18. Ask them whether the last sentence shows a key event in the story and have them give their reasons.

---

iELD Integrated ELD

Light Support

Preview the text. Students discuss the illustrations. Provide cognates, such as **potato/patata; poor/pobra.**

Choose, discuss, present, and then have students act out key vocabulary, such as **gathered around, move on, ourselves, place for the night.**

Students draw conclusions.

Since the old man didn't move on, he might _____.

The villagers gathered around, because _____.

Moderate Support

Preview the text. Choose, discuss, present, and then have students act out key vocabulary, such as **not enough, late one evening, looked tired, sparkled kindly, even better.** Students use key vocabulary to answer text evidence questions.

Ask: *What did the old man do, late one evening?*

Late one evening, the old man _____.

Ask: *What might make the stone soup even better?*

_____ might make the stone soup even better, because _____.

Substantial Support

Preview the text. Choose, discuss, present, and then have students act out key vocabulary, such as **beard, treat, stone soup, magician, cabbage.**

Ask simple questions.

Ask: *How might the old man make the stone soup? Why does the old man want a cabbage?*

RL.2.1 Ask and answer such questions as who, what, where, when, why, and how to demonstrate understanding of key details in a text. **RL.2.5** Describe the overall structure of a story, including describing how the beginning introduces the story and the ending concludes the action. **SL.2.1a** Follow agreed-upon rules for discussions (e.g., gaining the floor in respectful ways, listening to others with care, speaking one at a time about the topics and texts under discussion). **SL.2.1b** Build on others' talk in conversations by linking their comments to the remarks of others. **SL.2.1c** Ask for clarification and further explanation as needed about the topics and texts under discussion.

2018 Benchmark Education Company, LLC

Grade 2 • Unit 4 • Week 2   **169**

DAY 1

WRITING TO SOURCES

Write an Opinion Essay: Plan the Writing (15 MIN.) W.2.5

Student Writing Prompt

Is "Stone Soup" a story you would recommend to your friends? Why or why not? State your opinion in an essay. Supply reasons, based on details from the text, to support your opinion.

Student Objectives

I will be able to:
- Read and analyze a writing prompt.
- Read and analyze a checklist that includes key points to remember when writing an opinion essay.

Materials

Weekly Presentation: Unit 4, Week 2
- Student Writing Prompt
- Opinion Essay Checklist
- Opinion Essay Anchor Chart

Opinion Essay Anchor Chart

To write an informative report, writers…
State their opinion
- Clearly state their opinion in the first paragraph.
- Use a first-person point of view with pronouns such as *I* and *my*.
- Give reasons for their opinion.
- Include a conclusion.

Use facts and details from a source text
- Determine their opinion about the source text.
- Identify reasons for the opinion.
- Include facts and details from the source text to support their reasons.

Take notes on the source text
- Create an organized notetaking form.
- Record their opinion.
- Take notes in their own words about the facts and details.
- Note character dialogue that supports the opinion and reasons.

Provide a concluding statement
- Include key words and phrases from the opinion statement.
- Restate, but do not repeat, the opinion statement.
- Summarize, without adding new information.

Use conventions of English correctly
- Use adjectives to describe nouns.

Engage Thinking

Remind students that last week, you analyzed a prompt and an opinion essay that was written in response to the prompt. Help them recall that the essay was about the author's opinion of "The Blind Men and the Elephant."

Ask students to think about the opinion given in last week's essay and the reasons and details that supported the opinion. Then tell students that this week they will plan their own opinion essay in response to a prompt about "Stone Soup."

Review the Anchor Chart

Display the completed anchor chart from last week and review the key elements of writing an opinion essay.

Read and Analyze the Prompt and Checklist

Display and distribute copies of the Student Writing Prompt and Opinion Essay Checklist. Read aloud the prompt then use a think-aloud to model how you analyze it.

Sample think-aloud. *This prompt is similar to the one we analyzed last week. Instead of "The Blind Men and the Elephant," the prompt asks me to consider the story "Stone Soup" and give my opinion about recommending it to friends. Like last week, the prompt tells me to state my opinion and then provide reasons for it, based on details I find in the text.*

Draw students' attention to the checklist. Explain that this checklist reflects the important elements of an opinion essay as summarized on the anchor chart. Tell students they will refer to their checklists as they plan, draft, revise, and edit. Referring to the checklist will help them write a strong opinion essay.

170 Grade 2 • Unit 4 • Week 2 ©2018 Benchmark Education Company, LLC

Share Your Understanding

Bring students together and have them share their ideas about the prompt. Help students understand that the checklist is like a guide. Remind them to refer to the checklist and anchor chart as they write their opinion essays.

 Quick Write

During independent time, have students answer the following question: *What key elements do you need to keep in mind when writing an opinion essay?* Use students' writing to evaluate their understanding of an opinion essay.

> **iELD Integrated ELD**
>
> **Light Support**
> As you review the anchor chart and/or checklist, encourage students to build on the responses of others to demonstrate their understanding of the elements of an opinion essay.
>
> **Moderate Support**
> Guide students to ask and answer questions about the anchor chart and/or checklist, encouraging them to add relevant information in their responses. For example, a student might ask, "How do you begin an opinion essay?" Another student might respond with "An opinion statement." The first partner might then add information, such as, "Yes, you begin the first paragraph by stating your opinion."
>
> **Substantial Support**
> Ask yes/no questions about the anchor chart and/or the checklist for students to answer. For example: *Does an opinion essay use words such as I and my?* Reinforce students' correct responses by restating the question as a statement: *Yes, opinion essays use words such as I and my*. Reteach any information about opinion essays that students might be struggling with.

W.2.5 With guidance and support from adults and peers, focus on a topic and strengthen writing as needed by revising and editing.

DAY 1

PHONICS & WORD STUDY

r-Controlled Vowels ir Frieze Card

Student Objectives

I will be able to:
- Identify, blend, and spell words with r-controlled vowels **ear, eer, ere**.
- Learn high-frequency words.
- Read high-frequency words.

Additional Materials

- Letter cards: **a, e, e, f, h, r**

Weekly Presentation: Unit 4, Week 2
- r-controlled vowels /îr/ frieze card
- High-frequency word cards: **always, any, blue, buy, city, draw, four, great, how, live**
- Review high-frequency word cards: **long, now, our, some, them, through, upon, was, when, work**

For additional word study/decodable practice, see: *Fox and Cat, King and Grisly Beard,* and *Here or There.*

r-Controlled Vowels ear, eer, ere (20 MIN.)

RF.2.3b, RF.2.3e, RF.2.3f, L.2.2

Spelling-Sound Correspondences

Introduce: r-Controlled Vowels ear, eer, ere
Display the r-controlled /îr/ frieze card.

Say: *These sounds are /îr/. The /îr/ sounds are spelled many ways:* **ear, eer, ere.**

Model: ear, eer, ere
Point to each spelling on the card and provide a sample word: **ear** as in **year**, **eer** as in **deer**, **ere** as in **here**. Write each sample word and underline the r-controlled vowel spelling.

Say: *Look at the first word I wrote:* **y-e-a-r.** *I see the r-controlled vowel spelling* **ear.** *Listen and watch as I sound out the word: /yîr/,* **year.**

Run your hand under the word as you sound it out.

Practice: year, deer, here
Repeat the r-controlled vowel **ear, eer, ere** words one at a time. Ask students to write each word and underline the r-controlled vowel spelling.

Blend Words

Model: r-Controlled Vowels ear, eer, ere

Display the letter cards for **far**. Model how to blend the sounds together as you run your hand under each letter.

Say: *This is the letter* **f.** *It stands for /f/. These are the letters* **ar.** *They stand for /är/. Listen as I blend these sounds together: /fär/,* **far.** *Say the word with me:* **far.**

Model adding an **e** before the **a** to make the word **fear**.

Say: *I can add an* **e** *before the* **a** *to make the r-controlled vowel spelling* **ear.** *The* **ear** *spelling stands for the /îr/ sounds. Listen as I blend the new word: /fîr/. Say the word with me:* **fear.**

Continue modeling the words **here, hear**. Discuss their meanings.

Practice: cheer, dear, gear, near, clear, rear
Write each word. Have students blend the sounds aloud together. Provide corrective feedback, as needed.

172 Grade 2 • Unit 4 • Week 2

©2018 Benchmark Education Company, LLC

PHONICS & WORD STUDY

WEEK 2 • DAY 1

Spelling

Pretest

Say each spelling word. Read the sentence and say the word again. After the pretest, write each word as you say the letter names. Have students check their work.

year	There are twelve months in a **year**.
deer	We watched the **deer** run in the fields.
near	Do you live **near** our school?
clear	Tomorrow will be a **clear** and sunny day.
here	**Here** are the books you needed for your report.
cheer	We will **cheer** for our team.
fear	Do you have a **fear** of spiders?
ears	In winter my **ears** get cold if I don't wear a hat.
hear	What is that scary sound I **hear**?
steer	You can **steer** the car to the left to get to my house.

High-Frequency Words

Introduce: *always, any, blue, buy, city, draw, four, great, how, live*

Use the following routine: Write simple sentences using each high-frequency word. Underline the word and discuss important features about it. Say the word and have students repeat. Then spell the word with students as you point to each letter. Finally have students write the word as they spell it aloud.

Practice

Display the high-frequency word cards. Have students work with a partner to write sentences using the words. Then have volunteers read a sentence and identify the high-frequency word.

Review: *long, now, our, some, them, through, upon, was, when, work*

Review last week's words using the high-frequency word cards. Mix and display one word card at a time as students say each word aloud together.

**Integrate ELD**

Light Support
Pairs write two sentences using as many spelling words as possible in each sentence. Pairs use gestures or drawings to portray their sentences and show comprehension.

Moderate Support
Pairs write one sentence using at least two spelling words. Students act out the sentence to show comprehension.
This year, we are all here to cheer for our team.

Substantial Support
Review the spelling words and the r-controlled vowels **ear, eer, ere.**

Write the spelling words on cards. Students echo-read. Hold up a card. Students repeat the word, place it in the correct column of the chart below and present it to the group. Model presenting a word.
Say: *This is the word **deer**, d-e-e-r. In the word, **deer**, the letters -eer make the /ir/ sound. We saw so many **deer** in the forest.*

ear	eer	ere
year	deer	here
near	cheer	
clear	steer	
fear		
ears		

RF.2.3b Know spelling-sound correspondences for additional common vowel teams. **RF.2.3e** Identify words with inconsistent but common spelling-sound correspondences. **RF.2.3f** Recognize and read grade-appropriate irregularly spelled words. **L.2.2** Demonstrate command of the conventions of standard English capitalization, punctuation, and spelling when writing.

DAY 2

SHARED READING

Texts for Close Reading p. 16
"A Good Switch!"

Student Objectives

I will be able to:
- Read a fable about characters with different points of view.
- Identify important details and summarize key events.
- Recognize words I know in different texts.

Additional Materials

Weekly Presentation: Unit 4, Week 2

Shared Reading (15 MIN.) RF.2.3f, RF.2.4a, RF.2.4b, RF.2.4c

Reread for Fluency: Accuracy/Self-Correct

Partner Reading. Assign partners to read "A Good Switch!" aloud to each other, alternating paragraphs and then switching roles. Remind them to go back to correct themselves if they say words that don't seem to make sense.

Collaborative Conversation: Make Inferences and Predictions

Remind students that yesterday you demonstrated making inferences before reading—while you were previewing the story. Share that the reading strategy of making inferences is important for all literary and informational texts, but can be especially helpful when reading fables, which are often used to teach a lesson. Model making inferences as you read the text.

Sample modeling. *In paragraph 1, I read that Ralph doesn't like living in the city and wants to live on a quiet farm. In paragraph 2, I see that Ralph's cousin Max doesn't like farm life and would prefer to live in the city. While I read I can use this information from the text to infer that the two cousins would be happier if they switched places.*

Invite students to use sentence frames to help them make inferences.

- *While reading, I can make an inference about _____.*
- *The words _____ help me infer that _____.*

Transfer Skills to Context: Annotate Important Details (iELD)

Model underlining important details that help you summarize story events.

Sample modeling (paragraph 1). *I'll ask myself what is most important to understand about the beginning of this story. I'll underline the first sentence because it answers the questions **who?** and **where?** The answer to the question **What does the character want?** is important in any story, so I'll underline the last sentence. Here's one way I can summarize the key event in paragraph 1: "Ralph lives in the city. He wanted to live on a farm."*

Guide students to underline other details that lead them to summarize the events in paragraphs 2 and 3.

174 Grade 2 • Unit 4 • Week 2 ©2018 Benchmark Education Company, LLC

SHARED READING

WEEK 2 • DAY 2

Transfer Skills to Context: r-Controlled Syllable Patterns

Point to the word **here** in paragraph 3. Tell students to read the word aloud and then pronounce the syllable without the initial consonant: **/îr/**. Remind them that the consonant **r** can change the vowel sound that comes before it. Display these words, asking students to read each one aloud and name the letters that spell /îr/: **fear, cheerful, sincere, steering, dearly**.

Transfer Skills to Context: High-Frequency Words *city, live*

As you point to each of these previously taught words in paragraph 1, tell partners to say the word to each other: **city**, **live**. Remind students to look for words they know when they read a new text.

(iELD) Integrated ELD

Light Support

Display and review the text. Write key events on sentence strips. Students use the sequence words **first, then, finally** and sequence the sentence strips.

First	Ralph wanted to live on a quiet farm.
Then	Max thought city life would be better.
Finally	After Max wrote to Ralph, they switched places.

Pairs write two additional events on sentence strips, sequence the two events, and role-play them.

Moderate Support

Display and review the text. Write key events on sentence strips. Students use the sequence words **first, then, finally** and sequence the sentence strips with you.

First	Ralph was tired of dodging the noisy trains.
Then	Max was tired of dodging the loud, enormous horses.
Now	Ralph lives on the farm and Max lives in the city.

With students, add and correctly sequence a fourth event, such as *Max wrote to Ralph*.

Substantial Support

Display and review the text. Write key events on sentence strips. Students use the sequence words **first, then, finally** and sequence the sentence strips with you.

First	Ralph didn't like living in the city.
Next	Max didn't like living on the farm.
Last	Max and Ralph decided to switch homes.

Groups role-play events in the correct order.

RF.2.3f Recognize and read grade-appropriate irregularly spelled words. **RF.2.4a** Read on-level text with purpose and understanding. **RF.2.4b** Read on-level text orally with accuracy, appropriate rate, and expression on successive readings. **RF.2.4c** Use context to confirm or self-correct word recognition and understanding, rereading as necessary.

©2018 Benchmark Education Company, LLC

Grade 2 • Unit 4 • Week 2   **175**

DAY 2

EXTENDED READ 1 MINI-LESSON

"Stone Soup": Recount Story Events, Part 2 (15 MIN.) RL.2.1, RL.2.5, SL.2.1a, SL.2.1b, SL.2.1c

Texts for Close Reading, pp. 18–25
"Stone Soup"

Student Objectives

I will be able to:
- Read a folktale about characters with different points of view.
- Use the details to summarize key story events.
- Work cooperatively with a partner.

Additional Materials

Weekly Presentation: Unit 4, Week 2
- Details and Story Events Chart

Ways to Scaffold the First Reading

Use your observational assessment to determine the intensity of scaffolding your students need.

IF...	THEN consider ...
Students are English learners who may struggle with vocabulary and language demands...	**Read the Text TO students.** • Conduct a before-reading picture walk to introduce vocabulary and concepts. • Stop after meaningful chunks to define unfamiliar words and paraphrase difficult sentences.
Students are struggling readers who may decode with little comprehension...	**Read the Text WITH students.** • Stop after meaningful chunks to ask **who, what, when, where, how** questions. • Work with students to define unfamiliar words and paraphrase key ideas.
Students need some support to read unfamiliar texts with comprehension...	**Have students PARTNER-READ.** Partners should: • take turns reading aloud meaningful chunks. • ask each other **who, what, when, where, how** questions about the text. • circle unfamiliar words and define them using context clues.

Preview the Text

Remind students that they have already read the first part of "Stone Soup." Tell partners to skim the text again and discuss what the old man might do in Part 2 of the story. Remind students that they can make inferences about a story by using what they already know about a subject. Call on a few students to share their predictions and inferences with the class and explain how they arrived at them.

Read to Identify Key Story Events

Have students read paragraphs 19–30. Tell them to underline important details about the story events.

Give students time to read and annotate. Observe their annotations to assess their ability to distinguish details about key story events from other descriptive details.

Confirm Predictions

Give students an opportunity to tell how accurately they predicted the story events and outcome.

💬 Collaborative Conversation: Partner

Sample modeling. *When I am having a conversation with a partner, I listen to everything they have to say, and then I respond.*

Display and distribute the Details and Story Events Chart. Ask partners to write details and key story events in each section in the chart. Tell them to discuss the details they underlined as they decide how to summarize each event. Use your observations to determine if students need support in the form of guiding questions.

Paragraphs	Details (paragraph)	Story Events
Paragraphs 19–21	"added the cabbage to the pot" (19) "stone soup with cabbage and a piece of lamb... feast for a king" (20) "village butcher ... dropped the lamb into the pot" (21)	A villager adds a cabbage to the pot. After the old man tells about a soup with cabbage and lamb, a butcher drops a leg of lamb into the pot.
Paragraphs 22–26	"everyone could smell the soup" (22) "stone soup with ... carrots and turnips... truly tasty soup" (24) "villagers found a turnip or carrot and added them to the soup" (25)	The old man tells about a tasty soup with added vegetables. The villagers add more vegetables to the soup.
Paragraphs 27–28	"Everyone ... had a big bowlful" (27) "No one went to bed hungry . . ." (28)	When the soup is ready, the villagers share it and are not hungry anymore.
Paragraphs 29–30	"villagers begged the old man to stay" (29) "learned the magic of sharing" (30)	The villagers beg the old man to stay, but he leaves after teaching them about the "magic of sharing."

Sample Details and Story Events Chart

WEEK 2 · DAY 2

EXTENDED READ 1 MINI-LESSON

Share Your Understanding

Invite partnerships to share their key story events with the class. Tell listeners to decide if all the important events are included and to offer comments in respectful ways. Ask questions to confirm students' comprehension and to deepen their understanding.

Reinforce or Reaffirm the Strategy

If your students need support to understand the text, refer to "Ways to Scaffold the First Reading." Provide directive and/or corrective feedback as needed: For example:

- *What does the old man suggest adding to the soup after the cabbage?*
- *What does the old man suggest adding to the soup next?*

Choose one of the following based on your observations during partner collaboration.

IF...	THEN...
Students need support to identify the most important details and make summarizing statements about key events . . .	**Model to reinforce the strategy.** • *In paragraph 19, I read that the villager had a good crop this year. Does that detail help me keep track of story events? Not really—I'll underline details that tell what the villager did:* **added the cabbage to the pot.** • *In paragraph 20, the old man says "Wonderful!" and tells about "a feast for a king." But more important to the story events are his words about what he wants to add to the soup. I'll underline:* **stone soup with cabbage and a piece of lamb.** • *In paragraph 21, I read that the butcher was saving his leg of lamb for Sunday dinner. I think that detail is not important enough for a summary. I'll underline details that point to a key event:* **butcher, dropped the lamb into the pot.** • *I can use the important details I found to summarize the key story events:* **A villager adds a cabbage to the pot. After the old man tells about stone soup with cabbage and lamb, a butcher drops a leg of lamb into the pot.**
Students identify important details and make statements of key events . . .	**Invite partners to reflect on the strategy use by discussing the following question:** • *Why is it helpful for readers to think about key events in stories?*

☑ Show Your Knowledge

During independent time ask students to reread paragraphs 29–30 and write a sentence telling what the old man's secret was and why it was important.

Challenge Activity. Ask students to reread paragraphs 22–24 and find one sentence that seems most important to the story. Have them explain why they chose that sentence.

---

iELD Integrated ELD

Light Support
Preview the text. Provide cognates, such as **secret/secreto.** Choose, discuss, present, and then have students act out key vocabulary, such as **went hungry, elders, a piece of, as well, smacked his lips.** Students use key vocabulary to complete sentence frames and draw conclusions.
I guess nobody went hungry again, because _____.
The old man probably smacked his lips, because _____.

Moderate Support
Preview the text. Students discuss the illustrations. Choose, discuss, present, and then have students act out key vocabulary, such as **crop, rubbed, share, bellies, added, saving.** Students complete sentence frames to answer text evidence questions.
Ask: *Who added vegetables to the stone soup? Why?*
_____ added vegetables to the stone soup, because _____.

Ask: *How did the villagers share?*
The villagers _____.

Substantial Support
Preview the text. Students discuss the illustrations. Choose, discuss, present, and then have students act out key vocabulary, such as **meal, lamb, onion, turnips, carrots, villagers, butcher.**
Ask: *How did the butcher/villagers make the soup taste better?*
Help students answer the question. Provide a sentence frame.
The butcher/villagers _____.

RL.2.1 Ask and answer such questions as who, what, where, when, why, and how to demonstrate understanding of key details in a text. **RL.2.5** Describe the overall structure of a story, including describing how the beginning introduces the story and the ending concludes the action. **SL.2.1a** Follow agreed-upon rules for discussions (e.g., gaining the floor in respectful ways, listening to others with care, speaking one at a time about the topics and texts under discussion). **SL.2.1b** Build on others' talk in conversations by linking their comments to the remarks of others. **SL.2.1c** Ask for clarification and further explanation as needed about the topics and texts under discussion.

©2018 Benchmark Education Company, LLC

Grade 2 • Unit 4 • Week 2 **177**

DAY 2

WRITING TO SOURCES

Student Writing Prompt

Is "Stone Soup" a story you would recommend to your friends? Why or why not? State your opinion in an essay. Supply reasons, based on details from the text, to support your opinion.

Student Objectives

I will be able to:
- Identify and analyze events in a source text.
- Develop reasons based on a text to support an opinion.

Materials

Weekly Presentation: Unit 4, Week 2
- Opinion Essay Planning Chart

Write an Opinion Essay: Reread the Text to Develop Your Reasons (15 MIN.) W.2.8

Engage Thinking

Remind students that yesterday you read and analyzed a writing prompt. Reread the prompt and tell students that today you'll read aloud "Stone Soup." Then you'll guide them in analyzing the story to help them form an opinion statement for their essay and develop reasons for their opinion.

Model (iELD)

Display and distribute copies of the Opinion Essay Planning Chart. Also display "Stone Soup" and have students turn to this selection in their Texts for Close Reading. Read aloud the story.

Then return to the beginning of the story and reread paragraphs 1–5. Model how you use that text to develop reasons to support your opinion. Record each reason on the planning page as you identify it.

Say: *I've read the story and decided that I would recommend it to my friends. On my planning page, I'll circle "would recommend" in the center of the web. Now I have to identify my reasons for recommending the story. I reread the first part of the story and thought about how the villagers were not kind to the stranger. They judged him. I think it's important not to judge people based on their appearance, so I'll write "teaches not to judge" in the first Reason oval.*

Next, reread paragraphs 8–13 of "Stone Soup" and model how you develop a second reason to support your opinion.

Say: *Another thing I liked about the story is that the stranger has a mysterious or magical quality. I'll write "magical" in the second oval.*

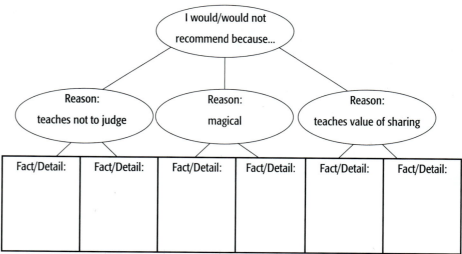

Sample Opinion Essay Planning Chart

178 Grade 2 • Unit 4 • Week 2

WRITING TO SOURCES

WEEK 2 · DAY 2

Peer Practice

Ask students to decide whether they would or would not recommend the story and circle the corresponding response on their planning page. Then have them work with a partner to identify reasons for their opinion. Explain that students should discuss their own ideas but the partners do not have to record the same reasons, as they may have differing views about why they arrived at their opinion.

Share Your Understanding

Bring students together and invite partners to share the reasons for their opinion with the class. Discuss students' ideas, then record this note for the last reason on your own planning page: "teaches the value of sharing." Tell students that they will fill out the rest of the planning page tomorrow.

☑ Quick Write

During independent time, have students respond to the following: *Use the information on your planning page to write the reasons you would give to support your opinion.* Keep in mind that your reasons should be based on information or details from the story. Use students' writing to evaluate their understanding that an opinion essay includes reasons that support the writer's opinion.

(iELD) Integrated ELD

Light Support
Remind students that as they identify reasons for why they would or would not recommend the story, they should refer to the story, rereading parts of it as needed. Have them think about the main idea, setting, characters, and important events: What did they like or dislike about these text elements? Encourage students to discuss their ideas and use them to state reasons in their own words.

Moderate Support
Provide sentence frames to help students use their own words in stating reasons for their opinion. Remind students that their reasons should be based on information from the text. For example: *One reason I recommend the story is that it _____.*

Substantial Support
Encourage students to think about the story elements in "Stone Soup" and how these might help them form the reasons for their opinion about the story. Use sentence frames, such as those in the chart, to help students develop and state their reasons.

Main Idea	A man makes _____. The villagers learn _____.	I like _____.
Characters	The main character is _____.	I like/don't like him because _____.
Setting	The story takes places _____.	I like the setting because _____.
Events	An important event is _____.	I like it because _____.

W.2.8 Recall information from experiences or gather information from provided sources to answer a question.

©2018 Benchmark Education Company, LLC

Grade 2 · Unit 4 · Week 2   **179**

DAY 2

PHONICS & WORD STUDY

r-Controlled Vowels ear, eer, ere (20 MIN.)

RF.2.3b, RF.2.3e, RF.2.3f, L.2.2d

Review r-Controlled Vowels ear, eer, ere

Display the r-controlled /îr/ frieze card. Review the r-controlled vowel sounds spelled **ear** as in **year**, **eer** as in **deer**, and **ere** as in **here**. Point to each spelling-sound.

Say: *What are the letters? What sounds do they stand for?*

Blend Words

Model: near
Display letter cards for near. Model blending.

Say: *This is the letter* **n**. *It stands for* /n/. *These are the letters* **ear**. *They stand for* /îr/. *Listen as I blend these sounds together:* /nîr/, *near. Say the word with me:* **near**.

Practice: fear, dear, year, hear, deer, here
Use the same routine to guide student practice. Discuss the homophones **deer/dear** *and* **hear/here**.

Build Words

Model: year, gear, dear, deer
Display the letter cards for year. Blend the sounds: /yîr/, year.

- Replace the **y** with **g** and repeat with **gear**.
- Replace the **g** with **d** and repeat with **dear**.
- Replace the **a** with **e** and repeat with **deer**.

Practice: far, fear, near, hear, here
Use the same routine to guide student practice.

r-Controlled Vowels ir Frieze Card

Student Objectives

I will be able to:
- Blend, build, and spell words with r-controlled vowels **ear, eer, ere**.
- Practice high-frequency words.
- Read contractions **'t, 's**.

Additional Materials

- Letter cards: **a, d, e, e, f, h, n, r, y**

Weekly Presentation: Unit 4, Week 2
- r-controlled vowels /îr/ frieze card
- **High-frequency word cards:** always, any, blue, buy, city, draw, four, great, how, live

For additional word study/decodable practice, see: *Fox and Cat*, *King Grisly Beard*, and *Here or There?*

180 Grade 2 • Unit 4 • Week 2

©2018 Benchmark Education Company, LLC

PHONICS & WORD STUDY

WEEK 2 · DAY 2

Spelling

Closed Sort: *year, deer, near, clear, here, cheer, fear, ears, hear, steer*
Write and display each word on an index card. Ask students to read and spell each word aloud together. Then make a three-column chart. Place a card for **ear** on the top of column 1, **eer** on the top of column 2, and **ere** on the top of column 3.

Have students place each card in the correct column. When completed, have students read and spell the words in each column aloud together. Ask them to use the words **deer**, **here**, and **hear** in sentences to confirm meanings.

High-Frequency Words (iELD)

Review: *always, any, blue, buy, city, draw, four, great, how, live*
Display the high-frequency word cards. Have students read and spell each word.
Focus on the spellings and meaning of homophones four/for and **blue/blew**. Point out that words ending in the /v/ sound, like **live**, add an **e** at the end (**give**, **love**, **glove**).

Contractions

Model: is not, isn't; he is, he's
Write the words **is not** and **isn't**. Point out **isn't** is a contraction, or shortened way to write the two words **is not**. Explain that when the two words are put together, the letter **o** in **not** is replaced by an apostrophe.

Repeat with the words **he is** and **he's**. Explain that when the two words are put together, the letter **i** in **is** is replaced by an apostrophe.

Practice: do not, don't; could not, couldn't; will not, won't; she is, she's
Use the same routine to guide student practice. Have students write sentences using the contractions.

(iELD) Integrated ELD

Light Support
Students echo-read the word bank below with the high-frequency words.

always	blue	city	four	how
any	buy	draw	great	live

Write the words on cards. Hold up a card. Volunteers point to the word in the word bank and read it aloud. Pairs alternate dictating the high-frequency words to each other, and self-check their work using the word bank.

Moderate Support
Students echo-read the word bank below with the high-frequency words.

always	blue	city	four	how
any	buy	draw	great	live

Dictate the high-frequency words. Students repeat after you. Write the words on cards. Hold up a card. Students echo-read. Volunteers point to the word in the word bank and read it aloud.

Substantial Support
Students echo-read the word bank below with the high-frequency words.

always	blue	city	four	how
any	buy	draw	great	live

Students read, spell, and write the words with you. Model using the words in sentences with **because** clauses. Have students complete sentence frames.
Ralph the rat didn't like the city because _____.
Max was having a great time on the farm because _____.

Pairs present original sentences using the target words and **because** clauses.

RF.2.3b Know spelling-sound correspondences for additional common vowel teams. **RF.2.3e** Identify words with inconsistent but common spelling-sound correspondences. **RF.2.3f** Recognize and read grade-appropriate irregularly spelled words. **L.2.2d** Generalize learned spelling patterns when writing words (e.g., cage →badge; boy → boil).

©2018 Benchmark Education Company, LLC

Grade 2 • Unit 4 • Week 2   **181**

DAY 3

SHARED READING

**Texts for Close Reading, p. 17
"Ira and Jeb"**

Student Objectives

I will be able to:
- Read a fable about characters with different points of view.
- Identify and annotate the fable's lesson.

Additional Materials

Weekly Presentation: Unit 4, Week 2

iELD Integrated ELD

Light Support

Choose and list key language from "Ira and Jeb."
played the fiddle, storeroom, winter came, invited him in
Write each phrase on a card. Groups say, write, read, and present original sentences using their assigned cards.

Moderate Support

Students echo-read "Ira and Jeb." Choose and list key language.
planted a garden, pulled the weeds, water it, worked too hard, for a meal
Students use at least two phrases in one original sentence.

Substantial Support

Students echo-read "Ira and Jeb." Choose and list key language. Students echo-read.
brothers, next door, fiddle, lively tune, plenty, porch
Use the illustrations and text and simple phrases and gestures to discuss vocabulary. Students role-play to show comprehension.
Write each phrase on a card. Groups present their assigned cards and then switch cards with another group. Model presenting a card.
Sample modeling: *This says "next door."*
Here it is in the story.
"Next door" means the house next to another house.
Our house is next door to Uncle Bob's house.

Shared Reading (10 MIN.) RF.2.4a, RF.2.4b, RF.2.4c

Introduce the Text

Display "Ira and Jeb." Read aloud the title as you point under the words. Invite students to turn to a partner and make inferences, using the title and illustrations to predict what the text may be about. If necessary, model how you preview a text.

Model Make Inferences and Predictions

Remind students that readers use various strategies when they read, including this unit's focus strategy: making inferences and predictions. Today they will make inferences and predictions before they read while previewing the text.

Sample modeling. The title names two characters. In the illustration, I see two men in front of their houses. One man is working on a garden, and the other is playing music. I predict that the story will be about two men named Ira and Jeb and different things they like to do. I can infer from the illustrations that one of the men is very relaxed and the other one is working hard.

Invite a few students to share their before-reading inferences or predictions with the class.

Model Fluent Reading: Accuracy/Self-Correct iELD

First Reading. Read the text aloud fluently and accurately. Remind students that to read accurately, readers listen for meaning and go back to fix any misread words or skipped words so that the sentences make sense.

Read Aloud. Ask students to read the story aloud with you. Remind them to self-correct as they read.

Transfer Skills to Context: Annotate Genre Feature

Explain to students that this story is a fable because it is short and teaches a lesson. Model rereading the paragraphs and annotating for details related to the fable's lesson.

Sample modeling. *To understand the lesson in this fable, I'll jot down notes about what each character does and thinks. Next to paragraph 1, I'll write:* **Ira works while Jeb plays**. *Next to paragraphs 2 and 3, I'll write:* **Jeb thinks Ira works too hard. Ira thinks Jeb won't have food in winter.** *Next to paragraph 4, I'll write:* **Ira is right!**

Ask students to write a sentence that states the lesson that Jeb learns. They may recognize this fable as a variant of "The Ant and the Grasshopper."

RF.2.4a Read on-level text with purpose and understanding. **RF.2.4b** Read on-level text orally with accuracy, appropriate rate, and expression on successive readings. **RF.2.4c** Use context to confirm or self-correct word recognition and understanding, rereading as necessary.

182   Grade 2 • Unit 4 • Week 2

©2018 Benchmark Education Company, LLC

Build Vocabulary: Identify Real-Life Connections Between Words and Their Uses (10 MIN.) RL.2.4, L.2.5a

EXTENDED READ 1 MINI-LESSON

WEEK 2 · DAY 3

Engage Thinking

We just read "Ira and Jeb." Now we will reread "Stone Soup."

Ask students to recall the story "Stone Soup" as you pantomime different actions, such as stirring the soup, sniffing it, and tasting it. Ask students to name a verb for each action. For example: **stir, mix, swirl, sniff, smell, breathe in, taste, sample, sip.** Explain that these words help readers picture a particular action and that readers can also use the words in their own speech and writing to tell about things they know.

Ask: *What other things can you stir? smell? taste?*

Model

Read aloud paragraph 2 of "Stone Soup." Model ways you can share.

Sample modeling (paragraph 2). *The old man tells the villagers he is looking for "a meal to share." I imagine the man and the villagers eating a meal together. What other things can I share? I can share toys, markers, or a big chair.*

Ask students to use the word **share** *in a sentence.*

Guided Practice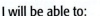

Reread selected sentences from the story. For each word, ask students to tell what the word means in the story's context and to suggest other sentences in which the word shows something they have seen in real life. Pose text-dependent questions and prompts to guide their thinking.

- **dropped** (paragraph 11): *What did the old man do when he "dropped the stone into the pot?" When have you dropped something?*
- **whispered** (14): *Show what the people did when they whispered. Who or what do you know that whispers?*
- **rubbed** (14): *Why did the people rub their bellies? Tell about a time that you rubbed something to clean it.*
- **tasty** (18): *What do you think tasty stone soup is like? What is a food that you think is tasty?*
- **delicious** (27): *The old man made a delicious meal for everyone. What meal have you had that was delicious?*

✓ Show Your Knowledge

During independent time, ask students to find the verb **begged** in paragraph 29. Have them explain what the villagers did when they begged, and write **beg** or **begged** in a new sentence about a real-life situation.

RL.2.4 Describe how words and phrases (e.g., regular beats, alliteration, rhymes, repeated lines) supply rhythm and meaning in a story, poem, or song. **L.2.5a** Identify real-life connections between words and their use (e.g., describe foods that are spicy or juicy).

©2018 Benchmark Education Company, LLC

Grade 2 · Unit 4 · Week 2   183

Texts for Close Reading, pp. 18–25
"Stone Soup"

Student Objectives

I will be able to:
- Understand real-life connections between words and their uses.

Additional Materials

Weekly Presentation: Unit 4, Week 2

iELD Integrated ELD

Light Support

Ask students to find key verbs from "Stone Soup" that show what is happening in the story. Assign verbs to student groups. Students write simple dialogues using their assigned verbs. Students present their dialogues and role-play them.

Moderate Support

Ask students to find key verbs from "Stone Soup" that show what is happening in the story. Assign verbs to student pairs. Pairs write, present, and role-play sentences using their assigned verbs.

Substantial Support

Ask students to find key verbs from "Stone Soup" that show what is happening in the story.

stir, mix, swirl, sniff, smell, breathe in, taste, sample, sip

Write the words on cards. Students echo-read. Discuss meanings. Students role-play to show comprehension.

Ask: *How do you think you would make soup?*
Assign groups verb cards, and have them use those verbs to act out making soup. Volunteers narrate as each group acts out making soup.

DAY 3

EXTENDED READ 1 MINI-LESSON

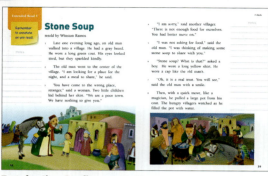

Texts for Close Reading, pp. 18–25
"Stone Soup"

Student Objectives

I will be able to:
- Answer questions about a story.
- Recognize the elements of a story.
- Share my thinking with peers.

Additional Materials

Weekly Presentation: Unit 4, Week 2
- Characters/Feelings Chart

Observation Checklist for Productive Engagement

Is the Productive Engagement Productive?

As groups discuss the structure and characters in the story, look for evidence that they are truly engaged in the task.

Partners are engaged productively if . . .
- ❏ they ask questions and use feedback to address the task.
- ❏ they demonstrate engagement and motivation.
- ❏ they apply strategies with some success.

If the discussion is productive, continue the task. If the discussion is unproductive, end the task and provide support.

Close Reading: Describe the Overall Structure of a Story (15 MIN.) RL.2.1, RL.2.5, SL.2.1a, SL.2.1b, SL.2.1c, SL.2.2

Engage Thinking

Remind students that when they read a story, they can look for answers to the questions **where? when? who? what?** and **how?** Point out that the answers to these questions are the elements found in many stories: setting, characters, problem, events, solution. These elements affect the overall structure of a story. Explain that knowing about story elements helps readers follow the story more closely.

Model

Display and read aloud the close reading prompt and annotation instructions. Model how you think about the prompt.

> **Close Reading Prompt:** In paragraph 1, the author writes "Late one evening long ago, an old man walked into a village." How does this help you visualize the setting at the beginning of the story?
> **Annotate!** Jot down notes in the margin.

Sample modeling (paragraph 1). *The prompt tells me to think about the setting of this story. The setting is where and when a story takes place. The first sentence has information about the setting. "Late one evening long ago" tells when the story happens. "Village" tells where it takes place. I will make a note that I learned about the setting at the beginning of the story.*

Productive Engagement: Peer Group

Organize students into groups of three or four. Each group should designate specific students to be the group's discussion facilitator, scribe, timekeeper, and encourager. Display and read aloud a second close reading prompt.

> **Close Reading Prompt:** The main character in this story is the old man. Who are the other characters in the story? What do their words and actions tell you about how they feel?
> **Annotate!** Underline details about the characters and jot down notes in the margin.

184 Grade 2 • Unit 4 • Week 2

©2018 Benchmark Education Company, LLC

EXTENDED READ 1 MINI-LESSON

Ask students to review the story and annotate it to respond to the prompt. Students should identify the different villagers who participate in the story events and decide on details to underline and margin notes.

Observe students' notes to determine if they need additional modeling or directive feedback. Ask students to use their annotations to fill out the Characters/Feelings chart.

What Characters Say and Do (paragraph)	What Characters Believe or Feel
One woman says the town is too poor to help the stranger. (3) She asks what the stranger is doing. (9)	She feels she can't help, but she is curious about the stone soup.
Another villager tells the stranger to move on because "There is not enough food for ourselves." (4)	The villager believes the town cannot share.
A boy asks what stone soup is. (6) He asks if it is "really for everyone." (15)	He is curious and hungry. He is surprised that a meal can be shared.
The villagers lick their lips and rub their bellies. (14) They are excited as they watch the pot. (18)	They are hungry and imagine a special soup.
One villager adds a cabbage to the pot. (19)	He believes he has enough and can spare one cabbage. He is curious about the stone soup. He feels generous.
The butcher adds a leg of lamb to the pot. (21)	He is curious about the soup. He wants to help.
The villagers beg the old man to stay. (29)	They believe he has the power to make a magic soup.

Sample Characters/Feelings Chart

Share Your Understanding

Call on students to share their answers to the close reading question. Guide a discussion of why the villagers act as they do at the beginning, middle, and end of the story. Remind students to listen carefully to each speaker and to ask questions if they need further explanation. Provide additional modeling, corrective feedback, or validation based on students' responses.

☑ Show Your Knowledge

During independent time, ask students to write two or more sentences explaining why the villagers bring items to add to the soup.

Challenge Activity. Provide a blank story map for students to fill out showing the elements of setting, main character, problem, events, and solution.

---

iELD Integrated ELD

Light Support
Say: *We are going to talk about story elements.* Present an outline of the chart below.

Story Element	Response

Discuss how to set up the chart. As you elicit responses, record the chart headings and story elements for the first column. Discuss story elements with students and elicit responses for the second column.

Moderate Support
Display the chart in Light Support. Elicit the story elements and record them on the chart in the first column. Students echo-read.
Discuss story elements with students and elicit responses for the second column.

Substantial Support
Review story elements using the chart below. Model formulating questions about the story elements, using the verb **to do** and the verb **to be.**
Ask: *What is the setting?*
Where does the story _____?
When does the story _____?
Who are the _____?
Who is _____?
What is the _____?
As you elicit responses, record them in the chart.

Story Element	Response
Setting (when/where)	
Main character	
Other important characters	
Important events	
Problem	
Solution	

Write sentence frames on the board. Students complete sentence frames to form responses about the story elements for "Stone Soup."
The setting is _____.
The story takes place _____.
The main character is _____.
Other important characters are _____.
The problem is _____.
The solution is _____.

RL.2.1 Ask and answer such questions as who, what, where, when, why, and how to demonstrate understanding of key details in a text. **RL.2.5** Describe the overall structure of a story, including describing how the beginning introduces the story and the ending concludes the action. **SL.2.1a** Follow agreed-upon rules for discussions (e.g., gaining the floor in respectful ways, listening to others with care, speaking one at a time about the topics and texts under discussion). **SL.2.1b** Build on others' talk in conversations by linking their comments to the remarks of others. **SL.2.1c** Ask for clarification and further explanation as needed about the topics and texts under discussion. **SL.2.2** Recount or describe key ideas or details from a text read aloud or information presented orally or through other media.

DAY 3

WRITING TO SOURCES

Write an Opinion Essay: Use Facts and Details to Support Your Opinion

(15 MIN.) W.2.5

Student Writing Prompt

Is "Stone Soup" a story you would recommend to your friends? Why or why not? State your opinion in an essay. Supply reasons, based on details from the text, to support your opinion.

Student Objectives

I will be able to:
- Take notes from a source to support reasons for an opinion.
- Share my ideas in collaborative conversation and in writing.

Materials

Weekly Presentation: Unit 4, Week 2
- Opinion Essay Planning Chart

Engage Thinking

Remind students that they have formed an opinion and developed reasons for why they would or would not recommend "Stone Soup" to friends. Tell them that now you'll show them how to use events and details from the story to support their opinion.

Model

Display "Stone Soup" and the Opinion Essay Planning Chart that you began filling out yesterday. Have students take out their copies of the planning page. Then think aloud to model how to use evidence from the story to support the reasons for your opinion.

Sample think-aloud. *Yesterday I used my planning page to note my opinion about recommending "Stone Soup" and jotted down reasons for my opinion. The first reason I listed is "teaches not to judge." Now I need to reread the story to find the text evidence I used to determine this reason and write those events or details in the Fact/Detail boxes. Here's what I'll write in the first box: "When the old man comes to the village, the people turn him away." I recall that the villagers have a different opinion about the man at the end of the story, so I write this in the second box: "At the end of the story, the villagers beg him to stay." I connected the events from the beginning and end of the story to support my reason that it teaches readers not to judge others.*

Sample think-aloud, continued. *The next reason I noted for my opinion is that the main character is "magical." I reread paragraph 8 and imagined the man's actions as being like a magician. He doesn't tell what he's doing as he pulls a large pot from his coat and takes a large stone from a bag. It's a mystery! I'll use my own words to write these details and events on my planning chart.*

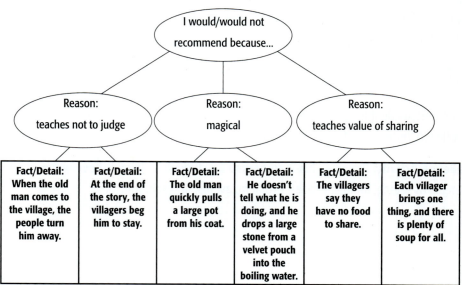

Sample Opinion Essay Planning Chart

Peer Practice

Have students work in small groups to find text evidence to support the reasons they noted on their planning page yesterday. Remind them to use their own words as they record the events and details that support and explain their reasons.

Share Your Understanding

Bring students together and invite partners to share the evidence they cited to support one of their reasons. Then point out and discuss the last reason on your own planning page and the text evidence that you recorded to support it.

 Quick Write

During independent time, have students answer this question: *Based on your planning chart, are you now ready to write an opinion essay?* Why or why not? Use students' writing to evaluate their understanding of the information that should be included in an opinion essay.

Light Support
Guide students, as needed, to connect and discuss related ideas found in the beginning and end of the story (people will not share food; people contribute items to create a soup). Encourage them to use their own words to record events/details such as these on their planning chart to note reasons for their opinion.

Moderate Support
Encourage students to identify and discuss details/events at the beginning and end of the story and help them connect the related events. Guide students in using complete sentences and key words to fill in the event/detail boxes in their planning chart. Provide sentence frames, as needed. For example:

At the beginning of the story…	At the end of the story…
The people do not _____.	Each person _____.

Substantial Support
Point out the third reason listed on your planning chart (teaches the value of sharing). Use words, pictures, and gestures to help students understand the meaning of share. Then help them locate relevant parts of the text to support and explain this reason for your opinion. Ask simple leading questions to help students cite text evidence. For example:
Did the villagers share their food with the stranger?
What did each person bring?
Did everyone get some soup?

W.2.5 With guidance and support from adults and peers, focus on a topic and strengthen writing as needed by revising and editing.

DAY 3

PHONICS & WORD STUDY

Texts for Close Reading, p. 26
"City Mouse and Country Mouse"

Student Objectives

I will be able to:
- Blend, spell, and read words with r-controlled vowels **ear, eer, ere**.
- Read word study (decodable) text.
- Practice high-frequency words.

Additional Materials

- Letter cards: **a, c, e, e, f, h, l, n, r**
- r-controlled vowels /ir/ frieze card

Weekly Presentation: Unit 4, Week 2
- High-frequency word cards: **always, any, blue, buy, city, draw, four, great, how, live**
- High-frequency word cards: **long, now, our, some, them, through, upon, was, when, work**

For additional word study/decodable practice, see: *Fox and Cat, King Grisly Beard,* and *Here or There?*

Monitor Student Reading of Word Study (Decodable) Text

As students read the word study (decodable) text and answer questions, ask yourself these questions:

Are students able to . . .
- ❏ blend and read r-controlled vowel **ear, eer, ere** words in the text?
- ❏ read new high-frequency words with automaticity?
- ❏ demonstrate comprehension of the text by answering text-based questions?

Based on your observations, you may wish to support students' fluency, automaticity, and comprehension with additional word study reading practice during intervention time.

r-Controlled Vowels ear, eer, ere

(10 MIN.) RL.2.3, RF.2.3b, RF.2.3c, RF.2.3e, RF.2.3f, L.2.2d

Blend Words

Practice: fear, near, here, cheer, clear
Display pocket chart letter cards for the word **fear**. Model how to blend the sounds to say the word. Use the same routine with other r-controlled vowel **ear, eer, ere** words to guide student practice.

Read Word Study (Decodable) Text

Introduce the Text
Read the title "City Mouse and Country Mouse" aloud. Ask students who have read or heard another version of the story to retell it.

Read the Text
Ask students to read the text. If students need modeling, guide them to blend decodable words and read high-frequency words. You may wish to conduct a second reading, having partners read to each other while you circulate and monitor the reading.

Connect Phonics to Comprehension
Ask some or all of the following questions:

- *What did the city mouse think of the country? Why?*
- *Where did the mice find food in the city?*
- *Why did the country mouse return home?*

Spelling

Word Clues
Write the word clues. Have students write the spelling word that goes with each clue.

1. parts of your head (**ears**)
2. 12 months (**year**)
3. close to (**near**)
4. an animal with horns (**deer**)

High-Frequency Words

Practice: *always, any, blue, buy, city, draw, four, great, how, live*
Draw a ladder with ten rungs. Write a high-frequency word on each rung. Have students take turns climbing the ladder by reading the words.

Review: *long, now, our, some, them, through, upon, was, when, work*

RL.2.3 Describe how characters in a story respond to major events and challenges. **RF.2.3b** Know spelling-sound correspondences for additional common vowel teams. **RF.2.3c** Decode regularly spelled two-syllable words with long vowels. **RF.2.3e** Identify words with inconsistent but common spelling-sound correspondences. **RF.2.3f** Recognize and read grade-appropriate irregularly spelled words. **L.2.2d** Generalize learned spelling patterns when writing words (e.g., cage →badge; boy → boil).

Shared Reading (10 MIN.) RF.2.3b, RF.2.4a, RF.2.4b, RF.2.4c

Reread for Fluency: Accuracy/Self-Correct (iELD)

Partner Reading. Assign partners to reread "Ira and Jeb" to each other. They may alternate paragraphs and then switch roles. Remind them to monitor their reading so that they can go back to correct any misread words.

Collaborative Conversation: Make Inferences and Predictions

Recall for students how you make inferences and predictions based on information from the text. Tell students that today they will work in pairs to make inferences and predictions themselves. If necessary, pose text-dependent questions to guide their thinking. For example:

- What can you infer about Ira after reading this fable?
- What is the lesson, or moral, of this fable? Use text evidence to support your inference.
- Based on the evidence in the text, do you think Jeb will work more or less in the future?

Transfer Skills to Context: Annotate to Identify Narrator

Model annotating for the voice of the narrator.

Sample modeling (paragraph 1). *The story begins with the words, "Once there were two brothers." The narrator sounds like a storyteller, getting listeners interested in learning more about these different brothers. I'll jot down a note in the margin about how to read this part:* **Show difference between brothers.**

Read aloud paragraph 1 to express the contrast between the work of one brother and the play of the other. Invite students to read aloud the first sentence of paragraph 4 to express a similar contrast.

Transfer Skills to Context: Long e Vowel Team Syllable Patterns

Point to the following words in paragraphs 1 and 2 of the story and ask students to read each word aloud: **each, weeds**. Ask students to identify the letter or letters that spell the sound /ee/. Then tell students to find more words with long **e** in paragraph 3 and name the vowel letter(s) that spell the sound (**eat, meal**).

RF.2.3b Know spelling-sound correspondences for additional common vowel teams. **RF.2.4a** Read on-level text with purpose and understanding. **RF.2.4b** Read on-level text orally with accuracy, appropriate rate, and expression on successive readings. **RF.2.4c** Use context to confirm or self-correct word recognition and understanding, rereading as necessary.

©2018 Benchmark Education Company, LLC

SHARED READING

WEEK 2 • DAY 4

Texts for Close Reading, p. 17
"Ira and Jeb"

Student Objective

I will be able to:
- Identify and annotate the narrator's voice.
- Recognize words with long **e** vowel team syllable patterns.

Additional Materials

Weekly Presentation: Unit 4, Week 2

iELD Integrated ELD

Light Support
If ELLs have trouble reading aloud to each other with accuracy and understanding, scaffold pre-reading lessons for "Ira and Jeb." As students participate in Shared Reading, assess their needs for future lessons. Write, discuss, and sequence key events with key vocabulary, such as **put them in the storeroom, had plenty to eat, work too hard.**
Partners read and discuss meaningful chunks, vocabulary, and language.

Moderate Support
Write, discuss, and sequence key events with key vocabulary, such as **lived next door, sat on his porch, played a lively tune, played the fiddle, winter came.**
Students echo-read key passages and partner-read.

Substantial Support
Write, discuss, and sequence key events with key vocabulary, such as **planted a garden, water it, pulled the weeds, gathered vegetables, invited him in, learned my lesson.**
Students role-play key vocabulary and key events to show comprehension.
Model reading aloud key chunks. Students echo-read.

Grade 2 • Unit 4 • Week 2   189

DAY 4

EXTENDED READ 1 MINI-LESSON

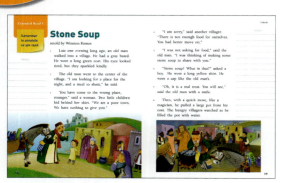

Texts for Close Reading, pp. 18–25
"Stone Soup"

Student Objectives

I will be able to:
- Describe the overall structure of a story.
- Share my ideas cooperatively with my peers.

Additional Materials

Weekly Presentation: Unit 4, Week 2
- Character's Challenge and Responses Chart

Close Reading: Describe How Characters Respond to Major Events and Challenges (15 MIN.) RL.2.1, RL.2.3, SL.2.1a, SL.2.1b, SL.2.1c

Engage Thinking

Remind students that stories often begin with a problem that a character wants to solve or a goal that a character wants to reach. The events in the middle of the story tell how the character tries to solve the problem or reach the goal. The end of the story tells whether the goal was reached or the problem was solved.

Model

Display and read aloud the close reading prompt and annotation instructions. Think aloud as you respond to the prompt, as shown in the sample.

> **Close Reading Prompt:** In paragraph 2, the old man says to the villagers, "I am looking for a place for the night, and a meal to share." What challenge is the old man facing?
> **Annotate!** Jot down notes in the margin.

Sample modeling (paragraphs 1–3). *To answer the question in the prompt, I'll start by rereading paragraph 2. I'll also reread the paragraphs before and after to find out more about his challenge. I learn that the old man's eyes "looked tired." I learn that when he asks for a place to sleep and a meal, a woman tells him that the poor village "has nothing to give you." The old man's challenge is clear to me. I'll jot a note in the margin:* **The old man is tired and hungry, but he has no place to sleep and no food. He asks for help and is turned down.**

Continue reviewing the story to analyze the old man's actions and to jot margin notes. You may want to show your observations in a Character's Challenge and Responses Chart.

Character's Challenge (Beginning)	Character's Responses (Middle)
The old man is tired and hungry, but he has no place to sleep and no food. He asks for help and is turned down.	1. He makes the villagers curious about his stone soup. 2. He adds a special stone to water boiling in a pot. 3. He describes a tasty soup that would be even better with added ingredients. 4. He slyly encourages the villagers to contribute vegetables and meat to the soup. 5. He shares the delicious soup with everyone.
Result (End): The old man is not hungry anymore, and he is invited to stay in the village.	

Character's Challenge and Responses Chart

WEEK 2 · DAY 4

⚙ Productive Engagement: Peer Group

Organize students into groups of three or four. Each group should designate specific students to be the group's discussion facilitator, scribe, timekeeper, and encourager. Display and read aloud a second close reading prompt.

> **Close Reading Purpose:** In paragraph 3, a villager responds to the old man by saying, "We are a poor town. We have nothing to give you." How does this response describe the challenges the villagers face?
> **Annotate!** Jot down notes in the margin.

Ask students to reread paragraph 3 and think about why the woman says they have nothing to give. Point out that they can use their ideas to make a statement of the villagers' challenges. After students jot down their margin notes, they can fill out a chart to identify "Characters' Challenges," "Characters' Responses," and "Results."

Share Your Understanding

Call on students to share their answers to the close reading prompt. Use this opportunity to provide additional modeling, corrective feedback, or validation based on responses.

Students should have noted that the villagers faced the challenge of being hungry and believing they had no food to share. With the stranger's help, they responded by joining together to contribute what they could and make a soup that could feed everyone. (middle of story) As a result, they learned the value of sharing, and "they never went hungry again." (end of story)

☑ Show Your Knowledge

During independent time, ask students to reread paragraph 26 and think about the old man's words, "That's all we need to make the best stone soup ever." Ask students to write a sentence explaining why the old man says those words.

RL.2.1 Ask and answer such questions as who, what, where, when, why, and how to demonstrate understanding of key details in a text. **RL.2.3** Describe how characters in a story respond to major events and challenges. **SL.2.1a** Follow agreed-upon rules for discussions (e.g., gaining the floor in respectful ways, listening to others with care, speaking one at a time about the topics and texts under discussion). **SL.2.1b** Build on others' talk in conversations by linking their comments to the remarks of others. **SL.2.1c** Ask for clarification and further explanation as needed about the topics and texts under discussion.

©2018 Benchmark Education Company, LLC

EXTENDED READ 1 MINI-LESSON

iELD Integrated ELD

Light Support

Use "Stone Soup." Have students echo-read the Character's Challenge and Responses Chart. Support students as they identify how the old man responds to his challenge. Review the following verb phrases that students might want to use when answering questions: **makes the villagers, encourages the villagers, is able to, make soup, probably thinks.**

Ask: *What is the old man's challenge/problem?*
List students' responses and have students echo-read.
Ask: *How does the old man handle his challenge? How does he succeed?*
Provide sentence frames.
The old man makes the villagers _____.
The old man encourages the villagers _____.
The old man is able to make soup, because _____.
The old man probably thinks _____ because _____.
Help students put it all together. Provide a sentence frame.
Since the old man was able to _____, he was able to overcome his challenge _____.

Moderate Support

Review and use verbs and verb phrases, such as **cooks, asks for, adds to the soup, probably thinks.**
Ask: *What is the old man's challenge/problem? How does the old man handle his challenge? How does he succeed?*
Provide and practice sentence frames that will help students answer questions.
The old man cooks _____.
The old man asks for _____.
The old man adds _____ to the soup because _____.
I guess the old man probably thinks _____ because _____.
Help students put it all together. Provide a sentence frame.
The old man overcomes his challenge _____ by _____.

Substantial Support

Review and use verbs and verb phrases, such as **says, looks, has, talks to.**
Ask: *What is the old man's challenge/problem? How does the old man handle his challenge? How does he succeed?*
Provide, have students echo-read, and practice sentence frames that answer the questions.
The old man says _____.
The old man looks _____.
The old man has _____.
The old man talks to _____.
The old man makes soup by _____.
Help students put it all together. Provide a sentence frame. *The old man's challenge is _____ and he succeeds because _____.*

Grade 2 • Unit 4 • Week 2   **191**

DAY 4

WRITING TO SOURCES

Student Writing Prompt

Is "Stone Soup" a story you would recommend to your friends? Why or why not? State your opinion in an essay. Supply reasons, based on details from the text, to support your opinion.

Student Objectives

I will be able to:
- Use a planning form to finalize a plan for writing an opinion essay
- Share my ideas in collaborative conversation and in writing.

Materials

Weekly Presentation: Unit 4, Week 2
- Opinion Essay Anchor Chart
- Opinion Essay Planning Chart

Write an Opinion Essay: Plan and Organize Your Opinion Essay (15 MIN.) W.2.5

Engage Thinking

Explain that students should now be prepared to write an opinion essay. During the week, they have formed an opinion, reread "Stone Soup" to develop reasons for their opinion, and found text evidence to explain and support each reason. Tell students that today you will show them how they can use their planning page as an organization guide for their essay.

Model iELD

Display and review the Opinion Essay Anchor Chart. Then display the Opinion Essay Planning Page and have students take out their copies. Use a think-aloud to show how you plan an opinion essay.

Sample think-aloud (opinion statement). *To begin, I reread the prompt then look at how I can use my planning page to organize my writing. I need an opinion statement that tells whether or not I would recommend "Stone Soup" and briefly explains why. I circled that I would recommend the story and I filled in three reasons for my opinion. So my opinion statement could be: "I would recommend "Stone Soup" to my friends because it teaches valuable lessons, and I like the mysterious main character." To help me organize, I'll write "Opinion Statement" next to the center hub of my page.*

Sample think-aloud (reason 1). *The prompt tells me to base the reasons for my opinion on details from the story. On my planning page, I filled in evidence from the story that supports each of my three reasons. I decide I have enough information to write one paragraph for each reason. These three paragraphs will make up the body of my essay. In the first paragraph, I'll focus on the first reason, "teaches not to judge," and use my notes under Facts/Details to give text evidence about that reason. I'll write "Body Paragraph 1" next to the first Reason oval as a reminder to take information from here for my first paragraph.*

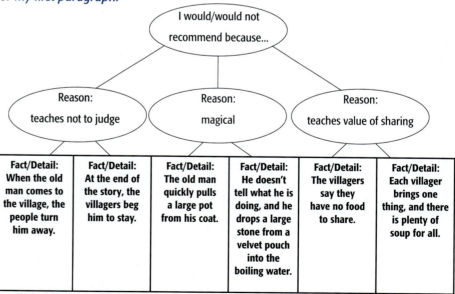

Sample Opinion Essay Planning Chart

192 Grade 2 • Unit 4 • Week 2

©2018 Benchmark Education Company, LLC

WRITING TO SOURCES

WEEK 2 • DAY 4

Peer Practice

Have students work with a partner to plan for writing their essay, following your model and using their own planning chart. Monitor the partners as they plan and discuss, reminding them to include all the parts of an opinion essay: an opinion statement, reasons for the opinion and text evidence to support each reason, and a conclusion.

Share Your Understanding

Bring students together and invite partners to share their plans for the opinion essay. Use this time as a reteaching opportunity if students need additional modeling or guidance.

Quick Write

Have students independently answer this question: *Why should you use your planning page to organize your writing before beginning the opinion essay?* Use students' writing to evaluate their understanding of the importance of planning their writing.

---

iELD Integrated ELD

Tell students they will need to use formal language in their essays, then help them understand the difference between informal and formal language in writing.

Light Support
Write a sentence that uses informal language, such as *I'd tell my friends they just have to read this story!* Ask students to restate the sentence using formal language. Then help them identify examples of informal language in their notes and restate them using formal language.

Moderate Support
Present a sentence, such as: *The new guy in town was a mysterious dude.* Help students identify the informal language in the sentence and then restate the sentence using formal language. For example: *The stranger was a mysterious man.* Provide additional examples to help reinforce students' understanding of informal and formal language.

Substantial Support
Tell students that they use different language when speaking with their friends than when speaking with adults. Likewise, their notes may be different from their actual writing of the opinion essay. Explain the difference between informal and formal language, then provide sentence frames to give students practice in changing sentences to formal language. For example:

> **Informal:** *I'd tell my pals to read the story.*
> **Formal:** *I would _____ "Stone Soup" to _____.*
> (recommend, my friends)

W.2.5 With guidance and support from adults and peers, focus on a topic and strengthen writing as needed by revising and editing.

DAY 4

PHONICS & WORD STUDY

r-Controlled Vowels ear, eer, ere (20 MIN.)

RF.2.3b, RF.2.3c, RF.2.3d, RF.2.3e, RF.2.3f, L.2.2d

Student Objectives

I will be able to:
- Blend and spell words with r-controlled vowels **ear, eer, ere**.
- Read high-frequency words.

Additional Materials

- r-controlled vowels /îr/ frieze card

Weekly Presentation: Unit 4, Week 2
- High-frequency word cards: **always, any, blue, buy, city, draw, four, great, how, live**

For additional word study/decodable practice, see: *Fox and Cat, King Grisly Beard,* and *Here or There?*

Read Multisyllabic Words

Model: hearing

Explain that when an r-controlled vowel spelling such as **ear, eer,** *or* **ere** *appears in a long word, the spelling acts as a team and must remain in the same syllable. Model using the word* **hearing**.

- Write the word **hear** and point out the r-controlled vowel spelling **ear**.
- Add the suffix **-ing**.
- Circle the vowel spellings **ear** and **i**. Tell students you will divide the word before the suffix (ending): **hear/ing**.
- Blend the syllables to read the word.

Practice: fearful, nearer, nearest, clearest, cheering, yearly

Use the same routine to guide student practice. Point out the suffix in each word.

Spelling

Categories

Write the groups of words. Read the words, and ask students to complete each category with a spelling word. Ask students to come up with other category groups for the remaining spelling words.

1. moose, bear, _____ (**deer**)
2. week, month, _____ (**year**)
3. scared, afraid, _____ (**fear**)
4. see, smell, _____ (**hear**)

High-Frequency Words

Review: *always, any, blue, buy, city, draw, four, great, how, live*

Display the high-frequency word cards. Read each word and have students repeat the word aloud together and spell it. Have students sit in a circle. Pass the cards, one at a time. Each student reads the word and uses it in a sentence before passing the card.

RF.2.3b Know spelling-sound correspondences for additional common vowel teams. **RF.2.3c** Decode regularly spelled two-syllable words with long vowels. **RF.2.3d** Decode words with common prefixes and suffixes. **RF.2.3e** Identify words with inconsistent but common spelling-sound correspondences. **RF.2.3f** Recognize and read grade-appropriate irregularly spelled words. **L.2.2d** Generalize learned spelling patterns when writing words (e.g., cage →badge; boy → boil).

Shared Reading (10 MIN.) RL.2.1, RF.2.4b, L.2.1e, L.2.6

Make Inferences and Predictions

Remind students that you showed them how you made inferences and predictions before and during reading. Students also practiced making inferences and predictions while they read the story. Tell them that today you will reread the fable and students will make inferences and predictions after they read.

Sample think-aloud. *In this fable, the Ralph lives in the city and longs for the country farm life and Max lives on a farm and longs for the city. Based on the fable, do you think Ralph and Max will be pleased with the "switch"?*

Transfer Skills to Context: Annotate Points of View

Explain to students that Ralph has a point of view about the city, and Max has a point of view about the farm. Underline the sentences that give Ralph's point of view: "Ralph didn't like city life. He wanted to live on a quiet farm." Ask students to underline the sentences that give Max's point of view. Together, write a sentence that describes how both characters' points of view change at the end.

Transfer Skills to Context: Adverbs (iELD)

Remind students that a word that tells how something is done is called an adverb. Tell students to reread the third sentence in paragraph 2. Then ask them to identify the word that describes how the horses neigh. Explain that **loudly** is an adverb in that sentence. Together, suggest adverbs that could describe how Max "prowled the barn" and "dodged enormous horses."

Build and Reflect

Ask students to review "Stone Soup" as they think about the villagers changing their points of view and have students complete the "Build, Reflect, Write" activity on page 27 of their Texts for Close Reading.

SHARED READING

WEEK 2 • DAY 5

Texts for Close Reading, p. 16
"A Good Switch!"

Student Objectives

I will be able to:
- Read a fable.
- Explain what adverbs describe.

Additional Materials

Weekly Presentation: Unit 4, Week 2

iELD Integrated ELD

Light Support
Ask: *What does an adverb tell us?*
Add the suffix **-ly** to each adjective in the chart below to create adverbs.

Adjective	Adverb
silent	
excited	
safe	

Groups complete sentence frames using the adverbs.
Ralph walked _____ in the barn _____, because _____. Max prowled _____ in the subway tunnels _____.

Moderate Support
Add the suffix **-ly** to each adjective in the chart below to create adverbs.

Adjective	Adverb
soft	
curious	
enormous	

Ask: *How did Ralph prowl the subway?* **How did the trains move?**

Substantial Support
Add the suffix **-ly** to each adjective in the chart below to create adverbs.

Adjective	Adverb
quick	
loud	
quiet	

Ask: *How did Max look for food? How did Ralph dodge the trains?*

RL.2.1 Ask and answer such questions as who, what, where, when, why, and how to demonstrate understanding of key details in a text. **RF.2.4b** Read on-level text orally with accuracy, appropriate rate, and expression on successive readings. **L.2.1e** Use adjectives and adverbs, and choose between them depending on what is to be modified. **L.2.6** Use words and phrases acquired through conversations, reading and being read to, and responding to texts, including using adjectives and adverbs to describe (e.g., *When other kids are happy that makes me happy*).

©2018 Benchmark Education Company, LLC

Grade 2 • Unit 4 • Week 2   195

DAY 5

CROSS-TEXT MINI-LESSON

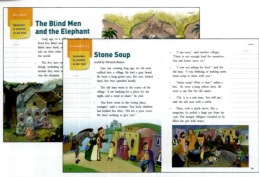

Texts for Close Reading, pp. 6–9 "The Blind Men and the Elephant" and pp. 18–25 "Stone Soup"

Student Objectives

I will be able to:
- Identify details in two stories that describe their lessons.
- Explain how the story lessons are alike.
- Follow the rules for group discussion.

Additional Materials

Weekly Presentation: Unit 4, Week 2
- Making Connections Chart

Close Reading: Compare and Contrast the Central Message in Two Stories (15 MIN.) RL.2.1, RL.2.2, SL.2.1a, SL.2.1b, SL.2.1c, SL.2.2, SL.2.3

Engage Thinking

Remind students that folktales often end with characters learning a lesson. Discuss with students what a "lesson" in a folktale is. Ask them to think about folktales and fables they have read independently. Confirm that they understand that the lesson is about how to behave—being honest, for example, or sharing with others.

Model

Say: *In paragraph 30 of "Stone Soup" the author states, "The villagers learned the magic of sharing and they never went hungry again." How is this similar to the lesson in "The Blind Men and the Elephant?" Annotate both selections by circling key details that identify the lessons.*

Reread to Find Text Evidence

Before students reread, ask them to circle the last sentence of each folktale. Suggest that they start thinking about the lesson that it teaches as they go back to find and circle related details.

Guided Practice

Display and distribute a blank Making Connections Chart. Give students time to fill out the chart. Observe students' conversations. Use your observations to determine the level of gradual release instruction your students may need.

Details about the Lesson in "The Blind Men and the Elephant" (paragraph)	Details about the Lesson in "Stone Soup" (paragraph)
"The Rajah was a kind and wise ruler. He encouraged the men to examine the elephant and learn more about it."(3)	"I am looking for a place for the night, and a meal to share." (2)
Each man felt a different part of the elephant and decided that the whole elephant was like that. (4–8)	"We are a poor town. We have nothing to give you." (3)
"Then the men began arguing, because each thought he was right." (9)	"There is not enough food for ourselves. You had better move on." (4)
"To know the elephant, you must put all the parts together." (9)	One villager added cabbage. (19) The butcher added a leg of lamb. (21) Several villagers "found a turnip or carrot and added them to the soup." (25)
	"Everyone in the village who wanted stone soup had a big bowlful." (27)
	"No one went to bed hungry that night." (29)
	"The villagers learned the magic of sharing and they never went hungry again." (30)
Connections: Both folktales teach the lesson that it's important to share and work together to solve problems. In "The Blind Men and the Elephant" the men argue because each one thinks he is right. But they're all right—if they share and combine their information and points of view, they succeed in gaining a better understanding of what an elephant is like. In "Stone Soup," each villager is hungry, and everyone feels poor. But when they combine their food together in a soup to share, they learn that they all have enough food.	

Sample Making Connections Chart

CROSS-TEXT MINI-LESSON

WEEK 2 · DAY 5

Share Your Understanding

Call on students to share their answers to the close reading question. Invite students to ask questions to clarify what speakers are saying. Remind students to follow classroom rules for discussion and to link their ideas to previous comments.

Reinforce or Reaffirm the Strategy

Provide modeling and/or engage students in self-reflection to build metacognitive awareness.

IF ...	THEN ...
Students need support to connect story details to the lessons in two stories ...	**Model to reinforce the strategy.** *I know that a story lesson is what characters and readers learn from the story. The lesson in "The Blind Men and the Elephant" is stated by the rajah. He tells the men that they must put their knowledge together to understand an elephant. From his words, I can tell that the story teaches us the importance of working together and sharing our points of view. In "Stone Soup," the story ends with a sentence about "the magic of sharing." I can tell that this story also teaches us the importance of putting together what we have so that everyone can share it.*
Students independently connect story details to the lessons in two stories ...	**Invite partners or small groups to reflect on or extend their ideas by discussing another question:** *If the rajah were to visit the village in "Stone Soup," what might he tell the villagers?*

☑ Show Your Knowledge

During independent time, ask students to reread paragraph 4 of "The Blind Men and the Elephant" and paragraph 4 of "Stone Soup." Ask them to write one or two sentences about how the points of view of the blind man and the villager are similar. Use students' writing to assess their ability to make a cross-text comparison.

---

iELD Integrated ELD

Light Support
Students echo-read and discuss the chart in Guided Practice. Students complete the sentence frames to compare the story lessons.
Even though both stories have lessons about _____, the lessons are different, because _____ is about _____, while _____ is about _____.

Moderate Support
Students read and discuss the chart in Guided Practice. Ask questions to check students' understanding of the chart.
Ask: *How does the chart help you? What information does the chart provide?*
Pairs complete the sentence frames to compare and contrast the story lessons. Assist as needed.
Both _____ and _____ are similar, because _____.
Since _____ teaches us _____, but _____ teaches us _____, the lessons are different.

Substantial Support
Students echo-read and discuss the chart in Guided Practice. Ask questions to check students' understanding of the chart.
Ask: *How does the chart help you? What information does the chart provide?*
Choose, list, explain, and have students echo-read key vocabulary, such as **lessons, work together, argue, thinks he is right, share their thoughts, share their food.**
Help students compare and contrast the story lessons.
They are similar, because both lessons teach the importance of _____.
The lessons are different, because _____ is about _____, while _____ is about _____.

RL.2.1 Ask and answer such questions as who, what, where, when, why, and how to demonstrate understanding of key details in a text. **RL.2.2** Recount stories, including fables and folktales from diverse cultures, and determine their central message, lesson, or moral. **SL.2.1a** Follow agreed-upon rules for discussions (e.g., gaining the floor in respectful ways, listening to others with care, speaking one at a time about the topics and texts under discussion). **SL.2.1b** Build on others' talk in conversations by linking their comments to the remarks of others. **SL.2.1c** Ask for clarification and further explanation as needed about the topics and texts under discussion. **SL.2.2** Recount or describe key ideas or details from a text read aloud or information presented orally or through other media. **SL.2.3** Ask and answer questions about what a speaker says in order to clarify comprehension, gather additional information, or deepen understanding of a topic or issue.

©2018 Benchmark Education Company, LLC

Grade 2 · Unit 4 · Week 2   **197**

DAY 5

WRITING TO SOURCES

Student Writing Prompt

Is "Stone Soup" a story you would recommend to your friends? Why or why not? State your opinion in an essay. Supply reasons, based on details from the text, to support your opinion.

Student Objectives

I will be able to:
- Form and use contractions.
- Identify informal and formal contractions.
- Share my ideas in collaborative conversation and in writing.

Additional Materials

Weekly Presentation: Unit 4, Week 2
- Chart paper and markers
- Formal Contractions Modeling Chart
- Informal Contractions Modeling Chart
- Revised Modeling Sentences
- Opinion Essay Rubric
- Opinion Essay Checklist
- Opinion Essay Anchor Chart

Opinion Essay Anchor Chart

To write an informative report, writers…
State their opinion
- Clearly state their opinion in the first paragraph.
- Use a first-person point of view with pronouns such as I and my.
- Give reasons for their opinion.
- Include a conclusion.

Use facts and details from a source text
- Determine their opinion about the source text.
- Identify reasons for the opinion.
- Include facts and details from the source text to support their reasons.

Take notes on the source text
- Create an organized notetaking form.
- Record their opinion.
- Take notes in their own words about the facts and details.
- Note character dialogue that supports the opinion and reasons.

Provide a concluding statement
- Include key words and phrases from the opinion statement.
- Restate, but do not repeat, the opinion statement.
- Summarize, without adding new information.

Use conventions of English correctly
- Use adjectives to describe nouns.
- Form and use contractions.

Conventions of Writing: Form and Use Contractions (15 MIN.) L.2.2.c, L.2.3a

Focus the Learning

Write and display the contraction **that's** for students to see. Explain that this word is a formal contraction—it's a shortened version of two words that have been joined together. Point out that the apostrophe means that one or more letters were removed when the two words were merged.

Have student volunteers tell which two words they think were put together to form the contraction **that's**. Then ask them to identify the letter that has been removed and replaced by the apostrophe.

Model

Display and distribute the Formal Contractions Modeling Chart. Then model how to form contractions.

Say: *This chart shows formal contractions. The contractions in each box are made from the word shown at the top of that box. Look at the word **I'm**. This contraction is formed with the words **I** and **am**. The two words have been joined together and the **a** removed to shorten the new word. An apostrophe sits where the missing letter used to be. Now look at **you'd** on the chart. This contraction can mean **you would** or **you had**. For **you would** the apostrophe replaces the letters **woul**. What letters are replaced when **you'd** means **you had**?*

am	are	is, has	would/had
I'm	we're	there's	you'd
	you're	what's	she'd
	they're	it's	I'd
		he's	that'd
have	**will**	**not**	
you've	you'll	wasn't	
we've	I'll	can't	
I've	he'll	don't	
could've	that'll	shouldn't	

Formal Contractions Modeling Chart

Say: *Sometimes when speaking casually to each other, we use informal contractions, such as **gonna**, which is a short way of saying **going to**. This chart shows other informal contractions. Authors rarely use informal contractions, but they might use informal contractions in dialogue so that the words their characters say sounds like real speech. Look at the second sentence in the second paragraph in "Stone Soup." Here, the old man uses the words **I am**, but the author could have used the contraction **I'm** instead to make the speech sound more natural.*

Informal Contractions	
going to	gonna
want a/to	wanna
am/is/are not	ain't
let me	lemme

198 Grade 2 • Unit 4 • Week 2

©2018 Benchmark Education Company, LLC

could have	coulda

Informal Contractions Modeling Chart

Peer Practice

Have students work with a partner to identify sentences on pages 18–19 in "Stone Soup" where a contraction might be used. Have them discuss how the contractions they suggest using are formed.

Paragraph	Sentence(s)	Rewritten Sentence
2	2	"**I'm** looking for a place for the night, and a meal to share," he said.
3	1	"**You've** come to the wrong place, stranger," said a woman.
3	3–4	"**We're** a poor town. **We've** nothing to give."
4	1–3	"**I'm** sorry," said another villager. "There's not enough food for ourselves. You'd better move on."
5	1	"I **wasn't** asking for food," said the old man.
6	2	"**What's** that?" asked a boy.
7	1–2	"Oh, **it's** a real treat. **You'll** see," said the old man with a smile.

Sample Revised Modeling Sentences

Share Your Understanding

Bring students together and invite the partners to share the sentences they found. Have them read aloud the original sentence then read it again, this time using the contraction.

Introduce the Rubric

Tell students that next week they will write their opinion essay and hand in a final copy. Explain that you will grade their final work using a rubric. Display the rubric and review how to use it. Point out that the rubric reflects the key points on the opinion essay anchor chart and writing checklist. Then tell students that they will use the rubric next week to evaluate their own writing before turning it in.

 **Quick Write**

During independent time, have students address the following: *Explain how to form a contraction. Then write two to three sentences containing contractions.* Use students' writing to evaluate their understanding of contractions.

iELD Integrated ELD

Light Support

Have students tell a partner their give their opinion of "Stone Soup." For example: *You've got to read "Stone Soup!" It's a great story.* Encourage them to jot down the contractions their partner uses, then talk about how these words were used in their opinion.

Moderate Support

Provide sentence frames for students to complete with contractions. For example:

The man _____ welcomed by the villagers. (wasn't)
They _____ want him in their village. (didn't)
They _____ share their food. (wouldn't)

Point out each contraction that students use and discuss how it is formed and the missing letter(s) in it.

Substantial Support

Label the front of note cards with contractions and the back with the words that are used to form the contractions. Have students identify each contraction, modeling the correct pronunciation, as needed. Then have them tell the words that form that contraction and look at the back of the card to check their response. Encourage students to use each contraction in a sentence.

Opinion Essay Rubric

L.2.2c Use an apostrophe to form contractions and frequently occurring possessives. **L.2.3a** Compare formal and informal uses of English.

DAY 5

PHONICS & WORD STUDY

Texts for Close Reading, p. 26
"City Mouse and Country Mouse"

Student Objectives

I will be able to:
- Build, read, and spell words with r-controlled vowels **ear, eer, ere**.
- Reread word study (decodable) text for fluency.
- Read high-frequency words.

Additional Materials

- Letter cards: **a, c, d, e, e, f, h, n, r, s, t, y**
- r-controlled vowels /**îr**/ frieze card

Weekly Presentation: Unit 4, Week 2
- Letter cards for each high-frequency word
- High-frequency word cards: **always, any, blue, buy, city, draw, four, great, how, live**

For additional word study/decodable practice, see: *Fox and Cat*, *King Grisly Beard*, and *Here or There?*

Review and Assess r-Controlled Vowels ear, eer, ere (20 MIN.) RF.2.3b, RF.2.3c, RF.2.3d, RF.2.3e, RF.2.3f, L.2.2d

Build Words

Model: near, hear, here

Display the letter cards for near. Blend the sounds: /nîr/, **near**.

- Replace the **n** with **h** and repeat with **hear**.
- Delete the **a**, add **e** at the end, and repeat with **here**.

Practice: year, dear, fear, deer, steer, cheer
Use the same routine to guide student practice.

Review r-Controlled Vowel or, oar, ore

Model: roar, roaring

Write the word roar and ask students to identify the vowel sound and spelling. Point out that the r-controlled vowel spelling **oar** must stay in the same syllable.

Write the word **roaring**. Model how to read the longer word. Point out the added syllable **–ing** is a suffix.

Practice: forest, before, shoreline, border, brainstorm, explore, soaring

Use the same routine to guide student practice.

Reread for Fluency: "City Mouse and Country Mouse"

Have students independently whisper-read "City Mouse and Country Mouse." Circulate and listen to their readings. Provide corrective feedback. For students having difficulty reading independently, have them read with a more skilled partner.

PHONICS & WORD STUDY

WEEK 2 • DAY 5

Spelling

Posttest

Use the following procedure to assess students' spelling of this week's words.

- Say each spelling word and use it in the sentence provided.
- Have students write the complete sentence on a piece of paper. Then continue with the next word.
- When students have finished, collect their papers and analyze any misspelled words.

1. In what **year** were you born?
2. Did that **deer** have long horns?
3. We are **near** my home.
4. It is **clear** to me that you are a good reader.
5. We are **here** to play a fun game.
6. Let's **cheer** for the best team.
7. I have a **fear** of big bugs.
8. My **ears** get cold in the winter.
9. I like to **hear** music all day.
10. Can you **steer** a large truck?

High-Frequency Words

Review: *always, any, blue, buy, city, draw, four, great, how, live*

Display the high-frequency word cards. Say each word and have students chorally repeat the word and spell it.

Place letter cards for one of the words in random order in a pocket chart. Have a volunteer beat the clock to form the word. Allow 15 seconds. Then have the rest of the class check the spelling and give a thumbs-up or thumbs-down.

Next have students turn to a partner and say a sentence using the word. Call on volunteers to check their sentences.

---

iELD Integrated ELD

Light Support
Review confusing language, such as **all year long, from the city, great apartment, nibble away, getting eaten**.
Partners read meaningful chunks of the text and discuss vocabulary and language to show understanding.

Moderate Support
Review key language, such as **life was good, big pile of corn, safe home, came to visit, without fear**.
Students role-play key language to show comprehension.
Students echo-read key passages and partner read.

Substantial Support
Discuss key language, such as **country, city, cousin, visit, trash cans, scratching**.
Students role-play to show comprehension.
Model reading key chunks of the text. Students echo-read.

RF.2.3b Know spelling-sound correspondences for additional common vowel teams. RF.2.3c Decode regularly spelled two-syllable words with long vowels. RF.2.3d Decode words with common prefixes and suffixes. RF.2.3e Identify words with inconsistent but common spelling-sound correspondences. RF.2.3f Recognize and read grade-appropriate irregularly spelled words. L.2.2d Generalize learned spelling patterns when writing words (e.g., cage →badge; boy → boil).

©2018 Benchmark Education Company, LLC

Grade 2 • Unit 4 • Week 2   **201**

Week 3 Mini-Lessons at a Glance

	Day 1	Day 2
Reading Mini-Lessons	Build Knowledge and Review Strategies (10 Min.), p. 204 SL.2.1a, SL.2.1b, SL.2.2, SL.2.3 Shared Reading (10 Min.), p. 205 RF.2.4a, RF.2.4b, RF.2.4c "The Stone Garden": Recount Story Events, Part 1 (20 Min.), p. 206 RL.2.1, RL.2.5, SL.2.1a, SL.2.1b, SL.2.1c,	Shared Reading (10 Min.), p. 212 RF.2.3f, RF.2.4a, RF.2.4b, RF.2.4c "The Stone Garden": Recount Story Events, Part 2 (20 Min.), p. 214 RL.2.1, RL.2.5, SL.2.2, SL.2.3
Writing and Language Mini-Lessons	Write and Opinion Essay: Draft an Effective Opening for Your Essay (15 Min.), p. 208 W.2.1	Write an Opinion Essay: Draft Body Paragraphs That Support Your Opinion (15 Min.), p. 216 W.2.1
Phonics/Word Study Mini-Lessons	r-Controlled Vowels air, are, ear, ere (15 Min.), p. 210 RF.2.3b, RF.2.3e, RF.2.3f, L.2.2d • High-Frequency Words: *another, boy, could, every, far, from, hurt, over, out, these* • Weekly Spelling Words: *where, hair, pear, care, share, stairs, square, bear, wear, chair*	r-Controlled Vowels air, are, ear, ere (20 Min.), p. 218 RF.2.3b, RF.2.3e, RF.2.3f, L.2.2d • High-Frequency Words: *another, boy, could, every, far, from, hurt, over, out, these*

Extended Read 2: "The Stone Garden"

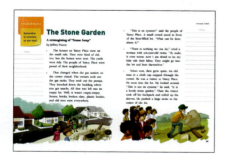

Fractured Folktale

Quantitative	Lexile® 520L

Qualitative Analysis of Text Complexity

Purpose and Levels of Meaning ②
- The story is essentially "Stone Soup" but with a twist, replacing the empty pot with a vacant lot and the need for a usable public space.

Structure ②
- The story has a chronological structure with events that build sequentially.
- Comprehending the resonance with "Stone Soup"'s similar structure is required for full interpretation.

Language Conventionality and Clarity ①
- Sentences are mostly simple, and with the modern-day setting the language is completely familiar.

Knowledge Demands ③
- Prior knowledge of "Stone Soup" is helpful for full appreciation of the narrative.

Total QM: 8
Moderate Complexity*

*The texts in *Benchmark Advance* are qualitatively evaluated based on their grade-level placement in the program. Reader maturity and age appropriateness are key considerations in the subjective use of the rubrics.

Day 3	Day 4	Day 5
Shared Reading (10 Min.), p. 220 RF.2.4a, RF.2.4b, RF.2.4c	**Shared Reading (10 Min.), p. 227** RL.2.4, RF.2.4a, RF.2.4c, L.2.1e	**Shared Reading (10 Min.), p. 233** RL.2.1, RF.2.4b, SL.2.2, SL.2.3, L.2.4a
Build Vocabulary: Describe How Words and Phrases Supply Rhythm and Meaning in a Story (10 Min.), p. 221 RI.2.4, L.2.4a, L.2.4e	**Close Reading: Compare and Contrast Two Versions of the Same Story (20 Min.), p. 228** RL.2.1, RL.2.9, SL.2.2, SL.2.3, SL.2.6	**Reflect on Unit Concepts (20 Min.) p. 238** W.2.6, SL.2.1a, SL.2.1b, SL.2.1c, SL.2.2, SL.2.3, SL.2.5, SL.2.6
Close Reading: Acknowledge Differences in the Points of View of Characters (15 Min.), p. 222 RL.2.1, RL.2.3, RL.2.6, SL.2.2, SL.2.3		
Revise the Writing: Revise to Include More Descriptive Words (15 Min.), p. 224 L.2.1e, L.2.6	**Write an Opinion Essay: Edit to Correct Use of Contractions (15 Min.), p. 230** L.2.2c, L.2.3a	**Review and Reflect (15 Min.), p. 234** W.2.1
r-Controlled Vowels air, are, ear, ere (10 Min.), p. 226 RL.2.3, RF.2.3b, RF.2.3c, RF.2.3e, RF.2.3f, L.2.2d • High-Frequency Words: *another, boy, could, every, far, from, hurt, over, out, these*	**r-Controlled Vowels air, are, ear, ere (20 Min.), p. 232** RF.2.3b, RF.2.3c, RF.2.3d, RF.2.3e, RF.2.3f, L.2.2d • High-Frequency Words: *another, boy, could, every, far, from, hurt, over, out, these*	**Review and Assess r-Controlled Vowels air, are, ear, ere (20 Min.), p. 236** RF.2.3b, RF.2.3c, RF.2.3d, RF.2.3e, RF.2.3f, L.2.2d • High-Frequency Words: *another, boy, could, every, far, from, hurt, over, out, these*

©2018 Benchmark Education Company, LLC

Grade 2 • Unit 4 • Week 3   **203**

DAY 1

UNIT REFLECTION

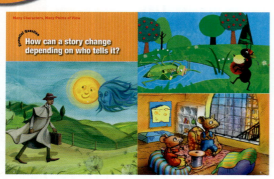

Texts for Close Reading, pp. 2–3
Unit Introduction

Student Objectives

I will be able to:
- Discuss my reading with a partner and a group.

Additional Materials

Weekly Presentation: Unit 4, Week 3

Integrated ELD

Light Support
Use "Stone Soup." Review using context clues to determine the meaning of unfamiliar words. Tell students to look for synonyms and antonyms of unfamiliar words. Choose unfamiliar words with students and complete the chart below.

Paragraph	Unfamiliar Word(s)	Context Clue
26	that's all we need	ready
29	move on	stay (antonym)

Moderate Support

Paragraph	Unfamiliar Word(s)	Context Clue
17	share	with everyone
14	whisper	grew louder (antonym)

I didn't understand _____. I continued reading, and found the context clue _____.
I think _____ means _____.

Substantial Support

Paragraph	Unfamiliar Word(s)	Context Clue
3	poor	nothing to give you

Ask: What words helped you understand _____?
Model: When I didn't know what _____ meant, I found the context clue _____. I think _____ means _____.

Build Knowledge and Review Strategies (10 MIN.) SL.2.1a, SL.2.1b, SL.2.2, SL.2.3

Discuss the Essential Question

Display the introduction to *Many Characters, Many Points of View*. Review the Essential Question and the selections for Weeks 1 and 2. Tell partners to listen carefully to follow these three-step directions:

1. Name two characters from the same story with different points of view.
2. Tell why their points of view differ.
3. Tell how a point of view changes from the beginning to the end of the story.

Ask partners to share their ideas with the class. Reinforce that attentive listeners ask questions to clarify others' comments. Explain that in Week 3, students will continue to think about characters' points of view as they read more stories.

Review Unit Strategies iELD

Identify Points of View. Remind students that they have been thinking about the points of view of story characters by looking at what the characters say and do.

Say: *When we read "The Blind Men and the Elephant" we saw that each man spoke with certainty. He was sure he knew what an elephant was like, even though he had touched only a part of the elephant. All five men needed to combine their points of view in order to get a true picture of an elephant.*

Ask volunteers to describe how the villagers changed their points of view in "Stone Soup."

Understand Story Structure. Remind students that they have learned to recount key story events and that stories have a beginning, middle, and end.

Say: *When we read "The Boy Who Cried Wolf" we saw that at the beginning of the story, the boy was bored and wanted excitement. In the middle of the story, he cried wolf when there was no wolf. At the end of the story, the villagers didn't answer his call when there was a wolf.*

Tell students that as they read the extended text this week, they will continue to identify points of view and recount key story events.

SL.2.1a Follow agreed-upon rules for discussions (e.g., gaining the floor in respectful ways, listening to others with care, speaking one at a time about the topics and texts under discussion). **SL.2.1b** Build on others' talk in conversations by linking their comments to the remarks of others. **SL.2.2** Recount or describe key ideas or details from a text read aloud or information presented orally or through other media. **SL.2.3** Ask and answer questions about what a speaker says in order to clarify comprehension, gather additional information, or deepen understanding of a topic or issue.

Shared Reading (10 MIN.) RF.2.4a, RF.2.4b, RF.2.4c

Introduce the Text iELD

Display "Why Owls Are Wise." Read aloud the title of the story as you point under the words. Invite students to preview the title and illustrations and make inferences and predictions about what the story will be about. If necessary, model make inference and predictions.

Model Make Inferences and Predictions

Remind to students that readers use various strategies when they read, including making inferences and predictions. Remind them that they practiced making inferences and predictions last week before, during, and after reading. Today they will make inferences and predictions before they read while previewing the text. Model making inferences and predictions for students.

Sample modeling (title/illustrations). *The title makes me think this will be a pourquoi tale—the type of folktale that explains why something came to be. Based on the title, I can infer that the tale will explain why owls are wise. The illustration shows an owl and a bear talking. So I can predict that the bear and the owl will be the main characters in this pourquoi tale.*

Invite a few students to share their before-reading inferences and predictions with the class.

Model Fluent Reading: Prosody/Phrasing

First Reading. Read the story aloud fluently and with appropriate phrasing. Point out that when you read a long sentence, you paused after words that belonged together, not between them. Read aloud the first sentence and hold your finger up to signal each slight pause, shown here with a slash: One day / as Great Bear lumbered through the woods / looking for berries, / he got lost.

Read Aloud Together. Invite students to reread the text with you. Tell them to listen for phrases and other words in groups.

Transfer Skills to Context: r-Controlled Syllable Pattern

Point to the word **here** in paragraph 2. After students read it aloud, ask them to name the letters that spell the /ir/ sounds. Then display the words **deer** and **clear**, and follow a similar procedure with each.

RF.2.4a Read on-level text with purpose and understanding. RF.2.4b Read on-level text orally with accuracy, appropriate rate, and expression on successive readings. RF.2.4c Use context to confirm or self-correct word recognition and understanding, rereading as necessary.

©2018 Benchmark Education Company, LLC

SHARED READING

WEEK 3 · DAY 1

Texts for Close Reading, p. 28 "Why Owls Are Wise"

Student Objectives

I will be able to:
- Read a pourquoi tale about characters with different points of view.
- Read a story with natural breaks between phrases.

Additional Materials

Weekly Presentation: Unit 4, Week 3

iELD Integrated ELD

Light Support
Display "Why Owls Are Wise." Conduct a pre-reading picture walk. Review **pourquoi tales**. Discuss key vocabulary and story events.
Choose and preview vocabulary, such as: **known for, sun would set, get back to, to this very day.**
Ask: *Bear knew the sun would set soon. What did he need to do?*
What are owls known for, to this very day?
Why do you think Bear needed to get back to his kingdom?

Moderate Support
Present as above and use: **rewarded, guide, lumbered, turned left/right, landed, up high.**
Ask: *What do you think Bear looked like as he lumbered?*
How/Why was owl rewarded?

Substantial Support
Present as above and use: **owl, wise, lost, nightfall, follow me, grateful, wisdom.**
Students act out terms and use the illustration to show comprehension.
Ask simple questions, such as:
Why did owl say, "Follow me?"
Why was Bear grateful?
Why do owls have wisdom?

Grade 2 · Unit 4 · Week 3 205

DAY 1

EXTENDED READ 2 MINI-LESSON

"The Stone Garden": Recount Story Events, Part 1 (20 MIN.) RL.2.1, RL.2.5, SL.2.1a, SL.2.1b, SL.2.1c,

Preview the Text (iELD)

Display and ask students to open to "The Stone Garden." Guide partners to preview the text together. As needed, prompt them to notice what the title, subtitle, and illustrations suggest about the type of text it seems to be.

Read to Find Key Details

Ask students to read paragraphs 1–12 to identify key story events. Have them annotate by underlining important details about the events. Give students time to read and annotate. Observe their annotations to assess their ability to identify important details that belong in a summary of story events.

Collaborative Conversation: Partner

Sample modeling. *I know it is important to speak clearly when you are having a conversation with another person.*

Draw students' attention to the subtitle, pointing out that the author has "reimagined" the folktale "Stone Soup." Ask students what kind of story they think "The Stone Garden" is. Some students may recognize it as realistic fiction based on the folktale. Others may offer support for viewing the story as a modern or original folktale.

Display and distribute the Details and Story Events Chart. Ask partners to compare the details they underlined and use them to fill out the chart by summarizing the key events for each noted section of the story. Remind students that a listener asks questions to clarify ideas, and also builds on the ideas of the speaker. Use your observations to determine if students need support in the form of guiding questions about "key events— the most important things that happen."

Texts for Close Reading, pp. 30–37
"The Stone Garden"

Student Objectives

I will be able to:
- Read a folktale about characters with different points of view.
- Identify and annotate important details.
- Work cooperatively with a partner.

Additional Materials

Weekly Presentation: Unit 4, Week 3
- Details and Story Events Chart

Ways to Scaffold the First Reading

Use your observational assessment to determine the intensity of scaffolding your students need.

IF...	THEN consider ...
Students are English learners who may struggle with vocabulary and language demands...	**Read the Text TO students.** • Conduct a before-reading picture walk to introduce vocabulary and concepts. • Stop after meaningful chunks to define unfamiliar words and paraphrase difficult sentences.
Students are struggling readers who may decode with little comprehension...	**Read the Text WITH students.** • Stop after meaningful chunks to ask **who, what, when, where, how** questions. • Work with students to define unfamiliar words and paraphrase key ideas.
Students need some support to read unfamiliar texts with comprehension...	**Have students PARTNER-READ.** *Partners should:* • take turns reading aloud meaningful chunks. • ask each other **who, what, when, where, how** questions about the text. • circle unfamiliar words and define them using context clues.

Paragraphs	Details (paragraph)	Story Events
1–4	"'This is an eyesore' … litter-filled lot. 'What can be done about it?'" (3) "There is nothing we can do." (4)	The people of Yancy Place don't like the litter-filled lot in their neighborhood. They think it is an eyesore, but there's nothing they can do about it.
5–7	A visitor to Yancy Place said, "It is a lovely stone garden." … "pushed a large stone to the center of the lot." (5) "A man … laughed… Others in the crowd laughed with him." (6) The visitor "placed each rock in a circle around the stone." (7)	A visitor tells the neighbors that the lot is really a "lovely stone garden." Everyone laughs at him, but he begins to place rocks in a circle around a big stone.
8–9	"Hmm … I do see the makings of a stone garden." (8) "… we might paint the rocks different colors. I saw that … in Paris." (9)	One woman sees "the makings of a stone garden." The visitor suggests painting the rocks.
10–13	"… painted with every color of the rainbow." (12) "… to make a stone garden a garden, it should have plants. It should have flowers." (13)	The neighbors paint the rocks. The visitor tells them that a stone garden should have plants and flowers.

Sample Details and Story Events Chart

206 Grade 2 • Unit 4 • Week 3

EXTENDED READ 2 MINI-LESSON

Share

Invite partnerships to share their statements about key events. Encourage group discussion of the summarizing statements and whether any details need to be added or deleted. Remind students to connect their comments to what they have heard from previous speakers and to agree or disagree in respectful ways.

Reinforce or Reaffirm the Strategy

If your students need support to understand the text, refer to "Ways to Scaffold the First Reading." Pose text-dependent questions to guide students' thinking. For example:

- *What event led to the lot becoming empty?*
- *Why wasn't the lot really empty?*

Choose one of the following based on your observations during partner collaboration.

IF...	THEN...
Students need support to identify the most important details and make summarizing statements about key events . . .	Model to reinforce the strategy. • As I read, I keep track of what is happening in a story–the key events. • In paragraphs 1–3, I learn that the story takes place in a neighborhood called Yancy Place. I learn what the story problem is–nobody likes the empty lot that is filled with litter and is dangerous. • In paragraphs 4–6, I meet the visitor who is the main character in the story. What does he do? He starts to persuade the neighbors that the empty lot is really a stone garden.
Students identify important details and make statements of key events . . .	Invite partners or small groups to reflect on the strategy use by discussing the following question: • *How did you decide on descriptions to include or leave out when summarizing key events?*

✓ Show Your Knowledge

Ask students to reread paragraphs 8–11 and summarize the key event.

Challenge Activity. Have students reread paragraph 6. Ask them whether they think the last sentence gives a key event in the story and give their reasons.

iELD Integrated ELD

Light Support
Preview the text. Students discuss the illustrations. Choose, discuss, present, and have students role-play language, such as **on the small side, kind of old, knocked down, all that was left, junkyard**.
Ask: *What happened when the owners knocked down the gas station?*
Why did the neighbor call the empty lot a junkyard?

Moderate Support
Preview the text. Students discuss the illustrations. Choose, discuss, present, and have students role-play vocabulary, such as **pump, eyesore, glowed, insulted, took out, rolled up, gas station**.
Ask: *What happened when the owners took out the pumps?*
Why did the neighbor call the empty lot an eyesore?
What happened after the visitor rolled up his sleeves?

Substantial Support
Preview the text. Students discuss the illustrations. Choose, discuss, present, and have students role-play vocabulary, such as **closed, owners, pushed, visitor, tidy, world-class, volunteered, neat**.
Elicit and record questions and answers. Students echo-read.
Ask: *What happened when the owners closed the gas station?*
How could the empty lot become world-class?

RL.2.1 Ask and answer such questions as who, what, where, when, why, and how to demonstrate understanding of key details in a text. **RL.2.5** Describe the overall structure of a story, including describing how the beginning introduces the story and the ending concludes the action. **SL.2.1.a** Follow agreed-upon rules for discussions (e.g., gaining the floor in respectful ways, listening to others with care, speaking one at a time about the topics and texts under discussion). **SL.2.1.b** Build on others' talk in conversations by linking their comments to the remarks of others. **SL.2.1.c** Ask for clarification and further explanation as needed about the topics and texts under discussion.

DAY 1

WRITING TO SOURCES

Student Writing Prompt

Is "Stone Soup" a story you would recommend to your friends? Why or why not? State your opinion in an essay. Supply reasons, based on details from the text, to support your opinion.

Student Objectives

I will be able to:
- Write an effective opening paragraph containing an opinion statement.
- Share my ideas in collaborative conversation and in writing.

Materials

Weekly Presentation: Unit 4, Week 3
- Example Opening Paragraphs
- Opening Paragraph Modeling Text
- Mentor Opinion Essay
- Opinion Essay Planning Chart
- Opinion Essay Anchor Chart
- Opinion Essay Checklist
- Opinion Essay Rubric

Write an Opinion Essay: Draft an Effective Opening for Your Essay

(15 MIN.) W.2.1

Engage Thinking

Ask students if they've ever heard someone speaking about a book with such excitement that they felt they just *had* to read it. Or perhaps someone gave such a negative review that they thought the book would be too terrible to read. Explain that today students will learn how to write an opening paragraph that includes an opinion statement interesting enough to make a reader want to continue reading the essay to learn more about their opinion.

Model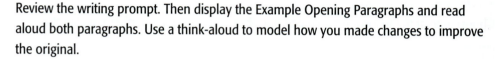

Review the writing prompt. Then display the Example Opening Paragraphs and read aloud both paragraphs. Use a think-aloud to model how you made changes to improve the original.

Sample think-aloud. *When I read my original opening paragraph, it was clear that I recommended the story, but I didn't tell much about it to make it interesting. I know that asking a question is one way to get a reader's attention. So I decided to begin the paragraph by asking, "Have you read 'Stone Soup' yet?" My question and the following exclamation, "If you haven't, you should!" suggest excitement and urgency, like the reader shouldn't wait any longer to read this great story.*

I felt that I now had the reader's attention, and I wanted to keep it. So I broke up the second sentence and told the reader more about why I thought the story was so worthwhile. Look at how I wrote the third sentence to state my opinion and give a strong reason for it. The next sentence also gives a reason, and suggests again that my reader should read "Stone Soup." Then I wrapped up my paragraph with another note of excitement.

Opening Paragraph Example

I would recommend "Stone Soup." It is a good story that teaches a lesson and has an interesting main character.

Improved Opening Paragraph

Have you read "Stone Soup" yet? If you haven't, you should! I would recommend you read the story because it teaches valuable lessons you need to have a happy life. You'll also really like the mysterious main character. I sure do!

Example Opening Paragraphs

---

208 Grade 2 • Unit 4 • Week 3

©2018 Benchmark Education Company, LLC

WRITING TO SOURCES

WEEK 3 · DAY 1

Peer Practice

Display and read aloud the following opening paragraph for an opinion essay. Ask partners to work together to improve the paragraph.

> I recommend "The Blind Men and the Elephant" to my friends. It's a good story. It's about blind men and an elephant.

Opening Paragraph Modeling Text

Share Your Understanding

Bring students together and invite partners to share their improved paragraph with the class. Help students understand that the opening paragraph of an opinion essay should clearly state the writer's opinion, but also draw readers in and make them want to understand why the writer thinks or believes what he or she does about the topic.

Independent Writing

During independent time, have students draft the opening paragraph of their opinion essay. Remind them to refer to the tools they have: mentor text, anchor chart, writing checklist and rubric, planning chart, and source materials.

☑ Confer and Monitor

As you monitor students' independent writing, provide feedback, as needed. For example:

Directive Feedback: *Your opinion is that you wouldn't recommend the story, because "It's not good." Can you give more information by giving reasons for your opinion?*

Self-Monitoring and Reflection: *Reread your opening paragraph. If you were a reader, would you recognize the opinion? Would you want to keep reading?*

Validating and Confirming: *You stated your opinion in an interesting way. I want to keep reading to learn more about the reasons you liked the story as much as you did.*

---

iELD Integrated ELD

Light Support

Have students explain why the improved opening paragraph is better than the original. Ask them to identify ways in which you shared your opinion and reasons in an effective way. Encourage them to suggest other changes that might make your opening more interesting.

Moderate Support

Use sentence frames to help students describe and compare the language used in the opening paragraph examples.

Opening Paragraph Example	Improved Opening Paragraph
The writer uses _____ language.	*The writer uses _____ language.*
The writer's opinion is _____.	*The writer's opinion is _____.*
I do/do not want to read the story because _____.	*I do/do not want to read the story because _____.*

Substantial Support

Ask questions about the original and improved opening paragraph to help students compare and understand the differences between them. For example:

Did I state my opinion? Which sentence includes my opinion?

Is my writing interesting? If so, what makes it interesting?

Does my writing make you want to read "Stone Soup?" What did I write to convince you?

W.2.1 Write opinion pieces in which they introduce the topic or book they are writing about, state an opinion, supply reasons that support the opinion, use linking words (e.g., because, and, also) to connect opinion and reasons, and provide a concluding statement or section.

©2018 Benchmark Education Company, LLC

Grade 2 • Unit 4 • Week 3   **209**

DAY 1 — PHONICS & WORD STUDY

r-Controlled Vowels air, are, ear, ere

(15 MIN.) RF.2.3b, RF.2.3e, RF.2.3f, L.2.2d

r-Controlled /âr/ Frieze Card and
Sound-Spelling Card r-Controlled /âr/

Student Objectives

I will be able to:
- Identify, blend, and spell words with r-controlled vowels **air, are, ear, ere**.
- Learn high-frequency words.
- Review high-frequency words.

Additional Materials

- Letter cards: **a, e, f, i, r, s t**

Weekly Presentation: Unit 4, Week 3
- r-controlled /**âr**/ frieze card
- Sound-spelling card r-controlled /**âr**/
- High-frequency word cards: **another, boy, could, every, far, from, hurt, over, out, these**
- Review high-frequency word cards: **always, any, blue, buy, city, draw, four, great, how**

For additional word study/decodable practice, see: *Two Boys, One Day; Manners in Tales;* and *Tell the Tale.*

Spelling-Sound Correspondences (iELD)

Introduce: r-Controlled Vowels air, are, ear, ere
Display the r-controlled /**âr**/ frieze card.

Say: *These sounds are /âr/. The /âr/ sounds are spelled many ways:* **air, are, ear, ere.**

Model: air, are, ear, ere
Point to each spelling on the card and provide a sample word: **air** as in **chair**, **are** as in **care**, **ear** as in **bear**, **ere** as in **there**. Write each sample word and underline the r-controlled vowel spelling.

Say: *Look at the first word I wrote: c-h-a-i-r. I see the r-controlled vowel spelling* **air**. *Listen and watch as I sound out the word: /châr/, chair.*

Run your hand under the word as you sound it out.

Practice: year, deer, here
Repeat the r-controlled vowel **air, are, ear, ere** words one at a time. Ask students to write each word and underline the r-controlled vowel spelling.

Blend Words (iELD)

Model: r-Controlled Vowels air, are, ear, ere
Display the letter cards for **far**. Model how to blend the sounds together as you run your hand under each letter.

Say: *This is the letter* **f**. *It stands for /f/. These are the letters* **ar**. *They stand for /är/. Listen as I blend these sounds together: /fär/,* **far**. *Say the word with me:* **far**.

Model adding an **i** after the **a** to make the word **fair**.

Say: *I can add an* **i** *after the* **a** *to make the r-controlled vowel spelling* **air**. *The* **air** *spelling stands for the /âr/ sounds. Listen as I blend the new word: /fâr/. Say the word with me:* **fair**.

Continue modeling the words **star, stare**.

Practice: hair, stairs, rare, share, square, wear, pear, where
Write each word. Have students blend the sounds aloud. Provide corrective feedback, as needed.

210 Grade 2 • Unit 4 • Week 3   ©2018 Benchmark Education Company, LLC

PHONICS & WORD STUDY

WEEK 3 • DAY 1

Spelling

Pretest

Say each spelling word. Read the sentence and say the word again. After the pretest, write each word as you say the letter names. Have students check their work.

where	**Where** do you live?
hair	Her **hair** is black and curly.
pear	I ate a **pear** for a snack.
care	Do you **care** if I borrow your crayons?
share	When you **share** the workload, you get finished faster.
stairs	We walked up twenty **stairs** to get to the top.
square	A **square** has four sides.
bear	The big brown **bear** growled in the forest.
wear	What will you **wear** to school tomorrow?
chair	Please sit in your **chair** until the bell rings.

High-Frequency Words

Introduce: *another, boy, could, every, far, from, hurt, over, out, these*
Use the following routine: Write simple sentences using each high-frequency word. Underline the word and discuss important features about it. Say the word and have students repeat. Then spell the word with students as you point to each letter. Finally have students write the word as they spell it aloud.

Practice
Display the high-frequency word cards. Have students work with a partner to write sentences using the words. Then have volunteers read a sentence and identify the high-frequency word.

Review: *always, any, blue, buy, city, draw, four, great, how, live*
Review last week's words using the high-frequency word cards. Mix and display one word card at a time as students say each word aloud.

iELD Integrated ELD

Light Support
Review rhyming words. Pairs write two sentences with rhyming words. Students present their sentences, and use gestures or simple drawings to show comprehension.
Since Bear and Hare have only one pear, they decided that they should share.

Moderate Support
Pairs write one sentence using at least two of the target words. Students act out the sentence to show comprehension. Assist as needed.
The bear sat on a chair next to the hare who wanted to share his pear.

Substantial Support
Present r-controlled vowel combinations **air, are, ear, ere**.
Write these words on cards: **chair, hair, stairs, fair, pair, care, share, square, hare mare, bear, pear, wear, there, where**. Hold up a card. Students repeat the word after you. Volunteers place the card in the correct column of the chart below.

air	are	ear	ere
chair	care	bear	there
hair	share	pear	where
stairs	square	wear	
fair	hare		
pair	mare		

Discuss word meanings using simple pictures, gestures, or phrases. Students role-play each word to show comprehension. Groups practice and present their assigned cards and then switch cards with another group.

RF.2.3b Know spelling-sound correspondences for additional common vowel teams. **RF.2.3e** Identify words with inconsistent but common spelling-sound correspondences. **RF.2.3f** Recognize and read grade-appropriate irregularly spelled words. **L.2.2d** Generalize learned spelling patterns when writing words (e.g., cage → badge; boy → boil).

DAY 2

SHARED READING

Texts for Close Reading, p. 28
"Why Owls Are Wise"

Student Objectives

I will be able to:
- Read a pourquoi tale about characters with different points of view.
- Identify and annotate important details to summarize key events.

Additional Materials

Weekly Presentation: Unit 4, Week 3

Shared Reading (10 MIN.) RF.2.3f, RF.2.4a, RF.2.4b, RF.2.4c

Reread for Fluency: Prosody/Phrasing

Partner Reading. Ask partners to take turns reading aloud "Why Owls Are Wise." They may alternate paragraphs and then switch roles. Remind them to pause only after reading a group of words that belong together.

Collaborative Conversation: Make Inferences and Predictions

Remind students that yesterday you demonstrated making inferences before reading– while you were previewing the story. Share that the reading strategy of making inferences is important for all literary and informational texts, including pourquoi tales and folktales like this. Model making inferences as you read the text.

Sample modeling. *In paragraph 1, I read that Great Bear is lost and can't find his way back to his kingdom. The text refers to him as "Great Bear" and mentions "his kingdom." From this information, I can infer that Bear is powerful.*

Invite students to use sentence frames to help them make inferences.

- *While reading, I can make an inference about _____.*
- *The words _____ help me infer that _____.*

Transfer Skills to Context: Annotate Important Details

Model underlining important details that help you summarize story events.

Sample modeling (paragraph 1). *I'll ask myself what is most important to understand about the beginning of this story. I'll underline the first sentence because it answers the questions **who?** and **where?** It also tells me Bear's problem: he is lost. I'll underline* **needed to get back to his kingdom before nightfall,** *because that detail describes Bear's problem. One way I can summarize the key event in paragraph 1 is: "Bear is lost in the woods and must get back to his kingdom before nightfall."*

Guide students to underline other details that lead them to summarize the events in paragraphs 2 and 3.

212 Grade 2 • Unit 4 • Week 3 ©2018 Benchmark Education Company, LLC

SHARED READING

Transfer Skills to Context: r-Controlled Syllable Patterns

Point to the word **Bear** in paragraph 1. Ask students to read the word aloud and then pronounce the word without the initial consonant: /âr/. Then point to the word **air** in paragraph 2, telling students to listen for the same vowel sound as they say the word. Remind them that the consonant **r** can change the vowel sound that comes before it. Display these words, asking students to read each one aloud and name the letters that spell /âr/: **pear, chair, fair, wear.**

Transfer Skills to Context: High-Frequency Words *over, from*

As you point to each of these previously taught words in paragraph 2, tell partners to say the word to each other: **over**, **from**. Remind students to look for words they know when they read a new text.

iELD Integrated ELD

Light Support
Preview "Why Owls Are Wise." Elicit and record key events on sentence strips. Students sequence the events.

One day	Bear couldn't find his way home.
After that	Owl landed in a tree, and offered to show Bear the way.
In the end	Bear was so grateful, he rewarded Owl with wisdom.

Pairs write two more events, sequence the two events, and present them.

Moderate Support
Preview "Why Owls Are Wise." Elicit and record key events on sentence strips. Students sequence the events with you.

All of a sudden	Bear noticed he was lost in the woods.
Then	Owl showed Bear the way home.
Finally	Bear gave Owl wisdom because she helped him.

Discuss, write, and sequence a fourth event. Students echo-read and present the events in order.

Substantial Support
Preview "Why Owls Are Wise." Elicit and record key events on sentence strips. Students echo-read and sequence the events with you.

First	Bear got lost in the woods.
Next	Owl found bear and helped him get home.
Then	Bear was grateful and made Owl wise.

Groups role-play events in the correct order.
Ask: *Why did Bear reward Owl?*

RF.2.3f Recognize and read grade-appropriate irregularly spelled words. **RF.2.4a** Read on-level text with purpose and understanding. **RF.2.4b** Read on-level text orally with accuracy, appropriate rate, and expression on successive readings. **RF.2.4c** Use context to confirm or self-correct word recognition and understanding, rereading as necessary.

©2018 Benchmark Education Company, LLC

Grade 2 • Unit 4 • Week 3   **213**

DAY 2

EXTENDED READ 2 MINI-LESSON

"The Stone Garden": Recount Story Events, Part 2 (20 MIN.) RL.2.1, RL.2.5, SL.2.2, SL.2.3

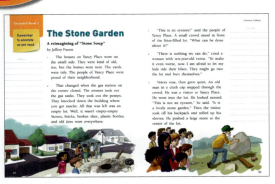

Texts for Close Reading, pp. 30–37
"The Stone Garden"

Student Objectives

I will be able to:
- Read a story about characters with different points of view.
- Use the details to summarize key story events.
- Work cooperatively with a partner.

Additional Materials

Weekly Presentation: Unit 4, Week 3
- Details and Story Events Chart

Ways to Scaffold the First Reading

Use your observational assessment to determine the intensity of scaffolding your students need.

IF...	THEN consider ...
Students are English learners who may struggle with vocabulary and language demands...	**Read the Text TO students.** • Conduct a before-reading picture walk to introduce vocabulary and concepts. • Stop after meaningful chunks to define unfamiliar words and paraphrase difficult sentences.
Students are struggling readers who may decode with little comprehension...	**Read the Text WITH students.** • Stop after meaningful chunks to ask *who, what, when, where, how* questions. • Work with students to define unfamiliar words and paraphrase key ideas.
Students need some support to read unfamiliar texts with comprehension...	**Have students PARTNER-READ.** Partners should: • take turns reading aloud meaningful chunks. • ask each other *who, what, when, where, how* questions about the text. • circle unfamiliar words and define them using context clues.

Preview the Text

Remind students that they have already read the first part of "The Stone Garden." Ask partners to skim and scan the first part of the story again and discuss what the visitor and neighbors might do in Part 2 of the story. Call on a few students to share their predictions and inferences with the class and explain how they arrived at them.

Read to Find Key Details

Ask students to read paragraphs 13–29 to identify key story events. Have them annotate by underlining important details about the events.

Give students time to read and annotate. Observe their annotations to assess their ability to distinguish details about key story events from other descriptive details.

Give students an opportunity to tell how accurately they predicted and inferred the story events and outcome.

💬 Collaborative Conversation: Partner

Display and distribute a blank Details and Story Events Chart. Ask partners to write the key story events in each section in the chart. Tell them to discuss the details they underlined as they decide how to summarize each event. Use your observations to determine if students need support in the form of guiding questions.

Paragraph	Details (paragraph)	Story Events
Paragraphs 14–18	"I am growing tomatoes … I can bring in some seedlings." (14) "… works in a flower shop … a good deal on plants." (16) "I'll help dig up the ground." (18)	Different neighbors offer to bring plants for the stone garden and dig up the soil.
Paragraphs 19–21	"'Sign us up,' said some teenagers." (19) "The teens … picked up the plastic bottles … rolled away the tires … built a slate walkway." (21)	Teenagers clean up the litter and build a walkway around the stone garden.
Paragraphs 22–26	"The people of Yancy Place worked …" (22) "The visitor gave direction … and encouragement." (23) "…we should add a string of paper lanterns." (24) "… 'it needs an outdoor brick oven.'" (26)	The visitor encourages the neighbors as they work. Two people add paper lanterns. Another suggests building an outdoor brick oven.
Paragraphs 27–31	"We have a huge pile of bricks … All I need is some help." (28) "one last look… finest stone gardens he had ever seen, and was on his way." (31)	As the neighbors begin work on the oven, the visitor looks at the fine stone garden and goes on his way.

Sample Details and Story Events Chart

214 Grade 2 • Unit 4 • Week 3 ©2018 Benchmark Education Company, LLC

EXTENDED READ 2 MINI-LESSON

WEEK **3** · DAY **2**

Share Your Understanding

Invite partnerships to share their key story events with the class. Ask listeners to comment respectfully about whether only the most important details are included in the summaries. Ask questions to confirm students' comprehension of the story and deepen their understanding.

Reinforce or Reaffirm the Strategy

If your students need support to understand the text, refer to "Ways to Scaffold the First Reading." Provide directive and/or corrective feedback as needed: For example:

- *What is the first plant people from the neighborhood offer to bring to the garden?*
- *What do the teens do to make the garden better?*

Choose one of the following options based on your observations during partner collaboration.

IF...	THEN...
Students need support to identify the most important details and make summarizing statements about key events . . .	**Model to reinforce the strategy.** • *In paragraphs 13–16, I read the conversation between the visitor and two neighbors. I ask myself what is most important to understand. I'll underline the details about the girl's offer to bring in tomato seedlings and the man's offer to bring in plants.* • *In paragraph 17, I'll underline the most important words about the young man's offer: "I'll help dig up the ground."* • *I can use the important details I found to summarize a key story event:* **Different neighbors offer to bring plants for the stone garden and dig up the soil.**
Students identify important details and make statements about key events . . .	**Invite partners to reflect on the strategy use by discussing the following question:** • *How can you tell which events belong in the beginning, middle, or end of a story?*

☑ Show Your Knowledge

Ask students to review paragraphs 13–27 and to write three sentences beginning with the words **First**, **Next**, and **After that**, to describe three key events in building the garden.

Challenge Activity. Ask students to think about special events a community might have together through the year such as an Independence Day celebration, a harvest festival, a winter wonderland, or one of their own. Tell them to draw a picture of the people of Yancy Place celebrating in their rock garden. Have students write a sentence or two describing their picture.

iELD Integrated ELD

Light Support

Preview the text. Choose, discuss, present, and then have students role-play word meanings for key vocabulary, such as **a good deal, sign us up, rolled away, electrician, instructions, teens, on his way, especially.**
Ask questions and elicit and record answers.
Ask: *How did the electrician help make the stone garden better? Why do you think the visitor decided to be on his way?*

Moderate Support

Preview the text. Choose, discuss, present, and then have students role-play word meanings for key vocabulary, such as **excellent, flower shop, good exercise, directions, finer, brick oven, turning out.**
Ask: *What directions did the visitor give the neighbors? How was the stone garden becoming finer?*

Substantial Support

Preview the text. Choose, discuss, present, and then have students role-play word meanings for key vocabulary, such as **seedlings, wonderful, dirty, teenagers, tires, walkway, cookouts, paper lanterns, fine.**
Ask: *How did the teenagers help make the empty lot better? How did the neighbors make it a fine stone garden?*

RL.2.1 Ask and answer such questions as who, what, where, when, why, and how to demonstrate understanding of key details in a text. **RL.2.5** Describe the overall structure of a story, including describing how the beginning introduces the story and the ending concludes the action. **SL.2.2** Recount or describe key ideas or details from a text read aloud or information presented orally or through other media. **SL.2.3** Ask and answer questions about what a speaker says in order to clarify comprehension, gather additional information, or deepen understanding of a topic or issue.

©2018 Benchmark Education Company, LLC

Grade 2 · Unit 4 · Week 3   **215**

DAY 2

WRITING TO SOURCES

Student Writing Prompt

Is "Stone Soup" a story you would recommend to your friends? Why or why not? State your opinion in an essay. Supply reasons, based on details from the text, to support your opinion.

Student Objectives

I will be able to:
- Cite text evidence to support my opinion in an opinion essay.
- Include dialogue to strengthen my opinion essay.

Materials

Weekly Presentation: Unit 4, Week 3
- Example Body Paragraph
- Body Paragraph Modeling Text
- Mentor Opinion Essay
- Opinion Essay Planning Chart
- Opinion Essay Anchor Chart
- Opinion Essay Checklist
- Opinion Essay Rubric

Write an Opinion Essay: Draft Body Paragraphs That Support Your Opinion (15 MIN.) W.2.1

Engage Thinking

Ask students to identify the parts of an opinion essay. As necessary, review that an opinion essay includes an opinion statement, one or more reasons, details that support the reasons, and a conclusion. Remind students that yesterday they drafted an opening paragraph for their opinion essay. Explain that today they will draft the body paragraphs and concluding statement.

Model

Display the Opinion Essay Planning Page from the previous week. Model how to begin drafting the body paragraphs by incorporating the reasons, facts, and details that support your opinion.

Say: *When I completed my planning page, I decided I would write three body paragraphs, one for each reason. I'll begin with the first reason. I would recommend "Stone Soup" because it teaches readers not to judge others. I'll include the events and details from the notes on my planning page. To make my essay stronger, I also want to include some dialogue, or words that characters speak, from the story. As I copy the dialogue, I need to remember to use quotation marks around the character's exact words.*

Display and distribute the Example Body Paragraph, then read it aloud. Model how to underline details from the text that are in your own words and circle the dialogue taken directly from the story. (This text should be set off by quotation marks.) Have students do the same on their copy.

> One reason you should read "Stone Soup" is it teaches a lesson about not judging others. When the man first comes to the village, the people turn him away. They think he only wants to take their food. One woman says, "You have come to the wrong place, stranger." Another villager tells him, "You had better move on." At the end of the story, the villagers know his true intentions. They beg him to stay. It is important for us not to judge a person before we know him or her.

Example Body Paragraph

Peer Practice

Display and read aloud the following sentence, then ask partners to add text evidence, including dialogue, to support the sentence.

> The best part of the story is when the villagers become interested in the soup.

Body Paragraph Modeling Text

216 Grade 2 • Unit 4 • Week 3   ©2018 Benchmark Education Company, LLC

WRITING TO SOURCES

WEEK 3 • DAY 2

Share Your Understanding

Bring students together and invite the partners to share the text evidence they found that supports the opinion in the practice sentence. Remind them that adding events and details from the text, including dialogue, helps to strengthen their opinion essay.

Independent Writing (iELD)

During independent time, have students continue to draft their opinion essay. Encourage them to focus on incorporating dialogue, along with events and details from the story in their own words, as they write the body paragraphs. Also, tell students to include a closing statement that restates rather than repeats, the opinion statement. Remind them to refer to the tools they have: mentor text, anchor chart, writing checklist and rubric, planning chart, and source materials.

☑ Confer and Monitor

As you monitor students' independent writing, provide feedback, as needed. For example:

Directive Feedback: *Look on your planning page at the notes you wrote for your first/second/third reason. Now go back to that part of the story. Can you find a detail you might use to support your reason?*

Self-Monitoring and Reflection: *Does your draft include events, details, and/or dialogue that support your opinion? Is there anything you can add to help explain your reasons?*

Validating and Confirming: *When you used the quotation, "_____," from the story, I really understood what you meant about _____.*

(iELD) Integrated ELD

Light Support
Remind students that an opinion essay should persuade people to think one way or the other. He or she should want/not want to read "Stone Soup" after reading the essay. Guide students to share specific events and details from the story to support their reasons in a convincing way.

Moderate Support
Work with students to provide more detailed events and facts from the text to support the reasons for their opinion. Ask leading questions, such as:
What else happened in the story that makes you think _____?
Where in the story does _____ happen?

Substantial Support
As students draft their body paragraphs, provide sentence frames, such as: *I think _____ because _____.* Guide students in using their planning page to state their reason and support it with specific details and events from the text.

W.2.1 Write opinion pieces in which they introduce the topic or book they are writing about, state an opinion, supply reasons that support the opinion, use linking words (e.g., because, and, also) to connect opinion and reasons, and provide a concluding statement or section.

©2018 Benchmark Education Company, LLC

Grade 2 • Unit 4 • Week 3   **217**

DAY 2

PHONICS & WORD STUDY

r-Controlled /âr/ Frieze Card and
Sound-Spelling Card r-Controlled /âr/

Student Objectives

I will be able to:
- Blend, build, and spell words with r-controlled vowels **air, are, ear, ere**.
- Practice high-frequency words.
- Read r-controlled vowels **ear, eer, ere**.

Additional Materials

- Letter cards: **a, b, c, e, e, f, h, i, p, r, r, s, t, w**

Weekly Presentation: Unit 4, Week 3
- r-controlled /âr/ frieze card
- Sound-spelling card r-controlled /âr/
- High-frequency word cards: **another, boy, could, every, far, from, hurt, over, out, these**

For additional word study/decodable practice, see: *Two Boys, One Day; Manners in Tales;* and *Tell the Tale*.

r-Controlled Vowels air, are, ear, ere

(20 MIN.) RF.2.3b, RF.2.3e, RF.2.3f, L.2.2d

Review r-Controlled Vowels air, are, ear, ere

Display the r-controlled /âr/ frieze card. Review the r-controlled vowel spellings **air** as in **chair**, **are** as in **care**, **ear** as in **bear**, and **ere** as in **there**. Point to each spelling-sound.

Say: *What are the letters? What sounds do they stand for?*

Blend Words

Model: share
Display letter cards for **share**. Model blending.

Say: *These are the letters **sh**. They stand for the sound /sh/. These are the letters **are**. They stand for the sound /âr/. Listen as I blend these sounds together: /shâr/, **share**. Say the word with me: **share**.*

Practice: scare, hair, where, wear
Use the same routine to guide student practice. Discuss the homophones **where/wear**.

Build Words

Model: rare, care, scare, stare
- Display the letter cards for **rare**. Blend the sounds: /râr/, **rare**.
- Replace the **r** with **c** and repeat with **care**.
- Add the **s** and repeat with **scare**.
- Replace the **c** with **t** and repeat with **stare**.

Practice: fair, pair, hair, chair, bear, pear, wear, swear
Use the same routine to guide student practice.

218 Grade 2 • Unit 4 • Week 3

©2018 Benchmark Education Company, LLC

PHONICS & WORD STUDY

WEEK 3 · DAY 2

Spelling

Closed Sort: where, hair, pear, care, share, stairs, square, bear, wear, chair
Write and display each word on an index card. Ask students to read and spell each word aloud together. Then make a three-column chart. Place the card for **hair** on the top of column 1, **wear** on the top of column 2, and **care** on the top of column 3.

Have students place each card in the column with the word that has the same vowel spelling. When completed, have students read and spell the words in each column aloud together. Ask students which word didn't fit into any of the columns (where).

High-Frequency Words (iELD)

Review: another, boy, could, every, far, from, hurt, over, out, these
Display the high-frequency word cards. Have students read and spell each word. Focus on common r-controlled vowel spelling patterns in **another**, **every**, **far**, **hurt**, and **over**. Compare the vowel spelling pattern -**ould** in **could**, **would**, and **should** to highlight this word family.

Review r-Controlled Vowels ear, eer, ere

Model: fear, deer, here
Write the words **fear**, **deer**, and **here**. Ask students to underline the r-controlled vowel spellings and read the words. Point out that these vowel spellings must stay in the same syllable of a longer word.

Write the word **fearful**. Underline each vowel spelling. Have a volunteer divide the word into syllables. Then have students use the syllables to read the word.

Practice: hearing, cheering, cheerful, dearest, clearest
Use the same routine to guide student practice.

(iELD) Integrated ELD

Light Support
Students echo-read a word bank with the high-frequency words:

another	boy	could	every	from
these	out	hurt	over	far

Students use the high-frequency words in sentences that contain **could**:
Could the <u>boy</u> see the owl flying **over** the tree?
These teens **could** move the bricks.

Moderate Support
Students echo-read a word bank with the high-frequency words:

another	boy	could	every	from
these	out	hurt	over	far

Students use the high-frequency words in compound sentences with **and**:
These teenagers rolled away the tires **and** a <u>boy</u> got some plants.

Substantial Support
Students echo-read a word bank with the high-frequency words:

another	boy	could	every	from
these	out	hurt	over	far

Write the words on cards. Hold up a card. Students echo-read. Volunteers point to the word in the word bank and read it aloud.
Students repeat, spell, and write the words with you.
Students use the words in sentences with **because** clauses.
The old man was far from home because _____.

RF.2.3b Know spelling-sound correspondences for additional common vowel teams. **RF.2.3e** Identify words with inconsistent but common spelling-sound correspondences. **RF.2.3f** Recognize and read grade-appropriate irregularly spelled words. **L.2.2d** Generalize learned spelling patterns when writing words (e.g., cage → badge; boy → boil).

©2018 Benchmark Education Company, LLC

Grade 2 · Unit 4 · Week 3   **219**

DAY 3

SHARED READING

Texts for Close Reading, p. 29
"Wind and Sun"

Student Objectives

I will be able to:
- Read a fable about characters with different points of view.
- Identify and annotate details that support the moral of a fable.

Additional Materials

Weekly Presentation: Unit 4, Week 3

iELD Integrated ELD

Light Support
Students echo-read "Wind and Sun." Choose and place key vocabulary in a chart. Students echo-read:

| mighty gusts | around himself |
| pulled his coat | gentle approach |

Students say, read, write, role-play, and present original sentences using the key language.

Moderate Support
Present as above.

| stronger | removed | shone |
| closer | to blow | tightly |

Students use and identify key words as they role-play a character from the fable.

Substantial Support
Present as above.

wind	contest	failed
sun	coat	warmly
feud	victorious	best

Write the words on cards. Groups present assigned words, and switch cards.
Model and practice:
This is the word **victorious**.
Here it is in the story.
Victorious *means winning.*
Our **victorious** *soccer team cheered.*

Shared Reading (10 MIN.) RF.2.4a, RF.2.4b, RF.2.4c

Introduce the Text

Display "Wind and Sun." Read aloud the title of the fable as you point under the words. Ask students to turn to a partner and predict and/or infer what the story will be about. If needed, model previewing and predicting.

Model Make Inferences and Predictions

Remind students that readers use various strategies when they read, including this unit's focus strategy: making inferences and predictions. Today they will make inferences and predictions before they read while previewing the text.

Sample modeling (title/illustrations). *The title makes me think that this story will be about the actions of the wind and the sun. The illustration shows faces on the wind and the sun, so I think they are characters in the story. Maybe the story will be about what the wind and the sun do to the man who is walking.*

Invite a few students to share their before-reading inferences or predictions with the class.

Model Fluent Reading: Prosody/Phrasing

First Reading. Read aloud the fable fluently, using natural phrasing.

Read Aloud Together. Invite students to read the fable with you. Remind them to think about natural places to pause within sentences.

Transfer Skills to Context: Annotate the Moral

Explain to students that like all fables, this one teaches a lesson, also called a moral. Model rereading the paragraphs and annotating details related to the fable's moral.

Sample modeling. *To understand the moral in this fable, I'll look for important details. I'll underline the last sentence in paragraph 1 because it shows what Wind thinks. In paragraph 2, I'll underline the third sentence because it shows why Wind's mighty gusts don't work. In paragraph 3, I'll underline the last sentence because it shows why Sun wins the contest. I'll jot a note that I think states the moral: "A gentle method can be stronger than a mighty one."*

Ask students to complete this sentence to state the moral in a different way: "If you want to persuade someone, try…"

RF.2.4a Read on-level text with purpose and understanding. **RF.2.4b** Read on-level text orally with accuracy, appropriate rate, and expression on successive readings. **RF.2.4c** Use context to confirm or self-correct word recognition and understanding, rereading as necessary.

220 Grade 2 • Unit 4 • Week 3 ©2018 Benchmark Education Company, LLC

Build Vocabulary: Describe How Words and Phrases Supply Rhythm and Meaning in a Story (10 MIN.) RI.2.4, L.2.4a, L.2.4e

Engage Thinking

We just read "Sun and Moon." Now we will reread parts of "The Stone Garden."

Display a page from a print dictionary. Use several entries with multiple definitions to point out each entry word and each numbered definition.

Say: *Many words have more than one definition. When we read, we decide which meaning fits with the way the word is being used. What should we do if the meaning we know for a word doesn't seem to make sense?*

Model (iELD)

Read aloud the first sentence of "The Stone Garden." Think aloud about the meaning of the word **side** as it is used in the sentence.

Sample modeling (sentence 1). *I know about a left or right side, or a back or front side, or a side on a team, but those meanings don't seem to fit with the word **side** in this sentence. The context makes me think that "houses on the small side" are houses that are somewhat small. I can use a dictionary to check my idea.*

Model using a print or digital dictionary to check the definitions of **side** to determine a meaning that fits with the context: "an aspect or a feature."

Say: *This meaning of **side** is the one that fits the context because "houses on the small side" are houses with the feature of smallness.*

Guided Practice

Ask students to reread paragraph 2 to find the word **lot**. Discuss the meaning of **lot** in its sentence, and ask students how they know **lot** doesn't mean "many" in this context. Ask a volunteer to look up **lot** in a print or digital dictionary to find the appropriate meaning.

Have students find each of the following words in the story, identify which meaning for the word seems to fit the context, and check their idea in a dictionary:

- **rose** (5)
- **plus** (18)
- **sign** (19)
- **direction** (23)

✓ Show Your Knowledge

During independent time ask students to reread paragraph 16 to find the phrase "a good deal" and jot down a note about what they think it means. They then look up **deal** in a dictionary to verify or revise their definition.

RI.2.4 Determine the meaning of words and phrases in a text relevant to a grade 2 topic or subject area. **L.2.4a** Use sentence-level context as a clue to the meaning of a word or phrase. **L.2.4e** Use glossaries and beginning dictionaries, both print and digital, to determine or clarify the meaning of words and phrases.

©2018 Benchmark Education Company, LLC

EXTENDED READ 2 MINI-LESSON

WEEK 3 • DAY 3

Texts for Close Reading, pp. 30–37
"The Stone Garden"

Student Objectives

I will be able to:
- Use context clues to find the meaning of a word.
- Check for the correct definition in a dictionary.

Additional Materials

Weekly Presentation: Unit 4, Week 3

iELD Integrated ELD

Light Support

Use "The Stone Garden." Review using a dictionary. Together, complete the chart below.

Paragraph	18
Unfamiliar Word	earth
Context Clue	ground, dig up
Dictionary Meaning	soil, ground, dirt

Pairs complete the sentence frames below to determine the meaning of one unfamiliar word from the text.

I didn't understand the word _____, but when I read _____, I thought it meant _____. The dictionary meaning is _____, so the meaning of _____ is _____.

Moderate Support

Paragraph	3
Unfamiliar Word	eyesore
Context Clue	lovely (opposite)
Dictionary Meaning	an ugly thing

When I didn't know what _____ meant, I found a context clue that meant (the opposite/same), _____. When I used a dictionary, I read that _____ means _____. I think _____ means _____.

Substantial Support

Paragraph	1
Unfamiliar Word	tidy
Context Clue	neat
Dictionary Meaning	neat; in order

The word _____ helped me understand _____. The dictionary meaning for _____ is _____. I think that _____ means _____.

Grade 2 • Unit 4 • Week 3

DAY 3

EXTENDED READ 2 MINI-LESSON

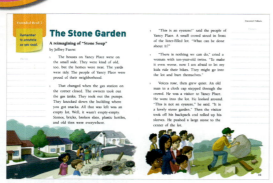

Texts for Close Reading, pp. 30–37
"The Stone Garden"

Student Objectives

I will be able to:
- Identify characters' points of view.
- Work cooperatively to discuss story characters.

Additional Materials

Weekly Presentation: Unit 4, Week 3
- Point of View Chart

✅ Observation Checklist for Productive Engagement

Is the Productive Engagement Productive?

As groups discuss characters' points of view, look for evidence that they are truly engaged in the task.

Partners are engaged productively if . . .
- ❏ they ask questions and use feedback to address the task.
- ❏ they demonstrate engagement and motivation.
- ❏ they apply strategies with some success.

If the discussion is productive, continue the task. If the discussion is unproductive, end the task and provide support.

Close Reading: Acknowledge Differences in the Points of View of Characters (15 MIN.) RL.2.1, RL.2.3, RL.2.6, SL.2.2, SL.2.3

Engage Thinking

Explain to students that they will continue working with "The Stone Garden." Remind students that a story character has a point of view—a way of looking at what is happening in the story. Explain that to understand a point of view, readers ask themselves questions, such as *What does this character believe? How does this character feel? What do you look for to understand a character's thoughts and feelings?*

Model

Display and read aloud the close reading prompt and annotation instructions. Model how you think about the prompt.

> **Close Reading Prompt:** Reread the last two paragraphs of the folktale. Why doesn't the visitor answer the man when he asks, "What do you think of this idea?"
> **Annotate!** Underline text evidence that explains why the visitor knew it was time to go on his way.

Sample modeling (paragraphs 30–31). *The prompt asks me to think about the man's question and the visitor's response. I'll underline those details:* **"What do you think of this idea?"** *…* **the old man … took one last look at one of the truly finest stone gardens he had ever seen, and was on his way."**

Sample modeling (paragraphs 5–7). *To figure out why the visitor leaves instead of answering the man's question, I need to think about the visitor's point of view. I'll go back through the story to see what the visitor says and does. In paragraph 4, I'll underline his comment,* **"This is not an eyesore. It is a lovely stone garden."** *I'll also underline his action:* **pushed a large stone to the center of the lot.** *After the crowd laughs at his idea, the visitor says,* **"Then you will see the makings of a fine stone garden."** *He places rocks* **in a circle around the stone.** *Those details help me understand that the visitor believes that people can change an ugly space into something beautiful.*

Use text evidence to determine the visitor's point of view at the end of the story.

Character	Text Evidence (paragraph)	Point of View at End of Story
Visitor	He tells the neighbors that the ugly lot is really "a lovely stone garden." He pushes a stone to the center. (5)	It is time for me to leave because the neighbors don't need my help anymore.
	He arranges rocks "in a circle around the stone." (7)	
	He suggests painting the rocks. (9)	
	He suggests adding plants. (13)	
	He says, "Excellent!" and "Wonderful!" as neighbors offer their own ideas. (15, 17)	
	"The visitor gave direction here and encouragement there." (23)	
	He is silent as the neighbors take over with their own ideas. (24–30)	

Sample Point of View Chart

222   Grade 2 • Unit 4 • Week 3   ©2018 Benchmark Education Company, LLC

EXTENDED READ 2 MINI-LESSON

WEEK 3 • DAY 3

⚙️ Productive Engagement: Peer Group

Organize students into groups of three or four. Each group should designate a discussion facilitator, scribe, timekeeper, and encourager. Display and read aloud a second close reading prompt.

> **Close Reading Prompt:** Reread paragraphs 23–27. What do the neighbors think about turning an ugly lot into a stone garden?
> **Annotate!** Underline details that help you explain the neighbors' point of view.

Ask students to reread paragraphs 23–27 to annotate the text and respond to the prompt. Clarify that they will look for what the characters say and do in order to tell about points of view. Observe students' annotations to determine if they need additional modeling or directive feedback.

Share Your Understanding

Call on students to share their answers to the close reading question. Remind listeners to ask questions to make sure they understand speakers' ideas.

Students should express their understanding that the characters in this story segment—an electrician, a woman, a "large man," a girl, and teenagers—have all become enthusiastic about the project. Each is participating by coming up with ideas, questions, and offers to help. Use this opportunity to provide additional modeling, corrective feedback, or validation based on students' responses.

✅ Show Your Knowledge

During independent time ask students to choose one of the characters from the story and tell how that character feels about what is happening. Ask students to read aloud the character's words as the character might say them.

---

iELD Integrated ELD

Light Support
Ask: *How can we use a Point of View Chart to organize our thinking on the visitor's point of view? Do the neighbors ever have the same point of view as the visitor? When? How do you know?*
Students complete the sentence frame below.
When I read _____ on page _____, this helped me understand that the neighbors' point of view was _____.

Moderate Support
Ask: *Why do we use a Point of View Chart? How does the chart help us organize information?*
Model determining the visitor's point of view.
Say: *I read _____ on page _____.*
I decided that this evidence shows that the visitor's point of view is _____.
Ask: *Do the neighbors have the same point of view as the visitor?*
Discuss the neighbors' point of view. Provide sentence frames.
I read _____ on page _____.
I decided that this evidence shows that the neighbors' point of view is _____.

Substantial Support
Students echo-read the Point of View Chart. Discuss and show students how to use the chart. Then discuss and model using the evidence in the chart to talk about the visitor's point of view.
Students present the visitor's point of view and use text evidence from the chart to support their answers. Provide sentence frames.
I think the visitor's point of view is _____, because I read _____.
These are the words in the story, _____.
Ask: *What do you think the neighbors' point of view is?*
Create a new column, and add text evidence to the chart. Substitute characters' names as students use the sentence frames to discuss the neighbors' points of view.

RL.2.1 Ask and answer such questions as who, what, where, when, why, and how to demonstrate understanding of key details in a text. **RL.2.3** Describe how characters in a story respond to major events and challenges. **RL.2.6** Acknowledge differences in the points of view of characters, including by speaking in a different voice for each character when reading dialogue aloud. **SL.2.2** Recount or describe key ideas or details from a text read aloud or information presented orally or through other media. **SL.2.3** Ask and answer questions about what a speaker says in order to clarify comprehension, gather additional information, or deepen understanding of a topic or issue.

©2018 Benchmark Education Company, LLC

Grade 2 • Unit 4 • Week 3   223

DAY 3

WRITING TO SOURCES

Student Writing Prompt

Is "Stone Soup" a story you would recommend to your friends? Why or why not? State your opinion in an essay. Supply reasons, based on details from the text, to support your opinion.

Student Objectives

I will be able to:
- Revise an opinion essay to include descriptive words.
- Share my ideas in collaborative conversation and in writing.

Materials

Weekly Presentation: Unit 4, Week 3
- Adjectives Chart (Week 1, Day 5)
- Example Draft and Revisions
- Descriptive Modeling Sentence
- Mentor Opinion Essay
- Opinion Essay Planning Chart
- Opinion Essay Anchor Chart
- Opinion Essay Checklist
- Opinion Essay Rubric

Revise the Writing: Revise to Include More Descriptive Words (15 MIN.) L.2.1e, L.2.6

Engage Thinking

Remind students that this week they have been drafting their opinion essays. Tell them that today they will begin to revise their writing, looking for opportunities to add more or stronger descriptive words to help readers better visualize what they describe.

Model

Display the Example Draft and Revision page. Read aloud the Draft version, then use a think-aloud to model how you evaluate and improve your draft in the Revision version.

Sample think-aloud: *When I wrote my draft of this paragraph, I used my planning page as a guide. In this body paragraph, I included events and facts from the story to support my reason, but I think I can improve it. I'll begin by connecting the first and second sentences using the word "because." The helps connect the reason to my opinion. I'll also look for places where I can add descriptive words, or adjectives. I'll underline these so when I look back at the text, I can make sure I used adjectives that correctly describe the events and details.*

Read aloud the Revision, pausing to compare it to the Draft and pointing out where you added adjectives. Talk about how the adjectives help readers get a better understanding of your meaning.

Draft
I like the main character. He is mysterious. He quickly pulls a pot from his coat. The villagers wonder what he's doing, but he only says, "You will see. You will see." He takes a stone from a bag and drops it into the pot. No one knows what he's doing.

Revision
I also recommend "Stone Soup" because the main character is mysterious. He quickly pulls a <u>large</u> pot from his <u>long, green</u> coat. The <u>curious</u> villagers wonder what he's doing, but he only says, "You will see. You will see." He takes a <u>big</u> stone from a <u>soft, velvet</u> bag and drops it into the pot. No one knows what he's doing.

Example Draft and Revision

Peer Practice

Display and read aloud the following sentences and ask partners to suggest adjectives to add or revise to make the writing more descriptive.

The villagers gathered around the pot of soup. It smelled good.

Descriptive Modeling Sentence

WRITING TO SOURCES

Share Your Understanding

Invite partners to share their revisions. Remind students that adding descriptive words helps readers visualize the ideas and events you are telling about. Tell students they can use the Adjectives Chart to help them think of descriptive words to add to their drafts.

Independent Writing (iELD)

During independent time, have students revise their draft, adding descriptive words to make their writing more interesting. Remind them to refer to the tools they have: mentor text, anchor chart, adjectives chart, writing checklist and rubric, planning chart, and source materials.

☑ Confer and Monitor

As you monitor students' independent writing, provide feedback, as needed. For example:

Directive Feedback: *I noticed you used a detail to support this reason. Now try to think of an adjective that might more accurately describe the detail.*

Self-Monitoring and Reflection: *Did you use descriptive words that help the reader get a clear picture of the events and details? What adjectives could you add to improve the essay?*

Validating and Confirming: *When I read the first body paragraph in your essay, I could picture exactly what the man did. It was easy to understand.*

---

iELD Integrated ELD

Light Support
Have students review the adjectives they used in their draft. Ask them to think about replacing more common adjectives, such as **good** and **big**, with stronger words like **terrific** and **huge**.

Moderate Support
Remind students that an adjective tells more about a noun. Help them identify nouns in their writing and discuss descriptive words they might use to help readers picture the person, place, thing, or idea.

Substantial Support
As students review their draft, guide them to identify a noun, then select a relevant adjective to describe that noun. They can refer to the Adjectives Chart for ideas. To help students select adjectives, ask leading questions such as:
How does ____ look?
What word can you use to describe how ____ feels?

L.2.1e Use adjectives and adverbs, and choose between them depending on what is to be modified. **L.2.6** Use words and phrases acquired through conversations, reading and being read to, and responding to texts, including using adjectives and adverbs to describe (e.g., *When other kids are happy that makes me happy*).

©2018 Benchmark Education Company, LLC

DAY 3

PHONICS & WORD STUDY

Texts for Close Reading, p. 38
"Goldilocks and the Three Bears"

Student Objectives

I will be able to:
- Blend, read, and spell words with r-controlled vowels **air, are, ear, ere.**
- Read word study (decodable) text.

Additional Materials

- Letter cards: **a, b, e, e, f, h, i, r, s, t**
- r-controlled /âr/ frieze card
- Sound-spelling card r-controlled /âr/

Weekly Presentation: Unit 4, Week 3
- High-frequency word cards: **another, boy, could, every, far, from, hurt, over, out, these**
- High-frequency word cards: **always, any, blue, buy, city, draw, four, great, how, live**

For additional word study/decodable practice, see: *Two Boys, One Day; Manners in Tales;* and *Tell the Tale.*

Monitor Student Reading of Word Study (Decodable) Passage

As students read the word study (decodable) text and answer questions, ask yourself these questions:

Are students able to . . .
❏ blend and read r-controlled vowel **air, are, ear, ere** words in the text?
❏ read new high-frequency words with automaticity?
❏ demonstrate comprehension of the text by answering text-based questions?

Based on your observations, you may wish to support students' fluency, automaticity, and comprehension with additional word study reading practice during intervention time.

r-Controlled Vowels air, are, ear, ere

(10 MIN.) RL.2.3, RF.2.3b, RF.2.3c, RF.2.3e, RF.2.3f, L.2.2d

Blend Words

Practice: fair, share, bear, there
Display pocket chart letter cards for the word **fair**. Model how to blend the sounds to say the word. Use the same routine with other r-controlled vowel words to guide student practice. Discuss the homophones **fair/fare** and **bear/bare**.

Read Word Study (Decodable) Passage

Introduce the Text
Read the title "Goldilocks and the Three Bears" aloud. Stop when you come to the word **Bears**. Point out the r-controlled vowel spelling **ear**.

Read the Text
Ask students to read the text. If students need modeling, guide them to blend decodable words and read high-frequency words. You may wish to conduct a second reading, having partners read to each other while you circulate and monitor the reading.

Connect Phonics to Comprehension
Ask some or all of the following questions:

- *Who lived in the home Goldilocks found?*
- *What did Goldilocks do inside?*
- *What happened when the bears returned home?*

Spelling

Write the word clues. Have students write the spelling word that goes with each one. Challenge students to come up with clues for other spelling words.

1. a fruit (**pear**)
2. an animal (**bear**)
3. a shape (**square**)
4. something you sit on (**chair**)

High-Frequency Words

Practice: another, boy, could, every, far, from, hurt, over, out, these
Draw a ladder with ten rungs. Write a high-frequency word on each rung. Have students take turns climbing the ladder by reading the words.

Review: *always, any, blue, buy, city, draw, four, great, how, live*

RL.2.3 Describe how characters in a story respond to major events and challenges. **RF.2.3b** Know spelling-sound correspondences for additional common vowel teams. **RF.2.3c** Decode regularly spelled two-syllable words with long vowels. **RF.2.3e** Identify words with inconsistent but common spelling-sound correspondences. **RF.2.3f** Recognize and read grade-appropriate irregularly spelled words. **L.2.2d** Generalize learned spelling patterns when writing words (e.g., cage → badge; boy → boil).

226 Grade 2 • Unit 4 • Week 3   ©2018 Benchmark Education Company, LLC

Shared Reading (10 MIN.) RL.2.4, RF.2.4a, RF.2.4c, L.2.1e

Reread for Fluency: Prosody/Phrasing

Partner Reading. Ask partners to take turns rereading "Wind and Sun," alternating paragraphs and then switching roles. Remind them to think about words that belong together as they decide where to pause within long sentences.

Collaborative Conversation: Make Inferences and Predictions

Recall for students how you make inferences and predictions based on information from the text. Tell students that today they will work in pairs to make inferences and predictions themselves. If necessary, pose text-dependent questions to guide their thinking. For example:

- *What can you infer about Wind and Sun while reading this fable?*
- *What is the lesson, or moral, of this fable? Support your inference.*

Transfer Skills to Context: Annotate Point of View

Remind students that the actions, thoughts, and words of a character show the character's point of view. Model underlining details that help you identify the point of view of the two main characters.

Sample modeling. *In paragraph 1, I learn about Wind's thoughts. Wind is sure that **his mighty gusts** will be stronger than Sun's power, and that he **would be victorious** in the contest. Wind believes that he can blow the man's coat off. Sun's words about a **gentle approach** show a different point of view. Sun prefers to slowly persuade the man to remove his coat.*

Ask students to think about the point of view of the man in the story: *What does he think when the wind blows? What is his point of view when the sun shines?*

Transfer Skills to Context: Use Adverbs

Remind students that an adverb can answer the question "How?" to tell about an action. Draw their attention to the adverb **tightly** in paragraph 2.

Ask: *How does the man pull his coat around him?* (**tightly**)

Point to the adverb **warmly** in paragraph 3 for students to read aloud.

Ask: *What question does this adverb answer?* (How does the sun shine?)

RL.2.4 Describe how words and phrases (e.g., regular beats, alliteration, rhymes, repeated lines) supply rhythm and meaning in a story, poem, or song. **RF.2.4a** Read on-level text with purpose and understanding. **RF.2.4c** Use context to confirm or self-correct word recognition and understanding, rereading as necessary. **L.2.1e** Use adjectives and adverbs, and choose between them depending on what is to be modified.

©2018 Benchmark Education Company, LLC

SHARED READING

Texts for Close Reading, p. 29
"Wind and Sun"

Student Objectives

I will be able to:
- Identify and annotate a character's point of view.
- Explain what an adverb does.

Additional Materials

Weekly Presentation: Unit 4, Week 3

iELD Integrated ELD

Light Support
Explain the words **closer** and **mighty**, and how to form the adverbs.

Paragraph	Adverb	Adjective
3	closely	(close)
1	(mightily)	mighty

Groups complete sentence frames using the adjectives and adverbs.
The wind blew _____. (mightily)
The wind blew with _____ gusts. (mighty)

Moderate Support
Together find adjectives and adverbs in the text, place them in the correct column of the chart, and write the missing adjective or adverb.

Paragraph	Adverb	Adjective
3	warmly	(warm)
1	(victoriously)	victorious

Students answer questions about the fable using the adjectives and adverbs from the chart.

Substantial Support
Together find adjectives and adverbs in the text, place them in the correct column of the chart, and write the missing adjective or adverb.

Paragraph	Adverb	Adjective
2	tightly	(tight)
3	(gently)	gentle

Students compose and echo-read sentences about the fable using the adjectives and adverbs from the chart.

Grade 2 • Unit 4 • Week 3   227

DAY 4

CROSS-TEXT MINI-LESSON

Texts for Close Reading, pp. 18–25 "Stone Soup" and pp. 30–37 "The Stone Garden"

Student Objectives

I will be able to:
- Identify similarities in two variant stories.
- Share my ideas and build on others' ideas in a group discussion.

Additional Materials

Weekly Presentation: Unit 4, Week 3
- Comparison Chart

Close Reading: Compare and Contrast Two Versions of the Same Story (20 MIN.) RL.2.1, RL.2.9, SL.2.2, SL.2.3, SL.2.6

Engage Thinking

Display "Stone Soup" and "The Stone Garden" and explain that students will now compare the two literary texts. Point out the subtitle in "The Stone Garden" and ask students what it helps them understand. Use students' responses to emphasize that both the old folktale and the modern story have many elements in common.

Model

Display and read aloud the close reading prompt and annotation instructions. Model analyzing the prompt and responding to it.

> **Close Reading Prompt:** How is the visitor in "The Stone Garden" like the old man in "Stone Soup"?
> **Annotate!** Underline evidence that displays each character's traits.

Sample modeling ("Stone Soup"). *The prompt asks me to look for similarities in both main characters. I'll start by reviewing "Stone Soup" to underline details that show me what the old man is like:*

- In paragraph 1, I'll underline words that describe his appearance.
- In paragraph 3, I'll underline the word **stranger**, because it shows that he does not live in this village.
- In paragraph 8, I'll underline **like a magician**, because it suggests that he has special knowledge.
- In paragraph 18, he mentions a way to improve the soup. I'll underline his words.
- As the story continues, the old man encourages the villagers to bring food items. I'll underline his encouraging words in paragraphs 20, 24, and 26.
- At the end of the story, the old man **needed to move on**, but before leaving, he **shared his secret** about **the magic of sharing**.

Sample modeling ("The Stone Garden"). *As I review "The Stone Garden" I'll focus on details that show me how the visitor is like the old man in "Stone Soup":*

- In paragraph 5, I learn that the visitor is also **an old man**. The words **a visitor to Yancy Place** show me that he is a stranger. The illustration shows his beard is gray.
- In paragraph 7, I'll underline his words telling that his travels have given him special knowledge.
- In paragraph 9, his words remind me of what the old man says in "Stone Soup"— suggesting a way to improve things.
- As the story continues, the visitor encourages the neighbors to bring items for the garden. I'll underline his encouraging words in paragraphs 13, 15, 17, and 23.
- At the end of the story, the visitor is **on his way**. He has seen the neighbors sharing ideas and work.

After annotating the texts, list similarities in a two-column Comparison Chart.

228 Grade 2 • Unit 4 • Week 3 ©2018 Benchmark Education Company, LLC

Old Man in "Stone Soup"	Visitor in "The Stone Garden"
old, with a gray beard	old, with a gray beard
a stranger in the village	a stranger in Yancy Place
tells about his special knowledge of stone soup	tells about his special knowledge of stone gardens
mentions a way to improve the soup	mentions a way to improve the garden
encourages the villagers to bring food items	encourages the neighbors to bring garden items
says "Wonderful" and "the best stone soup ever"	says "Wonderful" and "one of the finer stone gardens I have ever seen"
moves on after teaching the importance of sharing	moves on after teaching the importance of working together

Sample Comparison Chart

Guided Practice

Display and read aloud a second close reading prompt.

> **Close Reading Prompt:** How are the neighbors in "The Stone Garden" like the villagers in "Stone Soup"?
>
> **Annotate!** Underline evidence in both stories that shows what the characters are like.

Observe students' annotations to determine if they need additional modeling or directive feedback.

Share

Invite students to share their answers to the close reading prompt. Encourage students to restate classroom rules for discussion. Use this opportunity to provide additional modeling, corrective feedback, or validation based on students' responses.

Students should express their understanding of similarities between the characters in both stories, such as the inability of the villagers or the neighbors to see a solution to their problem at the start, the generous actions of a few individuals, the characters' responses to encouragement, and their changed points of view at the end.

☑ Show Your Knowledge

During independent time ask students to write two or three sentences explaining how the soup in "Stone Soup" is similar to the garden in "The Stone Garden."

Challenge Activity. Ask partners to write a new opening paragraph for "Stone Soup," in which the visitor from "The Stone Garden" arrives in the village.

RL.2.1 Ask and answer such questions as who, what, where, when, why, and how to demonstrate understanding of key details in a text. **RL.2.9** Compare and contrast two or more versions of the same story (e.g., Cinderella stories) by different authors or from different cultures. **SL.2.2** Recount or describe key ideas or details from a text read aloud or information presented orally or through other media. **SL.2.3** Ask and answer questions about what a speaker says in order to clarify comprehension, gather additional information, or deepen understanding of a topic or issue. **SL.2.6** Produce complete sentences when appropriate to task and situation in order to provide requested detail or clarification. (See grade 2 Language standards 1 and 3 on pages 26 and 27 for specific expectations.)

©2018 Benchmark Education Company, LLC

---

iELD Integrated ELD

Light Support

Have students review the Comparison Chart. Students complete sentence frames to tell how the characters from the two texts are similar.

Both old men are similar, because _____.

Since both old men _____, these characters are _____.

Pairs use the text to find additional information to add to the chart below.

Old Man in "Stone Soup"	Old Man in "The Stone Garden"
asks villagers for help	asks neighbors for help
taught the villagers a lesson	taught the neighbors a lesson

Ask: *What did you read in both stories that made you think these characters were similar?*

Moderate Support

Review and have students echo-read the Comparison Chart. Students complete a sentence frame to tell how the characters from the two texts are similar.

Both old men _____, so these characters are alike.

Pairs use the text to find additional information to add to the chart below.

Old Man in "Stone Soup"	Old Man in "The Stone Garden"
gets no help from the villagers at the beginning	gets no help from the neighbors at the beginning
is a visitor	is a visitor

Ask: *How do the pictures help you see the similarities between these characters?*

Substantial Support

Review and have students echo-read the Comparison Chart. Students complete a sentence frame to tell how the characters from the two texts are similar.

Both old men _____, so these characters are alike.

Help students use the text to find additional information to add to the chart below.

Old Man in "Stone Soup"	Old Man in "The Stone Garden"
helps the villagers	helps the neighbors
has a stone	works with stones

Ask: *How does the chart help you compare these two characters?*

DAY 4

WRITING TO SOURCES

Student Writing Prompt

Is "Stone Soup" a story you would recommend to your friends? Why or why not? State your opinion in an essay. Supply reasons, based on details from the text, to support your opinion.

Student Objectives

I will be able to:
- Edit a text to form and use contractions correctly.
- Consult reference materials to check and correct spelling.

Materials

Weekly Presentation: Unit 4, Week 3
- Contractions Modeling Text
- Formal Contractions Modeling Chart (Week 2, Day 5)
- Mentor Opinion Essay
- Opinion Essay Planning Chart
- Opinion Essay Anchor Chart
- Opinion Essay Checklist
- Opinion Essay Rubric

Write an Opinion Essay: Edit to Correct Use of Contractions

(15 MIN.) L.2.2c, L.2.3a

Engage Thinking

Remind students that yesterday they revised their drafts with a focus on ways to use and add adjectives to strengthen their essay. Tell them that today you'll show them how to edit your writing to make sure you use contractions correctly.

Model

Display and distribute the Contractions Modeling Text. Begin reading it, and model for students how you select the correctly formed contractions in the first two instances.

Sample think-aloud: *When I reread my draft, I look for errors, including contractions that might be formed incorrectly. Because I'm writing an opinion essay, I can use contractions. But I know I shouldn't use informal contractions unless they are in the exact words of a character that I'm quoting. In my first sentence, I know that **I's** is not a proper contraction, and I also know that a contraction isn't even called for. So I will circle **I**. The next one I see is supposed to be the contraction for **do not**, but **don'ot** is incorrect. The **o** is removed from **not** to form the contraction, and the apostrophe replaces it. So I'll circle **don't**.*

> A third reason **I's/I** think you should read "Stone Soup" is it teaches the value of sharing. At the beginning, the villagers say they **don't/don'ot** have food. Later in the story, the stranger begins to make soup and the villagers bring food. They **could've/coulda** shared before, but they did not. After they ate the soup, they learned **its/it's** important to share.

Contractions Modeling Text

Peer Practice

Have students work with a partner to identify the correct forms of contractions in the next two instances. (*could've; it's*)

230 Grade 2 • Unit 4 • Week 3

©2018 Benchmark Education Company, LLC

WRITING TO SOURCES

WEEK 3 · DAY 4

Share Your Understanding

Bring students together and invite the partners to share their edits with the class. Help students understand the difference between the informal **coulda** to the formal contraction **could've** and the insertion of the missing apostrophe in the contraction for **it is (it's)** in the last sentence.

Independent Writing (iELD)

During independent time, have students pay attention to their use and formation of contractions as they edit their drafts. Suggest they refer to a print or online dictionary, as needed, to check their spelling of contractions. Remind students to refer to the tools they have: mentor text, anchor chart, contractions chart, writing checklist and rubric, planning chart, and source materials.

✓ Confer and Monitor

As you monitor students' independent writing, provide feedback, as needed. For example:

Directive Feedback: *Look at this contraction. What two words does it stand for? Did you form the contraction correctly?*

Self-Monitoring and Reflection: *Read each sentence slowly, one word at a time. Is there any place you want to add a contraction? Are your contractions written correctly?*

Validating and Confirming: *I see you initially used the informal contraction* **gimme***. You changed it to* **give me***. That is the correct usage.*

(iELD) Integrated ELD

Light Support
Refer students to the Contractions Chart from Week 2, Day 5. Explain that using the chart can help them identify contraction errors and make corrections in their draft.

Moderate Support
As students review their drafts, guide them to focus on the contractions they used. Ask questions and provide sentence frames to help students make corrections. For example:
What two words does this contraction stand for? Did you form it correctly?
The words **did** *and* **not** *together make the contraction* _____ *.*

Substantial Support
Help students set up a chart to help them check contractions in their draft. Encourage them to list each contraction, check it's spelling in a dictionary, and make corrections, if needed.

L.2.2c Use an apostrophe to form contractions and frequently occurring possessives. **L.2.3a** Compare formal and informal uses of English.

©2018 Benchmark Education Company, LLC

Grade 2 • Unit 4 • Week 3   **231**

DAY 4

PHONICS & WORD STUDY

r-Controlled Vowels air, are, ear, ere

(20 MIN.) RF.2.3b, RF.2.3c, RF.2.3d, RF.2.3e, RF.2.3f, L.2.2d

Read Multisyllabic Words

Model: unfair

Explain that when an r-controlled vowel spelling such as **air**, **are**, **ear**, or **ere** appears in a long word, the spelling must remain in the same syllable. Model using the word **unfair**.

- Write the prefix **un-** and point out that it can mean "not" or "the opposite of."
- Add the word **fair**. Point out the r-controlled vowel spelling **air**.
- Circle the vowel spellings **u** and **air**. Tell students you will divide the word after the prefix: **un/fair**.
- Blend the syllables to read the word. Help students define it.

Practice: beware, compare, prepare, underwear, wearing, upstairs, hairless

Use the same routine to guide student practice.

Spelling

Categories

Write the groups of words. Read the words, and ask students to complete each category with a spelling word. Ask students to come up with other category word groups for the spelling words.

- eyes, ears, _____ (**hair**)
- deer, wolf, _____ (**bear**)
- table, couch, _____ (**chair**)
- circle, triangle, _____ (**square**)

High-Frequency Words

Review: another, boy, could, every, far, from, hurt, over, out, these

Display the high-frequency word cards. Read each word and have students repeat the word and spell it aloud together. Have students sit in a circle. Pass the cards, one at a time. Each student reads the word and uses it in a sentence before passing the card.

Student Objectives

I will be able to:
- Blend multisyllabic words with r-controlled vowels **air, are, ear, ere**.
- Spell words with r-controlled vowels **air, are, ear, ere**.
- Read high-frequency words.

Additional Materials

- r-controlled /âr/ frieze card
- Sound-spelling card r-controlled /âr/

Weekly Presentation: Unit 4, Week 3
- High-frequency word cards: **another, boy, could, every, far, from, hurt, over, out, these**

For additional word study/decodable practice, see: *Two Boys, One Day*; *Manners in Tales*; and *Tell the Tale*.

RF.2.3b Know spelling-sound correspondences for additional common vowel teams. **RF.2.3c** Decode regularly spelled two-syllable words with long vowels. **RF.2.3d** Decode words with common prefixes and suffixes. **RF.2.3e** Identify words with inconsistent but common spelling-sound correspondences. **RF.2.3f** Recognize and read grade-appropriate irregularly spelled words. **L.2.2d** Generalize learned spelling patterns when writing words (e.g., cage → badge; boy → boil).

Shared Reading (10 MIN.) RL.2.1, RF.2.4b, SL.2.2, SL.2.3, L.2.4a

Reread for Fluency: Prosody/Phrasing (iELD)

Partner Reading. Ask partners to reread "Why Owls Are Wise" aloud to each other, dividing the text as they wish. Remind them to pay special attention to groups of words that belong together.

Make Inferences and Predictions

Remind students that you showed them how you made inferences and predictions before and during reading. Students also practiced making inferences and predictions while they read the story. Tell them that today you will reread the fable and students will make inferences and predictions after they read.

Sample think-aloud: *In this fable, the text says that Great Bear is so thankful to Owl, that he rewards her with wisdom and that since then, all owls are known for their wisdom. Based on this, I can infer that Great Bear has the power to not only grant one single owl with wisdom, but grant wisdom to all species of owls.*

Transfer Skills to Context: Annotate a Pourquoi Tale

Remind students that a pourquoi tale explains why something in the world is the way it is. Tell them to find and underline the sentence in this story that shows why this is a pourquoi tale. Discuss their reasons.

Build and Reflect

During independent time, tell students to think about the Unit 4 selections, and ask them to complete the "Build, Reflect, Write" activity on page 39 to help them think more about how different characters have different points of view.

SHARED READING

WEEK 3 · DAY 5

Texts for Close Reading, p. 28
"Why Owls Are Wise"

Student Objectives

I will be able to:
- Read a pourquoi tale about characters with different points of view.
- Identify the reason that a story is called a pourquoi tale.

Additional Materials

Weekly Presentation: Unit 4, Week 3

iELD Integrated ELD

Light Support
If ELLs have trouble reading aloud with prosody and phrasing, scaffold pre-reading lessons for "Why Owls Are Wise." Assess their needs for future lessons.
Write, discuss, and sequence key events using key vocabulary and language, such as **before nightfall, up here, get back to**.
Partners discuss meaningful chunks for understanding, and then focus on reading aloud meaningful chunks with correct phrasing, intonation, rhythm, and stress.

Moderate Support
Write, discuss, and sequence key events using key vocabulary and language, such as **looking for, guided, so grateful**.
Model reading passages with correct intonation and phrasing. Students choral-read and then partner-read.

Substantial Support
Write, discuss, and sequence key events using key vocabulary and language, such as **should have, needed to, can see**.
Students role-play key language and events to show comprehension.
Model reading aloud key chunks with correct phrasing, rhythm, and stress. Students echo-read.

RL.2.1 Ask and answer such questions as who, what, where, when, why, and how to demonstrate understanding of key details in a text. **RF.2.4b** Read on-level text orally with accuracy, appropriate rate, and expression on successive readings. **SL.2.2** Recount or describe key ideas or details from a text read aloud or information presented orally or through other media. **SL.2.3** Ask and answer questions about what a speaker says in order to clarify comprehension, gather additional information, or deepen understanding of a topic or issue. **L.2.4a** Use sentence-level context as a clue to the meaning of a word or phrase.

©2018 Benchmark Education Company, LLC

DAY 5

WRITING TO SOURCES

Student Writing Prompt

Is "Stone Soup" a story you would recommend to your friends? Why or why not? State your opinion in an essay. Supply reasons, based on details from the text, to support your opinion.

Student Objectives

I will be able to:
- Evaluate my opinion essay using a rubric.
- Share my ideas in collaborative conversation and in writing.

Materials

Weekly Presentation: Unit 4, Week 3
- Mentor Opinion Essay
- Opinion Essay Anchor Chart
- Opinion Essay Writing Checklist

Review and Reflect (15 MIN.) W.2.1

Engage Thinking

Tell students today they will have an opportunity to evaluate the final draft of their opinion essay and decide if they are ready to turn it in. Explain that first you will model how you use the writing rubric to evaluate an opinion essay.

Model

Display the Mentor Opinion Essay from Week 1, and have students take out their copies of the same text. Reread the text aloud.

Review the selected criteria from the rubric evaluation form with students. Also review the scoring key. Remind students that the rubric aligns to the anchor chart and checklist they have used throughout the unit. Then use think-alouds to model how you evaluate four of the six criteria.

Rubric Criteria	Sample Think-Alouds	Sample Score
Includes an opinion statement with first-person pronouns	An opinion statement appears in my first paragraph. I clearly state that I would recommend "The Blind Men and the Elephant." I use the first-person pronoun **I**.	4
Bases writing on notes taken in writer's own words from the source text	To analyze this criterion, I need to make sure I don't use exact sentences from the story unless I'm using the exact words a character says. When I reread, I see that I have used my own words. I did include words two of the men speak in the story. I placed them in quotation marks. One example is, "He said, 'The elephant is like a rope!'" The quotation helps me express my opinion by giving readers a clear example from the text.	4
Includes a conclusion	I carefully read the requirements to get a score of a 4 in this criterion. I reread my conclusion. Did I include only key words and phrases from the opinion statement? Yes. I used the words **think about things in a different way** in the opinion statement, but I used **think about things from a different point of view** in the conclusion. I restated my opinion, but did not repeat it.	4
Includes adjectives	I used adjectives correctly to help my readers form a picture in their minds. I used the word **real** to describe the elephant. I used the word **long** to describe his trunk.	4

234 Grade 2 • Unit 4 • Week 3

Peer Practice

Ask students to independently evaluate and score their writing for one of the criteria on the rubric. Have them discuss their self-evaluation of the criteria with a partner. Then ask students to complete their self-evaluation using the rubric.

Share Your Understanding

Bring students together and invite the partners to share one thing about their evaluations with the class. Have students decide if they are prepared to turn in their final draft or if, based on their self-evaluation, they would like to revise or edit their writing further before turning it in.

✓ Quick Write

During independent time, have students respond to one of the following: *What do you think is the most important thing to remember when writing an opinion essay? What did you do to improve your opinion essay during the revise and edit process?* Use students' writing to evaluate their ability to review and reflect on their own writing.

Note: Each student should save a copy of their opinion essay to keep in a writing portfolio. They will have a chance to reflect on their writing portfolios at the end of the writing program.

---

iELD Integrated ELD

Light Support
Encourage partners to ask and answer each other's questions about the self-assessment process. For example:
Did you check to make sure you have an opinion statement?

Moderate Support
Demonstrate how to turn the criterion in the rubric into questions students can answer as they review their essay and share their self-evaluation. For example:
Did I include an opinion statement?
Encourage students to point out the text in their draft that answers the question.

Substantial Support
Help students evaluate their writing with sentence frames that guide them to describe the elements of an opinion essay. For example:
I begin with an ___ statement.
I state ___ reasons in my essay.

W.2.1 Write opinion pieces in which they introduce the topic or book they are writing about, state an opinion, supply reasons that support the opinion, use linking words (e.g., because, and, also) to connect opinion and reasons, and provide a concluding statement or section

DAY 5

PHONICS & WORD STUDY

Texts for Close Reading, p. 38
"Goldilocks and the Three Bears"

Student Objectives

I will be able to:
- Build, read, and spell words with r-controlled vowels **air, are, ear, ere**.
- Reread word study (decodable) text for fluency.
- Read high-frequency words.

Additional Materials

- Letter cards: **a, b, c, e, f, h, i, p, r, s, w**
- r-controlled /âr/ frieze card
- Sound-spelling card r-controlled /âr/

Weekly Presentation: Unit 4, Week 3
- Letter cards for each high-frequency word
- High-frequency word cards: **another, boy, could, every, far, from, hurt, over, out, these**

For additional word study/decodable practice, see: *Two Boys, One Day; Manners in Tales;* and *Tell the Tale*.

Review and Assess r-Controlled Vowels air, are, ear, ere (20 MIN.) RF.2.3b, RF.2.3c, RF.2.3d, RF.2.3e, RF.2.3f, L.2.2d

Build Words

Model: care, scare, share

Display the letter cards for **care**. Blend the sounds: **/kâr/, care.**

- Add the **s** and repeat with **scare**.
- Replace the **c** with **h** and repeat with **share**.

Practice: air, fair, pair, hair, chair, pear, bear, wear, swear

Use the same routine to guide student practice.

Review Multisyllabic Words

Model: wear, wearing

Write the word **wear** and ask students to identify the vowel sound and spelling. Point out that the r-controlled vowel spelling **ear** must stay in the same syllable in a longer word.

Write the word **wearing**. Model how to read the longer word. Point out that the added syllable **–ing** is a suffix.

Practice: air, airplane; hair, hairy; pair, repair; stair, stairway; care, careful; mare, nightmare

Use the same routine to guide student practice.

Reread for Fluency: "Goldilocks and the Three Bears" iELD

Have students independently whisper-read "Goldilocks and the Three Bears." Circulate and listen to their readings. Provide corrective feedback. For students having difficulty reading independently, have them read with a more skilled partner.

236   Grade 2 • Unit 4 • Week 3   ©2018 Benchmark Education Company, LLC

PHONICS & WORD STUDY

WEEK 3 · DAY 5

Spelling

Posttest

Use the following procedure to assess students' spelling of this week's words.

- Say each spelling word and use it in the sentence provided.
- Have students write the complete sentence on a piece of paper. Then continue with the next word.
- When students have finished, collect their papers and analyze any misspelled words.

1. **Where** will you sit?
2. I have black **hair**.
3. She ate a **pear** for lunch.
4. Do you **care** if I use your pen?
5. It is fun to **share** games with a friend.
6. We ran up more **stairs** than ever before.
7. Does a **square** have three or four sides?
8. The **bear** ran after the deer in the forest.
9. What do you **wear** when you play soccer?
10. Put that **chair** over here.

High-Frequency Words

Review: *another, boy, could, every, far, from, hurt, over, out, these*

Display the high-frequency word cards. Say each word and have students chorally repeat the word and spell it.

Place letter cards, in random order, for one of the words in a pocket chart. Have a volunteer beat the clock to form the word. Allow 15 seconds. Then have the rest of the class check the spelling and give a thumbs up or thumbs down.

Next have students turn to a partner and say a sentence using the word. Call on volunteers to check their sentences.

---

iELD Integrated ELD

Light Support

Revisit "Goldilocks and the Three Bears" before students independently whisper-read the text. Choose, write, discuss, and have students echo-read key vocabulary. Students role-play vocabulary to show comprehension.

far from home, broke into little bits, tapped on her arm, all the way home.

Monitor partners as they read meaningful chunks with fluency and discuss the text. Assist and model as needed.

Moderate Support

Choose, write, discuss, and have students echo-read key vocabulary. Students role-play vocabulary to show comprehension.

anyway, I don't care, splat, stared, mess.

Model reading meaningful chunks with fluency. Groups discuss story events. Assist as needed.

Substantial Support

Choose, write, discuss, and have students echo-read key vocabulary. Students role-play vocabulary to show comprehension.

golden hair, far, spotted, porridge, screamed, scared, broke, just right.

Model reading key chunks with fluency. Students echo-read and discuss the events. Assist as needed.

RF.2.3b Know spelling-sound correspondences for additional common vowel teams. **RF.2.3c** Decode regularly spelled two-syllable words with long vowels. **RF.2.3d** Decode words with common prefixes and suffixes. **RF.2.3e** Identify words with inconsistent but common spelling-sound correspondences. **RF.2.3f** Recognize and read grade-appropriate irregularly spelled words. **L.2.2d** Generalize learned spelling patterns when writing words (e.g., cage → badge; boy→boil).

©2018 Benchmark Education Company, LLC

Grade 2 • Unit 4 • Week 3   **237**

DAY 5

UNIT REFLECTION

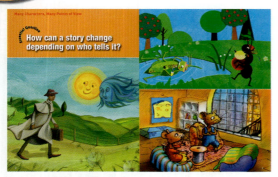

Texts for Close Reading, pp. 2–3
Unit Introduction

Student Objectives

I will be able to:
- Follow rules for a collaborative discussion.
- Discuss characters from different stories.
- Create an audio recording to present ideas.

Additional Materials

Weekly Presentation: Unit 4, Week 3
- Unit 4 Video
- Essential Question and Answer Chart

✓ Observation Checklist for Collaborative Conversation

As peer groups discuss the Essential Question, use the questions below to evaluate how effectively students communicate with each other. Based on your answers, you may wish to plan future core lessons to support the collaborative conversation process.

Do peer groups . . .
- ☐ stay on topic throughout the discussion?
- ☐ listen respectfully?
- ☐ build on the comments of others appropriately?
- ☐ pose or respond to questions to clarify information?
- ☐ support their partners to participate?

Reflect on Unit Concepts (20 MIN.) W.2.6, SL.2.1a, SL.2.1b, SL.2.1c, SL.2.2, SL.2.3, SL.2.5, SL.2.6

Engage Thinking

Encourage discussion of what students have learned from their reading. You may wish to display the titles from the unit.

Say: *In this unit, we have discovered many different characters and points of view in the fables, folktales, and other stories we have read. What are some things you have learned about the points of view of story characters?*

Display the introduction to *Many Characters, Many Points of View* and read aloud the Essential Question.

> How can a story change depending on who tells it?

Say: *By thinking about different points of view, we can see and understand events and ideas in new ways. In this lesson we will continue to share our understandings of points of view.*

▶ View Multimedia

Tell students that they will watch the same short video they watched at the beginning of this unit. After viewing, discuss how the video connects to the unit and the Essential Question. Encourage discussion of how this viewing experience was different for students from their first viewing.

💬 Collaborative Conversation: Peer Group (iELD)

Say: *When I am the assigned timekeeper in a conversation, I make sure everyone has a chance to speak, and nobody takes up the whole time.*

Assign students to peer groups. Guide the groups as they select a facilitator, a scribe, a timekeeper, and an encourager. Tell them that they will collaborate to develop a group answer to the Essential Question. Present the steps for groups to follow during their conversation.

Say: *We have three directions to follow for our conversation today:*

1. Choose one person to begin the conversation.
2. Raise your hand after a speaker has finished when you want the facilitator to give you a turn to speak.
3. Add to the speaker's ideas. Include details and ideas from the texts you have read to support your ideas.

Make sure that all students understand the steps. Ask a volunteer from each group to restate the steps in his or her own words. Monitor their conversations to ensure that they follow the directions and that all students have a chance to participate.

UNIT REFLECTION

WEEK 3 · DAY 5

Share

Give students about five minutes to share their ideas and develop an answer. Then bring the class together. Call on the scribe from each group to share the group's answer to the Essential Question. Review directions for participation as the groups share their ideas:

4. The scribe tells the group's answer to the Essential Question.
5. Classmates listen attentively.
6. Anyone with a follow-up question or comment raises a hand.

Capture each group's ideas in a chart. At the end of the unit, post the chart in your classroom.

How can a story change depending on who tells it?
- The shepherd in "The Boy Who Cried Wolf" would explain how he was just joking.
- The villagers in "The Boy Who Cried Wolf" would tell how annoyed they were.
- A character might tell only part of the whole story, like each man in "The Blind Men and the Elephant."
- The old man in "Stone Soup" might tell what he thinks of the villagers who say they can't help him.
- The neighbors in "The Stone Garden" might tell about the day a stranger showed them how to work together.
- Characters who learn a lesson might tell why they were mistaken and what they learned.
- Characters who teach a lesson might tell why the lesson is important.

Sample Essential Question and Answer Chart

Use Digital Media

Ask each group to choose a story character and turn him or her into the narrator of that story. They should write a script showing the new version of a short fable or folktale. Then they can use the script to make an audio recording.

Observe and Assess

As students reflect on unit concepts and present ideas, use the following questions to informally assess their understanding:

- Do students understand what a point of view is?
- Do students understand that story characters have different points of view and may change their points of view?
- Are students able to explain and support their ideas?

iELD Integrated ELD

Light Support
Choose, explain, and discuss key vocabulary for conversation directions, such as **follow-up question, listen attentively, respond to questions, ask questions, share, wait for a turn**.
Observe, monitor, assess, and evaluate students' conversation skills. Use the information to plan future conversation lessons.
Were students able to:
- *listen attentively and ask appropriate follow up questions?*
- *respond appropriately to peers' questions?*
- *act appropriately as a scribe or a facilitator?*
- *offer appropriate follow-up ideas?*
- *share and include appropriate details from the texts?*

Moderate Support
Discuss vocabulary for conversation instructions, such as **give you a turn, take a turn, details, ideas, comment, begin the conversation, listen respectfully, respond**.
Were students able to:
- *choose a scribe and a facilitator?*
- *build appropriately on the comments of others?*
- *share appropriate details during the conversation?*
- *ask and respond to questions appropriately?*
- *listen politely, wait for a turn to speak, and signal the facilitator appropriately by raising their hands?*

Substantial Support
Discuss vocabulary for conversation instructions, such as **raise your hand, facilitator, speaker, scribe, choose**.
Were students able to:
- *choose one person to begin the conversation?*
- *engage in proper turn-taking during a conversation?*
- *add appropriate details during the conversation?*
- *listen attentively, and offer appropriate comments?*

W.2.6 With guidance and support from adults, use a variety of digital tools to produce and publish writing, including in collaboration with peers. **SL.2.1a** Follow agreed-upon rules for discussions (e.g., gaining the floor in respectful ways, listening to others with care, speaking one at a time about the topics and texts under discussion). **SL.2.1b** Build on others' talk in conversations by linking their comments to the remarks of others. **SL.2.1c** Ask for clarification and further explanation as needed about the topics and texts under discussion. **SL.2.2** Recount or describe key ideas or details from a text read aloud or information presented orally or through other media. **SL.2.3** Ask and answer questions about what a speaker says in order to clarify comprehension, gather additional information, or deepen understanding of a topic or issue. **SL.2.5** Create audio recordings of stories or poems; add drawings or other visual displays to stories or recounts of experiences when appropriate to clarify ideas, thoughts, and feelings. **SL.2.6** Produce complete sentences when appropriate to task and situation in order to provide requested detail or clarification.

©2018 Benchmark Education Company, LLC

Grade 2 • Unit 4 • Week 3   **239**

Additional Resources

Table of Contents

Connect Across Disciplines Inquiry Projects AR1

Preteach/Reteach Routines AR6

Small-Group Texts for Reteaching Strategies and Skills AR18

Collaborative Conversation AR26

Access and Equity: Meeting the Needs of Students with
Disabilities and Students Who Are Advanced Learners AR32

Contrastive Analysis of English and
Nine World Languages AR48

Vocabulary with Spanish Cognates AR80

Managing an Independent Reading Program
and Recommended Trade Books AR81

Additional Resources